Haller's Polish Army in France

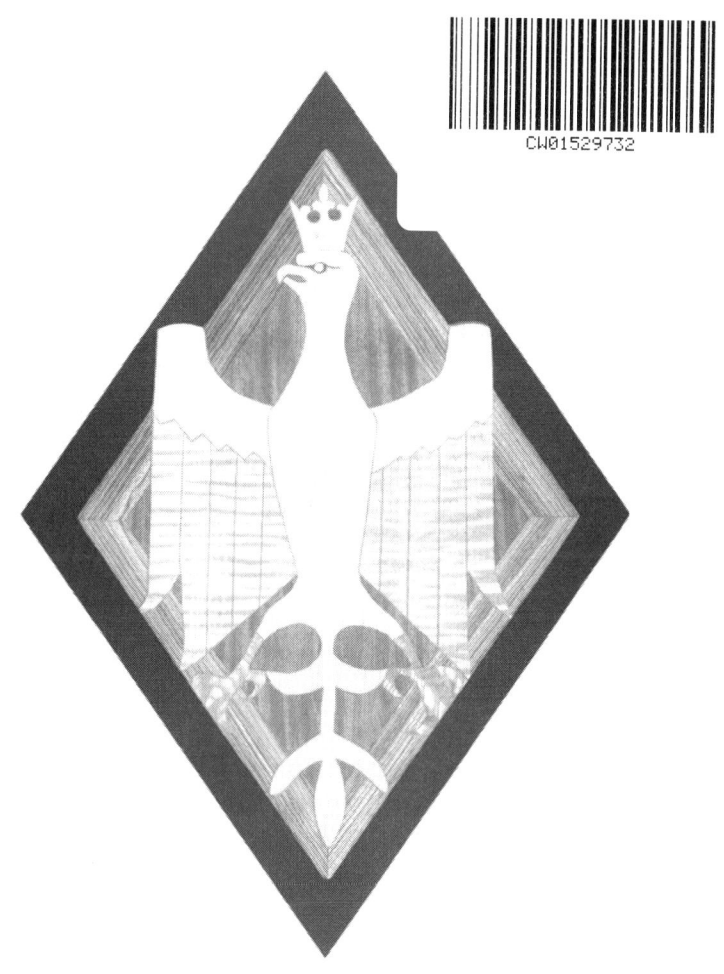

Paul S. Valasek

2006

Cover: The Many Faces of a *Hallerczyk*

Upper Left: Jan K. Kostrubała in Chicago soon after enlisting in October 1917. Since no uniforms had yet been issued, an available US Army issue was used for the photograph. Note the armband with the Polish eagle on it.

Upper Right: Jan K. Kostrubała wearing the Blue and Red of the Canadian Officer's Corp in training as an Officer Cadet at Camp Borden/ Niagara-on-the-Lake, Ontario, winter of 1917-1918.

Lower Left: Jan K. Kostrubała in France wearing the French Blue Uniform including the French Adrian helmet. ca. 1918.

Lower Right: Jan K. Kostrubała as a soldier of the Polish Legions after returning to Poland in April 1919. The uniform now sports a darker cap, the collar tabs are of the zig-zag Polish army style, and the epaulettes are renumbered according to Polish regimental numbers.

Center Eagle: Referred to as a "Haller eagle," this Art Deco-styled eagle was associated with General Haller and his troops. The example here is a wooden inlaid plaque created by Joseph G. Kostrubała DDS, MD in the early 1960's.

Back Cover: Though not directly connected to the recruitment process for the Polish Army in France in North America, this 1915 poster from Australia demonstrates the overdue awareness of Poland's suffering at the hands of its neighbors, which the world community was belatedly acknowledging.

Cover Design - Lisa A. Terlecki

Copyright © 2006 Paul S. Valasek
Printed in the United States of America by Whitehall Printing

ISBN 0-9779757-0-3

Best Wishes!

Haller's Polish Army in France

[signature] 6/27/24

To my grandfather

Jan Kazimierz Kostrubała

who shaped history

And

To my father

Charles E. Valasek

who taught me to appreciate it!

TABLE OF CONTENTS

Foreword 9
Introduction 15
Acknowledgements 18
City of Pittsburgh's Part in Formation of Polish Army: World War I
    1917-1920, *Joseph A. Borkowski* 21
Joseph A. Borkowski (1907-2003). A Brief Biographical Sketch by
    James Wudarczyk 2005 71
Physical Standards and Instructions for the Medical Examination of
    Recruits for the Polish Army in France 73
The Polish Army in France In Light of the Facts, *Wincenty Skarzyński* 80
Outline of the Wartime History of Polish Regiments, 1918–1920:
    The 43rd Regiment of Eastern Frontier Riflemen 150
Outline of the Wartime History of Polish Regiments, 1918–1920:
    The 44th Regiment of Eastern Frontier Riflemen 186
Outline of the Wartime History of Polish Regiments, 1918–1920:
    The 45th Regiment of Eastern Frontier Riflemen 228
The Blue Division, *Stanisław E. Nastał* 260
Index of Polish, Ukrainian, and Russian Names of Places Mentioned in
    the Regimental Histories 290
General Joseph de Hallenburg Haller, *Regina M. Kasaczun* 298
Polish Army Camp, *Col. A. D. LePan* 308
The Polish Force in Niagara, *Major C. R. Young* 320
The Polish Army in Niagara, *Janet Carnochan* 324
Polish Relief Work at Niagara, *Elizabeth C. Ascher* 332
With the Polish Autonomous Army (YMCA) 347
Interview with Walter S. Schutz (YMCA) 355
1921 YMCA Women's Letter from Poland 377
An Independent Poland: Why and How the Ancient Democratic Nation
    Should Be Resurrected for the Thirty-Five Million Poles Now
    Under Oppressive Foreign Rule, *Ignace Jan Paderewski* 382
Command of the Pomerania General District, Grudziądz, 29 April
    1920, Order No. 17 396
List of Haller's Army/Polish Army in France Recruitment Centers in
    North America: Map and List 398
Appendix — Troop Ships That Brought *Hallerczycy* to and from
    Europe 401
Appendix — The Emergence of the Polish Army in France 408
Index to Names of Persons and Places and Foreign Terms Found in the
    Text 410

FOREWORD

As a young child growing up in the early 60s in Chicago, many a time my sister Christine and I had spent a "sleep-over" at grandma's house. Now I know, many people will say, he should say "*Babcia's* house," but in reality, my Polish grandmother, Helen Dytkowska, born in Chicago in 1907, was always called "grandma." This was opposed to my Moravian grandmother, Marie Budinkova, who was born in Moravia in 1903, and was called *Babi*.

To pass the time, one of my special jobs was to place grandpa's medals in order. Out would come the leather covered cigar box, full of medals, ribbons, badges, and photos. Some heavy, some light, some golden, some silver, most with an attached white and red ribbon. As my grandfather, Jan Kazimierz Kostrubała, not only served in Haller's Army but also served as founding Vice-president of the Polish Army Veterans of America, *Stowarzyszenie Weteranów Armii Polskiej w Ameryce* (SWAP). He also served as President of the Polish Officer's Veteran Association, *Związek b. Oficerów Armii Polskiej w Ameryce*. He eventually served as the Executive Editor of the *Dziennik Chicagoski* until his death in September 1958, at the age of 58. It was his box of memorabilia which I would go through wondering what all of the medals and ribbons were about that is the reason this book has been created.

Some awards were from his days at the *Chicagoski* for covering national Presidential conventions in Chicago, participating at Conventions and *Sejm* of the Polish Falcons of America, the Polish National Alliance (PNA) and the Polish Roman Catholic Union (PRCU). These were interesting but the best were the heavy medals with soldiers, eagles and names and dates of battles on them. Unfortunately, I was of the generation which was becoming more and more Americanized, so my Polish was extremely limited. It also was not an aid attending an Irish Catholic Grammar School, St. Genevieve, as no material in the classrooms was in Polish, though approximately 40% of the pupils were of Polish heritage. Fruitless searches through all of the school's encyclopedias turned up nothing about any Polish General named Haller, nor of what I knew was called the Blue Army. None of the nuns, priests or teachers could help me out as well, this topic not being familiar to any of them.

Moving on to the Foreman High School library and a class on Modern European History yielded nothing more to my search. Poland was not a topic until it was dismembered by its neighbors in the late 18th century. A small blurb would be mentioned about Poland and Napoleon, and when the timeframe of Haller's Army was scheduled, we ran out of time at the year's end and no discussions took place.

Loyola University of Chicago classes on Modern European History were less informative. Once again, Poland would not be mentioned until its partitions, and when the time of World War I came into schedule, emphasis was always placed on the Western Front with little or no discussion about the Eastern battlefields. I can still remember the answer I received from the professor when I questioned him why discussions of European history would focus on the west, then jump over to Russian history, briefly mentioning Poland as a conquered country. His answer was that nothing of great importance took place in Poland until after the partitions. Thus started my serious quest for more information about Haller's Army.

When I had asked my grandmother what the medals meant, she could only give me a brief explanation, but always said how proud my grandfather was of them and especially his blue uniform. It was a rare treat to go down to the basement of her apartment building, unlock the large padlock on the storage shed, and dig out the box with his uniform and cap inside. I still vividly remember the day when my grandmother said over the phone that if I came to visit her on Saturday, she would let me take grandpa's uniform home. Unable to get someone to drive me over to grandma, I asked if I could walk to her apartment. No one objected so off I left for the two-mile walk to grandma's on a bright and sunny Saturday morning.

The uniform, though slightly soiled and a bit worn in places, still maintains its image of the days when Poles fought in French uniforms for the freedom of Poland. The tunic, cavalry britches, the leather belt with one strap over the shoulder and one leather legging remain, as well as one nickel plated spur. The hat is of a later vintage, grandpa's boy scout styled cap as well as his Adrian helmet had long ago gone missing. When grandpa enlisted in October 1917, he "deceptively" answered the question of when he was born by stating February 2, 1898. As a recent graduate of Weber High School in Chicago, and being fluent in Polish and English, he knew that had he stated the true answer of February 2, 1900, he would have been denied acceptance being under the minimum age of 18. So rather than waiting 5 more months to turn 18, he joined up at the "new age" of 19 going on 20.

Due to his recent diploma, and ability to read, write, and speak Polish and English, he was selected to attend officer's training school at Camp Borden, north of Toronto. It also benefited him that he was 6'1" tall when the average height of recruits was 5'6". Of the nearly 32,000 men who attempted to sign up for the Polish Army in France, he tied for 50th in height. Correcting his age, he also was within the 10 youngest recruits to serve in the Army. Soon, he was enlisted in the 3rd Class of Officer School Cadets, learning military techniques, science courses, and French. It has been stated that he first attended classes at Alliance College, the Polish College established in Cambridge Springs, Pennsylvania by the Polish National Alliance, before transferring to Camp Borden and eventually Camp Kościuszko at Niagara-on-the-Lake.

Arriving in France in the winter of 1918, he soon was placed in charge of a company of men in Mamers, in the Champagne region. Not seeing much action in France, he joined those men of what was originally called *Armia Polska we Francyi*, the Polish Army in France, and became known as *Armia Hallera*, or Haller's Army, after General Józef Haller took command in the late summer of 1918. This large group of men, some estimates as high as 75,000, were massed in France from recruits shipped over from the United States, Canada, Brazil and England. They also recruited from Poles living in France, as well as those soldiers who, though Polish in origin, had been drafted into the enemy armies of Germany and Austria. Many recruits came from the Allied POW Camps in France and Northern Italy. They readily joined the new Polish Army fighting for Poland's Independence on Polish soil under Polish command and under a new Polish flag.

When in Poland, these men of the Blue Army were co-mingled into Polish Regiments establishing at least three new regiments along the way. In France, most of the Army consisted of the 1st, 2nd and 3rd Regiments. But now in Poland, under Józef Piłsudski's Command, these regiments became the 43rd, 44th, and 45th Regiments of Borderland Riflemen respectively. The regimental histories of these three units are presented here in English for the first time and it is my hope that with success and interest in this book, more of the units' histories may be translated and added to the story.

These three regiments saw their most severe fighting after the Armistice of November 11, 1918, and not for the cause of establishing Poland's western borders, but in the fight against the rising Bolshevik menace in the East and the struggle to establish Poland's Eastern borders. This war, known both as the Russo-Polish War and the Polish-Soviet War, went on through 1920, until fighting was ended by the Treaty of Riga of 1921. Many of these Polish-American men found themselves fighting in the Ukraine and Volhynia, starting out from in and near the Polish city of Zamość. Some soldiers had reached as far as the capital city of Kiev, but eventually, they returned to Poland and a restored nation.

Now the problem of where these men would return was evident. Many still had close family in Poland, yet they wanted to return to family in the States or to that ideal of being a success in America. Others had their close families in the

United States and Canada and wished to return to them and continue their lives where they had left off.

I have heard from many people over the years of the pride these men exhibited when returning to America. They participated in memorial programs, banquets, ceremonies and parades, always wearing their blue uniforms. When the years took their toll on both original uniforms and the soldiers themselves, these veterans would order a veteran's uniform, also styled in the French blue to take the place of what they had fought with and for between 1917-1920. It is because of this reason I still have my grandfather's original uniform as he had eventually purchased a veteran's uniform in a larger size. He was no less proud of the veteran's uniform, so much so that when he died, he was buried in it.

The recruits from America were shipped back to the US using American military transports, a number of which were confiscated German ocean liners prior to World War I. Quite a number of these men originally immigrated to America on one of these German ships only to return to America on its renamed American version. My grandfather returned to New York in February 1921 aboard the *President Grant*. Had he returned on the *Antigone (ex Neckar)*, he would have sailed back to the United States on the same steamship he had originally emigrated from Poland in 1913. The *President Grant* was a Hamburg American ship which maintained its name both as a German steamship and as a US troop ship. Some of these ships started repatriating soldiers as early as November 1918, but most arrived during 1920-21. One voyage has been documented as arriving in 1922, with wives and children accompanying their soldier husbands and fathers. Many of these returning men are listed on the manifests of these ships, but due to illegible handwriting, may not be easily found using the Internet search engines.

I would very much like to hear from anyone who had a relative in Haller's Army and can also help those who may not know for sure if they did. Documents are constantly being "discovered" in North America and Europe, and I have dedicated much of my free time to indexing and data basing these rosters, rolls, and military correspondence. I have also created a database of nearly 32,000 potential recruits for Haller's Army from North America. This database has over 120 columns of information per recruit as more and more information is uncovered. Please consider sharing information of your *Hallerczyk*, as well as any information from your community which was established for the benefit of these men who fought for their motherland and adopted country.

Paul S. Valasek, DDS
2643 W. 51st Street
Chicago, IL 60632-1559
e-mail: Paval56@aol.com

Introduction

The Polish Army in France *(Armia Polska we Francyi)*—commonly known as Haller's Army *(Armia Hallera)*, in recognition of their commanding general, as well as the Blue Army *(Błękitna Armia)*, named for their French-issued blue uniforms—was a volunteer army recruited from 47 centers and Camp Niagara in the United States and Canada, starting in October 1917 and ending in March 1919. This fighting force was comprised predominantly of Polish nationals living in the United States and Canada who volunteered to fight in France towards the last year of World War I, and to continue fighting in Poland for its independence from all neighboring governments. What started out as part of the Great War to end all wars, ended up as the Polish-Soviet War of 1919-1921.

From the last decade of the 18th century, Poland as a political nation ceased to exist on the map of Europe. Its neighbors, Prussia, Austria, and Russia, over a period of nearly 15 years and three separate border divisions, conquered Polish lands and annexed pieces of these areas into each of the partitioning empires. Each partition was controlled differently, but a Polish citizen became an official minority within what previously was his own country. The official language spoken and written was that of the dominant empire, whether German or Russian, and rules for individual conduct were accorded to each citizen differently.

After more than a century of disharmony and oppression, the time was right to fight for Polish independence with the onset of the Great War. Polish militants in the United States, led by national and international leaders such as Roman Dmowski and Ignacy Jan Paderewski, sought out and developed the opportunity to form an independent Polish army from Poles living outside the historic boundaries of Poland, those areas collectively called Polonia. Countries such as the United States, Canada, Brazil, France, England, and Italy were prime sources for recruitment. This movement began a number of years before the outbreak of the First World War as leaders tried to form, through para-military organizations, fraternal aid societies, and the Roman Catholic Church, a 100,000-

man "Kościuszko Army," in tribute to a son of Poland who sought independence through the American Revolution.

Unable to form and build a foreign national army on U.S. soil, the founding leaders had to wait until final government approval came from President Woodrow Wilson allowing recruitment of resident aliens in the States. These men should not be eligible for the U.S. draft laws, and needed to demonstrate proof excluding them from service in the U.S. armed forces. The ideal age requirement was between 18-31 years of age, but upon review of recruitment records, some men as young as 16 and as old as 66 recruited and signed.

The first 10 recruitment centers were established by October 1917 and were formed in cities which had large Polish populations. As a result, the cities of Milwaukee, Chicago, Detroit, Cleveland, Buffalo, Pittsburgh, Wilkes-Barre, New York, Boston and Bridgeport started recruiting men (and a very small number of women) to sign up and form the Kościuszko Army. Large cities had multiple recruiting stations throughout the ethnically Polish neighborhoods. Some were located in parishes, in community buildings, in store fronts as well as backrooms of taverns and meeting halls. While some areas had great success, i.e. Chicago, a second recruitment center, in this case, South Chicago was established to attract additional Polish men from the southeast side of Chicago, as well as the steel mill industry of northwest Indiana. After a period of time, those centers which demonstrated low productivity were merged into larger neighboring centers which maintained the process and continued to recruit from a broader area. Even though the Armistice was signed on November 11, 1918, recruitment continued until February of 1919 building the Kościuszko Army for Poland's independence.

Because the training of a foreign army on U.S. soil was frowned upon by Washington, the Canadian government offered their officers and schools at both the University of Toronto and Camp Borden to train the "cream" of the newly formed army for service as its new corps of officers. The French government agreed to outfit and fund the army once trained and ready for war.

Enlisted men and non-commissioned officers set up base at Butler's Barracks, a Canadian training facility located at historic Niagara-on-the-Lake, Ontario. It was here that the new Polish troops, strange in their speech and manners, were cautiously (but later, enthusiastically) received by the local residents. After a crash course of training, on average 3-4 weeks, the first troops were to ship out of Halifax, Nova Scotia. However, due to that city's horrific explosion of December 6, 1917, these troops had to leave from American ports aboard U.S., British and Russian transports, the first two transports leaving December 16 and 19, 1917. Arrival in France began in the winter of 1917-8 and camps were quickly set up near Paris as well as in the Champagne region of France, near the often fought after Alsace-Lorraine region and the Marne. The first major action seen by the

Polish Army in France was in July 1918 at St. Hilaire-le-Grand, where casualties ran high as these new armed forces went up against more experienced German troops.

After the Armistice of November 11, 1918 and the subsequent Treaty of Versailles, new countries were being created from old empires. Poland's western borders were established by delegates to the Paris peace talks, but delineation of its Eastern borders was not yet set. Concurrent with the peace process in the west were the ravages in the east of the Russian Revolution and the invasion of the Bolshevik armies spreading from Russia to lands westward. With this in mind, the Polish Army in France, along with Polish prisoners of war released from French, German, Austrian and Italian prison camps, soon mustered together in Polish Silesia and organized with the Polish-based Piłsudski's Legions, to continue the war and eventually establish the Polish borders on the east. These were successful in keeping the spread of the Bolshevik armies and Communism within the Soviet borders until the onset of World War II.

Small villages, hamlets, and towns as well as major cities in the Ukraine, Belarus and Eastern Poland saw heavy action during battles in 1919-1920. The Polish army reached as far as the capitol city of Kiev before it was turned back by overpowering forces. Many heroic stories come out of this time frame including the battle for the city of Lwów and its defending "Young Eagles." Many of these heroes were buried at the Defenders of Lwów section of the Łyczakowski Cemetery, memorialized by their grateful nation. Included among these combatants were three American freedom fighting pilots, Graves, Kelly and MacCallum, who helped establish an air force via the Kościuszko Squadron for the fledgling Polish country and gave their lives for its struggle. As an act of retribution and for scores unsettled, the Łyczakowski Cemetery was destroyed during World War II to "eradicate" the memory of victorious armies and to establish a "new beginning" of Polish-Ukrainian relations. It is only in recent times that the cemetery has undergone some restoration to its former glory.

Upon conclusion of conflict, many of the *Hallerczycy* (men of Haller's Army) returned to America aboard the same ships which took them to Europe. Their families continued to live and prosper in North America, fitting into the existing American and Canadian societies. It is their descendants to whom this book is destined as many of them do not speak or read Polish through the American assimilation process our ancestors encouraged. It is meant to once again tell this story and appreciate the sacrifices these men made for their homeland, newly adopted country, as well as Western Society as a whole.

ACKNOWLEDGEMENTS

The purpose of this book was not to analyze, interpret, revise or re-write history. Those tasks can only be accomplished after the base material is readily available to scholars and researchers. This book is published to make little known, obscure and rare material accessible to those seeking information on the Polish Army in France, aka Haller's Army. Much of the Polish material is appearing here in English for the first time.

My gratitude goes first to the original authors of the compiled works. They took the time to write down their experiences not long after the fact. Many, having first hand knowledge and memories of those turbulent times, put them down on paper while still fresh in their minds.

For my own research, I would like to express particular appreciation to Michalina Byra of the Polish National Library in Warsaw, who has helped me locate hard to find material in Poland and make copies of these works for inclusion here. Her diligence has been much appreciated.

I also would like to thank Judge Edward Borkowski for allowing me to use his late father, Joseph A. Borkowski's manuscript on Pittsburgh's early role in forming the Polish Army and thus, the beginning of this tale. Also to be thanked are the Polish Falcons of America in Pittsburgh and their Vice-president Timothy Kuzma for assisting me in finding materials for use and allowing me to review their archival holdings.

The Niagara Historical Society and Museum graciously allowed me to reprint those articles created at Niagara-on-the-Lake which play an important role in the attitude of the local residents and the Canadian Officer's Corp to the over 23,000 Polish men who obviously were a strange sight from the start but later grew dear to the residents of Ontario.

The Polish American Veteran's Association (P.A.V.A., in Polish *Stowarzyszenie Weteranów Armii Polskiej — S.W.A.P.*) was quite willing to share Stanisław Nastal's memoirs and welcome this book on the Army for their English speaking supporters.

Appreciation also goes out to the Kautz Family YMCA Archives in Minneapolis for allowing use of the material demonstrating the very large yet little discussed role which the Y played in trying to rebuild and improve war torn Eastern Europe after the First World War and the later Polish Soviet War.

I also would like to show appreciation to the Gacek family for contributing the Order #17 of the Command of the Pomerania General District, Grudziądz which their *Hallerczyk* father, Wojciech (George), brought home with him from the war and proudly framed and hung in his home in Chicago for over 60 years.

Thanks as well go out to Leonard Kurdek of Chicago for putting me in touch with additional material especially newspaper articles for reference in this and future works.

And then comes the people who helped create this book to whom I am most indebted. To my wife Andrea, who has put up with me and "my blue army men" for the past six years which included extensive typing, paperwork review, traveling to many of the locations associated with Haller's Army as well as searching the Internet for articles and material, and helping me on Internet auctions for materials when they become available.

To my daughter Lisa A. Terlecki, who not only brought my vision for the cover of this book to life, but also retouched and enhanced those images found throughout the chapters. Visuals are as important as text and sometimes relate a more complete story.

And to my good friend, William "Fred" Hoffman, who is responsible for the excellent translations of the regimental histories and soldiers' memoirs which include out-dated military terms as well as those chapters which went from Polish to English. The extensive list of place names of villages in Polish, Ukrainian, and Russian when available was his idea and was truly welcomed. And for his laying out the book in its finished format I am much indebted.

And to all of the *Hallerczycy* who created this story and are no longer with us, their families should be proud!

Hotel Rider, Cambridge Springs, Pa.

Polish National Alliance College, Cambridge Springs, Pa.

City of Pittsburgh's Part in Formation of Polish Army
World War I
1917-1920

By Joseph A. Borkowski

Copyright 1956
Reprinted with permission from Judge Edward Borkowski
Published by Central Council of Polish Organizations of Pittsburgh, PA

Ignacy Jan Paderewski

The first Group of Volunteers leaving Pittsburgh, 1917

Background

Even though Poland was no longer on the European map following the infamous third partition in October 24, 1795, the Poles irrespective where located, lived in a hope of eventual restoration of Poland's independence.

Towards that goal many abortive attempts were made, particularly when Napoleon Bonaparte formed the Grand Duchy of Warsaw in 1807; Alexander I of Russia gave Constitution in 1815-30 and finally when serious revolts were staged against the Russian Czars in 1830, 1831, and 1863.

Development of New Type of Polish Leadership

The aftermath of Insurrection of 1863 was followed by a definite threat of smothering of Polish nationalism as many of the militant leaders who usually were of nobility or intelligentsia, were executed, imprisoned, or sent to Siberia.

The situation became all the more alarming in Prussia where Otto von Bismarck's "Kulturkampf" was introduced in an attempt to obliterate Polish Nationalistic spirit by germanizing schools and replacing the Polish landlords with German colonists. The Poles, led by clergy and political leaders rebelled only to have more stringent laws enacted.

Poles Seek More Hospitable Soil

When the Prussian pressure became intolerable and arrests threatened, the Polish leaders had no alternative but to migrate to more hospitable shores. As they sought asylum, there was one thought among them… to regain freedom and independence of Poland. It was also realized that only in a land which offered freedom of action and general tolerance could Poles nurture plans that would lead to liberation of Poland. Only the shores of the United States offered such opportunities, and whereto greater part of the Polish leaders migrated, settling usually in urban and industrial areas like city of Pittsburgh, Pennsylvania.

Polish Immigrants Organize

The Polish émigré was aware of this fact, that if Poland was to become an independent and free country again, it will come about only through effective leadership. To develop this type of leaders and to keep the freedom torch aglowing, numerous patriotic societies were organized.

At first it was collective leadership. To develop individual leadership was another task as each society assumed the role "that is was chosen to lead". However it was generally agreed that if Polish independence was to be gained it would be as a result of united military action.

An Organization that was Ready

Fortunately for the Polish inhabitants in the United States, there was an organization which was ready to assume that role. The Polish Falcons of America, both the eastern branch located in New York City, and the western situated in Chicago, have been sponsoring military training since their founding. As early as September 1, 1907, Dr. Teofil A. Starzynski of Pittsburgh, then the President of the Fourth District of the Polish Falcons, projected plans of forming rifle teams and field drills among the members located in the Pittsburgh district. On June 25, 1911, a special district meeting was called at Emsworth, Pa., where hundreds of Polish Falcons of the Pittsburgh area underwent special field maneuvers. On November 26, 1911, a number of qualified leaders were sent to Philadelphia, Pa., where the first formal military school was conducted under the auspices of the Polish Falcons with former officers of Austrian Army rendering the instructions.

On January 1, 1911, Dr. Teofil A. Starzynski of Pittsburgh, Pa., then a vice-president of the Eastern branch of the Polish Falcons Alliance of America, wrote the following letter to Professor Rudolph Tarczynski, Secretary of the Polish Falcons in Paris, France: "…let us construct a solid military foundation by sponsoring and conducting permanent military and gymnastic schools for purposes of training military leaders — the nucleus of officers without which no military action can be taken".

Polish Falcons Merge

To meet this situation a special convention was called to the city of Pittsburgh, Pa., on December 15, and 16, 1912, of the both branches of the Polish Falcons. The convention delegates met at the Mickiewicz Society Hall Nest 8, located at 97 S. 18th Street, South Side. The delegates voted to merge into the present

TYPICAL
POLISH ARMY WORLD WAR I — 1917
VOLUNTEERS

Captain W. A. Pawlak

Lt. Frank Bubacz

Sgt. Jan Rajchel

Sgt. Jacob Ryzowicz

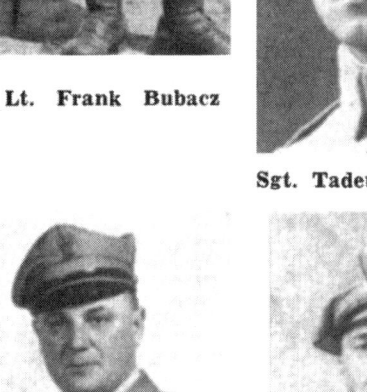

Sgt. Tadeusz Spychala

Sgt. Leon Kowalewski

Jan Kaczynski

Sgt. Ludwik Urban

organization and elected the following Pittsburgh resident officers: Dr. Teofil A. Starzynski, President; B. Mruczek, Vice-President; H. S. Listewska, Vice-President II; Adam Plutnicki, General Secretary; F. Posluszny, Treasurer; Victor L. Alski, F. Machnikowska, K. Olstynski, S. Zyglerowicz, as Members of the Executive Board of Directors. The city of Pittsburgh was picked as the official headquarters.

Military Training

With the Balkan Wars already in full force, the newly elected President Dr. Teofil Starzynski did not lose much time in realizing that "the hour has come", and immediately asked for an approval, "to appoint a special training and technical committee whose task was to formulate a training program for field use and was to be military in character".

The All Polish Convention in Pittsburgh, Pa.

At the same time Polish Falcons were meeting, a special call was issued to all Polish Organizations in the United States to meet in Pittsburgh, Pa., for the first time in the history of Polish immigration. The convention after being orientated to the impending European Conflagrations, resolved to form a united front. A special Committee was named, and became known as "Komitet Obrony Narodowej" (National Defense Committee), whose task was to collect funds and initiate pertinent action such as "promotion and support of military training".

The Pittsburgh National Defense Committee consisted of Attorney C.W. Sypniewski, President; Jan Ratajczyk, Vice-president; Ignacy Starzynski, Financial Secretary; Blazej Mruczek, Recording Secretary; Leopold Bucholtz, Treasurer; Directors: Jan Harenski, Marcin Galiszewski, Jan Maslowski, Jan Mielcarek, Jozef F. Bubacz, and Stanislaw Krall.

C. W. Sypniewski

The First Appeal and Training Units

On February, 1913, President Dr. Teofil A. Starzynski issued a call to all nests of the Polish Falcons of America, "to start training in basic military tactics and physical fitness". Among the first groups to respond in the

Pittsburgh area was the Society of Adam Mickiewicz, Nest 8, of 97 S. 18th Street, South Side. At a special meeting held on February 18, 1913, the members voted to purchase rifles and essential field equipment. Before the year ended, practically every Falcon nest was sponsoring physical training courses with emphasis on "Art of handling of manual arms.

Field Maneuvers and Training Courses

The first formal organized field camp for Pittsburgh district Falcons was opened on February 20, 1913, and continued until March 11, 1913. The training camp was located on the grounds of the Holy Family Institute, Emsworth, Pa. The training program attracted 34 men representing 23 nests from the Pittsburgh area. Dr. Adam Wolcyrz of Pittsburgh, was the sanitation and First Aid instructor. The purpose of the training program was to develop field leadership among the Falcons. This was followed by leadership training at Cambridge Springs, Pa., site of Polish National Alliance College. The courses were of two weeks duration and started on May 1, 1913, and ended June 30, 1914. W.A. Perry of the American Boy Scouts Executive Board also participated as an Instructor. These courses cost the Falcons $4,000.00.

The Mexican Border Incident

With a strong possibility that there might be a war as a result of border raids and killings by the marauding Mexican Bands under Pancho Villa, on March 9, 1916, the Polish Falcons feeling confident that its trainees were ready for military duties, on behalf of its organized membership, offered 10,000 trained recruits as an integral part of the Unites States Army. Most of these recruits would have been from the Pittsburgh area.

Telegrams Exchanged

The following telegrams were exchanged:

To the Secretary of War Garrison, Washington, D.C.

"Your Excellency - The President of Polish Falcons Alliance of America, representing 30,000 military training membership ask for audience to offer volunteers in Mexican War".

Dr. T.A. Starzynski, President.

Another set of telegrams were dispatched to Secretary of War Garrison on April 18, 1914.

The Secretary of War Garrison in reply dated 4-22-14 expressed his sincerest appreciation for the Falcons gesture, however further stated, "that there was no immediate need". The reply from H. Stestland, General Adjutant, was as follows: "I am empowered by the War Secretary to confirm the receipt of your telegram dated April 23, in which you offered the Falcons for military service with Mexico. However I am to inform you that if there is need that the National Guard will receive the first call". By no means was this an empty gesture for on May 7, 1914, the President of the Falcons instructed to compile a volunteer list which was to be ready when and if needed. The Falcons were still hopeful that the War Department would find need of volunteers as offered by their organization.

President Woodrow Wilson's Monument in Poznan, Poland

A Memorable White House Visit

Anxious more than ever to convince the diplomatic sources that Poles all over the world are ready for independence of their country and receiving little or no definite satisfaction from Allied Diplomatic sources, particularly France and England, the Polish Falcons of America delegation headed by Dr. T.A. Starzynski visited President Woodrow Wilson on February 10, 1915, to ascertain his views as to the future of the Independence of Poland. The President without hesitation informed the delegation that "when United States shall sit at the Peace Conference all efforts shall be made to see that Poland is free again". It was the first official utterance on behalf of Polish independence by a world power since partition of 1795.

Dr. T.A. Starzynski Urges Military Training

On January 6, 1916, in a special appeal he continued to urge the members to intensify their military drilling and establish such groups on permanent basis. He further asked the leaders to organize rifle clubs, sponsor field training and conduct first aid cources [sic]. All this was but a preliminary introduction to things to come.

Training School Approved

At a special plenary Board Meeting of the Polish Falcons held in Pittsburgh, Pa., from September 30 to October 1, 1916, the Falcons Technical Commission

Officers and Cadre Trainees at Polish National Alliance College Cambridge Springs, Pa.

composed of J. Sierocinski, W. Sulewski, and F. Boguszewski recommended an establishment of a training school for all potential officers and non-commissioned officers. Their proposal met with a unanimous approval and the Executive Board recommended a budget of $10,000.00. Among the contributors of the Military Training Course were Ignacy Jan Paderewski $1,000.00, his wife Helen Paderewski $500.00, and the family of Leonard Krajewski $1,000.00.

Drilling Performed Under Cover

Following the Plenary sessions, a call was made to all Physical Instructors to meet in Pittsburgh, Pa., November 28 to December 6, 1916. Under guise of Leadership Training, the trainees were given general training and instructions on military tactics. Fortified with this basic knowledge, they carried it to respective areas for promulgation and indoctrination of all Falcons membership. Because United States was still a neutral nation, all such training was described as "Physical Development Courses".

As a result of this training the Polish Falcons of America sent twenty most promising cadre candidates to the Officers Training School at University of Toronto, Canada. The men, all Falcons, arrived on about January 1, 1917. In this group were the following:

Adamczak, L.Z., Albrycht, W., Bogucki, J., Gawrys, T., Godowski, T., Klatt, A., Kresse, A., Krol, B., Kryze, J., Osielski, J., Rokicki, J., Seiler, J., Serge,

Polish Falcons Hall
South Side, Pittsburgh, Pa.

B., Sierocinski, J., Skarzynski, W., Sobczak, L., Szlachcinski, S., Szymanski, F., Wiecek, A., Wroblewski, J., Zielecki, K. - Chwalkowski, L. (first recruit killed in action)., Malkowski, A., (died).

Training School Opened at Cambridge Springs, PA.

In the meantime the training among the Falcons nests was intensified to such degree that there was a general clamour for a local training school. To meet the demand, the Polish Falcons of America formally opened a cadre training quarters at Polish National Alliance College, Cambridge Springs, Pa., on March 19, 1917, with Franciszek Dziob of Polish Falcons named as its Head Instructor.

Historical Meeting

When United States declared a War on Imperial Germany, April 6, 1917, the Polish Falcons of America were fully prepared both in man power and spirit. Up till that time, there were individuals and groups of all sizes and shades attempting to assume leadership in organizing "Polish Legions". Such endeavors only added additional confusion. Therefore it was obvious that if there was to be a Polish

Adam Plutnicki

Dr. Teofil A. Starzynski

fighting unit, it would come about as a result of influential leadership. To meet this need some guided action was pertinent.

Polish Falcons Call a Special Session

Since there was no longer a question as to the entry of United States on the side of the Allies, the Executive Board of Polish Falcons, headed by President Dr. Teofil A. Starzynski, called a special convention which convened on April 1, 1917, at Adam Mickiewicz Society Nest 8, 97 S. 18th St., South Side, Pittsburgh, Pa. There was a general enthusiastic response and 120 nests were officially accredited, represented by 187 delegates. The opening session was called to order on Sunday, April 1st at 10:00 A.M. by the President Dr. T. A. Starzynski, who outlined the purpose of the meeting viz: to decide what definite actions shall the Falcons take whenever United States declare war upon Germany.

Adam Plutnicki, Pittsburgh, Pa., Convention Chairman

Adam Plutnicki was elected Chairman of the convention and T. Samulski, General Secretary. After completing the usual conventional formalities of speechmaking by Mayor Joseph Armstrong, Dr. Kerr of City Council, the delegates took initial steps of projecting into discussion ways and means of initiating a formal recruiting of Polish Army. There appeared hesitancy on part of many delegates and questions were raised as to the feasibility of such a plan. It was motioned by delegate Henryk Lokanski to invite Maestro Ignacy Jan

Paderewski to address the delegates and advise on the practicability of recruiting of Polish Army in America. Dr. T.A. Starzynski was entrusted to contact Maestro Paderewski and which he did by phone. Subsequently the delegates were informed that the Great Paderewski will be in Pittsburgh April 2, 1917.

Ignacy Jan Paderewski Arrives

Ignacy Jan Paderewski

Promptly at 9:00 A.M., Ignacy Jan Paderewski with his wife, arrived at the Pennsylvania R.R. Station, Eleventh Street, Pittsburgh, Pa., where he was met by the Pittsburgh delegation headed by Attorney Frank A. Piekarski and escorted to Hotel William Penn, Pittsburgh, Pa. The news of Ignacy J. Paderewski's visit electrified the Pittsburgh's Polish colony. From all the areas around the City, people flocked to see and hear the Great Polish Patriot. Hours before his appearance, the Falcon Hall was jammed. Punctually at 7:30 P.M. the time for the evening session, Maestro Paderewski accompanied by his wife, arrived at the convention hall where throngs spontaneously greeted him in Polish "Niech Żyje Nam" (Long Live). At the doorsteps of the Convention Hall, he was welcomed in a traditional Polish manner "bread and salt" by Falcon member of Nest 8 - *Druh* J. Pozych. Unprecedented enthusiasm broke out on the convention floor when the Maestro made his platform appearance and for a while it appeared it would last indefinitely. Once the calmless restored, the renowned pianist began his memorable address. He outlined the contemporary alignments and the trend of the events and pointed out to the delegates that the future of Poland rests only in their "hands and bayonets". He went on to point out the necessity of such an army which would be a telling factor in winning the Polish Independence not only on the battlefield but also at the conference table, then urged the delegates to be loyal under all circumstances to the United States of America, stating in part, "I have full confidence in the United States, in its future and in their ideals upon which this great nation was built. Particularly let us be loyal to President Woodrow Wilson, the champion of the down trodden nations".

Proposes Formation of Kosciuszko Army to Fight Under Stars and Stripes

The hushed audience listened as the Artist proposed that the Convention go on record "To form a Kosciuszko Army for service under Stars and Stripes and to fight alongside with the Allies against the Imperial Germany which has infringed on the rights of almost all nations of the world. Furthermore permit me to send a wire to President Wilson offering an army of 100,000 men". When the great Patriot concluded his plea for the formation of the Kosciuszko Army, a thunderous cheer went up from the assembly that reverberated from the convention hall to the crowded street around the building. At the conclusion, Rev. Z. Rydlewski of the Immaculate Heart of Mary R.C. Church, Herron Hill, replied on behalf of Pittsburgh Poles to Maestro Paderewski's pleas, stating that "the Polish People in America will wholeheartedly respond to Polish Cause".

Historical Resolution

Then the convention proceeded to go on record and adopted the following resolution:

"We have reached a time when momentary deeds decide the fate of monarchies and nations, and which has brought our cause before the tribunal of the world. We realize that the existence of the nations depends upon their deeds, and being further aware as loyal Americans that it is our urgent duty to stand in the ranks of the defenders of liberty of the country, we the delegates of the convention of the Polish Falcons of America being aware of the existing state of war, do hereby promise allegiance to the United States of America, the country which takes up arms at this time against Imperial Germany, which has infringed on the rights of almost all the nations of the world.

Whereas war waged against the United States is war against the Polish race, of which the Prussians have been traditional foes for 1,000 years past, we resolve to create a Kosciuszko army and hereby appeal to the entire Polish people of this country unanimously to approve this move and lend a helping hand to the realization of this worthy cause. We further command our superior officers to commence without delay mobilization movements fully to prepare the army, expectant to accomplishing deeds to be added to the history of free Poland, the realization of which is now at hand.

We extend to our officers our utmost confidence, especially our president Dr. Starzynski, and to our man of the day, Ignace Paderewski, to whom we promise to stand by the colors of Kosciuszko, and never permit them to leave us until we have nobly and heroically defended our cause.

We appeal to you, our country men, scattered throughout the lands of your adopted country, to hasten to the ranks of the Kosciuszko Army that we may perform deeds which will lead us with triumphs to the realization of a free independent, undivided Poland".

Rush to Arms

The adoption of the resolution had a dynamic effect upon the local residents of Polish descent. There was immediately a rush to form a Polish Fighting Unit. However the cooler heads adopted a waiting policy pending the official approval by the United States Government. To re-emphasize the Polish Falcons position, President T.A. Starzynski sent the following telegram dated 4-6-1917 to President Woodrow Wilson: " Polish Falcons of America only ask and hope that the Government considering the glorious ties binding their ancestry with this country of ours allow the fighting force to bear the name of Kosciuszko's Army".

Dr. T.A. Starzynski.

Convention Recommendations

In its final session held on April 4th, the convention adopted the following recommendations: that the Polish Falcons of America through its Technical Commissions and District Physical Leaders assume all action pertaining to mobilization and training of the military; to sponsor on temporary basis officers training school until the needs are fully met; to mobilize all nests into active companies; establish recruiting offices and open training courses not only to the Falcons **but all eligible who have desire to join the Polish forces.**

**The Polish Relief Committee Functions-
United States Government Attitude**

To expedite the approval of recruiting in the United States, the Polish Relief Committee took on the task in contacting the U.S. Officials. In spite of persistent urgings there appeared a general reluctance on part of the United States authorities to take any formal action for the following reasons: — United States was at war and needed all the men it could muster, secondly, it would set a precedent for other nationalistic groups who also might be interested in recruiting their nationals and thereby jeopardizing the United war efforts, then the United States had no desire whatsoever to strain its diplomatic relations with the Russian Government who at different times looked with suspicion on any Polish Army. In the meantime, the Polish Falcons ranks were being depleted with eligibles joining with the American Army.

The Polish Cause Bolstered

The Polish Army cause in America was given an additional impetus when President R. Poincare of the French Republic issued a formal decree dated June 4,

1917, approving the formation of Autonomous Polish Fighting Forces in France under the Polish flag and Polish command. This decree was made possible when the Czarist Regime was abolished by the Bolsheviki in Revolution of 1917. President Poincare's decree created spontaneous enthusiasm for immediate formation of the Polish Army.

Special Meeting of Polish Leaders

Special session of Polish Central Committee representing all Polish major organizations was called at Chicago, Ill., April 11, 1917, with Attorney C.W. Sypniewski, and Dr. T.A. Starzynski of Pittsburgh, Pa., being present. It was presided by Maestro Paderewski who again urged the representatives of various Polish organizations to take immediate steps in line with the French decree. It gave unqualified approval of formation of the "Kosciuszko Army". The task of organizing a military force became an assignment of all Poles. As a result an Army Commission was formed which included Dr. T.A. Starzynski of Pittsburgh, Pa., and T.M. Helinski and A. Znamiecki whose task was to secure the official consent of the Unites States Government to permit recruiting of eligible and qualified Polish citizens.

First Military Commission in United States

One of the first actions following this meeting was to issue an order to synchronize all training and adopt a formal military procedure as well as to be alerted to anticipated approval of official recruiting. At a special called meeting of the Polish Falcon's Executive Board June 7, 1917, President Dr. T.A. Starzynski appointed the following members of the first military Falcons Commission viz: Jan Bartmanski, W.N. Skarzynski and Jozef Sierocinski, all Falcons and qualified officers and recent graduates of Canadian Officers Training School. They were to function on behalf of the Falcons until Polish Military Commission would take over the recruiting and financing of the Polish Army in America.

Call for Volunteer Officer Candidates

On June 7, 1917, the Executive Board of the Polish Falcons in the city of Pittsburgh, Pa., issued recruiting appeal to all eligibles for three hundred potential officer candidates. The candidates to qualify were required to be physically fit, be able to speak and write Polish and English, have a basic knowledge of mathematics, of good character and between the ages of 18-35. In addition he was to bring his OWN two military uniforms, belt, shoes, army shirts, two pairs of brown shirts, rifle and bayonet. Because of an enthusiastic response, a special announcement was made that on July 5, 1917, candidates would no longer be accepted.

British Government Intercedes

Additional pressure for recognition of the Polish Central Committee and its aims came from the British Government upon the urgings of the Polish Committee in Paris which was duly recognized by the British and French Governments. In a note dated July 23, 1917, to the State Department, the British Government expressed itself as following: –"As favoring free and independent Poland". It further asserted that "Poles living in countries of Allied Powers, whether German, Austrian or Prussian origin, should be granted open recognition as friends and potential allies". Such a step would crystalize the idea of a separate and free Polish state themselves of their claim of independence".

Robert Lansing, Secretary of State's Famous Reply

In a reply to above, Robert Lansing stated the United States position in a note dated 8-17-17:

"The Department has been considering for several months means to support the Polish people in their efforts to obtain their Freedom and to restore Poland as an independent state. It has been suggested that a great stimulus might be given to the Polish cause and indirectly to the general cause against Germany by establishment in this country of a Polish provisional government to be recognized by the Government and the Allied Governments as the Government of Poland. Upon such recognition this Government could legally loan the government so set-up funds for the military purposes secured by Polish bonds underwritten by this country and the Allies. The further suggestion has been made that such government thereupon recruiting Polish residents in this country. **The Army so recruited to be trained in Canadian Camps supplied by the English".**

Ignacy Jan Paderewski Pleads

Not desiring to wait for the formal recognition much longer, Ignacy Jan Paderewski as the General Chairman of the Polish Central Relief Committee on October 4, 1917, sent a telegram to President Woodrow Wilson, which read in part as follows: "On October 14th, the bells of the Polish Churches of those still remaining will call upon faithful to join in fervent prayers in memory of noble hero departed two hundred years ago, Thaddeus Kosciuszko, that the Polish National Committee in Paris has been recognized, the Polish National Army has been sanctioned, by our beloved President Woodrow Wilson, this would certainly give new strength, new hope, and new courage to the stricken nation that trusts but God and you".

President Woodrow Wilson Grants Permission

The Commission was finally successful in receiving a formal United States approval and on September 27, 1917, President Woodrow Wilson gave consent stating - "That recruiting to the Polish Army all those who do not fall in the category of potential recruitment into the United States forces is hereby approved without any impediments". However, it was now necessary to work out the details with the War Department.

The Official Approval of Recruiting of Polish Army in America

After prolonged negotiations with the Polish National Committee and the Allied Powers, the United States Government gave its official blessing to recruitment of Polish Army of America.

A note was issued by the War Department dated October 8, 1917, which is being quoted: "It has been brought to the attention of the War Department that the military Commission of the National Department of the Polish Central Relief Committee, located in Chicago, Illinois intends to start on October 7, 1917, an active campaign for recruiting for the Polish Army now fighting in the Western Europe in France. The War Department has been advised that no individual of Polish Nationality resident of the United States who is in any way subject to the draft will be accepted as a recruit by this Military Commission. Having in mind the attitude of this Government toward a united and independent Poland, the War Department is glad to announce that it is entirely in accord with the proposed plan of this Military Commission".

Falcons Surrender Recruiting Activities

When this data was made public, the Polish Falcons surrendered its recruiting activities to the Polish Military Commission who took on all the recruiting duties and assumed the obligations that were contracted by the Polish Falcons. The Commission received the official information on September 27, 1917 from French Mission that recruiting may commence. The recruiting offices were ready on October 4, 1917.

First National Recruiting Headquarters at Pittsburgh, PA.

Upon the announcement of approval, the Military Commission opened the first national recruiting headquarters in the city of Pittsburgh, Pa., on October

7th, 1917. The Bureau was located at the Farmers Bank Building located at Fifth Avenue and Wood Street. Offices were located on the eleventh floor viz: Room 1103-6 until December 31, 1917. On January 1, 1918, the offices were moved to 70 Fifth Avenue, New York City, N.Y.

To expedite recruiting the Military Commission divided the recruiting areas into twelve centers, each being headed by a Commissioned Military Personnel.

The Pittsburgh Recruiting Activities

To Pittsburgh's recruiting officer Dr. B.M. Zielinski a noted patriot and orator was assigned Number 1 and the recruiting center become known as "Centrum 6". Being energetic and zealous Dr. Zielinski lost no time in organizing the scattered Polish colonies into one smooth functioning recruiting unit.

Miss Helen (Pawlak) Adamczak

Assignment Number 2 was given to Miss Helen (Pawlak) Adamczak of 3017 Pulaski Way, Herron Hill, Pittsburgh, with a rank of "Recruiting Sergeant" of Center Number 6 of the Polish Army in France and with specific authority to open a recruiting station in Pittsburgh, Pa. The commission was signed by A. Znamiecki of the Military Commission. Miss Pawlak was the first and probably the only woman in the Polish Army recruiting ranks to receive a military commission.

Local Recruiting Stations

At first local recruiting activities were performed at Nest 8, 97 South 18th Street, subsequently transferred to Nest 176 in November, 1917, then located at 2813 Penn Avenue in the Strip area. Finally the Recruiting was transferred to 3402 Butler Street in Lawrenceville, where the activities continued until the closing of recruiting on February 15, 1919. The monthly budget for above bureau called for a minimum of $1,800.00.

Other Recruiting Officers in Pittsburgh, PA.

Others who were assigned at different times were: T. Zarewicz, Czeslaw Zulawski, Edward Szymorowski of Braddock, Pa., A. Curzytek, Stanislaw Rzewuski, Wladyslaw Sierocki, Idzi Piec, Wlodzimierz Kedzierski, Alfred

J. Debald

S. Pilchowski

Korzybski, A.F. Wilk, Lucjusz Kajko, Adam Kwasieborski, Jan Roskosz, F. Ryszkowski, S. Birstein, I. Zwolinski and P. Wrobel.

Center 6 Citizens Committee

The Polish Military Commission was aware of the fact that to get recruits, posting of appealing posters would not bring in even the most patriotic. A personal contact was to be the prime factor in promoting and encouraging the eligible to join with the Polish Army. Therefore under the auspices of the Polish Military Commission an auxiliary group known as "Citizens Committees" were organized. Their duties were to promote recruiting and solicit funds. The Pittsburgh Group was known as Citizens Committee of Center Number 6, and consisted of the following members: Jan Debald, President; Fr. Figura, Secretary; Antoni Karabasz, Treasurer, and the directors were representatives of local organizations. That this committee was achieving results is this fact that the one thousandth recruit was signed on or about April 8, 1918.

Local Recruiting Committee Reorganized

With the increasing demands for finances — as a result of unprecedented enrollment into the Polish ranks, more elaborate plans were to be formulated to handle the various demands. Consequently in September 1918 the following reorganized committee was named: Adam Plutnicki, President; Jan Domachowski, Vice-president; Stanislaw Pilchowski, Recording Secretary; Leon S. Kosmacki, Financial Secretary; Antoni Karabasz, Treasurer. The directors included Jan Debald, Jan Marciniak, D.G. Magnuski, Jan Panczyk, Jan Kadlewicz, R.S. Abczynski, Wojciech Kancelewski, Stanislaw Gawronski, Wiktor Borowicz, Ignacy Starzynski, Stanislaw Cwiklinski, Ignacy Sokolowski, Jan Maslowski, Jan Szelagowski, F. X.Kubiak, Ludwik Haduch, Marcin Galiszewski, and Piotr Kaminski.

The Citizens Sub-Committee: The Backbone of Polish Army Recruiting

The backbone of the Polish Army recruiting in the Pittsburgh area were the Polish Roman Catholic Churches and the Citizens sub-committees organized at the Parishes. The members of respective sub-committees were usually the outstanding and indefatigable citizens in their communities. To them the cause of Freedom and Independence of Poland was a sacred cause that demanded infinite self sacrifice and endless toil. "They were the shock troops".

Clergy a Prominent and Decisive Factor in Recruiting

That the clergy of Polish descent in Pittsburgh Diocese which also included present Greensburg, Pa. diocese was factor in promoting the recruiting, there is no better authority than the testimony of the Polish Military Commission as quoted in the Commissions official publication "Bulletin" dated April 11, 1918, Numbers 13 and 14: "The clergy in the Pittsburgh Diocese is steadily taking active and energetic part in promoting recruiting in this area". A further attestation of the fact is stated more specifically that a rally was held in West End (Guardian Angels R.C. Church), which resulted in recruiting twelve eligible men and in addition the Reverend A. Pniak asked those present to pledge themselves to pay a monthly assessment of fifty cents towards the Polish Army Recruits needs.

St. Joseph Union Contribution

Similar assessments were voluntarily agreed among many other parishes in the Pittsburgh area and Polish fraternal organizations like St. Joseph's Union, which assessed itself $50.00 per month. The Polish Roman Catholic Parish was the core of the recruiting and fund solicitation.

Polish Clergy on Active Recruiting List

Among others who were officially enrolled as volunteer recruiting sergeants who spearheaded the organization of recruiting and fund solicitation drives in their respective localities and parishes were Reverend P. Pilc, Lilly, Pa., Reverend F. Pilc, South Fork, Pa., Reverend J. Langer, Altoona, Pa., Reverend M. Habrowski, Portgage, Pa., Reverend John Wasyliszyn, New Castle, Pa., Reverend Wladyslaw Lipski, Everson, Pa., Rev. S. Zmijewski, Islen, Pa., Rev. F. Frania, Latrobe, Pa., Rev. B. Pawlowski, Uniontown, Pa., Rev. A Baron, Footdale, Pa., Rev. P. Glogowski, Republic, Pa., Rev. E. Pawlikowski, Oil City, Pa., Rev. T. Siadecki, Connellsville, Pa., Rev. J. Zdrojkowski, Rev. J. Rajs, Houtzdale, Pa., Rev. J. Trzetrzynski, Barnesboro, Pa.

Polish Clergy Indispensable

A. Curzytek, Pittsburgh recruiting officer, in his confidential report to the National Military Commission dated April 18, 1918, stated "That the recruiting can be successful only with the fullest cooperation of the local Polish Clergy".

Functioning Personnel of Sub-Committees

The following is the available list of Sub-Committees that functioned in the respective areas other than city of Pittsburgh:

Edward Szymorowski

Adams, Ohio - W. Zakrzycki, President, J. Borkowski, Secretary.
Ambridge, Pa. - Rev. Stanislaw Labujewski, Hon. President, Stanislaw Wroblewski, President, W. Pirozek, Secretary.
Arcadia, Pa. - P. Sierocki, President, J. Smigiel, Secretary.
Barnesboro, Pa. - Jan Bush, President, B. Blum, Secretary.
Barton, Ohio - J. Czyzewski, President, J. Bartnicki.
Beaver Falls, Pa. - P. Anuszkiewicz, Secretary.
Blaine, Ohio - M. Czyz, President, P. Miernik, Secretary.
Boswell, Pa. - Ignacy Stokowski, President.
Braddock, Pa. - E. Szymorowski, President, also served as organizer, V.C. Kolski, President, F. Jasinski, Secretary, A. Zylinski, Recording Secretary, W. Wardzinski.
Canonsburg, Pa. - Karol Frenik, President, B. Kotermanski, Secretary, Jan Dziedzik, Recording Secretary.
Carnegie, Pa. - S. Koczaja, President, Jan Pater, Vice-president, H. Mosna, Vice-president, S. Delinikajtys, Recording Secretary.
Charleroi, Pa. - Wojciech Stys, President, Edward Pyzynski, Secretary.
Claridge, Pa. - M. Puchalski.
Clarksburg, W. Va. - J. Duda, President, J. Pierzgalski, Secretary.
Conemaugh, Pa. - Andrew Kucharczyk, President, A. Hejnar, Secretary.
Crescent, Ohio - Bronislaw Tylka, Secretary.
Donora, Pa. - Jan Miller, President, Kazimierz Sobolewski, Secretary.
Dubois, Pa. - Adam Bachmurski, President.
East Vandergrift, Pa. - Joseph Guzirlek, President, Pawel Wichrowski, Secretary.

Elizabeth, Pa. - Bronislaw Skoniewicz, President, Stanislaw Bernadowski, Secretary.
Ellwood City, Pa. - A. Sawicki, President, Stanislaw Graczyk, Sec'y.
Everson, Pa. - Rev. Wladyslaw Lipski, Recruiting officer and organizer.
Fairpoint, Ohio - J. Stando, President, Z. Fabencikowski, Sec'y.
Farrell, Pa. - Joseph Dunaj, President, Michal Mularski, Sec'y.
Ford City, Pa. - P. Ziemianski, President, Andrzej Bilski.
Gallitzin, Pa. - Rev. P. J. Brylski, Honorary President, J. Zagorski, President, J. Kozlowski, Secretary.
Glassport, Pa. - Joseph Sierocki, President, Jan Tudek, Secretary.
Glen Campbell, Pa. - J. Gach, President, Ignacy Sowiski, Sec'y.
Glendale, Pa. - J. Kaszalowicz, President, J. Zwod, Vice-president, J. Stasiowski, Secretary.
Helvetia, Pa. - K. Lipinski, President, W. Guzy, Secretary.
Houtzdale, Pa. - K. Switala, President, Franciszek Sejmel, Sec'y.
Jerome, Pa. - Stanislaw Wilczewski, President, Andrzej Banasiewicz, Secretary.
Johnstown, Pa. - Antoni Furman, President.
Lafferty, Ohio - Jan Harkiewicz, President, Konstanty Bartciak, Secretary.
Latrobe, Pa. - J. Markiewicz, President, W. Homerski, Vice-president, Jan Serefiet, Secretary.
Lilly, Pa. - Rev. J. Pilc.
Leechburg, Pa. - Joseph C. Kunc, President, Jan Gruszka, Vice-president, Piotr Broda, Financial Secretary, Bronislaw Waszkiewicz, Recording Secretary, Jozef Mola, Treasurer.
Lyndora, Pa. - L. Rappa.
McKeesport, Pa. - Franciszek Michalski, President, Franciszek Figura, Secretary.
McKees Rocks, Pa. - Joseph Stepek, President.
Monessen, Pa. - Kazimierz Czelen, President, J. Filipowicz, Sec'y.
Mt. Pleasant, Pa. - Stanislaw Skibinski, Secretary, Rev. W.J. Osinski, President, W. Wielebski, Vice-president, A. Gorski, Treasurer.
Natrona, Pa. - H. Sieradzki, President.
Neffs, Ohio - Waclaw Wroblewski, President, Joseph Chmielewski, Secretary.
New Castle, Pa. - Franciszek Wrona, President. Stanislaw Litwinowicz, Secretary.
New Kensington, Pa. - Joseph Duda, President, Karol Duda, Secretary, J.J. Polcyn, Recording Sergeant [sic, Secretary?].
New Salem, Pa. - Rev. A. Baron.
Osceola Mills, Pa. - Franciszek Szatkowski, President, A. Kozlowski, Secretary.
Portage, Pa. - Stanislaw Wierzcholek, President, Jan Ligas, Sec'y.

Ralphton, Pa. - Feliks Uchman, President, Joseph Klimach, Secretary, Szczepan Wych, Treasurer.
Republic, Pa. - Rev. P. Glugowski.
Rossiter, Pa. - Jan Wrobel, Secretary.
Sagamore, Pa. - Fr. Pryszak, President, T. Bastecki, Vice-president, T. J. Malachowski, Secretary.
Scarbro, W. Va. - Blazej Kwasny, Pres., Edmond Walkowski, Sec'y.
Sharpsburg, Pa. - Aleksander Olszewski, Organizer and Rec. Sgt. [sic, Sec'y?]
South Fork, Pa. - Rev. Fr. Pilz, Pres., Jan Jachumowicz, Vice-pres. Joseph Jada, Secretary, Teofil Butkiewicz, Financial Secretary, Stanislaw Eizak, Treasurer.
Sprague, W. Va. - Antoni Pylka, Pres., Jan Turcza Skielton, Sec'y.
Steubenville, Ohio - F. Smogor, President.
Uniontown, Pa. - Rev. B. Pawlowski.
Washington, Pa. - Joseph Urbaniak.
Weirton, W. Va. - Konstanty Rybka, Pres., Aleks. Rogalski, Sec'y.
Wheeling, W. Va. - Pawel Jurczak, President.
Windber, Pa. - Joseph Wasniarski, Pres., Michal Roznowski, Sec'y., Antoni Grzeszek, Treasurer.
Youngstown, Ohio - M. Cztasz.
Yorkville, Ohio - J. Sadowski, Pres., J. Perglowski, Secretary.

First Recruit

The first recruit enlisted in Pittsburgh, Pa., was Jan Maguda.

Recruits Feted

The Polish Army in America, particularly in the city of Pittsburgh, has been created amid atmosphere of song, poetry and lofty patriotism. The recruiting meetings were almost religious festivals, the farewells of the Polish were marked by emotionalism and patriotic appeals. The united efforts on part of the Citizen's Committee and local clergy brought results and every week from 25 to 200 volunteers were recruited. At first the volunteers congregated at the Polish Falcons Hall Nest 8, 97 S. 18th Street, S.S. Pittsburgh, Pa., where they were given a physical examination and in the evening about the hour of seven they were filled with entertainment. Following the dinner, a parade was formed in which all societies, particularly those uniformed, escorted the recruits to Pennsylvania Railroad Station, where at 11:05 P.M. they were entrained for the training camps, arriving in Buffalo, N.Y., at 7:15 A.M., from where they were transported to the Canadian Camps. Similar affairs were also held at Polish Falcons Hall, 3028 Brereton Ave., Herron Hill.

The Ladies Auxiliaries of Center Number 6

The Ladies Auxiliary of Center Number 6 and their sub-committees played a part in making the recruiting a success particularly in supplying the enlistees with such necessities as shaving kits, tobacco, and other personal necessities.

The Ladies Auxiliary of Center Number 6 Executive Board consisted of: Mrs. Honorata B. Wolowska, President; Mrs. Wanda M. Skarzynski of Crabtree, Vice-president; Miss Alexandra Sophia Bednarko, Vice-president; Mrs. A. Zaucha, Recording Secretary; Mrs. Jadwiga Domachowska, Financial Secretary; Mrs. M. Piekarska, Treasurer.

Regional Sub-committees included Miss Angelina Leona Sikorska, Ladies Falcons Nest 161.

Mrs. M.M. Skarzynska, Polish Falcons Nest 260, Lawrenceville.

Miss Helen J. Synoradzka, President Number 4, South Side.

Mrs. Antoinette Spychala, representing Polish Queen Jadwiga Society 1511 P.N.A.

Mrs. Sophia Synoradzka, Emilia Plater Women's Society 546 P.N.A.

Mrs. J. W. Domachowska, President of Ognisko Domowe (Home Hearth Society) Group 526 P.N.A. of Lawrenceville.

Mrs. R. Zmudzinska, Daughters of Liberty, Branch 227 P.W.A. and Mrs. M. S. Piekarska.

Mrs. H. B. Wolowska

Three Holy Ghost Chaplains

Among the first to enroll to the Polish Army in America were three Pittsburgh Priests of the Congregation of the Holy Ghost Fathers. Reverend Joseph L. Jaworski was probably the first recruit chaplain to enlist. At the time of his enlistment he was pastor in Mt. Carmel, Pa. Prior to that he served as an assistant at Immaculate Heart of Mary Church, Brereton Ave., Herron Hill, and attended Duquesne University. In a letter to

Rev. Joseph L. Jaworski

Dziennik Chicagoski, dated March 31, 1917, Reverend Joseph Jaworski urged a formation of Polish Army.

Offers to Enlist

In April, 1917, Father Jaworski forwarded his application to the Polish Falcons of America. A reply dated April 10, 1917, acknowledged his application and finally on September 12, 1917, was officially notified that his offer of services as a chaplain was accepted.

Military Service

According to the official Polish Army Records, "Polowa Kurja Biskupa", dated April 14, 1931, Rev. Joseph L. Jaworski was in the active service as a volunteer from October 1, 1917 to December 26, 1917 in Canada, sailed with the first contingent on "Niagara" from the New York city port. A rather interesting incident is related by Rev. Jaworski. The Polish Army was originally scheduled to embark from Halifax, Nova Scotia. As the train reached the outskirts of Halifax, heavy snows fell, delaying the progress of the train. While waiting for the clearance of the roads, a terrific explosion shook the entire Halifax port area killing thousands of troops and workers. The explosion took place at the very hour, the first contingent headed by Rev. Jaworski was to board ship. With the port area totally demolished, the First Polish contingent sailing was transferred to New York City port, from where they sailed to France. – Father Jaworski returned to the United States on May 20, 1920, with a transport company of 2,165, demobilized and wounded, and upon landing was asked to promote the First Polish Loan of 1920. He with his committee was successful in raising $20,000,000.00. Upon returning to Poland, Rev. Jaworski continued the active service among the Regular Polish Army Forces until the time of his honorable discharge as of June 20, 1922. Among his numerous decorations received was Poland's highest medal of "Virtuti Militari".

In 1946, he volunteered his services as a chaplain with the United States Army, serving with the Chaplain Corps at Camp Upton and on July 10, 1947, received the following citation:

"The War Department expresses its appreciation for patriotic services to Reverend J. L. Jaworski of Immaculate Heart of Mary Church, Pittsburgh, Pa., for your active interest and assistance to the Chaplain Corps in the Welfare personnel at Camp Upton, N.Y.".

Reverend Zygmunt Rydlewski

At the time of his enlistment was an active pastor at Immaculate Heart of Mary R.C. Church, Herron Hill, Pittsburgh, Pa. He was one of the most zealous patriots priests on the Pittsburgh scene. When Ignacy Jan Paderewski spoke at the Falcon Hall on April 2, 1917 with reference to "Kosciuszko Army", Rev. Rydlewski occupied the same platform representing the Polish inhabitants of Pittsburgh. It was his duty to reply to the great oration which he did not only with words but also with deeds by joining the Polish Army, serving in France and Poland, where he decided to stay upon termination of Polish Wars. He died in Nazi Prison in 1946.

Reverend Jan. J. Dekowski

Rev. Jan J. Dekowski

Rev. Dekowski was one of those individuals that believed that serving a righteous cause is serving God. He distinguished himself on many occasions while serving as an assistant at Immaculate Heart of Mary R.C. Church as a priest and as a writer. As a literary man, he was prolific in his output of Polish poetry devoted to religious topics and in promoting a well known Polish Literary society known as Filarets. His military duties in the Polish Army with the Third Regiment in no way dettered him from continuing his literary efforts towards raising hopes and inspiring at times the faltering spirits of Polish Soldiers. Upon his discharge from the Polish Army he transferred his spiritual activities to Polish Settlement at St. Catherine's, Toronto, Canada, where he served until the time of his death. He was buried in the neighboring Polish Soldiers Cemetery, Niagara-on-the-Lake, where sleep many of his friends.

Other Volunteers

Other clergymen of Polish descent, who volunteered their services as Chaplains were: Rev. T. Siatecki, Connellsville, Pa., and Rev. Czeslaw Duszynski, who enlisted January 2, 1918.

Termination of Recruiting

With the ending of World War I, the French Government, being the godfather of the Polish Army in France, called "a halt to recruiting of the eligibles in United States in view of the fact that Polish Government no longer depends on the Allies for support". Consequently February 15, 1919, was the last enlistment opportunity and closing of all recruiting offices in the United States of America. From the time the recruiting was opened October, 1917, to closing date, approximately 38,088 volunteers joined the Polish Army, of which about 3,000 were from Pittsburgh areas.

Closing of Training Camps

With the closing of recruiting, came the termination of liquidation of training camps in Ontario, Canada. The official closing was on February 22, 1919. Reverend Stanislaus R. Labujewski, Ambridge, Pa., Chaplain of the Polish Falcons of America, represented the Falcons at this event and delivered appropriate remarks. Thus was the end of an act that had its inception in Pittsburgh, Pa., and blossomed into a Free and Independent Poland in 1919.

The Road Back - Home - U.S.A.

With the wars of World War I and the Bolsheviki Communist invasion brought to successful conclusion the question arose what is to be done with those desiring to come back to United States. It was mutually agreed that all those desiring to come to their USA home should be immediately repatriated. Consequently the men were brought to Camp Dix, N.J. and Camp Meade, Maryland, where demobilization was completed. Upon arrival in Pittsburgh they usually were greeted by the Citizen's Committee and feted and given a sum of money. The cost of transportation was borne by the Polish Government to the point of arrival at Hoboken, N.J. The names of vessels on which they returned to the United States were: The Antigone sailed from Poland March 30, 1920, arriving in U.S.A. April 18, 1920. Pocohontas sailed April 2, 1920, arriving in U.S.A. April 21, 1920; May 28, 1920, arriving June 16, 1920; July 26, 1920, arriving August 12, 1920. Princess Matoika sailed May 2, 1920, arriving May 23, 1920; July 7, 1920, arriving July 21, 1920. Mercury sailed June 16, 1920, arrived June 29, 1920. President Grant sailed January 28, 1921, arriving February 16, 1921. The last vessel included the veterans of these who fought in the Bolsheviki-Communist War of 1920.

Rev. Stanislaus R. Labujewski

Finale

It is doubtful if the cause of Independence of Poland would have had received such an unanimous and expeditious recognition from Allied Powers in World

War I if there was no Polish Army in France with the United States recruits forming its nucleus. In political and military sense it was in the United States that the activities of the Polish Patriots first brought fruit of Freedom. The overall success may be accredited to the united efforts of all Polish leaders in the United States with the City of Pittsburgh forming the spearhead. There were many outstanding leaders and zealous workers among both sexes. To give each individual his due credit would require volumes of writing but under present circumstances it is impossible, for we are limited in space and funds. When and if funds are available, additional details should be given to Dr. Teofil A. Starzynski's activities on behalf of the Polish cause, a full treatment should be rendered to Mrs. Honorata B. Wolowska and the Ladies Auxiliaries who played a vital part in recruiting drives and solicitation of funds for the personal needs of the recruits of the Polish Army.

Typical Grey Samaritan uniform as represented by Mrs. J. Rajchel

Judge Lois M. McBride of the Allegheny County Court and her contributions should be recorded in detail for posterity, particularly in training **Grey Samaritans**, dedicated to social and welfare work. Then we have a significant and indispensable role by Attorney C.W. Sypniewski, who as a president of the Polish Relief Committee and Polish Defense Committee solicited funds that were sorely needed to save the starving Poles and maintain the Polish Army.

The late Judge Frank A. Piekarski of the Allegheny County Court who used every occasion to champion the Polish cause, sacrificed his time and talents. Lest the local historians be deprived of one of the most active and colorful patriots of his day, we should not forget that robust Herron Hill pharmacist and personality of Anthony Karabasz who as a Censor of Polish National Alliance and treasurer of local Polish Recruiting Committee seemed to find source of endless energy and zeal in promoting the recruiting and solicitation of money for support of the Polish corps.

Finally, a detailed research should be made on J. M. Horodyski, a former Pittsburgher, who acted as a confidante of Premier Ignacy

Frank A. Piekarski

J. Paderewski. One of his last official recorded acts was his appearance before Col. House to plead "the tragic situation of Poland" in January 12, 1919. As a result, the Allied Diplomats approved the transfer of the Polish Army in France to Poland proper. It was this army that subsequently cleared the eastern and western borders and then culminated its military activities with a decisive defeat of the Communist Army at the gates of Warsaw in 1920.

Acknowledgement:

Central Council of Polish Organizations for financing the printing of this brochure.
Polish Falcons of America for supplying the pertinent data and original sources of references.
Mieczyslaw Wasilewski, Editor in Chief of the Polish Falcon, who devoted much of this time and effort in giving assistance to the author.
Arthur Waldo, author and publicist who offered many constructive suggestions.
Polish Roman Catholic Union Archives, Polish Army Association of America Circuit III, Pittsburgh, Pa.
Carnegie Library of Pgh., Lawrenceville and Oakland Branches.
Kamil Hupert, Mrs. Hedwig Siwicka, Mrs. Mary Pitakowska, Mrs. Heromina Cygnarowicz-Lewandowska, Mrs. Helen Pawlak-Adamczak - sources of original recruiting station references.

Pittsburgh Soldier's Diary with Polish Army - World War 1917

The following is a Diary of Michael Stypula, Pittsburgh, Pa., member of the Polish Army in France.

* * *

Enlisted with the Polish Army in France in Pittsburgh, Pennsylvania, November 16, 1917, entrained to Camp Kosciuszko, Niagara-on-the-Lake, Canada, December 3, 1917. Stopped and stayed in Buffalo, N.Y., for three days. After completing preliminaries proceeded to the training camp where I have arrived on December 6th, at 9:15 P. M. Re-assigned to Fort Niagara, N.Y. December 28th for further training … left camp on February 8, 1918 and proceeded our journey to France.

On the Way to France

Michael Stypula

Debarked from New York City Port on February 11, 1918, and subsequently arrived at Brest, France, February 28, 1918 ... greeted enthusiastically by the Polish, French, and American authorities.

Arrived at Mayenne, March 3, 1918, and on April 14th left for Cheutonouf. Departed for Camp St. Quentin June 1918, then marched to Brienne La Chatteu, reaching same on June 12, 1918, took four full marching days ... Brienne bombarded on June 13th, one killed outright and the wounded two died the following day. Presentation of regimental battle colors on June 22, 1918, somewhere in Champagne... it rained all day, but the ceremony went off as scheduled. Arrived in Paris July 12th, one and half of Second Battalion of Second Regiment, paraded in full review on July 14th, Bastille day, greeted enthusiastically by French and Parisian Poles. Returned to Brienne La Chatteu July 16th for training and conditioning. Given a furlough to Paris July 22nd, and spent 10 days ... Big Bertha is bombing Paris for four consecutive days. Joined my outfit at Camp St. Tanche, Champiegnie Front, August 1918 ... entrained for Crevachamp September, 1918.

Finally in Action

At last assigned battle position on an active front October, 1918, in Vosges Mountain terrain, where have taken part in action for sixteen consecutive days. Given a rest leave and returned to the reserve positions... On November 11th, reassigned to another sector near Metz... as we are traveling towards the front, at the village were informed that armistice is in the making... Returned to Horseville, a village near Strassburg... and subsequently transferred to Hosonville. In April, 1919, reassigned to St. Dizier, where preparations were made for hopeful transfer to our native Poland... this all depended on decision to be made by Allied Ministers.

On Way to Poland

Finally our dreams were about to be realized when informed that we are to leave for Poland and did on April 20, 1919. Trip was marked by occasional German rifle fire sniping. Arrived in Poland April 25, 1919, at station Kakolewo. Proceeded to Chelm and reached the town on April 26, 1919. Continued our training and orientation at a town of Wlodzimierz Wolynski … whence we reached on May 8, 1919.

Fight for Poland

May 15th witnessed our first Big Offensive against guerilla forces of general Petlura (subsequently joined the Polish Forces)… force march for four days … after severe fighting captured Luck on May 18, 1919 … town of Iwanowicz, capitulated May 15 … after four hour pitched battle … quartered at Jaroslawicze. Re-assigned to field positions at Ostrow, May 26, 1919 … promoted to rank of Company Adjutant July 29, 1919, and given a furlough. Returned to Rowno position August 18, 1919 …Town of Rowno captured August 12, 1919, after a three day battle … marched off to Kostopole, where was assigned to non-commissioned officers school for a period of three weeks as assistant instructor. Orders given to take positions at Olewsk front … battle started September 13th, and continued until September 14, 1919 … reassigned to town of Rowno for a rest. Transferred to Zwiahel … battle fought October 30, 1919. Marched off to Baranowski where we were stationed for three weeks and then proceeded by foot to Miropol, and after a two days rest returned to battle action. In Patrol Action December 22, 1919. Battle at Romanow … four casualties …captured Romanow February 21, 1920. Recalled to regimental school February 25th and assigned to non-commissioned officers school, as Junior officer commander … reordered to front … Battle at Zaborzycami … Budziskami … Romanowem … Wroblewka … Forced march 85 kilometers in thirty six hours on April 1st and 2nd, 1920 … marched to Lubar April 16, 1920, from where my battalion had made several surprising and successful attacks upon the Bolshevikis and Communists … in one particular instance my outfit captured twenty one prisoners and killed nine with only one casualty to our group of thirty men.

Return Home

Demobilized April 22, 1920 … spent six days in Luck … journeyed to Pomiechowek, arriving May 5th … given a furlough May 10, 1920, to visit my mother and sisters at my old home … returned May 18th. Transferred to Grupa May 24, 1920 … left Grupa June 14, 1929 (1920) … and embarked for the United

States June 16th, 1920, as second in command of the transport ... Landed at New York Port on June 29, 1920, and went directly to Camp Dix, N.J., where we underwent physical examination and processing.

Home - July 3, 1920.

Polish Army World War I
Honor Roll

**City of Pittsburgh
And Tri-State Area**

Akron, PA
    Markuszewski, Wladyslaw
Albana, PA
    Duploga, Jan *(Duplaga)*
Altoona, PA
    Hormanski, Kalisty *(Horomanski)*
Arnold, PA
    Andrzejewski, Stanislaw
Atlasburg, PA
    Pierzchala Ludwik
Ambridge, PA
    Brzozowski, Bronislaw
    Brzuska, Kazimierz
    Grzelka, Adam
    Grzywacz, Michal
    Kulczynski, Ignacy *(Kulczenski)*
    Ludwiczak, Maciej
    Mikolajczak, Jan *(Mikolajczyk)*
    Rykaczewski, Feliks
    Mrociek, Pawel
    Szczepanski, Antoni
    Szymanski, Jan
    Tuwalski, Feliks
    Tuwalski, Jan
    Wagner, Szczepan
    Wieloch, Zygmunt
    Zieja, Adolf
    Zmijewski, Antoni
Barnesboro, PA
    Bogacki, Ludwik
    Cieliczka, Jan
    Dziedzic, Wojciech
    Grzes, Jozef
    Haluch, Jozef
    Koscielniak, Jozef
    Mroczko, Ludwik *(Mroczka)*
    Noga, Walenty
    Oseliss, Karol *(Oselis)*
    Rachfal, Antoni
    Sander, Wincenty
    Trzaskus, Andrzej *(Trzaszkus)*
    Ziobro, Wincenty
Beaver Falls, PA
    Petterson, Czeslaw *(Peterson)*
    Pieczycha, Adam *(Pieczychna)*
    Konopka, Stanislaw
    Golota, Leon
    Flara, Leon *(Flera)*
    Chojnacki, Jozef
Berkertown, PA

Dusko, Szymon
Palka, Szymon
Salamon, Szymon

Brackenridge, PA
  Brzostek, Boleslaw
  Waskowski, Stanislaw
  Zaremba, Franciszek

Braddock, PA
  Chudecki, Wincenty *(Hudycki)*
  Dernacki, Wladyslaw *(Derucki)*
  Gorak, Antoni
  Jablonowski, Lucjan
  Jackiewicz, Jozef
  Jackowski, Teofil
  Kazmierski, Jozef *(Kazimierski)*
  Kepski, Jozef
  Krocin, Jan
  Krzywicki, Antoni
  Maszczak, Jozef
  Miezio, Aleksander
  Misialek, Rudolf
  Morcz, Lucian *(Moroz)*
  Nowakowski, Jan
  Nowakowski, Stanislaw *(Nowatkowski)*
  Olejniczak, Boleslaw
  Olejniczak, Boleslaw
  Oleksy, Stanislaw
  Puchalski, Tomasz
  Regula, Jan
  Sarna, Marcin
  Skoczylas, Franciszek
  Smalarz, Jozef
  Stanczak, Zygmunt
  Stolarczyk, Stanislaw
  Urbanowski, Wincenty *(Urbanowicz)*
  Wlaslowski, Barnaba *(Wloslowski)*
  Wlodarczyk, Stanislaw
  Styklinski, Bronislaw

No. Braddock, PA
  Chowaniec, Jozef *(Horoniec)*

Broughton, PA
  Slowinski, Jozef *(Slawinski)*
  Stysiak, Piotr

Beavendale, PA
  Mastalski, Jakob

Beadling, PA
  Mazur, Antoni

Brinketown, PA
  Cichon, Szymon

Brownsville, PA
  Mahaj, Antoni

Brownstown, PA
  Roskiewicz, Ignacy *(Reszkiewicz)*

Bruseton, PA
  Kalinowski, Jozef
  Orlowski, Jan

California, PA
  Bugaj, Franciszek
  Sienko, Ignacy
  Wenc, Jozef

Carbondale, PA
  Hanusiak, Michal

Connonsville, PA
  Hydzik, Pawel

Castle, PA
  Nilik, Antoni *(Hilik)*
  Zylewicz, Feliks
  Zylewicz, Stanislaw

Castle Shannon, PA
  Konsikas, Konstanty *(Kornikas)*

Coneville, PA
  Koszyk, Jozef

Cuddy, PA
  Malinowski, Stanislaw

Conifer, PA
  Omieszko, Aleksander *(Oniszko)*
  Szymanski, Jozef

Charterak, PA
  Kupindlowski, Jan *(Kupidlowski)*
  Lechowski, Franciszek *(Lachowski)*
  Tomkiewicz, Antoni
  Wodejko, Jan

Charleroi, PA
  Gurzynski, Jan
  Laskowski, Antoni
  Stasiak, Antoni *(Stasziak)*
  Tomaszewski, Jozef

Conemaugh, PA
  Goralski, Wasyl *(Gorasik)*
  Janiak, Piotr
  Paliszewski, Jozef
  Suprun, Michal

Canonsburg, PA
  Flis, Jan
  Leszczynski, Wladyslaw
  Mrugac, Ignacy *(Mrugacz)*
  Paszek, Stanislaw
  Rusiewski, Piotr

Rzadkowski, Jakob
Skowronski, Kazimierz
Wiloszewski, Teodor *(Miloszewski)*
Wojczyk, Jozef *(Wojcik)*
Zimmerfald, Franciszek *(Zimmerfeld)*

Carnegie, PA
   Czop, Feliks
   Czop Jan
   Howniecz, Antoni
   Handzak, Stanislaw *(Handzel)*
   Jagilewski, Jozef
   Kantek, Jan
   Jaworski, Michal
   Kedzierski, Kazimierz *(Kendzierski)*
   Ligenza, Michal
   Marszal, Michal
   Paczek, Jakob
   Pasek, Franciszek
   Pater, Wojciech
   Piotrowski, Wladyslaw
   Seres, Jozef
   Skocz, Jozef
   Tarsza, Stanislaw *(Tarsa)*
   Trzeciak, Jozef
   Wojcik, Adam
   Wojciechowski, Jozef
   Zaradzki, Jozef
   Zelek, Jan

Cassandra, PA
   Gawlowski, Marcel
   Kunka, Antoni
   Kurowski, Feliks

Donora, PA
   Bury, Jozef
   Cwiklinski, Ludwik
   Olesko, Piotr
   Poloncarz, Antoni
   Ryzowicz, Jakob
   Sowinski, Stanislaw
   Skrocki, Aleksander
   Suski, Jan
   Zajdek, Antoni *(Zajdel)*
   Zarnowski, Pawel

Delonville, PA *(Dillonvale, OH)*
   Lorkowski, Jan

Dhrenfeld, PA   *(Ehrenfeld)*
   Kamienski, Antoni

Dubois, PA
   Hibaszek, Jan *(Hilaszek)*
   Jatczak, Jan *(Jatszak)*
   Karolewski, Stanislaw
   Naradka, Jan
   Skrzypiec, Jan
   Slomkowski, Stanislaw
   Sychalski, Stanislaw *(Spychalski)*

Elwood City, PA
   Dermatowicz, Stanislaw *(Dermontowicz)*
   Wosiak, Jozef

Emeigh, PA
   Pyiek, Franciszek *(Pyjdyk)*
   Rachfal, Tomasz
   Waliszak, Michal *(Waliczek)*
   Wolonia, Jakob *(Wolonin)*

Etna, PA
   Skrzypaszek, Jakob
   Tuskau, Mikolaj *(Tuskau)*

Elizabeth, PA
   Cieslik, Jozef

West Elizabeth, PA
   Zembicki, Jan *(Zebicki)*

Elenora, PA
   Warian, Jakob *(Waryan)*

Eritan, PA
   Debek, Bronislaw

Everson, PA
   Jaworski, Ignacy

Fairpoint, PA
   Kowalski, Wladyslaw

Fayette City, PA
   Bytnar, Wojciech
   Sobek, Piotr
   Zurowski, Mateusz

Farrell, PA
   Bober, Jan
   Delinski, Jozef
   Magusiak, Jozef
   Malenda, Stanislaw *(Molenda)*
   Prejsnar, Franciszek *(Prajsner)*
   Sidor, Pawel
   Wojtowicz, Franciszek
   Wratny, Jan *(Wrotny)*
   Wrona, Franciszek

Footdale, PA
   Banek, Jakob
   Sosieu, Jan *(Sosien)*
   Trybon, Jakob

Ford City, PA
   Folcik, Wladyslaw *(Folczyk)*

Folta, Hieronim
Godzik, Pawel
Graca, Franciszek
Kaspryk, Jozef *(Kasprzyk)*
Kenia, Jan *(Kania)*
Klocek, Michal
Kochanski, Andrzej
Kornasiewicz, Stanislaw
Krempulec, Piotr
Lysakowski, Jan
Sigut, Jan
Szafran, Jan
Ziemianski, Marcel

So. Fork, PA
Grochowski, Franciszek
Krzemienski, Jozef *(Krzemien)*
Mazur, Feliks
Poczatek, Jacenty
Skiba, Antoni
Surowicz, Feliks *(Surowiec)*
Swider, Antoni
Sycz, Jan
Walczak, Jan
Waskiewicz, Wincenty
Zdunczyk, Franciszek
Zaremba, Stanislaw *(Zareba)*

Gallitzen, PA
Dembski, Jan *(Debski)*
Dida, Jan *(Dyda)*
Gunie, Franciszek *(Gonia)*
Kalinowski, Ignacy
Kozubal, Franciszek
Krol, Jan
Kubrah, Jozef *(Kubrak)*
Machanski, Piotr
Maciejewski, Piotr
Pirwota, Stanislaw *(Pierwola)*
Slawik, Stan. Antoni *(Slowik)*
Slowik, Marjan
Szymaika, Franciszek *(Szymusiak)*

Glassmere, PA
Ugodzinski, Stanislaw

Glassport, PA
Bidzinski, Adam
Guzikowski, Pawel
Kipowski, Jozef *(Kijowski)*
Michalski, Jan
Sobieszanski, Bronislaw *(Sobieszinski)*

Glendale, PA
Adamiec, Michal
Niemiec, Wojciech

Glenwhite, PA
Abrecki, Andrzej
Giblah, Andrzej *(Giblak)*

Heidelberg, PA
Mazur, Walenty

Heilwood, PA
Adamczak, Wojciech
Ronczka, Wojceich

Hoboken, PA
Ginka, Antoni *(Glinka)*

Homer City, PA
Boczar, Andrzej
Cislo, Jozef

Homestead, PA
Baranowski, Wladyslaw
Bednarski, Waclaw
Chwal, Michal
Czyz, Tomasz
Gladkowski, Jan
Gorczyca, Stanislaw
Gwordos, Wladyslaw
Janowski, Aleksander
Kalisz, Wladyslaw
Kumega, Feliks *(Kumiega)*
Markiewicz, Bronislaw
Milewski, Jozef
Piwowar, Henryk
Rakowski, Jan
Sitek, Franciszek
Sudo, Antoni
Wawrzacz, Jozef *(Wawrzac)*

Hermine, PA
Mokolanic, Antoni *(Mikolanic)*
Roszak, Konstanty

Irwin, PA
Kwiatkowski, Franciszek

Indiana, PA
Body, Stanislaw
Grabowski, Konstanty
Jezewicz, Michal

Jamison, PA
Abramowicz, Franciszek

Johnstown, PA
Adamski, Bartlomiej
Bazan, Franciszek *(Bazon)*
Ceslik, Andrzej *(Cieslik)*
Cochara, Franciszek *(Czochara)*

Cyrek, Walenty
Czekaj, Ludwik
Dembowski, Walenty
Depa, Stanislaw
Fabiezewski, Jozef
Florek, Wojciech
Gac, Andrzej
Gomulka, Andrzej *(Gamulka)*
Gaszynski, Wladyslaw
Golojuch, Kazimierz
Grzesik, Walenty
Gurka, Wojciech
Guzek, Piotr
Guzik, Wojciech
Hoboda, Marcin *(Hebda)*
Jagielo, Stanislaw
Jakubowski, Jozef
Jarosz, Franciszek
Jaszczak, Wojciech *(Jastrzab)*
Juraszewski, Jan
Kaminski, Wincenty
Kaminski, Wladyslaw
Klimowicz, Michal
Klenk, Stanislaw
Krajenko, Segeniusz *(Kroneijko)*
Krok, Michal
Kubala, Ferdynand
Kulbida, Longius *(Kulbera)*
Kusniar, Jan
Lachman, Jan
Lasota, Dominik
Lech, Andrzej
Magurski, Wojciech *(Magierski)*
Marziusz, Jan
Mis, Aleksander
Mroczka, Michal *(Mrocka)*
Mucha, Lukasz
Nowak, Wincenty
Misiewicz, Michal
Pachowicz, Antoni
Pieconka, Wojciech *(Piecaka)*
Pieklo, Jan
Piekarski, Stanislaw
Piklo, Jan *(Pieklo)*
Psychocki, Stanislaw *(Przychodzki)*
Pukala, Jozef
Pulka, Jozef *(Palko)*
Rasmus, Franciszek *(Rozmus)*
Rusin, Jan
Siwy, Jozef
Skomielski, Stanislaw
Skuba, Jakob
Slezak, Feliks
Slonka, Stanislaw
Sowa, Stanislaw
Smiti, Szczepan *(Smith)*
Stadler, Rudolf
Stec, Jan
Stepien, Jan
Sutyla, Wladyslaw
Swal, Marcin *(Szwal)*
Swart, Andrzej *(Szwaszt)*
Szciechowicz, Franciszek *(Szczechowicz)*
Szczur, Jan
Szostek, Jan
Szostek, Jozef
Trzeciak, Jan
Urban, Jozef
Walitko, Wojciech
Walkowicz, Ludwik
Wozniak, Antoni
Zelkos, Jozef *(Zolkos)*

Lafayette, PA
   Kaminski, Piotr
   Lach, Wojciech

Loupux, PA
   Rozems, Jozef *(Rozmus)*

Latrobe, PA
   Fic, Franciszek
   Rynkowski, Aleksander

Leechburgh, PA
   Zelman, Jan

West Lebanon, PA
   Kozlowski, Aleksander

Lupurees, PA
   Handzlik, Antoni

Lyndora, PA
   Janik, Walenty
   Nowoczynski, Konstanty
   Rajchel, Jan

Lilly, PA
   Jendrzejewski, Feliks
   Paskiewicz, Wincenty *(Paszkiewicz)*
   Platta, Wojciech *(Plata)*
   Semet, Julian *(Sement)*

Marstelar, PA
   Kluska, Kazimierz
   Marczak, Jozef

Miznik, Mateusz *(Mytnik)*
McIntyre, PA
    Kontrynowicz, Boleslaw *(Kontrymowicz)*
    Olchowski, Jan
    Wiencek, Michal
    Wienciak, Franciszek
Mollenauer, PA
    Zuzanski, Jan
Mouchal, PA
    Szymboras, Jan *(Szymbara)*
McKeesport, PA
    Adamek, Jozef
    Bocian, Antoni
    Bolawajder, Ludwik *(Balawajder)*
    Borowiec, Antoni *(Borowicz)*
    Burzynski, Jozef
    Cubowski, Jozef
    Curek, Jozef *(Cwiek)*
    Debski, Franciszek
    Dudek, Jan
    Grochocinski, Ignacy
    Grochocinski, Wojciech
    Grochowski, Stanislaw
    Golebiewski, Jan
    Gorelanski, Stanislaw *(Gorzelanski)*
    Gorzelanski, Franciszek
    Jaworowski, Wiktor
    Kalcicki, Stanislaw
    Karolewski, Franciszek
    Kowalewski, Wladyslaw
    Kijowski, Jozef
    Kolanowski, Jozef *(Kolakowski)*
    Kondratowicz, Wiktor
    Konopka, Wiktor
    Konkel, Jan
    Kozlowski, Piotr
    Krawiec, Antoni
    Krzeminski, Jan
    Kujatkiewicz, Karol *(Kwiatkowicz)*
    Kustra, Leon
    Lewandowski, Leon
    Lewandowski, Stanislaw
    Lozzela, Kazimierz *(Koszela)*
    Lopaczynski, Jozef *(Lopacinski)*
    Matczak, Waclaw
    Mazurek, Rafal
    Michalek, Tomasz
    Mikrut, Pawel
    Niedzwiecki, Pawel
    Olejniak, Piotr *(Olejnik)*
    Osalinski, Erazo *(Osolinski)*
    Palka, Jozef
    Piskorski, Stanislaw
    Ptaszczynski, Ignacy *(Ptaszcinski)*
    Pociosk, Franciszek *(Pociask)*
    Rozanski, Jan
    Rybka, Wiktor
    Stanaszek, Jozef
    Sykala, Ludwik
    Synas, Jozef *(Synos)*
    Szczap, Franciszek
    Szczap, Wladyslaw
    Szlachetka, Wawrzyniec
    Wisocki, Andrzej *(Wysocki)*
    Wisocki, Jan *(Wysocki)*
    Wisocki, Marjan *(Wysocki, Marcin)*
    Wladkowski, Stanislaw *(Wlodkowski)*
    Wojnarowski, Waclaw
    Wozniak, Stanislaw
    Wrotecki, Tomasz
    Wysocki, Michal
McKees Rocks, PA
    Bednarowski, Stanislaw
    Brzezinski, Jan
    Dyczeski, Piotr *(Dyczewski)*
    Dzidowicz, Jan *(Dziadowicz)*
    Dziengelewski, Szymon *(Dziengielewski)*
    Dyckowski, Edward *(Dyczkowski)*
    Hnat, Piotr
    Golembiowski, Mikolaj *(Golebiowski)*
    Jurkiewicz, Stanislaw
    Karmazinski, Antoni
    Kwasny, Jozef
    Kwiatkowski, Franciszek
    Liss, Boleslaw *(Lis)*
    Robert, Feliks
    Rodakowski, Franciszek
    Rozewicz, Wincenty
    Rutkowski, Teofil
    Sawicki, Franciszek
    Smigielski, Walenty
    Wasielewski, Stanislaw *(Wasilewski)*
Middland, PA
    Kwiatkowski, Aleksander *(Kulakowski)*
    Krutulis, Jozef
    Ruskowski, Jozef *(Ruszkowski)*
Monessen, PA
    Beck, Jan

Demanczuk, Pawel *(Dymanczyk)*
Demnianczuk, Pawel *(Demianczuk)*
Drzewinski, Stanislaw
Feliga, Franciszek
Gasiorowski, Antoni
Gasiorowski, Teofil
Kantor, Jozef
Karpinski, Leon
Karwinski, Bronislaw *(Korwinski)*
Kielczewski, Ksawery
Konieczny, Konstanty
Kusiniak, Edward
Lewandowski, Antoni
Nartowicz, Kleofas
Niebojenski, Jan *(Niebojewski)*
Nowinski, Ludwik
Olejnik, Stanislaw
Osinski, Aleksander
Pekala, Teofil
Radzikowski, Franciszek
Sajewski, Adam
Swieczasek, Wladyslaw *(Swieciaszek)*
Szterc, Boleslaw *(Sztorc)*
Wojtkowski, Julian
Zdancewicz, Aleksander
Zub, Bronislaw
Zmijewski, Wladyslaw *(Zijewski)*

Mt. Pleasant, PA
Bryja, Stanislaw
Chowaniec, Jan
Garbarz, Antoni *(Garbasz)*
Kuczkowski, Zygmunt
Oleksy, Jan
Spenczar, Szymon
Zawora, Szczepan

Natrona, PA
Andrzejewski, Tomasz
Antkowiak, Antoni *(Antokowiak)*
Baranowski, Julian
Bastecki, Jozef
Bartnikowski, Stanislaw
Baziutowski, Stanislaw *(Badziulowski)*
Binkowski, Boleslaw
Bojakowski, Ludwik
Boros, Jan
Brodowski, Marcel
Brzozowski, Franciszek
Bulwicki, Wladyslaw
Cicholski, Jozef

Chrzanowski, Boleslaw
Czarnecki, Zygmunt
Dabkowski, Zygmunt *(Dombkowski)*
Dobrzynski, Edward
Domurat, Aleksander *(Domurad)*
Falencki, Aleksander
Ferczyk, Stanislaw
Filipiak, Boleslaw
Furmanski, Leon
Girlewski, Jan
Gorski, Aleksander
Grzewinski, Jan
Jackowski, Wladyslaw
Jankowski, Bronislaw
Kolankowski, Stanislaw
Konopka, Wladyslaw
Koprowski, Stefan
Krasnicki, Franciszek *(Krosnicki)*
Krukowski, Wladyslaw
Kuczynski, Jozef
Kwiatkowski, Jozef
Kwiatkowski, Stanislaw
Liszewski, Antoni
Malecki, Wincenty
Malicki, Jan
Masalski, Waclaw
Narzedziewski, Jozef
Nawotko, Cyprjan *(Nawotka)*
Modzelewski, K. Jozef
Mozelewski, Jan *(Modzelewski)*
Nowak, Antoni
Nowakowski, Henryk
Nowicki, Konstanty
Nowoczynski, Antoni *(Nowocinski)*
Oglecki, Boleslaw
Oglecki, Jozef
Ogrodowski, Wladyslaw *(Ogrodowczyk)*
Osiecki, Wladyslaw
Pawlak, Jozef
Pawlowicz, Stanislaw
Pilkowski, Jan
Piotrowski, Jan
Pokusinski, Boleslaw
Przewrocki, Wladyslaw *(Przewlocki)*
Pysiewicz, Antoni
Pyrzewski, Stanislaw
Rudnicki, Adam
Rusinski, Boleslaw *(Rucinski)*
Sadowski, Feliks

Skibicki, Waclaw
Skowronski, Walenty
Stando, Franciszek
Suchowski, Jan
Szkalewski, Jozef
Szarewicz, Jozef
Szczesny, Franciszek
Szydlik, Aleksander *(Szydik)*
Wasilkowski, Stanislaw *(Wasilowski)*
Wendereusz, Jozef
Wosniewski, Adam *(Wolniewski)*
Wysocki, Jozef
Zbryski, Antoni

New Castle, PA
Bak, Alojzy
Bocek, Antoni
Cichon, Franciszek
Cychon, Franciszek *(Cycon)*
Cychon, Stanislaw *(Cycon)*
Data, Ignacy
Fitz, Jozef *(Filtz)*
Gierlach, Piotr
Gorgacz, Stanislaw *(Gorzach)*
Herbut, Stanislaw
Hunia, Franciszek
Jagielski, Stanislaw
Karski, Jozef
Kobiatka, Andrzej *(Kobialka)*
Krupa, Michal
Mastyk, Jozef
Nowak, Stanislaw
Rajchel, Franciszek
Sekcinski, Stanislaw
Skrzypski, Boleslaw
Sniezek, Ignacy
Swiezek, Jozef *(Sniezek)*
Szelest, Izydor
Wilusz, Piotr
Wolawin, Franciszek *(Wolanin)*
Wroblewski, Adam

New Kensington, PA
Adamkiewicz, Stanislaw
Bagienski, Leon
Baranowski, Stanislaw
Baranowski, Stanislaw
Benedykt, Jakob *(Benedyk)*
Bujalski, Jan
Dziekonski, Antoni *(Dzienkonski)*
Dzwonkowski, Mieczyslaw
Gizinski, Jozef
Gudkowski, Stanislaw *(Gutkowski)*
Gulowski, Stanislaw *(Gutowski)*
Handzyski, Adolf *(Hadzynski)*
Jackowski, Stanislaw
Janukiewicz, Tomasz *(Janulewicz)*
Kaczor, Kazimierz
Kaluba, Stefan
Kantorski, Leon
Karp, Jan
Koper, Jan *(Kopec)*
Kordelski, Jozef
Kubit, Jan
Lipka, Edward
Maliszewski, Jozef
Materski, Aleksander
Mazur, Jan
Nowotka, Clemens *(Nowodka)*
Panko, Antoni *(Painko)*
Pawlowski, Szymon
Pelczarski, Jan
Pelczarski, Kasper
Prusinski, Ignacy
Przybystowski, Aleksander
    (Przybyslawski)
Radomski, Franciszek
Ratynski, J. Kazimierz
Sarczuk, Aleksander *(Szacuk)*
Sitkowski, Stanislaw
Siuta, Jan
Siuta, Stanislaw
Szepietowski, Konstanty
Szoda, Stanislaw *(Sroda)*
Szydlowski, Stanislaw
Tasinski, Wladyslaw *(Tosinski)*
Tomczak, Aleksander
Tupac, Michal *(Tupaj)*
Tylinski, Boleslaw
Wasikowski, Franciszek
Waskiewicz, Wincenty
Wisniewski, Wladyslaw
Wloch, Stanislaw
Zdanczyk, Jan

New Salem, PA
Kogut, Stanislaw
Wozniak, Jan

Osciola, PA
Ciezarkiewicz, Jozef
Dolnaczko, Stefan *(Dolniaczko)*

Goral, Antoni
Kwiatkowski, Jozef
Plata, Wladyslaw
Wrobel, Jan
Osciola Mills, PA
    Konski, Rudolf
    Wisnaj, Jan *(Wisniol)*
Oakdale, PA
    Sosnowka, Wojciech
Oil City, PA
    Seborowski, Jan
Olmsbry, PA
    Gabys, Jan *(Gabrys)*
Orient, PA
    Biduko, Marcin *(Bienko)*
    Gac, Wladyslaw *(Gec)*
Penn Station, PA *(Pittsburgh)*
    Sienkiewicz, S. *(Stanislaw)*
Philadelphia, PA
    Stankiewicz, Czeslaw
    Staniszewski, Stanislaw
Puritan, PA
    Malisz, Bartlomiej *(Malik)*
Portage, PA
    Boltowski, Jan
    Buczynski, Jozef
    Gladysiewicz, Wojciech
    Hajduk, Pawel
    Halish, Pawel
    Kaczmarski, Jan
    Kaczynski, Jan
    Kuta, Antoni
    Mieldziuk, Michal
    Podasznik, Jozef *(Potasnik)*
    Rutkowski, Antoni
    Wajsak, Jan
    Waksmulski, Jozef *(Wakomulski)*
Republic, PA
    Fiolna, Jozef
    Markiewicz, Andrzej
    Pasierb, Ignacy
    Penkowski, Jan
    Sieradzki, Tomasz
Ranton, PA
    Gorski, Jan
Reynoldsville, PA
    Cymont, Aleksander
Rochester, PA
    Piotrowski, Jan
    Rudnicki, Teodor
Rossiter, PA
    Blajer, Jozef
    Gloty, Wladyslaw
    Gregorczyk, Jozef *(Gregorczuk)*
    Grymacz, Jozef *(Grzymacz)*
    Mogielnicki, Jan
    Osika, Kasper
    Pelc, Jozef
    Pelc, Ludwik
    Stopor, Izydor *(Stopa)*
    Stuperski, Antoni
    Turek, Walenty
    Wiernik, Jan
    Zebrowski, Bronislaw
Russelton, PA
    Dobrowolski, Jozef
Scranton, PA
    Polkowski, Aleksander
Sharpsburg, PA
    Brzezinski, Zygmunt
    Bzibziak, Antoni
    Ciski, Stanislaw *(Ciszki)*
    Cirupka, Teofil *(Ciupka)*
    Czapski, Piotr
    Dawideusz, Tadeusz *(Dawidenasz)*
    Dymkowski, Boleslaw
    Jaronski, Zygmunt
    Jendrzejewski, Jan
    Kaczor, Fabisz
    Krupowicz, Boleslaw *(Kropowicz)*
    Mialki, Jozef
    Miecznikowski, Marceli
    Podgorski, Jan
    Olszewski, Adam
    Przysierzny, Jozef
    Rekowski, Adam
    Srorut, Jozef *(Skorut)*
    Stachura, Zygmunt
    Swietonowski, Jan
    Szymanski, Jozef
    Tobik, Julian
    Wielegowski, Zygmunt
Soman, PA *(Sonman)*
    Cyrmos, Wojciech *(Cyrwos)*
    Zabczyk, Jozef
Spring Alley, PA *(Pittsburgh)*
    Wisniewski, Jozef
Sturgeon, PA

Polapa, Adam
Sylly, PA *(Lilly)*
    Deptula, Jozef
Tarentum, PA
    Brzozowski, Leopold
Timblin, PA
    Borys, Piotr
    Jagiello, Wawrzyniec
    Markiewicz, Jozef
Tyre, PA
    Zylak, Michal
Uniontown, PA
    Bielecki, Andrzej
    Gawel, Jozef
    Grzeslik, Jozef *(Grzesik)*
    Ozimek, Jan
    Pasiut, Jozef *(Pasiul)*
    Sprysz, Michal
Vandergrift, PA
    Wladkowski, Kazimierz *(Wlodkowski)*
East Vandergrift, PA
    Nieiwerdowski, Franciszek
    Wozniak, Jan
Vataburg, PA *(Vestaburg)*
    Stebnicki, Stanislaw
Vestaburg, PA
    Kaczor, Pawel
    Soroczynski, Kazimierz *(Soroszynski)*
Walkers Mills, PA
    Gosiewski, Aleksander *(Gasiewski)*
Washinton, PA
    Dopirata, Jozef *(Dopirala)*
    Galka, Stanislaw *(Palka)*
    Jankowicz, Jozef
    Szewc, Jozef
Wilmerding, PA
    Dembiec, Jan
    Dlugosz, Jan
    Grondalski, Wojciech
    Janos, Jan
    Keiler, Jan *(Kielar)*
    Kielas, Stanislaw
    Kijowski, Jozef
    Klamut, Wojciech
    Liebiedz, Florjan *(Lebiedz)*
    Penar, Jan
    Ryniak, Stanislaw
    Sleds, Wladyslaw
    Szmit, Antoni
    Wegrzynek, Wojceich
    Wojnar, Marcin
Windber, PA
    Barczak, Leopold *(Bartczak)*
    Bruszewski, Konstanty
    Brzozowski, Jan
    Cyrnek, Jakob *(Czyruch)*
    Fularz, Piotr *(Fulasz)*
    Fularz, Wawrzyniec
    Gielas, Jan
    Kasperek, Jan
    Kaszewski, Waclaw *(Kraszewski)*
    Kocharczyk, Jakob *(Kucharczyk)*
    Kolas, Jakob *(Kotas)*
    Kostro, Kazimierz
    Kozinski, Leon
    Krok, Piotr
    Krol, Jan
    Kwiatkowski *(Jozef)*
    Malek, Ludwik
    Niezwa, Wojciech *(Miezwa)*
    Nowicki, Henryk
    Panek, Stanislaw
    Perkowski, Aleksander
    Perkowski, Antoni
    Rog, Wojciech
    Rusmicz, Marcin *(Busnicz)*
    Smecinski, Tomasz *(Smiecinski)*
    Stypulkowski, Jozef *(Styputkowski)*
    Styka, Jozef
    Szepietowski, Waclaw *(Sepetowski)*
    Woync, Jan *(Wojno)*
    Wozniak, Stanislaw
    Zdrogowski, Jan *(Zdrodowski)*
    Zywicz, Jan *(Zywicz)*
Woodlawn, PA
    Czaszowski, Pawel *(Czaszenski)*
    Drebis, Pawel *(Drobis)*
    Pribicko, Pawel
Youngstown, OH
    Balabuch, Waclaw
    Baran, Marcin
    Bzilziak, Wladyslaw
    Domica, Aleksander *(Domicz)*
    Fedorek, Stanislaw
    Habuda, Michal
    Jablonski, Marcin
    Kacak, Walenty
    Kaminski, Jan

Karwowski, Zygmunt *(Karwoski)*
Krukowski, Stanislaw
Maszaz, Jan *(Maziarz)*
Oltarzewski, Marcin
Romanowski, Stanislaw
Rudzik, Jan
Rybczak, Ludwik
Stahoryk, Andrzej *(Stachoryk)*
Wawrzynor, Jozef *(Wawrzynow)*
Wozniak, Franciszek
Paterson, NJ
Soroczynski, Stanislaw
Buffalo, NY
Zebrowski, Jan
New York, NY
Dembowski, Gustaw
Salamanca, NY
Rzucek, Jan
Adena, OH
Fortuna, Franciszek
Kozlowski, Boleslaw
Adono, PA
Pawlikowski, Piotr
Barmoch, OH
Pawlasek, Andrzej
Blair, OH
Bartnik, Tomasz
Lafferty, OH
Ochab, Stanislaw *(Ochap)*
Zaleski, Szymon *(Zalezki)*
Maynard, OH
Pasejewski, Andrzej *(Padjewski)*
St. Clairsville, OH
Kozlowski, Stanislaw
Steubenville, OH
Kotowski, Julian *(Kulowski)*
Wolak, Wladyslaw
Ziarko, Stanislaw
Tiltonsville, OH
Potocki, Pawel
Warren, OH
Jazwinski, Jan
Benwood, WV
Andrzejewski, Andrzej *(Andrzejanczyk)*
Fullerton, WV
Ignaciuk, Witold
Moundsville, WV
Kolodziejski, Feliks
Rebowski, Jan *(Rebecki)*
Weirton, WV
Jagiello, Jozef *(Jagiela)*
Lenard, Michal *(Lenart)*
Slawinski, Wladyslaw *(Stawinski)*
Wheeling, WV
Beger, Jan
Galka, Wawrzyniec
Gatuszka, Wiktor *(Galuszka)*
Kania, Karol
Kontara, Jozef
Miroslaw, Jan
Naplocowski, Wladyslaw *(Naplacowski, Wladyslaw/ Stanislaw)*
Pawliszak, Michal *(Pawlasek)*
Pawelczyk, Jan *(Pawelczak)*
Placha, Franciszek
Zakzgowski, Antoni *(Zalegowski)*
Zdankiewicz, Wlad. *(Zdanowicz)*
Ziulkowski, Jan
Lansing, OH
Regec, Franciszek
Martins Ferry, OH
Buczek, Jan
Grzyb, Stanislaw
Mich, Jozef
Pittsburgh, PA
Centrum Reckrutacyjne No. 6

Abramowicz, Franciszek
Adamczyk, Franciszek
Adamczyk, Lucjan
Adamczyk, Ludwik
Adamczyk, Tomasz
Adamski, Feliks
Akuratny, Janusz
Albrycht, Wojciech
Ambroziewicz, Wincenty
Andruszkiewicz, Stanislaw
Andrzejewski, Waclaw
Aniola, Ludwik
Antczak, Piotr
Antoniak, Mieczyslaw
Armalowicz, Teofil
Baczkowski, Wladyslaw
Bagdan, Franciszek *(Bogdan)*
Bajniak, Nikodem
Bajorek, Franciszek
Bakowski, Jozef
Blaha, Stanislaw

Balisz, Stanislaw
Baltuszewski, Antoni
Banajski, Stanislaw
Banaszewski, Mieczyslaw
Bandurski, Antoni
Baniszewski, Wincenty
Baran, Stanislaw
Barczak, Jozef
Bartmanski, Jan
Bartczak, Wladyslaw
Bartoszek, Ludwik
Baczadlo, Leon
Bejna, Jozef *(Bejma)*
Bentkowski, Antoni
Bernaszek, Wladyslaw *(Bernaczek)*
Bielecki, Antoni
Bilecki, Marcin
Bielecki, Stanislaw *(Bialecki)*
Bieniek, Wladyslaw
Bienkowski, Kazimierz
Bilecki, Pawel *(Bielecki)*
Bilewicz, Franciszek
Bibikowski, Wladyslaw
Bilinowski, Wladyslaw
Blas, Stanislaw *(Blaz)*
Blejwas, Walenty
Blocki, Wladyslaw
Bobrowski, Antoni
Bogacz, Jozef
Bogucki, Antoni
Bolek, Andrzej
Bombich, Stanislaw *(Bombick)*
Bordak, Jan
Borden, Antoni
Borkowski, Ignacy
Borodenko, Franciszek
Borowski, Jan
Borowski, Michal
Bosiak, Julian
Bougard, Jozef
Bozek, Franciszek
Bozym, Wladyslaw
Bronowski, Jozef
Brozowski, Jan *(Brzozowski)*
Brzecki, Jan *(Brzezicki)*
Brzezinski, Jan
Brzoski, Jozef
Brzozowski, Stanislaw
Brzynski, Stanislaw

Buchalski, Stanislaw *(Bucholski)*
Bufalski, Wladyslaw
Buczkowski, Julian
Budzinski, Wladyslaw
Bujanowski, Wladyslaw *(Bujnowski)*
Bukowski, Bronislaw
Butkiewicz, Jozef
Byczak, Gustaw
Bykorz, Franciszek
Cechawski, Franciszek *(Cechowski)*
Ceglarski, Jan *(Ceglarz)*
Chabrzynski, Jozef
Chajko, Maurice *(Chojko)*
Charzynski, Wincenty *(Charzenski)*
Chlebowski, Michal
Chmiel, Jan
Chmielewski, Anastazy
Chmielewski, Jozef
Chmielewski, Jozef
Chowaniec, Jozef
Chranek, Andrzej
Chrzanowski, Antoni
Ciemielewski, A. Wladyslaw
Ciminski, Aleks.
Ciesielski, Jozef
Cisielski, Jozef
Clender, Stanislaw
Cwajan, Wojciech
Cyglarz, Jan
Cyrulik, Jozef
Czajka, Marcin
Czarnecki, Leon
Czarnecki, Stanislaw
Czarniak, Wojciech
Czecko, Wincenty *(Czeczko)*
Czernik, Jan *(Czarnik)*
Czerwinski, Bronislaw
Czuba, Jozef
Czurak, Daniel
Czwerw, Piotr *(Czerw)*
Czyczyn, Jozef
Dabrowski, Jozef
Danielewicz, Michal
Dembinski, Mieczyslaw
Dimarski, Konstanty
Disman, Jozef
Dobrowolski, Kazimierz
Dobrzynski, Antoni *(Dobrzyski)*
Domalewski, Bronislaw

Domanczyk, Jan
Dombrowski, Franciszek
Dombrowski, Wladyslaw
Domino, Franciszek
Dresewski, Tomasz
Dretkiewicz, Leopold
Drozdowski, Jozef
Duchmowski, Pawel
Durbas, Jan
Duzinski, Czeslaw *(Duszynski)*
Drzewiec, Stanislaw *(Drzewicz)*
Dziedzic, Mateusz
Dziegielewicz, Jan *(Dziegielewski)*
Dziengelewski, Waclaw
Dzierzgowski, Polikarp *(Dziergowski)*
Dzilinski, Jozef *(Dzilenski)*
Ejsmont, Waclaw *(Ejzymont)*
Farmer, Henryk Robert
Fedor, Pawel
Felinski, Konstanty *(Falinski)*
Filipien, Jozef *(Filipiak)*
Filipo, Michal
Filipowski, Kasper
Fondakowski, Franciszek
Franczak, Wladyslaw
Fuks, Karol
Gajdisz, Stefan *(Gajdysz)*
Gajkowski, Antoni
Galka, Jan
Gancarz, Jan
Gapinski, Mieczyslaw
Garbacik, Jozef
Gawel, Wojciech
Gawinski, Konstanty
Gawron, Tomasz
Gedrog, Jozef *(Giedrog)*
Gefort, Franciszek *(Gefert)*
Gierla, Piotr
Gizinski, K. Roman *(Karol Roman)*
Girzycki, Piotr
Glaszewski, Piotr *(Glazewski)*
Glarzewski, Boleslaw *(Glasieski)*
Glodowski, Dam. *(Adam)*
Gluszkowski, Jan
Gniewek, Pawel
Goczkowski, Jozef
Godek, Jozef
Godlewski, Edmund
Golacinski, Edward
Golenia, Sebastyn
Golebiewski, Stanislaw
Gorka, Bronislaw
Gorka, Jan
Gosk, Jan
Goy, Piotr
Goszczynski, Boleslaw *(Goszczycki)*
Grabowski, Bronislaw
Grabowski, Wincenty
Grabowski, Wladyslaw
Grabczyk, Kazimierz
Graczyk, Kazimierz
Graczyk, Piotr
Gralazny, Jozef
Gregorczyk, Antoni
Gregorak, Jan *(Grzegorczak)*
Grochowski, Jozef
Grochowina, Szczepan
Grochowski, Stanislaw
Grodzielski, Kazimierz *(Grodzicki)*
Grodzki, Adam
Grodzki, Antoni
Gronczewski, Antoni
Gronczewski, Stanislaw
Gruszka, Stanislaw
Grygenc, Antoni
Grys, Jan
Grzelak, Edmund
Guter, Adam
Gwardzinski, Wincenty
Gwodz, Stanislaw *(Gwozdz)*
Gzik, Blazej
Habowski, Franciszek
Hausner, Stanislaw
Hehelski, Jozef
Hirzinski, Jozef
Holewa, Wladyslaw
Hozempa, Gabryel
Hrynicki, Jan *(Hrywicki)*
Hujczejk, Andrzej *(Hucek)*
Indeczowski, Jan *(Indyczowski)*
Ipnar, Jozef
Iwanski, Stanislaw
Jablonski, Bronislaw
Jablonski, Edward *(Jablonowski)*
Jablonski, Jozef
Jackowski, Stefan
Jakubaszak, Jan *(Jakubaszach)*
Janiak, Andrzej

Janiecek, Jakob
Janicki, Antoni
Janiszewski, Bronislaw
Jankowski, Wladyslaw
Janowicz, Andrzej
Jargielo, Andrzej
Jarosz, Jan
Jasinski, Marcel
Jaworski, Andrzej
Jaworski, Jozef
Jedrzejewski, Jozef
Jedrzejewski, Leon
Jesien, Waclaw
Jeziorski, Franciszek
Jerzewski, Zygmunt
Jozdzio, Antoni *(Jodzio)*
Jozwiak, Franciszek *(Jozwik)*
Jozwiak, Jozef
Julkiewicz, Jozef
Junasik, Wawrzyniec
Jurkiewicz, Michal
Jurkowski, Aleksander
Kaczmarczyk, Jan
Karczmarski, Alojzy
Kaczynski, Antoni
Kaczynski, Jan
Kaczynski, Jozef
Kalas, Franciszek
Kalinowski, Jozef
Kalis, Michal *(Kulis)*
Kaminski, Albin
Kaminski, Antoni
Kaminski, Andrzej
Kaminski, Antoni
Kaminski, August
Kaminski, Franciszek
Kaminski, Franciszek
Kaminski, Michal
Kaminski, Stanislaw
Kania, Wincenty
Kaplan, Stefan *(Kaplon)*
Karbon, Wawrzyniec *(Karbol)*
Karwowski, Czeslaw *(Karwoski)*
Kasperowski, Michal *(Kasperoski)*
Kateusz, Wladyslaw
Kawczynski, Stanislaw
Kawinski, Wladyslaw
Kwiatkowski, Stanislaw
Kedzierski, Karol

Keller, Zygmunt
Kendziorek, Ludwik *(Kendzierski)*
Keps, Piotr
Kiciszewski, Jan
Kiljan, Adam
Kiljan, Stanislaw *(Kilian)*
Kisczynski, Wincenty *(Kiszczynski)*
Kisielewski, Jan
Kiriaczyk, Ignacy *(Kirionczyk)*
Kiruc, Adolf *(Kiurc)*
Kitlinski, Adam
Klawon, Bernard
Klupinski, Kazimierz
Knap, Wladyslaw
Kobecki, Jan
Kochan, Jan
Kochanski, Stanislaw
Kociszewski, Franciszek
Kociuba, Jan
Koda, Boleslaw
Kodaszewski, Apolinary *(Kardaszewski)*
Kodek, Jan
Kogucz, Jan
Kolkis, Hieronim
Koluba, Teodor *(Kaluba)*
Komic, Leon
Komorowski, Jan
Komorowski, Mikolaj
Konopka, Aleksander
Kopac, Ignacy
Kopczyk, Jozef
Kopura, Lucian *(Kepura)*
Kopysz, Michal
Korolski, Stanislaw *(Karolski)*
Koscielny, Henryk
Kosinski, Jozef
Kosinski, Wincenty
Kosmalski, Franciszek
Kossakowski, Pawel
Kotlinski, Stanislaw
Korenkiewicz, Antoni *(Korynkiewicz)*
Kowalski, Stanislaw
Kowalski, Wladyslaw
Kowalczewski, Feliks
Kowalczyk, Wladyslaw
Kowalski, Marcin
Kowlaczewski, Feliks
Kozakiewicz, Kazimierz
Koziel, Andrzej *(Koziol)*

Kozlowski, Szczepna
Kozlowski, Wojciech
Krajewski, Edmund
Krajewski, Stanislaw *(Krejewski)*
Krolikowski, Franciszek
Kropiewicki, Teofil *(Krupiewnieski)*
Kropiewicki, Aleksander *(Kropiewinski)*
Krondy, Wladyslaw
Krosnicki, Hieronim
Kruk, Jan
Krupiewski, Jan *(Kropienski)*
Krupka, Jozef
Kruszewski, Boleslaw
Krzyzanowski, Waclaw
Kubas, Jan
Kubica, Pawel
Kuchanski, Jan *(Kuchienski)*
Kucharzewski, Franciszek
Kujanowicz, Ludwik
Kukuczka, Jan
Kulesza, Aleksander
Kupisinski, Czeslaw
Kupski, Marcin
Kurczma, Wawrzyniec *(Kuczma)*
Kurek, Wladyslaw
Kurowski, Antoni
Kurowski, Jozef
Kurpatwa, Stanislaw *(Kuropatwa)*
Kurzych, Antoni
Kusiak, Jozef
Laba, Wojciech
Labunowski, Boleslaw
Lacek, Jan
Lacki, Wladyslaw
Lakomski, Wladyslaw
Lan, H. Henryk Stan.
Laniewski, Wladyslaw
Lapinski, Edward
Las, Wojciech *(Los)*
Lash, Stanislaw
Laska, Franciszek
Lasowski, Piotr
Latawski, Jozef
Lazkiewicz, Aleksander *(Laszkiewicz)*
Lech, Jan
Lengizowski, Antoni
Lepkowski, Franciszek
Leszner, Karol
Lewaniowski, Michal *(Lewandowski)*
Lewandowski, Jan
Lewandowski, Piotr
Lewandowski, Stanislaw
Lewandowski, Szczepan
Lewandowski, Waclaw
Listopad, Feliks
Liszewski, Franciszek
Litkowski, Roman
Litwicki, Wincenty
Lotarski, Jan
Lotarski, Jan
Lotusewski, Andrzej *(Latuszewski)*
Luniewski, Witold
Lyska, Jozef
Machnik, Jan
Machnikowski, Leon
Magnowski, Wincenty
Maciejewski, Jozef'
Maciejowski, Tadeusz *(Maciejewski)*
Majewski, Jozef
Makowski, Stanislaw
Malinski, Antoni
Malinowski, Aleksander
Malinowski, Jakob
Malinowski, Wladyslaw
Malek, Michal
Matejko, Jozef *(Matejka)*
Matuszek, Piotr
Matuszewski, Wincenty
Matynia, Jozef
Matyszczak, Tomasz *(Matysczuk)*
Marchwinski, Jozef
Marczak, Franciszek
Marges, Antoni *(Margas)*
Markowski, Marjan
Marlanga, Szczepan
Marlanga, Jan *(Marlenga)*
Marlenga, Piotr *(Marlenga)*
Maros, William
Mazur, Jozef
Mazur, Stanislaw
Mazur, Wladyslaw
Medrzunski, Stanislaw
Mendlowski, Jan
Michalski, Stanislaw
Michalski, Stefan
Michura, Jozef
Midlowski, Michal
Mikulski, Ignacy *(Mikucki)*

Miradzinski, Jan
Misielski, Wincenty
Mizerek, Jozef
Moskiewicz, Jakob
Moskiewicz, Jakob
Moskot, Franciszek
Moszcinski, Jan
Mroczkowski, Feliks
Mroczka, Jozef
Musial, Antoni
Nabruzuchowski, Andrzej *(Nabrzuchowski)*
Nadolny, Leon
Nadolny, Leon
Nadolski, Walenty
Napierkowski, Feliks
Napierkowski, Jan
Napierkowski, Stanislaw
Napierkowski, Wladyslaw
Napierkowski, Wladyslaw
Nawracaj, Wojciech
Nowracki, Franciszek *(Nawrocki)*
Nawrocki, Jozef
Niedzwiecki, Franciszek
Niemiec, Jan
Nierzbicki, Boleslaw *(Wierzbicki)*
Niga, Tomasz
Noga, Feliks
Nowak, Wawrzyniec
Nowakowski, Jan
Nowicki, Franciszek
Nowinski, Pawel
Nowak, Franciszek
Nowak, Jozef
Nowak, Konstanty
Nowak, Michal
Nowak, Zygmunt
Nycz, Franciszek *(Nysz)*
Obierek, Jan
Obremski, Antoni
Ochman, Wincenty
Ogrocki, Jozef
Oklota, Stanislaw
Okonski, Konstanty *(Okomski)*
Olejniacz, Antoni *(Olejniasz)*
Olejniczak, Jan
Olszewski, Adam
Olszewski, Aleksander
Olszewski, Antoni
Olowiak, Jozef
Orlowski, Aleksander
Osowski, Aleksander
Ostaszewski, Jan
Ostrowski, Bronislaw
Ostrowski, Dominik
Owsiany, Franciszek
Paczewski, Piotr
Pachulski, Wladyslaw *(Pakulski)*
Pakulski, Waclaw
Paluch, Michal
Parkowski, Bronislaw *(Perkowski)*
Pawliszyn, Franciszek
Pawlowski, Ludwik
Pawlowski, Wladyslaw
Pazkowski, Antoni
Pendich, Jozef *(Pendzich)*
Pepera, Jozef
Perzanowski, Dominik
Piatek, Wladyslaw
Piecychna, Jan
Piecyna, Stefan *(Puczyna)*
Pieczkowski, Jozef *(Pieczykowski)*
Piejak, Wojciech
Piekutowski, Konstanty
Pieszewski, Tomasz *(Piesewski)*
Pietrzak, Jozef
Pilszak, Jozef
Pietrzyk, Kazimierz
Pingielski, Adam
Piontek, Marcin *(Marek)*
Piotrowski, Bronislaw
Piotrowski, Feliks
Piotrowski, Franciszek
Piotrowski, Stanislaw
Pirowski, Stanislaw
Piskorski, Alexander *(Piskorowski)*
Plackowski, Michal
Ploszaj, Stanislaw
Pokorski, Jan
Podlaski, Jan
Podlaski, Jan
Pokorski, Maksymilian
Polacki, Jozef
Polec, Wladyslaw
Positowski, Szymon
Pozor, Michal
Primas, Ignacy
Probolia, Jan *(Probola)*

Prorok, Marcin
Prorok, Pawel
Pruchniewski, Boleslaw
Przybyszewski, Ignacy
Pugaczewski, Boleslaw
Rakoczy, Feliks
Rakoczy, Jozef
Renkiewicz, Wladyslaw
Rewiak, Antoni
Rewiak, Jozef *(Rewiako)*
Ritter, Stanislaw
Rodusha, Stanislaw *(Roducka)*
Rofala, Jan *(Rogala)*
Roginski, Antoni
Roginski, Jan
Rogowski, Kajetan
Rodnicki, Jozef *(Rudnicki)*
Romankiewicz, Marcin
Romanowski, Stanislaw
Rostkowski, Wincenty
Rozanski, Aleksander
Rugiel, Jozef
Rugut, Andrzej *(Rugiel)*
Rusin, Stanislaw
Ruszkowski, Aleksander
Ruszkowski, Jan
Ruszkowski, Piotr
Rybak, Antoni
Rychert, Teofil
Rydlewski, Jan
Rydzewski, Waclaw
Rygalski, Stefan
Rygalski, Wladyslaw
Rygiel, Ignacy
Rzepczynski, Pawel
Rzepinski, Piotr *(Rzeplinski)*
Sadowski, Jan
Sajewski, Franciszek
Sajler, Jan
Sak, Stanislaw
Sakowicz, Waclaw
Samselski, Aleksander
Samulski, Tadeusz
Sarakowicz, Marian Piotr
Sawicki, Andrzej
Sekcinski, Piotr
Sekulski, Antoni
Seremat, Andrzej
Scharzynski, Michal

Siemientowski, Jozef *(Siemientkowski)*
Siepiakowski, Jan *(Siepialowski)*
Sierocinski, Jozef
Sikora, Franciszek
Siwkowski, Wawrzyniec
Skarzynski, Wincenty
Skierkowski, Andrzej
Skadzien, Roman *(Skladzien)*
Skonieczny, Stanislaw
Skorski, Antoni
Skuratowicz, Leonard
Slencka, Michal
Slesonski, Jan *(Slesinski)*
Slonicki, Agustine
Slowecki, Ignacy
Smolenski, Wojciech
Smolinski, Wojciech
Smolucha, Jan
Smorag, Wladyslaw
Sobolak, Feliks
Sobolewski, Piotr
Sobolewski, Stanislaw
Sokolowski, Adam
Solida, Jan
Solinski, Jan
Sondej, Feliks
Sosnowy, Mateusz
Sparaga, Jan
Sprezynski, Wadclaw
Spychalski, Jozef
Sroka, Jozef
Stachowicz, Franciszek
Stachowicz, Jan
Stachowicz, Stanislaw
Stanczyk, Mikolaj
Stanek, Stanislaw
Staniszewski, Jozef
Staniszewski, Stanislaw
Stankiewicz, Anastazy
Stankiewicz, Jozef
Staszkiewicz, Wincenty
Stawicki, Antoni
Stawienski, Franciszek *(Stawinski)*
Stawinski, Lukasz
Stawicz, Jozef *(Stawisz)*
Stawowczyk, Piotr
Stefanski, Ignacy
Stepniewski, Antoni *(Stempniewski)*
Stypula, Michal W.

Sternik, Stanislaw
Stolowski, Franciszek
Sudlowski, Kazimierz
Sulkowski, Jozef
Sundej, Andrzej (Sundey)
Superczynski, Jozef
Surmacz, Andrzej
Sywiec, Wiktor
Szablewski, Zygmunt
Szajkowski, Jan
Szalajka, Andrzej
Szarnos, Adolf (Szaronos)
Szatkowski, Michal
Szelong, Jozef
Szerszen, Jozef
Szczucinski, Wincenty (Szczecinski)
Szczebele, Piotr (Szczebelek)
Szczepaniak, Jan (Szczepanik)
Szczypa, Franciszek
Szmyd, Bartlomiej
Szmyd, Pawel
Szponder, Julian
Szubielski, Szczepan
Szurnicki, Antoni
Szychowski, Wladyslaw
Szydlowski, Wladyslaw
Szymczak, Jozef (Szymczyk)
Szymal, Franciszek (Szynal)
Szymal, Piotr
Szwajnos, Jacek
Szczepanski, Antoni
Szwalkowski, Jan
Szwed, Mikolaj
Szweda, Stanislaw
Talak, Jan
Taluciak, Piotr (Talusciak)
Tampowicz, Jan (Tarnapowicz)
Tarakiewicz, Konstanty (Tereskiewicz)
Tarnowicz, Michal
Tarrowski, Boleslaw (Tarnowski)
Tepien, Jozef
Tereciakowski, Jozef (Trzeciakowski)
Tomczak, Franciszek
Tomczak, Ignacy
Tomkiewicz, Jan
Trojanowski, Szymon
Trojna, Marcin (Trojnar)
Trojna, Marcin
Tulisiak, Marian

Tyburski, Czeslaw
Tyminski, Hipolit
Tyra, Andrzej
Urban, Ludwik
Uszka, Jan (Uszko)
Walas, Wladyslaw
Wlawski, Michal (Walawski)
Walowski, Hipolit
Walkowski, Dominik
Wanderlich, Antoni
Wardzinski, Wladyslaw
Watylko, Michal (Walitko)
Wasik, Jakob
Watras, Andrzej
Weklar, Antoni
Wesolowski, Ignacy
Wiacek, Franciszek
Wiater, Karol
Wielenczyk, Tomasz (Wilenczyk)
Wienczkowski, Antoni (Wiczenkowski)
Wieszkowski, Jozef
Wierzchowski, Franciszek
Wiercienski, Jozef
Widewica, Feliks (Widiewicz)
Wigniewicz, Kost.
Wilk, Antoni
Wilinski, Czeslaw
Wlorkowski, Stefan
Witek, Piotr
Witka, Grzegorz
Witkowski, Adam
Wisniewski, Adam
Wisniewski, Aleks.
Wisniewski, Bronislaw
Wisniewski, Jozef
Wisniewski, Stanislaw
Wisniowski, Franciszek
Wlodarski, Michal
Wochadlo, Jozef (Wohadlo)
Wohadlo, Stanislaw
Woncik, Jozef
Wojcicki, Zygmunt
Wojcik, Antoni
Wojcik, Jozef
Wojciechowski, Aleksander
Wojciechowski, Stanislaw
Wojna, Wiktor (Wojnar)
Wojszak, Andrzej
Wojtowicz, Wladyslaw

Wolenski, Stanislaw
Woroniec, Jan
Wos, Andrzej
Wozniak, Jozef
Wozniewski, Wladyslaw
Wroblewski, Jozef
Wroniak, Franciszek
Wybraniec, Franciszek
Wyrostek, Jozef
Wyszynski, Kazimierz
Zabawski, Antoni
Zablocki, Franciszek
Zabrzewski, Jozef *(Zabrzeski)*
Zachowski, Antoni
Zachowski, Jozef
Zagurski, Franciszek *(Zagorski)*
Zagrzezewski, Ksawery *(Zegaczewski)*
Zajda, Feliks
Zak, Walenty
Zakrzewski, Maciej
Zakrzewski, Roman
Zales, Franciszek
Zales, Jozef
Zalewski, Antoni
Zalewski, Jan
Zalewski, Piotr
Zaporowski, Wladyslaw
Zaremba, Antoni
Zbrzezny, Jan
Zelazowski, Antoni
Zielinski, B.N. dr.
Zielinski, Jan
Zielinski, Piotr
Zielinski, Stanislaw
Zielinski, Wladyslaw
Ziemieniak, Michal *(Ziemianek)*
Ziemniak, Stanislaw *(Ziemianek)*
Zirnoch, Adam *(Zimnoch)*
Zlotkowski, Boleslaw
Zwoniarek, Jozef
Zubek, Jozef
Zuchowski, Wladyslaw *(Zukowski)*
Zurawski, Adam
Zydler, Kazimierz
Zylinski, Jozef
Zyra, Jozef
Zoltanski, Jozef
Zurawski, Aleksander
Bednarczyk, Wladyslaw
Filip, Michal
Kowalewski, Leon
Rosiak, Julian
Urbaniak, Jan

Published by Central Council
of Polish Organizations of
Pittsburgh, Pennsylvania
1956

In the preceding list the surnames in italics were recorded as they appear on the recruitment records. These documents themselves demonstrate variable spellings. The version listed is judged to be the most accurate until further research justifies changing the spelling.—P. S. V.

Joseph A. Borkowski (1907-2003)
A Brief Biographical Sketch by James Wudarczyk 2005

According to an obituary written by Harry Tkach for the *Post Gazette*, Joseph Borkowski was born March 27, 1907, received his elementary education at Immaculate Heart of Mary School and Holy Family, graduated from Duquesne University with a bachelor's degree in economics, and earned a master's degree in history at the University of Pittsburgh. He was employed by the city of Pittsburgh for 27 years as an auditor-accountant, supervisor of the parking tax department, and manager of wage tax. He also worked for the Allegheny County controller's office.

In the role of Polish historian, Mr. Borkowski was instrumental in obtaining a number of historical markers and plaques. These included ones honoring Anthony Sadowski (Allegheny County Court House), Polish Volunteers in American Civil War (City Council Building), Marcella Sembrich (William Penn Hotel on the corner of Oliver Ave. and Strawberry Way), Polish Army Recruitment (97 S. 18th St., site of old Falcon Hall), Three Polish Army Chaplains (Immaculate Heart of Mary Church), Casimir Pulaski's First Battle at Brandywine (marker on Highway #1 Chadd's Ford), Pulaski's Training and Recruitment Site (York, PA), Pulaski Banner Site (Bethlehem, PA), and Marie Sklodowska Curie (Graduate School, University of Pittsburgh, O'Hara St., Pittsburgh). The Polish prelate, Karol Cardinal Wojtyła, who would later become Pope John Paul II, dedicated the last plaque listed.

Joseph Borkowski was also instrumental in obtaining a plaque marking the 50th anniversary of the participation of American pilots in the Polish-Russian War. To obtain the markers, Mr. Borkowski, who served as Chairman of the Polish Historical Commission of the Central Council of Polish Organizations, researched and provided the necessary documentation. His writings included materials on Polish Pioneers of Pittsburgh; Anthony Sadowski; Christian Frederick Post; Marcella Sembrich; Madame Modrzejewska; Ignace Jan Paderewski's first Pittsburgh Concert; Stanislaus Parzyk, the first Polish priest in Pittsburgh; Pittsburgh's Part in the Formation of the Polish Army in France; History of St. Stanislaus Kostka Parish and Cemetery; Madame Marie Sklodowska Curie's visit to Pittsburgh; History of Holy Family Parish; Colonial and Pre-Revolutionary Poles; and the Poles of Jamestown. It is unclear at this point how many of these pieces were published and how many were submitted as required source documents.

Used with permission from James Wudarczyk. More information can be found on the website of the Lawrenceville Historical Society at **www.LHS15201.org**.

Doctor's Instructions No. 1

PHYSICAL STANDARDS

AND

INSTRUCTIONS FOR THE

MEDICAL EXAMINATION OF RECRUITS

FOR THE

POLISH ARMY IN FRANCE

1917

PITTSBURGH, PA

Doctor's Instructions No. 1

RULES FOR MEDICAL EXAMINATION OF RECRUITS.
PRINCIPAL POINTS IN MEDICAL EXAMINATION OF RECRUITS.

In the inspection of recruits the principal points to be attended to are:

- That the recruit is sufficiently intelligent.
- That his vision with either eye, is up to the required standard.
- That his hearing is good.
- That his speech is without impediment.
- That he has no glandular swellings.
- That his chest is capacious and well formed and that his heart and lungs are sound.
- That he is not ruptured in any degree or form.
- That his limbs are well formed and fully developed.
- That there is free and perfect motion of all joints.
- That the feet and toes are well formed.
- That he has no congenital malformation or defects.
- That he does not bear traces of previous acute or chronic disease pointing to an impaired constitution.
- That he is between the ages of 18 and 40 years.

General Grounds for Rejection.— Men presenting any of the following conditions will be rejected:—

- Indication of tubercular disease; constitutional syphilis;
- bronchial or laryngeal disease;
- palpitation or other diseases of the heart;
- generally impaired constitution;
- under standard of vision;
- defects of voice or hearing;
- pronounced stammering;
- contraction or deformity of chest or joints;
- abnormal curvature of spine;
- defective intelligence;
- hernia, hemorrhoids;
- marked varicose veins or varicocele;
- inveterate cutaneous disease;
- chronic ulcers;
- fistula;
- traces of corporal punishment;

- or any disease or physical defect calculated to unfit them for the duties of a soldier.

N.B. - Varicocele will be considered severe when the mass of veins is so great that it hangs down in front of the testicle when the candidate stands up, or if the cord is so elongated that the testicle hangs abnormally low.

Mental Capacity.— Great care is to be taken in ascertaining the mental capacity of a recruit.

Correlation of height, weight, chest measurement and age.— The height, weight and chest measurement of a recruit should accord with each other, and with his age, agreeably to the table of standards laid down in the Recruiting Regulations. So far as concerns weight, this table is to be regarded as a guide only, and the medical officer is to exercise his own judgement as to the general fitness of the man under examination.

Determination of Age by Physical Development— Should a recruit, on presenting himself for enlistment, bring no satisfactory proof of his age, the medical officer who exams him, will by comparing the height with the weight and general development, and also from the recruit's appearance, decide his age, which will be entered on the second page of the attestation "apparent age."

Position of recruit.— When not required to approach the recruit for special objects, the medical officer should always take his place at a distance of about six feet from him. The recruit should be placed so that the light may fall upon him.

Directions for general examination, and objects.— The recruit having, if possible, had a bath, or been washed, and being wholly undressed, the following should be the order in which the examination is carried out:—

- He is measured.
- His weight is ascertained.
- His chest measurement is taken.
- His vision is tested.

If he satisfies requirements in these respects, and appears otherwise eligible, the general examination will be thus proceeded with:—

- He is directed to walk up and down the room smartly two or three times, to hop across the room on the right foot, and back again on the left. (The hops should be short and upon the toes.)
- He is halted, standing upright, with his arms extended above his head,

while the medical officer walks slowly round him carefully inspecting the whole surface of his body.
- An estimate is formed of the general physique, of his age, and whether he presents the appearance of having served before.

The objects to be observed and noted in this part of the examination are the following: —

- The general physical development;
- the formation and development of the limbs;
- the power of motion in joints, especially in the feet and hips;
- extreme flatness of the feet; formation of the toes;
- skin disease;
- varicose veins;
- cicatrices of ulcers;
- and any special marks from congenital or accidental causes, and tattoo marks.

If no disabling defects are found, the second part of the examination will be proceeded with.

Examination of the trunk.— The trunk will be examined from below upwards. The recruit stands with his arms extended above his head, the backs of the hand being in contact. The following will be the order of inspection: -
- The medical officer notes indication of venereal disease.
- He examines the scrotum to ascertain if the testicles have descended and are normal, or if there be varicocele or other disease. He inserts the point of his finger by invagination of the scrotum in the external abdominal ring of each side, and desires the recruit to cough two or three times, to ascertain if he be ruptured or liable to the condition.
- He examines the abdominal walls and parietes of the chest.

Examination of the chest.— He desires the recruit to "take in a full breath" several times, while he watches the action and notes the capacity of the chest. Careful stethoscopis examination of lungs is made.
- He examines the action of the heart, and notes its sounds.

The upper extremities.— The examination of the upper extremities will be made from below upwards. Time is saved by the medical officer himself acting as well as telling the recruit the movements he desires to be made.

The following are the directions:-

- Stretch out your arms with the palms of your hands upwards.
- Bend the fingers backwards and forwards.

- Bend your thumbs across the palms of your hands.
- Bend your fingers over your thumbs.
- Bend your wrists backwards and forwards.
- Bend the elbows.
- Turn the backs of the hands upwards.
- Swing your arms around at the shoulders.

Marks of vaccination.— The medical officer will examine the recruit for marks of vaccination.

This comprehends the inspection for loss or defects of the fingers, thumbs, wrists, elbows and shoulder joints; power of rotating the forearm, and vaccination. If not vaccinated, the circumstance should be stated on the medical history sheet.

The lower extremities and back.— The inspection of the lower extremities and back will be made from below upwards. The recruit first faces the medical officer, afterwards turns his back to him.

The following are the directions given facing:—

- Stand on one foot, put the other forward.
- Bend the ankle-joint and toes of each foot alternately backwards and forwards.
- Kneel down on one knee.
- Up again.
- Down on the other knee.
- Up again.
- Down on both knees, and up from that position with a simultaneous spring of both legs.
- Turn round.
- Separate the legs.
- Touch the ground with the hands.

While the recruit performs these movements the medical officer will observe the action of the knee-joints, the conditions of the perineum and of the spinal column. This includes the inspection for defects of the toes, ankle and knee-joints; for hemorrhoids, prolapsus ani, fistula in perinaeo and spinal deformity.

The head and neck.— The examination of the head and neck will be made from above downwards. The medical officer will note the intelligence, character of voice of and power of hearing of the recruit by his replies to the questions put to him. The following are the directions:

- Have you had any blows or cuts on the head?

- Are you subject to fits of any kind?
- He examines the scalp.
- He examines the ears.
- He examines the nostrils.
- He examines the mouth, teeth palate and fauces and then tells the recruit to say loudly "who comes there?"
- He examines the neck.

This comprehends the inspection for injuries of the head, deafness, disease of the ears, defect of voice; polypus of nose; tubular ulceration; glandular enlargements and defects of the eyes and the teeth.

Teeth.— An examining officer should not reject a recruit on account of the condition of his teeth, provided that the physical condition of the recruit is good in other respects. The condition of the mouth will received attention from the C.A.D.C. [Canadian Army Dental Corps] subsequent to enlistment.

The following are the instructions for the measurement of recruits:-

Height.— The recruit will be placed against the standard with the feet together, and the weight thrown on the heels, and not on the toes or outside of the feet. He will stand erect, without rigidity, and with the heels, calves, buttocks and shoulders touching the standard; the chin will be depressed to bring the vertex of the head level under the horizontal bar and the height will be noted in parts of an inch to eights.

Chest.— The recruit will be made to stand erect with his feet together, and to raise his arms over his head. The tape will be carefully adjusted round the chest with its posterior upper edge touching the inferior angles of the scapulae, and its anterior lower edge, the upper part of the nipples. The arms will then be lowered to hang loosely by the side, and care will be taken that the shoulders are not thrown upwards or backwards so as to displace the tape. The recruit will then be directed to take a deep inspiration several times, and the maximum expansion of the chest will be carefully noted. It is often attempted to conceal the true minimum measurement, but it can be obtained by a little manipulation and by drawing off attention from the examination by a few questions.

The maximum expansion rarely exceeds the average minimum by more than 2 or 2.5 inches.

The maximum and minimum will be recorded thus:- 34/36½, 33/35 etc.

In recording the measurements, fractions of less than half an inch should not be noted. The maximum is the standard measurement, and a recruit must also reach the range of chest expansion laid down in the table of physical equivalents.

Vision.— (See Appendix I.)

Hearing.— (See Appendix II.)

Nasal conditions.— (See Appendix III.)

Standards for chest measurements.— At least 33 inches around the chest, if between 18 and 30 years of age and 34 inches around the chest if between 30 and 45 years of age.

Height.— At least 5 feet in height for infantry, 5 feet 4 inches for Artillery and Cyclists Corps, and 5 feet 2 inches for other Corps.

APPENDIX I. *STANDARDS OF VISION.*
In examining a recruit's vision he will be placed with his back to the light, and his visual acuteness will be tested by means of test types placed in ordinary daylight, at a distance of twenty feet (six metres) from the recruit. The visual acuity of each eye in the case of approved recruits will be entered on the Medical History Sheet. If vision can be improved by glasses they should be ordered and worn.

Any morbid condition of the eyes or lids of either eye, liable to risk of aggravation or recurrence, will cause the rejection of the candidate.

APPENDIX II. *HEARING.*
Ears should be tested separately with the ordinary voice. Ear not under test to be closed firmly with the finger, and the candidate not to look at the officer speaking. The approximate distance at which the voice is heard by each ear, should be entered on the Medical History Sheet.

The following may be accepted:-

(a) Any man who can hear the ordinary voice at fifteen feet or better, in each ear, and who has no organic disease of the ear.

(b) Any man who has hearing at twenty-one feet in either ear, but with little or no hearing in the other ear, but without active organic disease.

N.B. - No man with a discharge from his ear shall be accepted for overseas service.

APPENDIX III. *NASAL CONDITION.*
Men suffering from severe nasal obstruction should not be enlisted, as it is found that such cases find it difficult or even impossible to wear respirators.

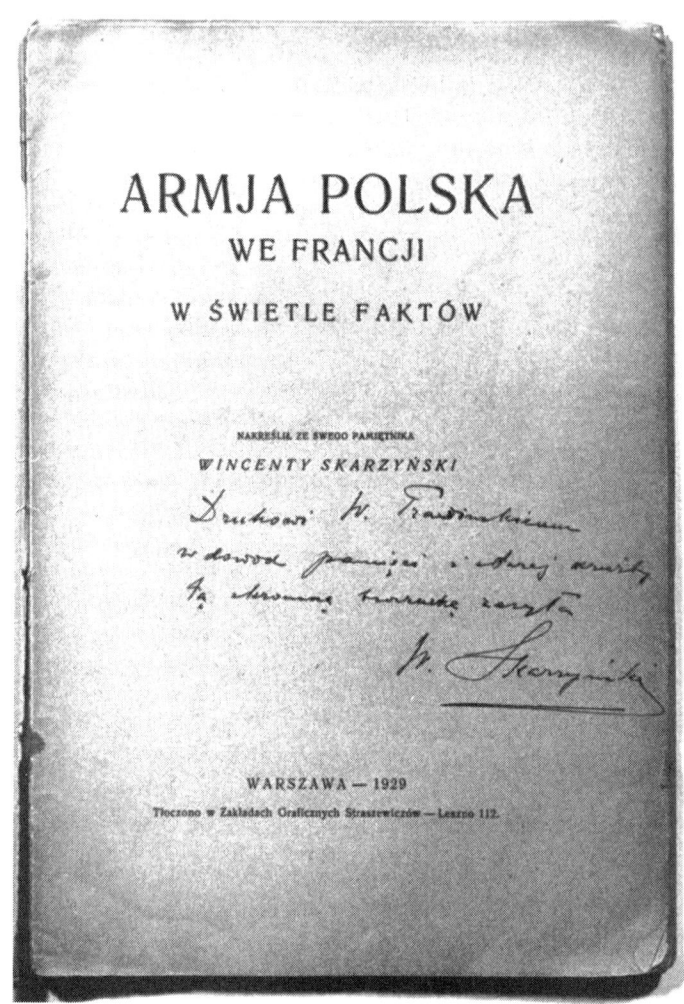

Original printing of Skarzyński's manuscript as autographed by the author to his friend Witold Hilary Trawiński. This copy, in turn, was given by Trawiński to his good friend Jan K. Kostrubała.

WINCENTY SKARZYŃSKI

THE POLISH ARMY IN FRANCE

IN LIGHT OF THE FACTS

WARSZAWA — 1929

Józef Piłsudski, First Marshal of Poland, Creator of the Polish Army, Commander-in-Chief of the Nation, the Great Architect of Poland Reborn

FOREWORD

The trade rivalry between England and Germany, the natural decay of a thoroughly bureaucratized Austria, the fall of the Czarist government in St. Petersburg, the political equilibrium of Europe, the Versailles treaty… Is that the whole of it? No. Those are only variable and accidental conditions, that is only the position on the chessboard of history at the time when the game was won for Poland.

Won by whom? By the Skarzyńskis. The constant, essential, unfailing factor in the Resurrection of the Republic and its Rebirth were those like Skarzyński, with their concern first and foremost for Poland, their concealed ambition to serve Poland, their mystical and spontaneous longing for Poland—a Poland wise in a practical context, fair in an international context, and great in a historical context.

The emigrant exile, the legionary soldier—from Mickiewicz to Piłsudski, whether from "the land of Italy" or from the coal mines of Pennsylvania or above the lakes of Canada, from the forests of Siberia, from the Murmansk shores of the Arctic Ocean, from the lakes of Odessa—it was always the same, the one striving for Polish territory, over the heads of the indecisive politicians, cutting through the intrigues of obtrusive careerist intermediaries, despite the disgrace of partisanship and artificial divisions of the living Polish soldier into individual formations.

The Polish Army in France, which originated on American soil, was the expression of just such a spontaneous striving on the part of Polish emigrants, a striving for a Polish land in the spirit of the historical traditions of the legions.

And it is in this that the secret lies of the Resurrection of Poland—which never died in the hearts of Poles.

Skarzyński—a *Hallerczyk [member of Haller's Army]*, and a legionnaire of the First Brigade—put his life on the line, a life that was a tangle of political prisoners, of vagabonds in exile, of work and service abroad—just as it was with so many other fighters for freedom.

He differs, however, from his predecessors. He is no 18-year-old hothead who rushes to war as if to a girl, for whom that war first opens the horizons of the broad world. He is also not one of life's castaways, not an emigrant rebel worn out by exile, ill-used by foreigners. No, Skarzyński is the modern Poland, conscious of the virtues of his race, knowing the price of those virtues on the international market. He said bluntly to the "Tiger of France," "Mr. Clemenceau—Santo Domingo will not be repeated!"* Was it not in this same spirit that the Commander refused to swear allegiance to the Kaiser? And thereby refused the Germans his legions for cannon fodder.

And in this, too, lies the secret of the Resurrection of Poland—neither Santo Domingo nor "Bartek the Conqueror"** was repeated.

GRZEGORZ PIOTROWSKI
Commander of the Polish Naval Reserve

**Translator's Note: This refers to the Polish Legions in Italy, who joined the French Revolutionary forces from 1797-1803 to struggle for the rights of man, only to lose 6,000 men putting down a revolt by black slaves in Santo Domingo (now in the Dominican Republic) in 1802-1803. This information comes from Iwo Cyprian Pogonowski's* Poland: A Historical Atlas, *Dorset Press, 1989, p. 283.*

***Translator's Note: "Bartek Zwycięzca" is the name of an 1882 short story by Henryk Sienkiewicz in which unified German immigrants in America take advantage of Polish immigrants' dissension.*

INTRODUCTION

The number of Polish source publications on the Great War is comparatively small; we do not possess the historical works on this period that the French or Germans have. True, a few books have appeared that discuss this era, but they shed light primarily on historical incidents from the viewpoint of individual political groups. Scattered in these works are comments and judgments, some of them rather deep, but not supported by appropriate documents. They are, in effect, political treatises, or personal partisan polemics, such as appear in large numbers during great moments in history, and then, after a dialectical duel of shorter or longer duration, are forgotten and swell the graveyards of library stacks.

Of the first type of source works, among the most prominent Polish books on the Great War in terms of content and composition must be placed J. J. Sosnowski's *Księga Prawdy Dziejowej [Book of Historical Truth]*. Unfortunately, the fate of this book has been the same as that of its author. To this day lack of appreciation of its value, and lack of interest in its subject—the conditions in which our national independence arose—leave unanswered the question of whether the revivers of our independence really were the officially and generally accepted "establishments," or whether the author of *Historical Truth,* dependent on no one, a champion of Polish independence, was not correct in showing the actual role of these establishments to be that of rubber stamps.

Besides this, there also exists among us a series of diaries and memoirs written by participants and eyewitnesses who experienced the battles and events. This sort of work is undoubtedly very important for all who study the past, and is all the more valuable for us because Polish patriots, divided by the partitions, scattered in all corners of the earth, each tried in their own way to contribute to the building of our Fatherland's independence. Particularly interesting in every respect are the wartime memoirs of those who found themselves outside its geographic boundaries, or those who were cast by fate into distant lands, inasmuch as they were able to preserve far more objective and sober judgment on contemporary events, not yielding to the hypnosis of unfortunate orientations that tore Poland apart into the camps of the Entente and the Central Powers.

The division of Polish society and its division by leaders into two factions was tragic in its blindness, because neither side was based on Polish reasons of state, but rather those of foreign interests that were fundamentally hostile to Poland. Neither arose from the depths of the Polish spirit. Neither relied—as befits a great nation—on active, aggressive enterprise. Neither built its political plans on conviction of its inner strength. Neither drew comfort and faith from the inspiration of national philosophy. Neither was able to tear away from the stifling yoke of foreign psyches, from the conceptions of the political powers that created the partitions. Neither knew how to create the beginnings of a truly Polish government. To fill the emptiness of their plans for building an independent state, both political factions employed a shallow pre-war Machiavellianism, which counted on their opponents' naïveté. Both sides strove for minimal gains.

The passivity of the masses, always patriotic but wholly unprepared for events of world importance (the end of their bondage), made these masses, in the hands of leaders juggling the noblest ideals, slow to raise their persons to the pedestal of national heroes. Only one, Marshal Piłsudski—along with a handful of proponents of independence who were, in the judgment of most Poles, madmen—regarded armed action by Poland as necessary by historical logic at the time when the struggle of the peoples foretold by Mickiewicz broke out. Being, however, physically restricted, Piłsudski unfortunately had to deal with the conditions imposed by the Central Powers, the more so because Polish society in general was ill-disposed toward him at the beginning of the war.

If we brought up J. J. Sosnowski's *Księga Prawdy Dziejowej* first, we did so because it is a joyful and exceptional proof of an impartial and truly Polish expression of political affairs at the time the Central Powers were struggling with national freedom, as our bard foretold with his prophetic insight.

On that same plane is this book entitled *Armja polska we Francji w świetle faktów*. It is a short, modest tale, drawn from the diary of a soldier, episodes from the experiences of a freedom fighter, Wincenty Skarzyński. The author has no pretensions of imposing pompous theses, but shows us in all honesty the fervor with which his heart burned at the thought that fighting for Poland was not a myth or an absurdity, but an essential part of forging national independence. The author shows us details hitherto completely unknown to the Polish public, details concerning the Polish Army in America, later called the "Polish Army in France" or, as a popular name, "Haller's Army."

The author—in his boyhood years the prototype of S. Żeromski's *Syzyfowe prace [Labors of Sisyphus]*, a fearless fighter in the first early spring days of liberation in 1905 and 1906—grew up in the patriotic atmosphere of a family settlement. A disciplined member of the Polish Falcons from the dawn of his social activity, he escaped from exile in Siberia to America, where his character was formed in the hard school of life and, a born soldier, he advanced through the school of professional military experience in the American and English armies. The Falcons are always for him the focus of national organization and the best mainstay of social discipline, and here, too, at the decisive moment he finds the most suitable material for the cadres of the Polish Army.

In his work he encounters much opposition, especially and almost exclusively on the part of his compatriots, not so much for their lack of enthusiasm for the national cause, but rather due to the way this enthusiasm was quenched by circles connected with the Polish National Committee in Paris for views of the so-called "Great Policy," which frequently ran counter to the healthy instincts of a Polish soldier. This convulsive embracing of foreign policies meant to throw a chill into our young army at its very first step on French soil, when Roman Dmowski asked the author "What have you come here for?" And when prisoners from the Central Powers' camps and volunteers from the faraway Murmansk Coast began to gather as around a magnet, and the Poles' wave of martial ardor for their country's cause could no longer be chilled, showing itself actively, on both sides of the eastern front, in the march of the Second Brigade and in Polish formations in the Russian army, culminating in the organization of General Józef Dowbor-Muśnicki's Army—then the National Committee, rejecting the idea by which the army's creator in America was guided, hastily tried to attach party etiquette to it.

The description of the arrival of the American ship with the first battalion is truly moving; no less striking with their energy are the scenes from the French front and the tragedy of the Polish Army's fruitless waiting for return to the Fatherland by way of either Berlin or Gdańsk. General Haller's greeting of the envoys of Józef Piłsudski, at that time the head of the government, is the final episode in the memoirs and is, as it were, a symbol of the military and political consolidation of the reborn Republic, for which Polish blood was shed on all fronts of the gigantic struggle, for which that blood flowed in a red stream in the heroic defense of Lwów and Warsaw.

The author tries always to remain out of sight, and never puts himself forward for honors and decorations—he did not know how, or did not want support for such... He surely did, however, acquire one conviction, that he served the fatherland with all his might, and that conviction means more to him than any reward from others. In such cases the soldier's confession, though public, is a requirement of the soul, understood by every one who is capable of feeling the sincerity of his compatriot's words and who, having listened intently to the pulse of great historical events, feels the beating of a kindred heart.

Dr. M. Nałęcz-Dobrowolski

Wincenty Skarzyński, in the field uniform of the Army of the United States of America.

THE POLISH ARMY IN FRANCE

IN LIGHT OF THE FACTS

My dream from childhood days was the army. Always and everywhere I sought ways of acquiring military knowledge, so that at the right time I could step forward as an experienced soldier to battle with the enemies of my oppressed Fatherland. Thus when I arrived on American soil after various ordeals, imprisonment, exile, and so forth, I enlisted as a volunteer for service in the regular army of the United States of America during the Mexican campaign. In 1913 I finished that voluntary military service in Eagle Pass, Texas, on the Rio Grande, the border of Mexico and the United States. I had not fared badly, but I had never forgotten about Poland and the principles I learned in my parents' home. I had been a Falcon since 1905, and I remained loyal to its traditions and ideals, and when in the spirit of those ideals I organized a Falcons' Nest in my battery, the foremost Falcon activists in America—chiefly *druh** Rylski, at the time the head of the Polish Falcons Alliance of America—influenced me to reject the attractive prospect of a career in the American Army and direct my energies toward organizational work and militarization of the Falcons.

I began my work in this direction full of zeal, beginning with Detroit, Michigan, where I was named the head of Nest 79 and 576. At the Falcons convention in Buffalo in 1914, as a delegate from my Nest, I strongly opposed pro-German and pro-Muscovite attempts to spread dissension and sow the seeds of hatred and mutual accusation in the bosom of Polish society beyond the

---

**Translator's Note: the term* druh *appears frequently in this account. It is a title given Falcons, and comes from a root meaning "friend, comrade." The usual English rendering is "scout" or "boy scout," but that does not reflect adequately the military connotation—for the Falcons were largely devoted to training young men so they might be fit to fight for Poland's independence. There is no adequate term in English, so* druh *is simply left untranslated.*

Ocean. I regarded people from both these factions of "unfortunate orientations" as blind slaves, directed by shrewdly hidden foreign organizations hostile to all that is Polish, hostile to every right idea of our national independence, and I chose the Falcon cadres for my socio-political work, inasmuch as in North America only the Falcon organization sprang from the native soil of my people.

At the Buffalo convention already mentioned I was appointed by chief Samulski to supervise the camp. In a short time the president, Dr. Teofil Starzyński, who wished to revive the Falcons' ranks with new spirit and had apparently noticed my social and military activities, brought me into the administration, and I was chosen inspector of the Nests and Districts of the Polish Falcons Alliance of America.

During the years 1914-1915, on the basis of the Falcons Administration's authorization, I made an inspection of the Nests and Districts. It is my impression that I performed this work to the benefit of the Falcons and the satisfaction of my superiors, but unfortunately at the same time I also aroused the envy of some members of the Falcons, namely those who did not sufficiently understand their duties. It was for this reason, out of a desire not to provoke private disputes, that I stepped down from the position I occupied and settled in Pittsburgh in 1915. There I performed the duties of secretary of the Alliance's Technical Committee, also with complete devotion. This must have produced an appropriate result in the life of the individual nests of Falcons, inasmuch as one of them (Nest No. 429), in a desire to express its gratitude to its chief, an artilleryman in the American army (namely, me), had a cannon made for maneuvers in McKees Rocks, Pennsylvania. And when the head of the Falcons Alliance, *druh* Bartmański (who died a colonel near Ostropol in 1920 in battle with the Bolsheviks), came to that Nest, it also offered him a sword. On this occasion *druh* Bartmański said a few stirring words and promised that he would not rest until, before his death, he soaked the sword they had given him in the enemy's blood.

As head of District 6, at the plenary convention of the Polish Falcons Alliance of America in 1916, I proposed creating a School of Cadets (later located at the school of the Polish National Alliance in Cambridge Springs, Pennsylvania) and offered the first contribution for beginning this work. This idea was accepted enthusiastically. My heart was filled with joy that the plan which I had nourished in the depths of my soul was beginning to come to life.

In order to convert further measures into reality, it was necessary to train officer candidates. I approached this work with determination, but I owe its future successful course to an accident. While I was crossing the border between Canada and the United States in Windsor, Ontario, one of my comrades-in-arms in the American army recognized me. I had previously done him some small service that made it easier for him to cross into Mexico at a time when he found himself in serious danger. Wishing to show his gratitude, he took me

At right: Dr. Romuald Ostrowski, Chapter Master of the Legion of Honor of Polish Falcons in America, at the time chief medical officer of District 6 of the Polish Falcons Alliance of America.

At left in this photo is the late druh *Andrzej Małkowski, father of Polish scouting. To the right is Wincenty Skarzyński, in their officer's school uniforms at the University of Toronto, Canada.*

almost by force to his house in Canada, where I got to know his whole family and his acquaintances, influential people. At the time this comrade's father, Colonel Sir William Price, was organizing his own regiment at his own expense. Conversations in the Colonel's home centered on the unfolding events of the war; on my side I presented the desperate situation of Poland. Sir William Price listened attentively to my arguments, and when I had finished, stated that at first he had wished to see me in his own regiment; but when he recognized and understood the patriotism of the Polish people expressed through my mouth, he quickly came to the conclusion from my arguments that Poles in America could provide up to 100,000 volunteers—so he became convinced that in his regiment I would have less effect in comparison to what I could do by organizing perhaps 25,000 such soldiers as the Polish soldier had always been in the history of war. "A soldier of this kind," as Sir William expressed himself, "will surely perform invaluable service in the struggle with the Germans. "I will give my wealth and property, my own dear boys for my beloved England," he continued.

Hearing this, tears welled up in my eyes, and I jumped up from my chair and cried, "Colonel, what can I, a poor exile, give my unhappy, torn, bleeding Poland? Only my own neck. Take me with you, I am at your disposal."

At this Sir William approached me and said, "You do not have the right to give your own neck, but you are obligated to give your mind and your organizational talent, and now I am at your disposal. For my part I will try to carry out what you propose, and turn it into action, as best my strength and relationships allow." I understand that this was a decisive moment, and so I answered with zeal, "Good! Colonel, command me!" At this Sir William Price picked up the telephone receiver and called the Minister of War, Sir Sam Hughes, who granted me an appointment to see him six days later.

In the meantime, the father of Polish scouting, the late Andrzej Małkowski, answered my call to come to Ottawa. After he arrived in Canada and was informed of the events that had taken place, he responded enthusiastically to my plans, encouraged me urgently to take advantage of the moment, and offered himself as ready to serve as my secretary.

At my audience with the Canadian Minister of War, in the presence of members of the General Staff, I was asked whom I represented. I answered, "Only myself and the gentleman sitting beside me, Mr. Małkowski. Beyond that I am no one's representative and do not wish to speak for anyone else. My steadfast intention, which I have begun to make a reality, is to create an armed Polish force here in Canada, and then go to France, according to the traditions of my forefathers, so that with weapon in hand I can take part in the battle with the barbaric German hordes." Then, wishing to take advantage of the War Minister's exceptional courtesy, I tried to convince him of the need to create Polish cadres, and thus as a first step a Polish military school—for I explained

Convention and course of district heads of the Polish Falcons in America, in Pittsburgh, Pennsylvania, 28 November – 6 December, 1916.

Standing left to right: W. Sulewski, District VIII; F. Boguszewski, District VII; W. Skarzyński, District VI, A. Albrycht, District V; J. Zaucha, District IV; F. Zabrowski, District III; Fr. Gnutkiewicz, District II; Fr. Dziób, District I.

Seated center: J. Bartmański, manager of the Association; T. Starzyński, President of the Association; A. Małkowski, Scoutmaster.

Seated front row: Unidentified

that first and foremost it was necessary to take advantage, as soon as possible, of Great Britain's agreement to declare for the independence of Poland in its historical boundaries, including the Gdańsk region and Kaliningrad.

This last statement effected the Englishmen like a thunderbolt; they were simply stunned. "Yes," I continued without confusion, "even Berlin lies on our Slavic soil. I understand, Mr. Minister, that we cannot reach too far, but we should reach as far as that part of our patrimony that really is essential for life as a great power. Currently, due to the partitioners' persecutions in Poland, we possess beyond the borders of our country a large and valiant national reserve, trained in Anglo-Saxon schools, numbering about five million. The Anglo-Saxon brain should be combined, as quickly as possible, with the brain and exuberant nature of the Slavs, especially the Polish people, who occupy the foremost position in the Slavic lands. Only then can your practicality and realism, combined with our idealism, create the real power and might capable of opposing the barbarians of the West, just as we have done through the whole course of our glorious history, when we protected the West with our own bodies from the hordes of the East. If we possess an armed force, such as we can create both for our sake and yours, only then will we be in a position to fight your opponent and our ancient mortal enemy."

When I finished, Minister Hughes stood up and asked if I had served in an army. When I answered that I had previously served as a volunteer and non-commissioned officer in the army of the United States, he said "In that case I will appoint you as a colonel." I answered, "General, thank you for your kindness, but I prefer to go to school first and be better prepared before receiving such a rank, because the cause might suffer for it—so I cannot at present accept this appointment." The audience lasted some time longer, with discussion of technical details involving army matters.

After it was over, when I had written down the protocol of the conference and drawn up a proposal and organizational conditions for a Polish legion, I informed the president of the Polish Falcons Alliance of America about all this, and at the same time informed him of a second conference which was to take place in the Ponchentrain Hotel [*sic*] in Detroit, Michigan, with the participation of officers of the English General Staff. Appointed semi-officially as delegates to these proceedings on behalf of the Falcons Alliance were Andrzej Małkowski and Franciszek Dziób (the latter was at the time the head of the Polish Falcons Alliance of America). Due to *druh* Dziób's incompetent presentation of the matter and his lack of fluency in English, this conference produced little in the way of results.

At the same time the Falcons were being terrorized by the National Defense Committee. The reason was as follows. Five young Falcon hotheads, led by *druh* Sobczak, had heard from *druh* Małkowski that a fellow named Skarzyński was doing something in Canada, and set out to find the Canadian legions, to join the ranks of the Polish legion. At the Canadian border they were detained and told that there was no official information about any such action. This was perfectly natural, because the action was not yet complete and thus had not yet been announced. Disappointed in their hopes, the would-be legionnaires came under the care of the opposite camp. Soon, in the columns of American daily newspapers that supported the National Defense Committee, articles appeared about the betrayal to the Czar of Falcon youth by Wincenty Skarzyński, at that time the head of District VI (bordering on Canada) of the Polish Falcons Alliance of America, supposedly on the rationale that this Polish legion in Canada was to be part of the English Army.

The first such article appeared in the *Dziennik Polski* in Detroit, Michigan, and I will quote its text:

National Crime of the Falcons Administration
Many youths from the Detroit district betrayed to the Czar!
Eight Falcon districts will go to New York for a convention on saving the Falcons' organization

> We have learned that a number of youths from districts VI, II and IV of the Polish Falcons *went to Canada, headed by 6th district chief Skarzyński*. Probably several hundred Falcons have gone.
>
> On Sunday, 29 October, there will be a Falcon conference from the eastern districts, I, III, V, VII, VIII, IX, X and XII in New York, in the National House, 404 E. 15th Street, beginning at 2 p.m. The representatives of these districts are meeting to consult on rescuing the Falcon organization. Down with Russia! It is time to serve Poland and preserve the remnants of our strength for her! Down with the Judas Department that wishes to betray the Falcons wholesale to Russia! Let us rescue the Falcon youth!

The future course of the relations we had established was discussed with the Falcons' Administration, mainly with president Starzyński. At that point, as a result of dispatches sent by Małkowski to Władysław Zamoyski in Paris, a man named J. N. Horodyski came to him. This gentleman, supposedly sent on the authority of Roman Dmowski, managed to install himself so firmly among the Falcons that president Starzyński, who had summoned me to Pittsburgh (the headquarters of the Administration of the Polish Falcons Alliance of America), demanded from me, as a disciplined Falcon, my complete obedience, and required that henceforth I would take no steps on my own authority, but only with the consent of Mr. Horodyski, who was supposedly Roman Dmowski and I. J. Paderewski's ambassador. Since I did, in fact, consider myself a disciplined Falcon, I submitted to the demands of president Starzyński and chief Franciszek Dziób and gave my word of honor that I would remain inactive for three months. In the meantime Horodyski, who was, as I later learned, in the diplomatic service of Great Britain, was informed in detail about all my actions and those of *druh* Andrzej Małkowski in Canada; he went to Ottawa and began to conduct the work I had begun there himself. Since I initially had no idea who Horodyski really was, but believed that president Starzyński was acting in good faith (as he was, in fact), I did nothing, but awaited orders from above. At last in November, 1916, *druh* Małkowski, his patience exhausted by the wait, slipped off to join the ranks of the English in Canada.

His impatience due to the idle waiting for concrete information is reflected in one of the late Andrzej Małkowski's letters (shortly after this letter he joined the ranks of the Canadians):

6 October 1916
180 Second Ave., New York, NY

Druh W. Skarzyński,

Dear *druh*,
I am disturbed by your silence and that of *druh* D. in the Canadian matter. Personal affairs do not allow me to await a decision any longer than a few more days. For this reason I ask you to report back to me by special delivery on how the Canadian authorities received the project of ours, known to you.
With a hearty handclasp and the cry 'Be prepared!'
Andrzej Małkowski

In the meantime I had received from president Starzyński and chief Dziób orders to prepare the people in my District for departure to Canada. Carls Rite Hotel in Toronto was designated as our assembly point. Horodyski showed up and officially stated that he himself was taking over the organization, which was equivalent to seizing the work he had not begun and taking advantage of my initiative.

Though I was not without my suspicions, I submitted obediently and, in the spirit of my given word to my president, I accepted the events passively. Not wishing to waste time in inactivity, I enrolled in the school, along with all the *druh*'s I had previously recruited.

Since I had three years of military experience in the American army, I completed officers' training school at the University of Toronto before my comrades, and then became my former colleagues' instructor. Soon all had completed their studies—they all plunged eagerly into action—and in the meantime our "messiah," Horodyski, had not made an appearance. In view of this wholly unexpected turn of affairs, I had to salvage the situation. I made an arrangement with the head of the school and at my own expense sent three colleagues to the general convention of Falcons in Pittsburgh in April, 1917, that is, after the United States of America had declared war on Germany.

At this convention, everything came to light. The Polish-American community learned of the existence of the military school, but no one could or would get seriously involved with it, so that I had to take everything into my own hands. I began by reaching an understanding with president Starzyński, but unfortunately neither the president nor Dziób, the head of the Polish Falcons Alliance of America, who was still completely under the influence of Horodyski (he had vanished into thin air) was willing to take any steps toward concentrating their efforts for the military school. This reluctance to promote such a promising cause was due to Paderewski's proposal to the Falcons in America that they create a "Kościuszko's Army" in the United States. This idea—it is not known exactly who came up with it—was unrealistic. If the American government had agreed to a separate Polish national army, it would also have had to let others organize national military units, which, in my opinion, would obviously be counter to the interests of the United States. I had a fairly good orientation regarding the conditions and relations of America, and I foresaw the impracticality of this idea. I was determined to continue working to maintain and develop the action that had been begun in Canada, on the soil of the British Empire. Horodyski, the self-proclaimed confidant of Paderewski sent by Roman Dmowski, and an official of Great Britain, was no longer in charge of us and disappeared from view.

To save the school and the whole plan for organizing the Polish American army in Canada, I will admit that I had to resort to a ruse to capture Starzyński, tear him away from Pittsburgh and the Horodyski-Paderewski circle, and drag him to Toronto and Ottawa, Canada. So I made arrangements with five of my more eminent colleagues, namely Albrecht, Adamczak, Osielski, Sierociński, and Wiącek, and I went to Pittsburgh, prepared for anything, even abducting Starzyński and taking him to Canada. It was high time to do something decisive, because even the lads had begun to be agitated, there were more and more applications to the school—and the Canadian authorities had no idea how to proceed. But I finally succeeded in inducing Starzyński to travel to Toronto. At the same time I worked out a plan of action, to which both president Starzyński and Colonel LePan, commandant of the Officers Training School at the University of Toronto, agreed completely.

The group of the first volunteers in the officers' training school in Canada, with two Canadian instructors, in front of the University building in Toronto, Canada.

First alumni of the Canadian Officers' Training Corps at the University of Toronto, Canada

1) Adamczak, L.
2) Albrycht, W.
3) Bogucki, J.
4) Chwałkowski, L.
5) Gawryś, T.
6) Godowski, T.
7) Klatt, A.
8) Kresse, A.
9) Król, B.
10) Kryze, J.
11) Małkowski, A.
12) Osielski, J.
13) Rokicki, J.
14) Seiler, J.
15) Serge, B.
16) Sierociński, J.
17) Skarzyński, W.
18) Sobczak, L.
19) Szlachciński, S.
20) Szymański, F.
21) Więcek, A.
22) Wróblewski, J.
23) Zielecki, K.

The first volunteers of the Canadian Officers' Training Corps in Canada, with Rev. Hincman, the pastor of the Polish parish in Toronto, Canada. The August 1977 issue of Weteran Magazine, *a SWAP Veterans' publication, gave the following caption to this photograph: "A Group of the 'Lost Ones' — The First Officers in Canada. When they left, sent by Dr. Starzynski to the Officer's School in Canada, the Falcons were accused of 'losing' the flower of Polish youth. From them came the first officers of the Polish Army in America, later in France. Seated are, from left: Osielski, Sierocinski, Rev. Hintzman, Skarzynski, Adamczak. Second row, from left: Zielecki, Wiacek, Godowski, Chwalkowski, Krol, Sejler, Sobszyk, Kresse, NN. Last row, from left: Gabrys, NN, Klatt, Wroblewski, Albrycht, Szlachcinski, Rokicki. Three are missing."*

I also informed my five comrades, mentioned above, of Starzyński's arrival. We met at the house of Rev. Hincman, the pastor of the Polish parish in Toronto, to discuss our next steps. The result of this meeting was our forming a committee which was to undertake first and foremost translating English military regulations into Polish.

It must be noted that, thanks to the rendering of the English drills in Polish, on 3 May 1917, before we set out for church, we put on a sort of exhibition of the military school's Polish unit, to the enormous amazement of the Englishmen. This exhibition took place with the sounds of commands in Polish. The school's commandant, Colonel LePan, reproached me strongly for not having warned him of my intention to issue commands in Polish. He himself received a sharp reprimand from higher authorities for allowing this. The English could not restrain their agitation that a foreign tongue could be heard officially in an English military school, the like of which it had never seen from its earliest history.

This incident, later smoothed over, proved to the English that this small handful of "desperadoes" came there not as mercenaries, but as men of ideals, Polish patriots, who risked all in their determination to make their way to Canada and create the foundation of a Polish national military unit, not losing heart at any obstacle, just to reach this longed-for goal of unfortunate exiles, provided that they remained soldiers of their mother Poland. And here president Starzyński became convinced of the true state of affairs, of the position in which these "desperadoes" found themselves, that is, the first alumni of the school known officially in English as the "Canadian Officers' Training Corps" (C.O.T.C.).

After he had seen all this, president Starzyński let himself be talked into going with me to Ottawa. We received an appointment to see the chief of the General Staff, General Gwatkin; I introduced him to the president of the Polish Falcons Alliance of America, Dr. Teofil Starzyński, and, in order to save Polish "prestige"—which had been damaged by the disappearance of Horodyski—I tried, as best I could, to explain that fact. I immediately brought up the necessity of getting permission to increase the number of students at the Officers' School mentioned above. After long and grueling arguments and consultations, and the solemn assurance that Horodyski would no longer be the man responsible, but that president Starzyński would thenceforth be that man, the chief of the Canadian General Staff agreed to my proposal to enlarge the school, and entrusted its organization wholly to me. Thus ended the tiresome uncertainty over the fate of the effort, begun with such labor, to build in America the basic unit of a Polish army, an effort interrupted by Horodyski's intrusion and attempts to seize the whole plan in his hands.

On the way back from Ottawa I received president Starzyński's approval of my plan for the school's further development. The idea was that those who had completed their training in Toronto should go as instructors to Cambridge Springs, Pennsylvania, where the Polish Falcons Alliance of America, thanks to the grant of a location by the existing College of the Polish National Alliance of America, had already begun training volunteer candidates for future officers. I pushed Sierociński for the position of commandant of that school in Cambridge

Springs (I did so due to personal liking) despite considerable opposition on the part of president Starzyński, who was opposed to all change and wanted to see the school's long-time commandant, Dziób, in that post. I, on the other hand, was a supporter of change, and precisely because of the changes I proposed, the same system was introduced in both schools.

There was great joy among the lads at the officers' school in Canada when they learned that after finishing it they could go to the States. I gave some of them rest leave and allowances, others I ordered to go to Cambridge Springs under the protective wing of the Falcons Alliance. I myself received an order from president Starzyński, ignoring Paderewski's and Horodyski's fantasies on the army, to go to Chicago, Milwaukee, South Bend and Detroit and increase the officers' cadres by attracting to it the senior Falcons; I was aided by the chief of Falcon District II, *druh* Wład. Sulewski. I carried out the order completely, after which strenuous training began. Difficulties arose, mainly due to insufficient knowledge of the English language on the part of many candidates, and to the exorbitant ambitions of some individuals.

W. Skarzyński in the uniform of a lieutenant in the Canadian army, and the late druh Bartmański in the uniform of a student at the University of Toronto's Canadian Officers' Training Corps.

In Detroit I met the former chief of the Polish Falcons Alliance of America, *druh* Bartmański, a former first lieutenant of the Austrian infantry. He had resigned as head of the Polish Falcons Alliance due to a personal conflict during the course of the senior Falcons of District VI in South Bend, due to differences of opinion with the president in regard to the matter of the Polish Army. I wanted to assemble the greatest possible number of former military men, so I tried very hard to bring in him and his subordinates. So when I caught sight of Bartmański, I stood before him at attention, military-style, and said, "*Druh* Bartmański, my captain, I wish to report obediently that that work of which you used to dream, the creation of a Polish armed force, is truly begun. I beg you, before God, to hear this report in peace and join us in this work." Since this meeting took place after a number of bombs in the press—in which I was defamed as having betrayed the Falcons to the Czar, as I mentioned earlier—Bartmański thought about it for a while, then extended his right hand and answered that before he joined the ranks, he had to find out where, with whom, and in what manner the work was being conducted. After exhaustive explanations and a long discussion, he gave me his word of honor that he would appear at the agreed spot on the Canadian border, which he did, in fact. As an expert officer, in all the work he was a most useful agent.

Before driving the boys from the States into Canada, I had them swear a pledge, a kind of oath that was required by the Canadian authorities and was in Polish, thereby getting around the problems that could have resulted from using the original English text, which would have required each of the volunteers to swear allegiance to the King of England and thereby to serve in the English army. With the purpose of avoiding this, I changed the English oath to the promise shown on pages 34 and 36 *[these page numbers refer to the original manuscript; in this book see pages 104 and 107]*.

When class after class began to arrive at the school and the number of students grew to a sizeable figure, the work, which was very vigorous, began, and soon

---

Members of the second group of the Canadian Officers' Training Corps, University of Toronto, Canada

Bartman, A.
Bartmański, J.
Bauer, F.
Bednarz, J. J.
Borek, S.
Chwastyk, J.
Dombrowski, K.
Janeczko, P.
Kendziorek, F.
Klich, F.
Krzysztawkiewicz, Z.
Kuraszkiewicz, S.
Kusjorski, P.
Lewandowski, M.
Liss, J.
Łabędzki, S. K.

Łączkowski, S.
Matecki, J. K.
Michniewicz, Z.
Nastał, S.
Oleksy, E. J.
Organisty, W.
Pasternak, F.
Pawłowicz, E.
Pela, J.
Pieprzny, G.
Piasecki, W.
Piotrowski, Z.
Pryba, W.
Roskosz, J.
Rogoziński, S.
Rowiński, Z. J.

Rupiński, J.
Rzewuski, W. W.
Szembarski, S.
Sulewski, W.
Szymański, J.
Trawiński, W. H.
Turkowski, W.
Urban, L.
Urbaniak, J. H.
Walaszczyk, W.
Wojciechowski, S.
Wójcik, F.
Wronowski, S.
Żydanowicz, P. F.

took all the English instructors at the school's command. In summer, 1917, the school was transferred from Toronto to Camp Borden, and that is where it was actually transformed into a Polish school. At my request, specialized courses were introduced for those who had completed the infantry school, courses on machine-guns, field engineering, bomb-throwers, etc.

At the end of May, 1917, I was made a first lieutenant, to the great joy of the school's students, and began as an instructor of a captain's course (see the photograph on page 101). After completing the course, I traveled to the States, to the administrative offices of the Polish Falcons Alliance, so that, with the participation of the president, Dr. Starzyński, I could conduct efforts to mobilize the first Falcon regiment. The Falcons' administration agreed to my further plans to appoint a military committee, and on 27 July 1917 I appointed to it the president, Dr. Teofil Starzyński, and *druh*'s Jan Bartmański and Józef Sierociński.

The commandant of the Canadian Officers' School, Colonel A. D. LePan, expressed his opinion of Lieutenant W. Skarzyński in a letter addressed to Major F. E. Fronczak of the Polish National Committee:

Polish National Committee   Paris, 17 February 1919
Department of Public Welfare
47 bis, Ave Kleber, Paris   Major F. E. Fronczak
                                   Director, Dept. of Public Welfare

    <u>W G</u>
    2426   To: Lieutenant Skarzyński
                                   Headquarters N.D.A.P.

I am forwarding to you a letter, enclosed, sent to me by Colonel LePan, commandant of the Polish Camp, Niagara-on-the-Lake, Ont., Canada, in your matter, which may be helpful to you.
FEF/WMS
1 Enclosure   *Franciszek E. Fronczak*

And WG 2117 S 16/II 1919.

                 Re Lt Skarzyński- Important.
<u>M. F. B. 239.</u>   **MILITIA AND DEFENCE.**
1½ million—3-18.   *Polish Army Camp*
H. Q. 1772-39-194.   *Niagara-on-the-Lake, Ont., Jan. 31st,*
                             1919.

                    To: Major Francis E. Fronczak, MC USA,
                    Director—Dept of Public Welfare

The Polish-language version of the oath taken by the Polish cadets; it says "I, as a member of the class of the Officers' Training Corps and a disciplined Falcon, hereby pledge my word of honor to obey in a disciplined manner and fulfill in a soldierly manner all orders of the commanders of the Military School in Canada and to conform to all the schools' rules and regulations, which I affirm with my signature in my own hand." The cadets' signatures follow. On the right margin is written "Received 29 May 1917, W. Skarzyński, First Lieutenant."

Polish National Committee
47 bis, Avenue Kleber, Paris, France.

Dear Major Fronczak,

I was glad to receive your letter of Jan 4th and to have the opportunity at your request of giving you my appreciation of the work of Lieut. W. N. Skarzyński in as far as it came under my observation.

Skarzyński arrived at the School of Infantry, Toronto on Jan. 3rd. 1917 with the first class of Polish boys to be qualified. You will readily appreciate that the situation was an unusual one and even with devotion and patriotism on the part of the Poles and a sympathetic attitude on the part of Canadians it took time to come to a complete understanding of each other. During this period Skarzyński was of very great value and stood out as a leader. It was with him that often I discussed matters of procedure and had it not been for his assistance many difficult situations might have arisen.

After qualification he stayed at the School for a while as an instructor and later a good deal of his time was spent in assisting organization in the States. During all this time we considered Skarzyński a most useful man, and had the greatest admiration for his patriotism and energy. All his efforts seemed to be directed in furthering the Polish cause, and we never had any reason to believe that he had any selfish motives in this work. He was continually making trips between our camp and points in the United States on matters connected with the Polish Army. Whether he was recompensed for these expenses I do not know, but I do know that he never hesitated to spend money, apparently his own when he thought the Polish cause would be benefited.

I can only add that Skarzyński was of the very greatest assistance to us in the early stages of the Polish Army in America, and that his devotion and energy were important factors in enabling us to arrive at a working arrangement. I am glad to be able to make this statement for I feel that he certainly is entitled to some consideration for these efforts.

As you of course know this camp will shortly be broken up, a circumstance we view with regret for our relations with all the Poles have been most pleasant and we have developed the greatest admiration for the splendid men who have come through our camp. However we will follow with the greatest interest the events of Poland and we hope with you that the realization of the Poles will be speedily realized and that Poland will again occupy its former and rightful place among the great nations of the world.

ADL/S

Yours sincerely
A. D. LePan, Lt-Col
Commandant Polish Army Camp.

Members of the third group of the Officer's Training Corps at the University of Toronto, Canada

Andruszkiewicz, P.
Basowski, M.
Baśkiewicz, F.
Białas, F.
Blacha, S.
Bratuszewski, S. B.
Brzeziński, B.
Budziak, L.
Butlak, S. A.
Ciapa, J.
Ciecierski, W.
Cieślicki, A.
Czaban, W. A.
Czaczkowski, B.
Czajkowski, W.
Dąbrowski, J
Dombrowski, A.
Drączkowski, S.
Dudek, W.
Dworzecki, F.
Dzierzgowski, P.
Galasiewicz, F.
Galiński, W. J.
Gawałkiewicz, W.
Godziszewski, R.
Gołaszewski, W.
Gorczyca, W.
Gosiewski, J.
Górecki, F.
Grecki, J.
Gruchacz, L.
Gut, J. L.
Jędrczak, J.
Karczewski, S.
Kargol, W.
Kawszewicz, J.
Klimczewski, H.
Kogut, G. J.
Kolasa, S. J.
Kordecki, W.
Kosiński, F.
Kostrubała, J. K.
Kowalczyk, A.
Kowalewski, A.
Kowalski, M.
Koźlakowski, A.
Kozłowski, J. F.
Kukuczka, J.
Kuźmiński, F. S.
Kwaśniewski, T.
Ławcewicz, G.
Łuczywo, B.
Łyczak, A. B.
Malinowski, A. T.
Marszewski, M.
Matejkowski, A.
Matuszkiewicz, J.
Mierzejewski, W.
Miller, L. R.
Miller, R.
Minoga, J.
Misiewicz, P.
Młochowski, K.
Mulak, J.
Niemiec, P. J.
Niski, B.
Nowak, Z. F.
Nowakowski, S.
Pajewski, M.
Paluch, M. K.
Pałaszewski, S.
Partyka, S.
Paśniewski, J. R.
Pawlak, W. A.
Pawłowski, W.
Perzan, J.
Pospuła, J.
Przybyłowski, S.
Pszczółkowski, K.
Pułaski, S.
Radziwanowicz, A.
Rolka, I.
Ruciński, J. H.
Rumiński, J. A.
Rutkowski, S. R.
Sielawa, S.
Smakosz, V. T.
Smieciński, F.
Sobieski, I.
Solon, S.
Sosien, S.
Sosnowski, C. A.
Stach, L. S.
Staniszewski, A.
Stępkowski, J.
Stygar, W.
Szczepański, P. A.
Szwagiel, W.
Szwejkowski, J.
Tenerowicz, J.
Truszkiewicz, F.
Twardowski, S. J.
Wenda, B.
Wenglicki, J. W.
Wienckus, Z. F.
Wojtylak, B.
Zajączkowski, W.
Zarzecki, W. L.
Zegarski, F. R.
Żebrowski, S.

Polish-language form of the oath sworn by the Polish cadets to the Officers' School on 16 July 1917 in Toronto, literally: 'As a true Pole and a cadet of the third class of the Officers' Training School of the Polish Falcons Alliance of America, I voluntarily consent to all regulations of the Canadian Army, as well as the rules of the C.O.T.C. school currently at Camp Borden. As a true and disciplined Falcon, I will abide by them in everything I do, and I promise to persevere to the completion of my courses. I give with my word of honor to this, and affirm it with my signature in my own hand.' At bottom right is noted, 'Received 16 July 1917, W. N. Skarzyński, First Lieutenant, C.O.T.C.'

A delay in further progress of further work was caused by new interference on the part of Horodyski in Washington. In the meantime, however, president Starzyński, who was in constant contact with the president of the West European Falcons Alliance, *druh* Wacław Gąsiorowski in Paris, received news from *druh* Gąsiorowski that thanks to his efforts and the magic word "America," he had succeeded in obtaining a decree establishing the Polish Army in France, which read as follows:

The President of the Republic of France
as a result of the report of the President of the Council of Ministers, the Minister of Foreign Affairs, and the Minister of War,
has determined:
Article I. An autonomous Polish Army is to be formed in France during wartime, under the supreme command of France, fighting under the Polish flag.
Article II. The organization and maintenance of the Polish Army are guaranteed by the French government.
Article III. The rules in force for the French army regarding organizations, ranks, administration, and military judiciary, will apply to the Polish Army as well.
Article IV. The Polish Army will be created from
  a) Poles serving at this time in the French Army;
  b) Poles in other categories, authorized to enter the ranks of the Polish Army in France, or to enlist during wartime under the standard of the Polish Army
Article V. The President of the Council of Ministers and the Minister of War are instructed, each in his own competence, to carry out this decree, which will be published in the Official Journal of the Republic of France and in the Journal of Laws.
Article V. Further ministerial orders will regulate the application of this decree.

Issued in Paris on 4 June 1917

> *By the President of the Republic: R.* POINCARÉ
> *President of the Council of Ministers*
> *Minister of Foreign Affairs: (signed) A.* RIBOT.
> *Minister of War: (signed)* PAUL PAINLEVE.

This move was obviously coordinated among the Allies, as was the matter of the Polish Army and its relationship to France.

Frenzied joy overcame the pupils of our school in Canada when the news of these events reached us. It was an important moment, because, due to Horodyski's

Photograph of the second class of Polish cadets at the Officers' Training Corps in Canada, taken at Camp Borden on the occasion of the arrival of Dr. T. A. Starzyński, president of the Polish Falcons Alliance in America. Seated from left to right: Lt. W. Skarzyński, Dr. T. A. Starzyński, druh J. Bartmański, druh W. Sulewski.

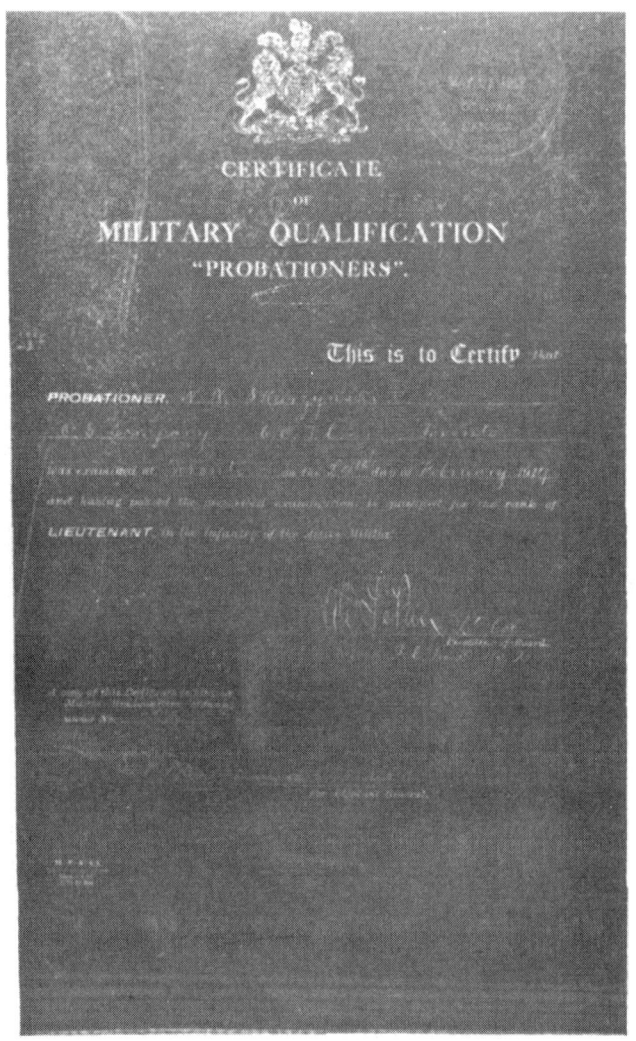

Certificate of Military Qualification for Wincenty Skarzyński

Second class of Polish volunteer cadets to the Canadian Officers' Training Corps at the University of Toronto. In the first row is the school's staff; seated, right to left, are the following English officers: Lieutenant Lewis, Captain Kenrick, Major Madill, school adjutant Major Young, school's commandant Colonel A. D. LePan, Major Branford, Major Kirk, Lieutenant Parr, Lieutenant W. Skarzyński.

Participants in the third group at the Canadian Officers' Training Corps, Toronto, Canada, with Colonel A. D. LePan and Lieutenant W. Skarzyński.

Aerial photo of Camp Borden, Ontario, circa 1917.

Machiavellian maneuvers and the delays that resulted from them, desertion had begun to creep into the ranks of our pupils. I tried with all my might to curb it; I attempted to oppose the decline in energy by every means including entreaties referring to the sacred nature of our effort and descriptions of images of a free Poland.

At this point an inspection committee of the Canadian government was touring military schools, and among them, therefore, visited the school in Camp Borden. After the inspection was completed, Vice-Minister of War Frazet, whom I was visiting, told me of the extremely positive impression that the condition of the school had made on the authorities, and assured me that as a result the school and its alumni could count on the authorities' broadest support, since at that point there was already a full battalion of those alumni. It should be noted that the Canadian Officers' Training Corp (C.O.T.C.) had been wholly transformed into a purely Polish military school, run obviously by Englishmen, but there was not a single English student in it.

Shortly thereafter I traveled to the States, to Pittsburgh; there president Starzyński summoned me to appear at a reception by the Falcons for Wacław Gąsiorowski, who was then visiting America. Afterwards I went to Washington to report on the alliance of the Polish Army to the representative of France, Franklin Bouillon, who headed a special mission created by the French government, in which Wacław Gąsiorowski also took part. I reported with him for an audience with Franklin Bouillon.

No one in Europe had any real idea of the current state of organization for the beginnings of the Polish Army in America. This matter was intentionally passed over in silence, or else completely distorted, by some agents, like Horodyski. The chief French and Polish activists were uninformed, so that the most enthusiastic supporters of this army came up with various bizarre ideas, e. g., they wanted to transport several hundred people at a time in civilian clothes from America to Europe. There were ten such proposals in all, among them the project of Gutowski, who wanted to see the Polish Army formed in some neutral country (in the end he was one of the Poles who agreed to my plan, the eleventh).

When I laid out my plan for Franklin Bouillon, who had steadfastly opposed all the others, he cried out with evident satisfaction, "Oh, it's so good that I finally get to deal with a soldier on a military matter" (I reported for the meeting dressed in an English uniform).

What I said was as follows, more or less: "Mr. Minister, we have so far, under the supervision of the Polish Falcons of America, one school for non-commissioned officers in the United States, at Cambridge Springs, Pennsylvania, numbering more than 250 students and directed by officers already trained in Canada. In Canada, on the other hand, we have about 400 officers capable of leading a company, and of that number about 200 could boldly lead a battalion.

First Mission of the Polish Army of France to the United States. From left: Włodzimierz Szaniawski, Lieutenant Prince Stanisław August Poniatowski, and Henryk Rzekiecki. In the middle, seated, First Lieutenant Wacław Gąsiorowski.

In addition, infantry specialist courses are being conducted. They can produce officers fully competent to organize, train, and man at least two hundred battalions, and more fighting units, with training that is hard and amazingly practical, which is how the English do it. If further recruiting is filtered through these schools, it will have a very positive influence on the course of further enlistment, the more so if it is organized ostentatiously, with a simultaneous review of existing cadres. Soon the results of this kind of behavior must become evident, because the site designated for the camp by the Canadian Vice-Minister of War, Frazet, in Niagara-on-the-Lake, is located not far from the enormous Polish settlement in Buffalo, where seven Polish newspapers are published. When the Poles see that Polish work is actually being carried out, and when they are convinced with their own eyes that the Polish army exists, it will create an enormous impression. And I have Vice-Minister Frazet's promise that if need be, the Canadian authorities will create a Neutral Zone exclusively for the use of the Polish Army."

Franklin Bouillon was extremely pleased by my argument. But he asked me whether conducting a similar plan in the States would be required. I answered that it would be desirable to take such measures, "but, in my opinion, I doubt that it could be put into effect." Then Franklin Bouillon picked up his telephone and called Secretary of State R. Lansing and asked him about this matter. As I had foreseen, Lansing gave a negative answer. This short episode was yet another proof of my good information regarding the whole matter of creating a Polish army, such that after our conversation was over, Franklin Bouillon was wholly of my opinion and became a wholehearted supporter of, as he said, this one truly military, matter-of-fact plan. Immediately after our conversation he issued appropriate instructions, entrusting the completion of my plan to a member of his mission, French Army Second Lieutenant Prince Stanisław A. Poniatowski, with whom I immediately left for Canada, to Camp Borden, introduced him to the authorities, and handed over command of the school. Colonel LePan, seeing finally that my plan was beginning to be fully realized, became even more enthusiastic for our work and invested all his skill and talent in organizing the school and battalions, and became an unparalleled friend to the Polish soldiers. The results crowned his labor, as in a relatively short time, on foreign soil with a foreign element, he accomplished a magnificent deed: he laid the cornerstone for building the Polish Army in France.

I returned to Pittsburgh and, with Dr. Starzyński and *druh* Samulski, secretary of the Polish Falcons Alliance of America, I worked out a recruitment plan. We divided the whole area of the States into twelve districts and, having chosen twelve exceptional, trustworthy men, we appointed them to those twelve centers, for the purpose of beginning immediate conscription and transportation of volunteers straight to the camp, which as a result of my insistence had been moved from Camp Borden to Niagara-on-the-Lake. After a meeting directed by *druh* Bartmański, the Falcons' Military Committee completed its activity, inasmuch as president Starzyński, with a view toward concentrating the efforts of all the Polish immigrant community, coordinated the past preparatory work of the Falcons with the National Department, which represented all the Polish immigrant community in America, and therefore all the Polish national organizations that existed there, such as the Polish National Alliance, the Polish Falcons' Alliance, the Roman Catholic Union, the Polish Women's Alliance, and others. As a consequence of this coordination the National Department appointed a Military Committee, which consisted of: 1) *druh* Dr. T. A. Starzyński, as the Falcons' representative; 2) T. M. Heliński, of the Polish National Alliance; and 3) A. Znamięcki, specially recommended by maestro Paderewski for this enormous work, a well-connected man and one of best of the Poles in America in terms of understanding financial matters. The National Department entrusted to this committee the immediate commencement of recruiting volunteers on American and Canadian soil for the Polish Army in France, in the spirit of the plan worked out by the Polish Falcons Alliance of America.

After I completed my activity on the Falcons' Military Committee, on president Starzyński's instructions I set out for the largest center of America's Polonia, Chicago; in the course of three weeks I sent from there to the camp at Niagara-on-the-Lake the first 1,500 volunteers, and arranged noisy national demonstrations during their departure by special trains.

I must mention here that when I was in Chicago and was first invited to a meeting of the Polish National Alliance, I addressed the presidium of the Alliance with these words: "Dear sirs! The Falcons, as the vanguard in the work of creating the Polish Army, came up against an obstacle; without your help and substantial efforts we could not have gotten past that obstacle. For this reason I, in the name of the Falcons, turn to you, Alliance members, at whose head stands one of the first Falcons in America, *druh* Kazimierz Żychliński, and I ask you to designate a certain sum of money for the beginning of that great work, before the French Mission settles all money matters. For we must get the volunteers to the designated site as soon as possible, as they are becoming impatient due to the delay in summoning them to the ranks; because of the delay a great many volunteers have already joined the American ranks. If we wish to create a Polish force, we must give the Falcons, and other Poles not in that organization, a chance to go into battle against our Fatherlands' ancient enemy under the standard of the White Eagle!" At this summons the Polish National Alliance, the largest Polish national organization of Polish immigrants in America, and the one that cared for the Falcons, assigned money and made it possible for me to take the first

The First Falcons' Military Committee, headed by President T. A. Starzyński; in Falcon field uniforms are druh's J. Bartmański and J. Sierociński; W. Skarzyński is in the uniform of the Canadian army. The picture was taken in front of the Alliance School building in Cambridge Springs, Pennsylvania.

steps in Chicago, which soon echoed across all America. The contribution of spreading news of the whole course of this meeting and the Alliance's resolution fell to the part of the mobilized and disciplined Polish-American press.

Besides the meeting I have described, another meeting, of Polish women, was called by Mrs. Paderewski in Chicago. The proceedings became so stormy, due to the opposition, that I was summoned by the president and secretary of the Polish Women's Alliance, Mrs. Napieralski, to calm down the disturbance, which threatened at any moment to degenerate into a serious scandal. Fortunately, I succeeded in calming things down, and then immediately withdrew. On the next day I received an invitation from the Paderewski's. The maestro was not feeling well and was in bed, but he received me very courteously. During the conversation he was greatly surprised that I was still a lieutenant in the Canadian army, when I should have been at least a captain, and he said he was prepared to write at once to one of the generals, so that I could be promoted immediately. I thanked him sincerely for his courtesy and said that I did not want this, I would prefer to attain higher rank by way of my military service. During the course of further conversation, not sensing that this was a sensitive issue, I touched on the errors and behavior of Horodyski, indicating that he was the one who had hindered the whole organization of the Polish Army. "If it were not for him," I continued, "we would have already had several thousand trained officers and non-commissioned officers." "What do you mean? After all, he is a very influential man in Great Britain," Mrs. Paderewski cried out. Disregarding this, I spoke on.

There ensued a discussion unpleasant for the Paderewski's, and highly unpleasant for me; as it dragged on, I excused myself, citing a mountain of work, and left the Paderewski's house. I left them with an opinion of me as a troublemaker, simply because, despite regarding Paderewski as a great Polish patriot, I could not agree with the type of people by whom he was surrounded—individuals who served foreign powers for foreign pay, or who wanted to promote their own interests in recruiting.

In contrast to the latter, I must stress that both in Chicago and in other Polish centers, the organizers of the Polish Army distinguished themselves by their determination and total selfless devotion to this sacred cause. They worked from conviction, not for money, as was done later, when agitators were paid five dollars a day. Among these men of ideals were *druh*'s Adamczak, Dziób, Osielski, Sulewski, Wróblewski, Zielecki, and many, many other students of the Canadian Officers' Training Corps.

In describing my work recruiting the first volunteers in Chicago, there is an event I cannot pass over in silence; it took place in October, 1917, in Walsh's Hall, when opponents of the Polish Army in France, grouped together in the so-called National Defense Committee, called a meeting for the purpose of counteracting

The first Polish volunteers recruited in Chicago, Illinois. In the center, Lieutenant W. Skarzyński.

The colors presented to the Polish Army in France by Polish Women in America, Chicago, Ill., October 14th, 1917.

the organization of the Polish Army in France on the soil of the United States of America. As an advocate of "creating a Polish armed force, even with the devil," as Józef Piłsudski, First Marshal of Poland, said at one time, I went to the promised meeting, determined to explain to these gentlemen that they were acting wrongly. But when one of them—as best I can recall, Mr. Rajzacher —in his speech began uttering nonsense such as "Not one drop of Polish blood should be shed in the battle against the Germans," and later—for what reasons or what cause I don't know—called on Poles to enlist in the American army rather than the Polish Army in France, I could no longer bear to hear such statements and began to protest firmly against them. As a result, enormous confusion broke out in the hall, and before I could get the floor again or could look around, volunteers of the Polish Army in France who had already been recruited took over the hall and, outraged by the statements of the meetings' organizers, forced them off the stage, thus turning what had been a meeting of opponents of the Polish Army in France into a meeting of advocates of that Army, and in addition gaining new recruits at that same meeting. Obviously, the opponents of the Polish Army in France, ascribing to me the intention of organizing the whole attack on their meeting, tried to have me arrested by the local police, but failed to do so. They later took me to court, where they also lost their case, as their pro-German activities were proven. This verdict was at the same time an exoneration of me and a source of satisfaction that, as an impartial man, I had nothing else in mind but working for Poland, exerting all my efforts toward creating an armed force, irregardless of whether I offended some groups or individuals.

Overcoming numerous difficulties, I completed all the difficult work of recruiting the first Polish volunteers in Chicago; since the first period of that work was now finished and I felt myself somewhat more at liberty, I asked Dr. Starzyński to promise that I could go to France with the first unit. He did not want to agree to that, he intended to go on using me for organizational work here in America. But I felt that I could not stay in America any longer: my heart was eager to go to Poland, I simply could not wait for the time when, along with our Polish Army from America, I would stand on European soil, to fight and win back Poland's independence there. Carried away by patriotism, I was in no position to think about myself. I didn't think about how I would be leaving my young, recently married wife behind in another hemisphere; nor did I give any thought to how I would lose my rank as a lieutenant and become a private once more, for I wished with all my heart to depart as soon as possible for Europe with our freshly organized Polish Army, whose foundations I had laid. It was all the same to me, I wanted to encounter the enemy as quickly as possible, I wanted to tear away from him that which he had stolen from our Fatherland...

At that point the organization of the Polish army was taken over by Colonel Martin, newly arrived at the camp at Niagara-on-the-Lake from Washington, a

Second group of Polish volunteers recruited in Chicago, Illinois. The photograph was taken on the steps of Holy Trinity Church in Chicago, with maestro Paderewski.

member of the *Mission Militaire Française* [French Military Mission], that is, a representative of the French General Staff in the United States. In my desire to depart as soon as possible, I resigned my rank of Lieutenant in the Canadian Army and placed myself, as a simple private, at Colonel Martin's disposition. On Colonel LePan's recommendation I was put on the first list as leader of one of four companies of the first Canadian battalion, as leader of which I went, with my whole battalion, to St. Johns in Quebec province, to prepare the battalion for departure. I was appointed second-in-command to the commander assigned us, Prince Stanisław August Poniatowski.

The long awaited moment finally arrived. On 16 December 1917 the ship *Niagara* was bidden farewell by those who knew about the departure of the first battalion, consisting of about 1,000 Polish volunteers, and set sail from the port of New York for France. The journey of this first unit of the Polish Army to France should surely be numbered among the most magnificent moments of that period. The faces of our boys were always smiling, it didn't occur to anyone that we might be in any danger; we rejoiced to be headed for the other hemisphere, there to avenge the wrongs done our ancestors and hoist the flag of liberty on our native lands. It should be noted that at this time it was not at all unusual to encounter enemy submarines, mines, or other surprises. I remember we spent Christmas Eve and the first day of the Christmas holidays very joyfully on that ship. During our voyage the chaplain, Rev. Jaworski, celebrated Holy Mass with a devout congregation on the deck of the ship, and Midnight Mass on the first day of the holiday in the ship's dining room, and that made a great impression on our boys.

On 27 December 1917 we arrived at Bordeaux. The next morning we began to disembark. There to greet us and welcome us were the chief of staff of the French-Polish Mission, Colonel Mokiejewski, Major Radziwiłł, Captain Jagniątkowski, and Lieutenant Rodzyński, with twelve buglers specially sent to play a fanfare, along with a battalion of Senegalese—it seems they were originally designated by the French military authorities to keep control over unruly Poles—and finally the authorities' representatives. It was a magnificent and unforgettable moment when the ship approached the shore where the buglers stood playing *"Jeszcze Polska nie zginęła" [which was to become the Polish national anthem]* and on the deck the mass of volunteers, already drawn up in ranks, began singing the words to the hymn in time with the bugles. Another stirring moment came when the ship was secured and the signal to disembark given, the battalion lined up at my command in close order, and I reported to the chief of staff, Colonel Mokiejewski, and received the order to lead the battalion to barracks. At the command "Battalion, attention!" the sound of heels clicking came in a single bang, like

Above: Review of the first battalion of volunteers from America by Colonel Mokiejewski in Bordeaux, France. Below: General Archinard.

the discharge of a cannon—on signal the unit set out for their assigned barracks with extraordinary verve. The breaking of ranks into columns of four, the beat of feet striking the earth, the dressing and covering were so adroit that one got the impression that the old guard of Napoleon's Vistula Legion had come. On the faces of the soldiers and officers arriving from across the ocean was painted an expression of enormous joy, and it seemed that the mouths of these true patriots were saying "We are now near the goal of realizing our dreams, the creation of a genuine Polish military force!"

The officers of the French-Polish Military Mission were amazed by the battalion's training and appearance, as they confided later, after the battalion was quartered in barracks, at supper in the Hotel Bayon. There it was decided that on the following day Lieutenant Rodzyński would take command of the battalion and lead it to Laval, and the chief of staff of the French-Polish Military Mission proposed that I should go to Paris, so that they could present me to the head of that Mission, General Archinard.

When I reported in at the Mission, I was informed that an audience with the Premier and Minister of War, Clemenceau, was granted for the 4th of January, 1918. From that point on a tangle of intrigue began to coil about my person; Colonel Mokiejewski prohibited any contact with the Polish National Committee… All this was the reason that—after reaching an understanding with the lawyer K. Sypniewski, whom the National Department in the United States had sent to France to observe what they would do with us and what would happen to the money collected by America's Polonia—I made my way directly to the Polish National Committee in Paris, at 11 Kleber Avenue, to the residence of the heir to the Zamojski estate *[Translator's note: presumably this means Count Władysław Zamoyski,]* and there I bluntly presented my situation, in hopes of cutting through all the misunderstandings, hints, and intrigues.

First and foremost, the members of the National Committee painted Colonel Mokiejewski in the darkest colors and asked directly, "Why did you come here without our knowledge? Gąsiorowski isn't a usurper, is he?" Not comprehending the question or the whole content of these arguments, I answered like a soldier, "After all, in America Ignacy Paderewski is acting and managing things in the name of the National Committee … We, that is, Starzyński in Pittsburgh and Gąsiorowski in Paris, actually compelled him to support the Falcons' actions … It was no joking matter. Things were urgent; could we joke around, for instance, with the 50,000 Poles who gathered in Chicago's Humboldt Park, demanding the creation of a Polish armed force, 'even with the devil, as soon as possible?' Then a telegraph was sent to Paderewski to alert him, and thus, having volunteers and the masses of the Polish people ready for action, we had to cooperate with Paderewski. The irresolute or hesitant can only be made to act by an accomplished fact."

At this point I turned to Roman Dmowski, Marjan Seyda, Prof. Rozwadowski, and Count Zamoyski, and said, "One must take into account the will of the people, those individuals who without any foreign help whatsoever, organized Polish armed action by themselves on another hemisphere, and perhaps understood no less than you gentlemen its value and essence; I would say, therefore, that what was necessary was not to make difficulties in this matter, but rather to coordinate the efforts of everyone who has the good of the Fatherland at heart..."

I continued to bring up a series of technical and financial details, and stated categorically that it was badly done to hand over the organization of a Polish armed force to the French without reservations. "Personally I say that as far as the organizational technique of the army goes, the results would be better if English or American instructors were used, coordinating the details of their own training with the French; for in my judgment the French are lackadaisical in organization work, and will only delay us in our cause. Due to their sluggishness, hundreds of thousands of Poles had joined the American army instead of enlisting in our ranks. It is difficult, for I, as a disciplined Falcon, cannot refuse orders and must defer to others. But by God, Mr. President, you must deal with this existing army, for up to now there has been absolutely no decision or plan whatsoever. We, for our part, especially attorney Sypniewski, will do all we can so that the Polish-Americans will give carte-blanche to the National Committee in Paris."

On 4 January 1918, the day of my appointment with the premier of France, I presented myself punctually. Entering his office, I saw an old man, still lively and in good condition, with quick eyes and lively movements. The premier began by greeting me courteously in French. I begged his pardon, saying I had better command of English, and would make so bold as to use that language. Clemenceau answered in excellent English, saying that that was not a problem, and immediately began to praise the Polish unit and its fitness, and asked, "Surely when you were on the other side of the ocean you prepared for battle with our common foe?" I answered in the affirmative, and added that we could supply far more volunteers if the French Mission in America were better organized, and said, "One more thing, Mr. Premier, namely, if we had assurances that Santo Domingo will not be repeated this time or ever again!" *[Translator's note: see page 84 for explanation of this reference]*.

"That cannot happen again in any case," the Old Tiger responded briskly, "these are no longer the days of Napoleon."

Then matters of military organization were brought up, on which the Premier, who was also Minister of War, laid special emphasis. After that we once more got to talking about politics. Clemenceau asked me whom we regarded as our national leader. I thought for a moment and answered, "Unfortunately, it is difficult to name a single one, for the first is imprisoned by the Germans, and the second is in Paris." *[Translator's note: a reference to Piłsudski and Dmowski, respectively]*.

After these words I noted amazement on the premier's face; with a quick, nervous gesture he adjusted the cap on his head and said briskly, "This is the first time I have heard such an opinion from the mouth of a Pole, because all the ones I have encountered put forward only one. For instance, Dr. Motz was devoted only to Piłsudski, and others, such as Count Zamoyski, regard only Dmowski as their national leader." I saw that my objective point of view pleased the "Tiger." He ended by adding, "With such a point of view you can, in my judgment, achieve far more among Poles than hitherto."

The premier said goodbye to me—quite cordially, if I may say so—and I did not realize that the normal period of time allotted an official audience had long since passed. I was regarded with amazement, as the interview had lasted almost 30 minutes. Among some of the members of the French-Polish Military Mission this aroused a certain kind of envy, of which I had an inkling.

When I reported to lawyer Sypniewski on my talk, he agreed completely with me, and, thanks to his connections in the American Embassy in Paris, he sent a report immediately to America. In February of 1918 the Military Committee headed by Dr. Starzyński sent to the French Minister of Foreign Affairs, Pichon, authorization for Roman Dmowski to speak in the name of his countrymen, who had come to the field of battle to show by risking their own necks that Poland was among the nations fighting against the Germans. Soon, as a result of all these moves, Colonel Vaschoux was appointed chief of staff of the French-Polish Mission, in place of the previous chief, Colonel Mokiejewski—and as things turned out, at the moment Dmowski, visiting General Archinard, entered the Mission by one door, Colonel Mokiejewski left it for good by another.

It should be noted that the latter was the victim of his own political naïveté. On the one hand he was very useful to Gąsiorowski, using his own influence and contacts in the best of faith with Russian diplomats, who were still quite powerful in Paris at the time, and it was he, no one else, who persuaded Milukov to send dispatches to the French government that made it possible to form Polish units in France. But on the other hand Ignatyev counted heavily on succeeding in getting a hold on fervent Poles, with Mokiejewski at their head, by creating "Slavic Legions" for his own subsequent and exclusively Russian goals. This was the opinion of Mokiejewski held by Gąsiorowski and other idealistic individuals who worked with him. Mokiejewski soon received orders to go to the front, enlisted in the French ranks, and from that point his connection with the French-Polish mission was ended. Mokiejewski was, unfortunately, one of many examples of the lack of coordination at the very outset of Polish efforts to rebuild their nation; but, in my opinion, he was genuinely devoted to the cause of a Polish army, but wounded—and badly—by Polish partisan ferocity.

The bad example came from above and caused dissonance among the community, which was reflected in the army. One example of the lack of determination in the front line was the following episode. Once a delegation arrived at the Mission, from the first regiment from America, consisting of Second Lieutenants Matecki, Trawiński, and Wronowski and hostile to Mokiejewski—for his person was, to the less initiated, a symbol of lack of faith in the realization of a Polish army. Their violent dislike for Mokiejewski became apparent immediately after he was presented to the newcomers, to such an extent that one of the lieutenants (born in America) was ready to shoot Mokiejewski. For safety's sake I had to hold onto this comrade, who was ready to pounce, by the arm. After a short conversation I took the delegates to the National Committee and to president Dmowski, which had a very soothing affect on them. Dmowski reprimanded the officers vigorously, after which the delegates, placated, returned to their regiment. Soon a second delegation headed by Second Lieutenant Rowiński arrived and underwent the same process of pacification.

When I saw Dmowski's triumphant entry into the French-Polish Mission, I was very glad that the period of instability was ending and that real, coordinated work was beginning—for I was being drawn to the regiment, to the front, I missed those I had summoned not long ago to battle with the foe. So I reported to General Archinard and asked him to send me to the regiment. I considered my action advisable for this reason, too, that I saw how extraordinarily patriotic and disciplined this Polish element was that we had recruited from immigrant masses, but at the same time I also knew it was not receiving intellectual preparation, which gives birth to distrust and suspicion, which appeared in the glaring incidents mentioned earlier, and the basis for these incidents was one and the same: fear that the French would sell living Polish blood. In any case I was certain that once I arrived at the front I would be able to put the camps in order; every few weeks another 1,000 volunteers, more or less, were arriving from America, and time and again disturbing news about them (always exaggerated) was coming in. I was told of the volunteers' improper behavior, but no one said anything about the fact they were being inadequately organized by the French, or by French Jews, for it was to them, mainly, that the camp and companies' bookkeeping was entrusted. The position of bookkeeper was important because he kept all accounts on supplying the camps with provisions, and he abused his authority hideously, exploiting their lack of local contacts and ignorance of the French language.

With me at the audience with General Archinard was Professor Wincenty Lutosławski. When I explained to him my motives for asking to return to the regiment, the general consented and provided me with a document as an envoy on a *Mission Speciale* to inspect the camps.

Colonel Mokiejewski. The inscription reads "Greetings to [my] brother Falcons. Mokiejewski, Paris 10 August 1917."

MINISTERE DE LA GUERRE   REPUBLIQUE FRANCAISE
—
État-Major de l'Armée
—
Mission Franco-Polonaise
— **ORDRE DE MISSION**

  Monsieur SKARZYŃSKI Sous-Lieut. au 1-er Regt. de Chasseurs Polonais detachée de la Mission Militaire Franco-Polonaise est chargé (1) de Mission Speciale à Laval, Mayenne et Sillé-le-Guillaume.

  Il partira de Paris par (2) dan fevrée le 4 Fevrier 1918 à 20 heures 8´.

  Il rentrera à Paris, sa mission terminée (3) le….. partant de (4) Sillé-le-Guillaume (Sarthe).

  Il aura droit aux indemnités prévues par le règlement sur les frais de dèplacement.

№ de l'ordre de transport: aller
délivré   :retour
Retour à Paris le . . . .
à . . . . h . . . .
 Le Titulaire
 S/Lt. W. Skarzyński

      Paris, le 4 Fevrier 1918.

     Le Général *Archinard*
    Chef de la Mission Militaire
      Franco-Polonaise.

    Le Chef d'État Major *Vachoux*

(1)—Enumérer sommairement la mission
   à remplir ou le service à exécuteur.
(2)—Voie ferrée, voiture, automobile, etc.
(3)—Mention à biffer s'il y a lieu.
(4)—Indiquer la gare de départ au
   retour.
(5)—A complèter par le titulaire à son
   retour.

  After touring the camps for a week and calming troubled minds here and there, I gave my report to the general and brought up the necessity of appointing a Pole as their leader, an experienced soldier, at least a colonel in rank, and one with a purely Polish name, because the volunteers would not trust anyone else. Such a leader, in my opinion, had to finally take over the whole organization and bring it under the iron control of military discipline. I must note that Colonel Mokiejewski, whom I mentioned earlier, was very helpful to me in presenting my comments; at that time he was still chief of staff, and, understanding my intentions and showing a great deal of good will, he helped in appointing the leader of the first regiment, Colonel Jasiński, one of the most capable Poles in the French army, possessing all the virtues of a commander, broad vision and a famous talent for organizing. Unfortunately, once again the National Committee blundered badly. Since Colonel Jasiński, as a true soldier, did not understand how to conform to every partisan direction, the National Committee tried with all its might to disqualify him. On this account I had a harsh squabble with Dmowski and the French, telling them outright, "Poles are not Senegalese, but a nation, just like the French."

Colonel Jasiński returned to the French army after giving the first division of the Polish army excellent training. That division (currently the 13th) later gave proof of its valor in its battles with Budionny at Dziunków, Ostropol, Stary Konstantynów, and Lwów, thwarting him at Zamość. It was there that the fruits of Colonel Jasiński's zealous work were harvested. It was also, in my opinion, a great injustice that the Polish military, instead of seeking foreign gods, did not propose to this valiant leader, the descendant of an officer of 1831 [*referring to the 1831 Uprising against Russian rule*], that he take part in the work of strengthening and organizing the Polish armed forces.

When the political leadership was in the hands of the National Committee, and the military leadership was assumed by the French-Polish Military Mission, I felt that my place henceforth was in the regiment. When I explained my resolution to Colonel Vaschoux, whom I have already mentioned, I was appointed to the position of Colonel Mokiejewski, and was detached back to the first regiment; I arrived there on 3 April 1918. There Colonel Jasiński assigned me to the 5th company, where I was simultaneously second in command to company commander Lieutenant Krzywkowski-Wolański.

On the day of my arrival, the regiment set out from Laval and Mayenne to "Camp de Mailly dans la Zone des Armées," to the operational zone in the region of the 4th Army, active in Champagne under the command of General Gouraud.

After our regiment took up its position and got organized, General Franchet d'Esperey, commander of a group that was part of the 4th Army, arrived for its first inspection. When Colonel Jasiński informed us that this general was coming to see us, the regiment was busy as a beehive with frantic preparations to receive such a notable guest. The next day our whole regiment formed ranks as if by the line and awaited the arrival of General Franchet d'Esperey. Finally a

The creator of the first regiment of the Polish Army in France, Colonel Jasiński, and his successors, Col. Korszun-Osmołowski and Col. Piekarski.

vehicle appeared in the road, and in it was our honored guest, accompanied by his chief of staff and several other officers. When he was greeted by our colonel, he began to approach our regiment with him, and the colonel's order sounded, "Commanding officers, please order arms presented in turn." Immediately the first battalion's commander's order raised a forest of bayonets shouldered by our Polish lads, and as the general approached, battalion after battalion presented arms. When the general had finished his review, the whole regiment began to sing *"Boże coś Polskę,"* after which the general summoned all officers of the whole regiment, asking each of us personally where we came from and what military experience we had. Then he addressed us, saying "Today the world has understood the situation of Poland; France, in particular, has understood it, and therefore gives Her the opportunity to form an armed force." He continued, "Gentlemen, I gave you one of the best officers of the whole French Army, your compatriot, Colonel Jasiński, and knowing you, I must emphasize that you who have laid the cornerstone for the Polish army must understand that great truth, that this army will only be an army and will only serve its country well if it maintains discipline. I emphasize that in my address to you officers because you Poles, having a broken thread of tradition of a national army, must pay special attention to strict observance of that discipline, and must take it as your chief watchword for your whole military organization and the foundation of the strength and future of your Fatherland. I bring this particularly to your attention, Officers of the First Regiment, so that you will shine as an example of soldierly virtues to all Polish fighting units that will be organized after you…" He finished his speech with the statement that he fully believed that Poles, fighting today for their and all of civilization's equality and independence, side by side with France, will recall how once they fought for the freedom of other nations….

A parade followed. The whole regiment marched before the general and his staff, and after the parade all officers were summoned and one of the staff officers took a photograph of the whole group. While we were standing for the picture, I cast my eye over our whole regiment. The sight of it at that moment deeply touched my heart. My soul was overcome with joy that this first regiment was the cornerstone of the Polish Army, and, unable to hold back tears of joy, I whispered joyfully, "Finally, finally, I am in a real Polish army!"

Events now came more quickly. A French lieutenant educated in Poland, Le Doux, was sent to give the junior officers final specialized training. Then Colonel Jasiński brought in from the 4th French Army a group of English-speaking specialists to complete the officers' training.

At the end of April, 1918, the regiment was transferred to Somepuis. There on the feast of the 3rd of May a Field Mass was celebrated by the regimental

Group of officers of the First Division of the Polish Army in France with Colonel Jasiński, commander of the 1st Regiment.

chaplain, a great patriot, Rev. Więckowki. This famous preacher knew how to bring the greatest rascals to repentance and turn them into obedient lambs. The collaboration of this chaplain and Colonel Jasiński produced splendid results with the formation of combat personnel of the Polish Army in France. In time the first regiment covered itself in immortal glory in the battles of Champagne, in Fabre Sector, where the first American died, my close friend (who took my place in 5th Company), Second Lieutenant Chwałkowski, who once belonged to the first group of those popularly called the "Canadian desperadoes" in America. At St. Hiller [*sic, almost certainly should be St. Hilaire*] on 25 July 1918, the 5th Company of this regiment was mentioned in the Army's orders of the day, its pennant received the decoration of the French *Croix de Guerre,* and the battalion's second-in-command, Captain Piekarski, was then mentioned in the Army's orders of the day and decorated with the French Cross of the Legion of Honor and the *Croix de Guerre* with palm. It should be mentioned that this Captain Piekarski, now a colonel, showed a great deal of coolness, calmness, and tact. Once trained for national work among the ranks of conspirators, he understood the spirit of a soldier and felt the spiritual needs of that mass collected from various corners of America and the whole world, and as one of the most educated officers, knew how to transform them into disciplined ranks. Soon he was promoted to commander of the first regiment.

Lieutenant Lucjan Chwałkowski, who was the first of the American volunteers to fall in the fields of Champagne.

Our First Regiment consisted of a dozen or more volunteers from Bayonne, of Polish Falcons from America, natives of Poznań, and later several hundred so-called "Dutch" were incorporated into the regiment—these were young Poles, mainly from Warsaw and Łódź, who had been forced to go work in Germany.

Group of officers and guests at the celebration of the second anniversary of the First Regiment in Zwiahel, headed by Colonel Wacław Piekarski (in the middle of the first row).

When these "Dutch" learned of the existence of the Polish Army in France, at every opportunity that presented itself they fled through Holland to England, where they made their way to the offices of the French-Polish Military Mission and joined the ranks of the Polish Army in France. They were a restless element, but one valiant in battle. Finally there were in the regiment Poles from former Russian formations in Thessaloniki, with their own commander Piekarski, later a colonel. Polish-Americans (75%) were the founding element and the magnet drawing all other groups and individuals to the Polish Army in France.

Group of volunteer Russian soldiers, Poles, from Thessaloniki, led by Lieutenant Piekarski.

More and more volunteers were arriving from America. The transport ships arrived about every two weeks, and so more and more new regiments, and later divisions, were being formed from them. The Second Regiment, under the command of Colonel Berecki from the French Army, and the Third Regiment, under the command of Colonel Pachucki from the Russian Army, comprised with the First—now led by Colonel Korszun-Osmołowski—the First Division, under the general command of General Vidallon. Colonel Jasiński headed the division infantry. Also at that time the processing center at Sillé-le-Guillaume, under the command of Captain Jagniątkowski, sorted through the volunteers and, in view of its character and its commander's understanding of affairs, became a sort of maternal center and cell of all the Polish units in France. As for special kinds of weapons, we should mention the First Light Artillery Battery, organized by Lieutenant Markus. He developed that branch of arms in the full sense of the word, and his students in the First Division proved by their deeds what school they had graduated from.

In April, 1918, Colonel Jasiński, wishing to finally produce full responsibility on the officers' part, began to assign them—especially the younger ones from America who did not know the front—to companies in French regiments, to get a practical introduction to the terrain and the newest forms of fighting. I was sent with the first such party. I was assigned to the 87th Regiment of the French Infantry, and there, for the first time, I came face to face with the "Boche." I was in the trenches of the most advanced outpost with 28 French soldiers, commanded by a French second lieutenant. Suddenly the sentry reported to the lieutenant that the Boche were in the wire. With great coolness and gallantry the lieutenant asked me if I would like to see the Germans for myself. I answered eagerly that I would like to very much. At that point my comrade officer issued instructions to the soldiers to fire a rocket and ordered more fired every dozen seconds or so. I obeyed the order and saw the Germans' heads. They were helmeted and were cutting the wire that had been run, every so often falling to the ground… Time and again the rockets light up with a bloody glare their dark forms crawling along the ground, and at the same time from the French side several score of grenades, popularly called *"les citrons,"* were thrown, showering the German unit with fire. The lieutenant shot off another rocket, a signal to the artillery and an indication of the direction from which the enemy was attacking. Immediately after the first salvo of grenades, we jumped out of the trenches, hopping along the way into various holes, to protect ourselves from the hail of German hand grenades that fell into our trenches. Now, less than two minutes after the rocket signal, the lovely "roses" of French shrapnel appeared, spattering with a bang, again and again throwing columns of dirt in the air, tumbling together in one terrible heap the bodies of Germans, wire, stones, and concrete… During the next ten minutes or so, under the barrage of French artillery shells, all trace of the Germans disappeared. The enemy's small but well thought out attack on the French outpost was actually a reconnaissance, shrewdly discovered in time and thwarted by the French—a score or more Germans lost their lives in the effort.

The next day the French attacked the German trenches, overwhelmed them, and took prisoners. The Germans took vengeance by attacking again three days later, supporting the attack with a whole battalion of infantry and the artillery fire of a division. The attack was so terrible that it was impossible to emerge from the ground. A hurricane of bursting iron whistled on all sides, and to the deafening bang was added the incessant moan of those wounded and killed, creating a hellish image of destruction. I must bring up here the heroic defense of the 5th Company of the 2nd Battalion of the French 87th Regiment. This company, seeing the great losses of their neighboring company and seeing that its commander was wounded, put up superhuman resistance with the help of machine guns and individual groups throwing grenades, violently assailing the Prussian grenadiers—for the rest of the regiment was cut off by the German artillery barrage and was totally unable to come to the aid of their companies heroically standing firm.

The attempts to train the officers, carried out according to plan before the first regiment's departure to the line, proved that Colonel Jasiński's method was turning out splendidly. For when the regiment received the order to depart for the front on 31 May 1918, the officers had already had a taste of fire and were superbly informed on means of activity on the front line. They led their units to battle so skillfully and coolly that even senior French instructors were amazed.

On 3 June 1918 the regiment set out for Verzy, Verzenay, Bouzy and Ambronay, the center of Champagne, not far from Fort Pompel, which was occupied several times by the Germans, in the vicinity of Reims, where the actual front line was the little river Velle, and where, on the anniversary of the decree's publication, namely 4 June 1918, the regiment entered the second line of trenches as a fighting unit, replacing a French regiment.

At this time I was in command of this regiment's 7th Company. After a stay of several weeks in this sector, the regiment was divided into battalions, and our second battalion, under the command of Major Haciski and his second-in-command, Captain Piekarski, marched out to the assembly point for the whole regiment; there it was assigned the Fabre sector, made famous by the laudable deeds of the whole regiment in July, 1918. When we were in position, I received an order from the battalion commander to go with Lieutenants Matecki and Nastał to Ambronay to take command of 8th Company in the so-called *Centre d'Instruction Divisionaire (C.I.D.)*, the First Division Instruction Center, to act simultaneously as an instructor at the N.C.O. school there.

I was appointed commandant at the C.I.D. school in le Mont sur Aube, and I learned that the commander of the Second Legion Brigade, General Józef Haller, had arrived in Paris. The whole Falcon brotherhood rejoiced enormously at this news. Soon after, in August, 1918, we learned that General Haller was to be named Division General and Chief Commander of the Polish Army in France (the appointment took place after presentation to the French authorities of the appropriate proposal by the Polish National Committee), and that he would soon arrive to visit the army at the front. I remember as if it were today how General Haller arrived in the afternoon, along with Roman Dmowski and Colonel Vaschoux, the Chief of Staff of the French-Polish Mission, with adjutants Captain Bajer and Captain Tadeusz Malinowski. I had the honor of first presenting to General Haller my non-commissioned officers' school as the only unit there at the time, since my 8th Company, along with the other units under the command of Lieutenant Cybulski, were at exercises in the field. General Haller had within him a large supply of optimism and faith in the creation of a national armed

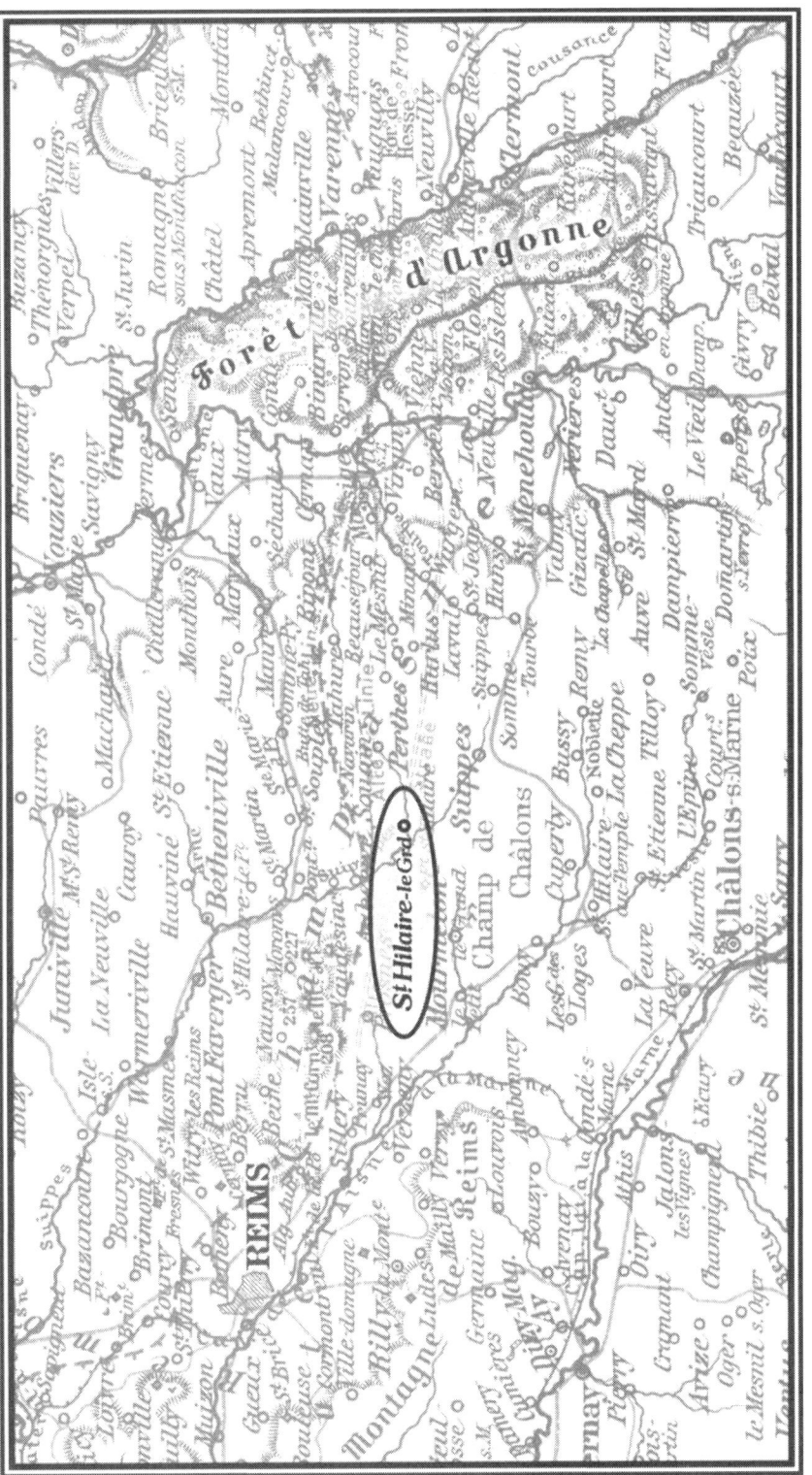

The Champagne-Vosges region.

Nomination of General Józef Haller as Chief Commander of the Polish Army, 4 October 1918. The caption below the original photo read: "J. Rozwadowski, Major Fronczak, General J. Haller, Count Maurycy Zamoyski, J. Wielowiejski, St. Graski, St. Kozicki."

force in France, and zealously encouraged us to work hard. He returned that same evening to Paris.

On 6 October 1918 General Haller took the military oath as Chief Commander of the Polish Army in France. Our division and various other units assembled not far from Nancy on the fields of Lorraine. It was a very beautiful day. One of the actual organizers of the whole demonstration, Major Giżycki, arrived with the general. Colonel Korszun-Osmołowski read the oath aloud; General Haller repeated its words clearly. The regiments, drawn up at attention, listened to the words in a solemn mood and with concentration; an aerial squadron, like a flock of soaring eagles, glided and rustled in the blue expanse….

Another event that tore the soldiers away from their daily concerns was the ceremony of handing the standard over to the First Regiment; it will never be erased from my memory. It took place before the arrival of General Haller. A number of French towns, such as Verdun, Paris, Belfort, and others, had paid for standards for the Polish regiments. Paris contributed the standard for the first Regiment of Polish Riflemen. For the First Regiment's ceremony, several companies of that regiment assembled, with delegations of officers from each company, as well as four cadre companies. Also present was Roman Dmowski, the president of the National Committee, accompanied by delegates of all the Allied Armies on the Champagne front. (German artillery fire did not prevent the sending of individual delegates to attend the ceremony).

The solemn moment brought tears to the scarred cheeks of the oldest soldiers. I stood at the head of 8th Company with my eyes fixed on the podium, where a field Mass was being celebrated at the altar, after which came the whole ceremony of handing over the standard—and to this day that image brings tears to my eyes… In his speech Dmowski, who handed the standard to General Goureaux, the commander of the 4th French Army (it was handed next to Colonel Jasiński), emphasized the importance of events and ended with the words "May this standard lead the Polish army to victory and to regaining the independence of the Fatherland in its historical boundaries."

The President of France himself, Poincare, handed the donated standards to the other regiments, supposedly with extraordinary pomp and in the presence of delegates of all the Allied armies. But I never witnessed these ceremonies, since I was with the First Regiment.

After breaking the Germans' final offensive in Champagne, at the request of the National Committee, the First Regiment was withdrawn, since in the battles that had taken place it had already experienced serious losses of killed officers

General Haller's oath on the standard.

Handing of the standard to the 1st Regiment of Polish Riflemen. R. Dmowski, Baron Degrand, General Gouraud, General Archinard, Major Fronczak, General Capdepont.

and soldiers. The regiment made a particularly bloody sacrifice on 25 July 1918, along with the 4th French Army, in a furious counterattack on the Germans. This was in retaliation for their attack on the French line on the French national holiday, Bastille Day. There at St. Hiller [*sic, probably should be St. Hilaire*] the 2nd Battalion of the First Polish Regiment utterly crushed the 66th Regiment of the Prussian Guard and took 213 prisoners of war (among them about a dozen Poles) and significant spoils in the form of more than a dozen machine guns—and also took almost a kilometer of the enemy front.

Soon afterward the regiment was withdrawn to Saffais. There began preparation not just for the First Regiment, but for the whole First Division of the Polish Army in France, to occupy the fighting line. At that point, at my request submitted to General Vidallon, I received the order to leave the Division Instruction Center and take command of 10th Company, to set out with it and the whole division commanded by our beloved Colonel Jasiński for the Vosges, to release the Americans' so-called "Wildcat Division of Tennessee" [*the 81st*], who were in the trenches of Lorraine, and encounter the enemy in that sector.

The Polish soldiers' hearts were filled with joy, the more so that they saw that for the first time since 1831, they would be appearing as a Polish fighting unit in such sizeable numbers—namely a whole division, consisting of infantry, artillery, engineering, cavalry and trains—to occupy a sizeable area of French soil, drive our common enemy from it, and get as quickly as possible to our Fatherland.

Our division's sector was relatively quiet. Only from time to time did small artillery encounters take place. The infantry's activity was limited to small sorties—Polish battalions were relieved every so often by ... Polish battalions ... This lasted till 5 November 1918, when the order came to hand the sector over to the French. It was said quietly that the Polish division, along with 15 Allied divisions, was to be used to attack Metz, strike a decisive blow on the Germans, break their line, and force the Rhine, and the ultimate purpose of these movements was to smash utterly the German army.

In terrible nervous tension, the Polish soldier waited to enter battle with the ancient enemy. By the 10th of November loaded trucks were standing on the roads, to redeploy our whole division upon first fire. With each hour rabid enthusiasm seized the officers and soldiers, the minutes were counted ... morning came, everything was ready ... the army was like a tiger ready to pounce ... alongside the road a vehicle speeds from the side of the German line, and shout was heard that was most unwelcome to the Polish soldier: *"Armistice est signé—la guerre est finis!"* ("The armistice has been signed, the war is over!"). A French officer in the vehicle cried out for joy, the Polish soldier set his teeth and cursed that moment—convinced of his own might, he had only one desire: to advance in triumphant march as a Polish army of a hundred thousand across all Germany to Poland—and there is no doubt that only that soldier identified the whole sense, the whole essence, the whole real goal of the war! ....

After the armistice the division was transferred to Luneville, where under Colonel Jasiński's resilient direction it was readied to fight the Germans for mastery of towns in Poland—because such a possibility was foreseen, with Gdańsk foremost. The probability of battle in the open field was also assumed.

As for myself, about two weeks after the armistice was signed, I received orders from General Haller to report to the Staff Headquarters of the Polish Army in France in Paris, which had existed since that general assumed command of the Army.

3rd Battalion

Second Lieutenant SKARZYŃSKI WINCENTY is to go to the detail officer for travel orders.

By General Haller's orders he is to appear immediately at the Supreme Command of the Polish Army in France (15 avenue d'Iéna—16c arrond).

26 XI 1918

By order of Colonel
J. Le Doux, Regimental Adjutant

I was ordered first and foremost to organize the staff units. I carried out the order, and as I got into the details, I traced how beautifully the organization of the Polish Army developed. I saw how far Major Radziwiłł advanced the organization of Polish prisoners of war in Italy, how much Lieutenant Kleczkowski had accomplished by bringing in Poles from the German army who had been prisoners of war of the French in processing centers in France. There I witnessed the origin of the second division, became acquainted with the whole of further recruiting of American Poles, which had already brought in 25,000 volunteers; I saw how the ranks had shot up. Regiments came into being, and a second division, a third… then Żeligowski's division from Odessa was designated as the Fourth and was incorporated into the Polish Army in France and handed over to the command of General Józef Haller, as was the one from Siberia, numbered as the Fifth, and finally a Sixth Division from France—they all comprised what was later called popularly "Haller's Army."

Joy filled the heart when in the Officers' Club on Bois de Boulogne street civilians began to be attracted to the military group, and a nest arose to which eagles began to fly from all corners of the earth. Time and again we received groups who came in, men from Murmansk, or fugitives from the Russian army. All these units came to one place, the growing Polish Army. It was constantly

Citation of Wincenty Skarzyński for intelligence, energy, and his cold blood and initiative in difficult situations.

said that we would disembark in Gdańsk. A strategic line was drawn from Kołobrzeg, to Krzyż, to Piła. Oh, what joy there was in this kind of soldier talk! But something—the clumsy diplomacy of our would-be men of state, the weakness of the activists over us, a lack of faith in our own powers, unfortunately repeated so many times in our history—something paralyzed the whole campaign; those activists were afraid to send a Polish division to our country in a manner categorical and worthy of a Nation, of the sacrifices of blood spilled and loyalty to ideals—they did not take advantage of the chance to disembark in Gdańsk, which was promised many times to the army, and the one advantageous moment was overlooked, Poland was harmed so as not to give offense! ... Who bears the blame? ... I will not venture to say firmly... But from what I know, I conclude that the National Committee's moves, not coordinated with Piłsudski, the formation of great political moves from the viewpoint of persons acceptable or not acceptable to the parties, caused this great defeat—our failure to seize Gdańsk and the historic Polish borders and permission to impose a plebiscite.

I observed the National Committee's very damaging battle with Piłsudski's government, the abuses and mutual defamation, which reached a point that more than once I, as a Pole, was simply ashamed to hear the various attacks, especially on the Head of State, caused most often only by partisan ferocity.

During these struggles and preparations for departure to Poland, envoys came to Paris of Józef Piłsudski, who was then the Head of the Polish Government and the Commander-in-Chief of the Polish Army in our Fatherland, in the persons of Professor Dłuski, Professor Sujkowski, cavalry Captain Wieniawa-Długoszewski, and Second Lieutenant Michał Mościcki, for the purpose of making contact with the National Committee. Deeply engraved in my memory is the moment during General Haller's address welcoming the envoys from Poland in the name of the Army of Polish Volunteers in France—gathered no longer from America but from the whole world—when, in spite of the intentions of various ambitious politicians, he cried out, "Long live the Polish Head of State and Commander-in-Chief of the Army of Poland, Józef Piłsudski!" At this exclamation I simply felt the moment our national armed force was cemented into a single great solid body united under the leadership of one commander. I whispered joyfully to Major Jagniątkowski, standing next to me, "How good it is that God inspired our General to say that, for what's at stake here is not the ambitions of individuals, but a single mainstay of Poland's freedom, a guarantee of our independence, the Polish Armed Forces! Isn't that right, Major?" And Major Jagniątkowski whispered back, "God grant that it come true and last for ages!"

Weeks passed. April, 1919 arrived—then plans were changed: it was decided irrevocably to transport our army to Gdańsk instead by trains, through Germany.

Many officers came from Poland, among them Major Górecki, to coordinate technical details with General Haller. The major asked General Haller to assign me to the Purchasing Mission under the command of General Romer.

> ARMÉE POLONAISE   *Paris, le 7 Avril 1919.*
>   ÉTAT MAJOR
> 15, avenue d'Iéna   **ORDRE DE SERVICE**
>
>   Le Lieutenant SKARZYŃSKI WINCENTY, mis à la disposition de la Mission Militaire Polonaise, est chargé d'organiser la Service des convois des transport du matériel, transportés en Pologne.
>   Dans le but de recruter le personnel nécessaire, il doit se rendre dans les dépots de SILLE LE GUILLAUME et DOMFRONT pour choisir des Officiers, Sous-officiers, et soldats nécessaires à l'organisation du service en comptant I officier, I sous-officier et soldats par train.
>   La liste nominative du personnel choisi doit être remise par le Lieutenant SKARZYŃSKI à l'E. M. de l'Armée Polonaise et au président de la Mission Militaire Polonaise, Général ROMER.
>   *Gen. J. Haller*

It was very painful for me to remain in France when the first officers and soldiers who had helped lay the foundation for the accomplished work were being transported to the Fatherland, when everything dear to my heart was in Poland—my mother, whom I had not seen for 15 years, even my wife, whom I had left in America when I departed for France and had not seen since, but who now made it to Poland before me, as the secretary of the Commissioner of the American Red Cross Mission. It was a hard one, that order! But I had to obey it.

Assigned by General Romer as a liaison officer to the Liquidation Commission of the United States Army in France* [*see note on page 148*], I worked hard and took advantage of my American connections and acquaintances (some of whom I knew from the days of my service in the U. S. Army during the Mexican campaign), and was able to get for Poland all the supplies of the American camp in Gevre, which was being liquidated, on long-term credit, including locomotives, cars, and enough supplies for a dozen or more divisions on four years of campaign. But to my astonishment and the Americans', due to the blindness of some of our individual Poles who had the deciding voice in this matter, this deal, which amounted almost to giving the supplies away, was declined; thanks only to the personal initiative of General Romer I did succeed, simply by illegal means, in sending several trains loaded with these supplies to Poland. I learned later, to my great distress, that the Americans, who wanted to get rid of their problems and return home as quickly as possible, burned some of these items, of great value to us, and sold some to French businessmen, from whom the Polish government later bought back a small amount, paying large sums.

After some time I received permission from General Romer to go to Poland as a courier; I arrived in Warsaw on 9 May 1919. There, after receiving from General Majewski of the Ministry of Foreign Affairs (which is where I reported) 48-hour leave (hardly enough for me to see my wife, who at that time was in the Eastern *kresy [borderlands, the eastern part of Poland]* with the American Red Cross Mission), I received an order from General Romer, Chief of the Purchasing Mission in Paris, to depart for America with the Mission for Purchasing Horses, as a liaison officer between that Mission and the American authorities, with orders to help organize transports as well. Colonel Ostrowski headed the Mission. After a two-month stay in America—compulsory and directly against my wishes—I saw what nonsense was going on and firmly requested the Minister of War by telegram to recall me to the regiment, first sending him a report with the reasons for my request.

I returned to Poland in September, 1919, and cheerfully headed back to the

---

*The order by which I was assigned to the Liquidation Commission reads as follows:

ARMÉE POLONAISE *Paris, le 9 Avril 1919.*
—
État-Major
1º Bureau
Section du Personnel
No 1864/1—P
— **ORDRE DE SERVICE**

Le Lieutenant SKARZYŃSKI Wincenty du Q. G. de l'E.-M. de l'Armée Polonaise est détaché en qualité d'expert à la Commission d'Achats du Général ROMER à la date du 7 Avril 1919.

Le présent ordre tiendra lieu à cet officier de lettre de service dans l'exercice de ses fonctions.

Le Général Haller
DESTINATAIRES: Commandant en Chef de l'Armée
Polonaise
Commandant du Q. G. n/o Les Chef d'État-Major
Lieutenant Skarzyński *Perchenes*

First Regiment, which in 1919 and 1920, as a part of the First Division of the Polish Army in France (now the 13th Division) acquitted itself gloriously in its actions during the Polish-Russian War as the 43rd Regiment of the Borderland Riflemen. There are many more events and very interesting details I could stress in describing the heroic deeds of the First Regiment, the foundation of the Polish Army in France—but that is another page of my life's story.

Wincenty Skarzyński

Witold Hilary Trawiński

*Born January 14, 1894, Tupadły Czarne, Lipno
county, Płock province, Poland
Died February 1976, Chicago, Illinois, U.S.A.*

OUTLINE OF THE WARTIME HISTORY OF POLISH REGIMENTS, 1918–1920

THE 43RD REGIMENT OF EASTERN FRONTIER RIFLEMEN

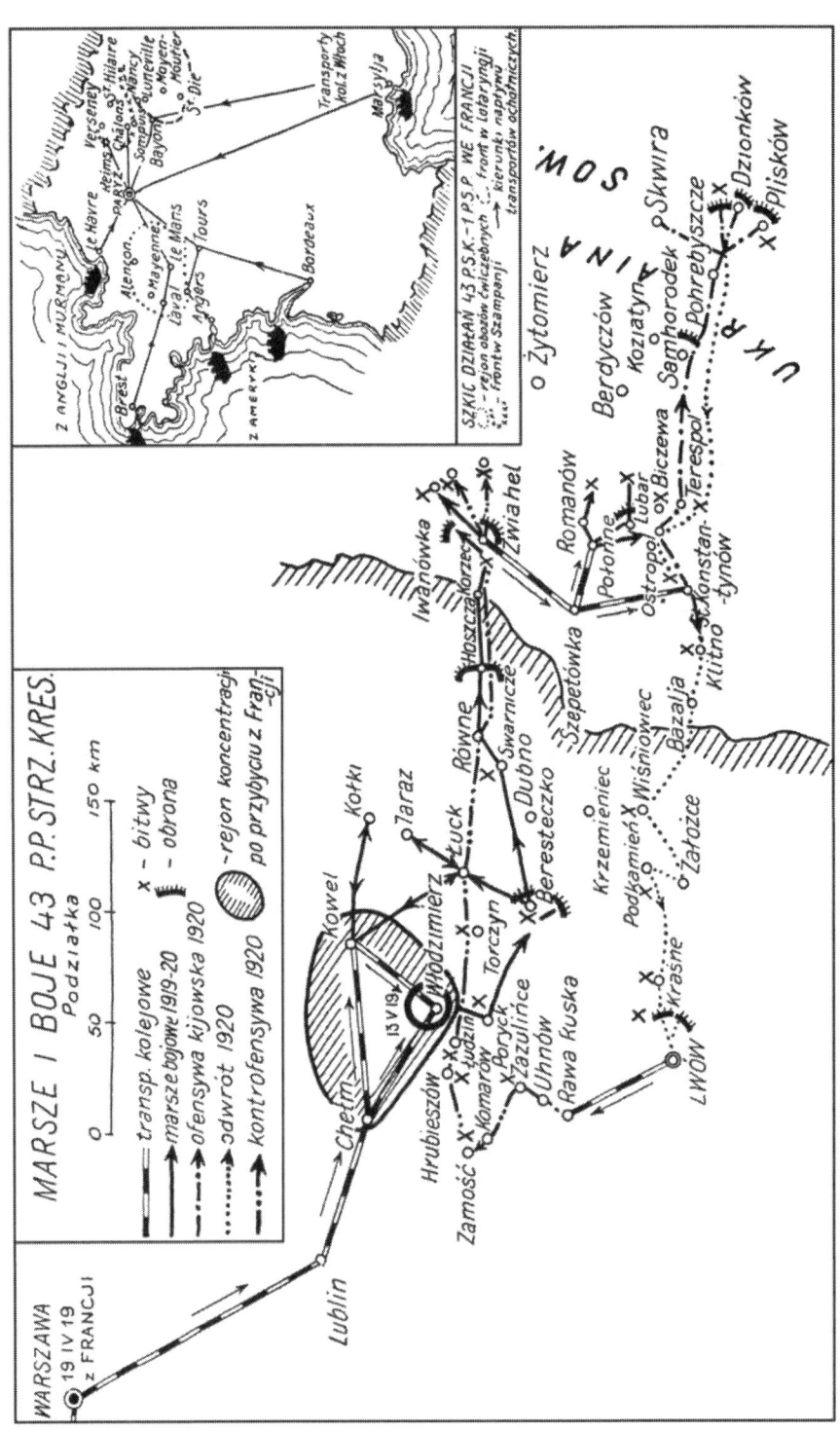

OUTLINE OF THE WARTIME HISTORY OF THE 43RD REGIMENT OF THE EASTERN FRONTIER RIFLEMEN

AS COMMISSIONED BY THE MILITARY HISTORICAL OFFICE

compiled by

MAJOR STEFAN WYCZÓŁKOWSKI

WARSAW

1928

THE REGIMENT AS THE FIRST INDEPENDENT UNIT OF THE POLISH ARMY IN FRANCE

THE LEGION OF THE *BAJOŃCZYCY* IN 1914, AS THE FIRST POLISH MILITARY FORMATION IN FRANCE

The idea of armed conflict for freedom and independence of the Fatherland, raised by the First Marshal of Poland, Józef Piłsudski, found response among all Poles in exile beyond the borders of the nation as well.

A few years before the outbreak of the World War the first riflemen's associations formed in Paris, organized in accordance with orders from the Commander of the Chief Riflemen's Association, Józef Piłsudski.

From the moment the World War broke out, the young men of these associations, hungry for action, wanted to make their way to Poland, so that they could fight. The course of events at the beginning of the war, however, rendered impossible their original intention, as only a small number of riflemen were able to join the ranks of the legions.

Then these young men, with the active support of the entire French Polish community, created a committee of Polish volunteers and decided to form a Polish unit with the French Army.

After the Minister of War's decree on 21 August 1914, which allowed foreigners to enter the French army, about a thousand Poles—youths from the associations, students, and workers—rushed to join the army's ranks and committed themselves to fight alongside the French.

At first the Polish volunteers were incorporated into the 1st Regiment of the Foreign Legion and sent to training camp in Bayonne, that same Bayonne through which the Polish Legions had once passed on their way to Spain. The Polish unit, wishing to document that it was taking up the fight against Germany primarily on behalf of the cause of Poland, wanted to fight under their national standard. French society spontaneously supported the Poles' aspirations, and the town of Bayonne offered the Polish volunteers a standard with the Polish eagle. The publicity that resulted provoked a protest to the French government from the Russian embassy. The French government yielded to Russia's demands and split off the Polish volunteers' unit, from then on called the Legion of the *Bajończycy* ["ones from Bayonne"], to the 1st Moroccan Division, and stopped the influx of volunteers from joining the legion. The legion's standard, as the standard of the company, accompanied the *Bajończycy* in their further heavy trials, becoming a relic of the unit and the sole visible sign of its ideal of *polskość* ["Polishness"]. After several weeks of exercises the *Bajończycy* legion left for the front in the vicinity of Reims, in Champagne, where it fought for half a year as part of the 1st Moroccan Division. During these battles, on the anniversary of the November uprising, the legion's first *chorąży* [Chief Warrant Officer], Władysław Szujski, son of the noted historian, perished, among others.

At the end of April 1915 the 1st Moroccan Division, and along with it the *Bajończycy* Legion, was shifted to the Arras area in anticipation of the offensive that was to ensue.

On 9 May 1915 the *Bajończycy* Legion charged in the front line of the "Berthonval" sector against the hill "Vimy," where it suffered heavy losses during the course of the day; but on the other hand it took four lines of German trenches in less than 2 hours. The next day, due to its heavy losses, the remnants of the Legion were withdrawn to the reserves. In its order of the day the French command recognized and commended the behavior of the *Bajończycy* Legion in this battle. A few years later the President of the Republic of France, in recognition of the Legion's services, personally decorated the *Bajończycy* standard with the Croix de Guerre with palm.

On 16 June the decimated *Bajończycy* Legion fought in the Nôtre-Dame de Lorette sector, where it was almost completely wiped out in a bayonet charge at the cemetery of the little town of Souchez.

Thus ended the epic of the handful of legionnaires from Bayonne, who after long months of combat sealed their ideal with their blood before the world, and once more proved with deeds that the Pole is ready to sacrifice all that is dearest to him for the freedom of his Fatherland.

The Legion ceased to exist, and those legionnaires who remained alive were scattered among various regiments, dreaming that they would once again be gathered under their own standard, a relic preserved with reverence in expectation of a better fate.

Not until 1917 were the dreams of the *Bajończycy* realized. Polish units were formed. Incorporated into the 1st Regiment of Polish Riflemen, being formed in America and subsequently in France, were the rest of the *Bajończycy*. A common ideology blended these formations.

The standard, their relic, frayed by shells, had a new army. Under it the 1st Regiment of Polish Riflemen received its baptism of fire and shed its blood on the fields of Champagne.

In an amazing coincidence, Fate, directing the bullets that shredded the cloth of the standard, created 43 holes—which is today the Regiment's number.

After the war the Supreme Commander decorated the standard of the *Bajończycy* with the Military Cross *Virtuti militari* 5th class in recognition of the services.

THE ORIGIN OF THE POLISH ARMY IN FRANCE

In early 1917 the Allied powers' situation underwent fundamental changes. The Russian Revolution broke out; the Kerensky government declared the freedom of the nations. Taking advantage of this new political situation on the part of the Polish emigrants was the famous literary figure Wacław Gąsiorowski, and on the part of the French government Painlevé and Ribot. Their efforts resulted in the 4 June 1917 proclamation of a decree by the President of the Republic of France, Raymond Poincaré, which called for the creation of an independent Polish Army.

This decree motivated a significant number of Poles, whether already fighting in the ranks of the Allies or ready to join the ranks of the Polish army, in accordance with the intention of the governments of the Allied nations to rebuild a Polish state, which would most easily be accomplished by admitting Poles to battle under their national standard.

As the decree said, it was "the moral obligation of France to undertake the stirring and laudable mission of creating a future Polish army, arising from the kinship of the races and the Poles' steadfast loyalty to the French nation."

The executive order issued with this decree established in the newly-created Polish army all the regulations regarding organization, administration, hierarchy and military courts, as in the French army, with this difference, that the light blue French uniform underwent the following characteristic variations:

    1) all services wore the four-cornered cap;

    2) the Polish eagle on an amaranthine field was on the shoulder-straps of the jacket and coat;

    3) the Polish eagle was on the caps, helmets and buttons;

    4) all officers were to wear an eagle made of white metal on the right side of their chest, medal-high;

    5) in addition to the distinctions detailed above, on the collars of their jackets and coats the battalions of riflemen (regiments) were to wear cloth tabs of a light-blue color with the number of the battalion (regiment) and a cornet cut from green cloth.

RECRUITING VOLUNTEERS

As a result of the President's decree, in June 1917 a specially organized French-Polish military mission was created under the command of General

Archinard. This mission, in strict consultation with the Polish National Committee—created as a result of the June decree on organizing the Polish Army in France and under the direction of Maurycy Zamoyski and Roman Dmowski—on the one hand dealt with informing Poles about the existence of an independent Polish Army and recruiting men into its ranks for battle on behalf of the cause of the Fatherland's independence by sending representatives to the United States of North America, Canada, and Holland, and on the other hand undertook organizing a camp for the Polish soldiers already recruited in northwestern France, at Sille le Guillaume. This camp was already organized by 27 June 1917.

Poles from all the places of their forced exile rushed to join the ranks of the army above which the standard of the white eagle was to wave.

And so there were Poles from the ranks of the French Army (the former *Bajończycy*); Poles from the Russian Expeditionary Corps; Polish emigrants from Holland; some of the Polish prisoners of war from the German and Austrian armies; and, most of all, Poles from Canada and the United States.

The Polish emigrant community in America, upon hearing the signal that came from the mouth of Paderewski, "To arms for our Fatherland's freedom!", gave the most and the best of its sons, repaying the debt they owed the Fatherland and confirming that, even though they were separated from their homeland and Americanized, they had not lost the feelings of native Poles.

The largest centers of the Polish emigrant community, such as Chicago, New York, Philadelphia, Boston, and Detroit, rushed with truly American vigor to acquire the greatest possible number of volunteers for the Polish army being organized.

Hundreds of volunteers—mostly Falcons, since they were the ones best organized by military standards—went to the recruiting offices, "committing themselves to serve in the Polish Army for an undetermined period of time, until the independence of Poland is won, and to bear all the consequences of military life." Since Americans did not want their citizens to go join a foreign army, the first few hundred volunteers had to steal across the border to Canada. In Niagara on the Lake and St. John, Canada, Polish camps were organized by English authorities.

The civilians of yesterday, today volunteers in Canadian uniforms, all red or black, trained to be soldiers, competing to do their military duty.

Transports of 250 to 800 soldiers arrived in France at Bordeaux, Brest, and Le Hâvre.

THE REGIMENT'S BEGINNING

At the end of December 1917 larger and larger groups of volunteers were arriving at the camp from all over. The influx was so great that the organization of the Polish Army, based on battalions of riflemen, was changed by decree of the French Minister of War. Regiments were formed, each of three battalions and one supernumerary company (communications platoon, pioneers, camp, orchestra, craftsmen and commissariat). Each battalion numbered three companies of riflemen and a company of heavy machine guns. The lowest combat unit was the half platoon.

In accordance with this decree, the head of the French-Polish military mission, General Archinard, by order 554/I dated 12 December 1917 ordered the formation of new battalions for the future regiment of riflemen.

In anticipation of the arrival of more volunteers, the camp at Sille le Guillaume was becoming too cramped. On 12 December 1917 the cadres of the 1st, 2nd, and 3rd Battalions were transferred to Laval and Mayenne.

The work that had lasted half a year had achieved its goal: on 10 January 1918 was formed a completely organized 1st Regiment of Polish Riflemen, today's 43rd Regiment of Eastern Frontier Riflemen, with its first commander, Lt. Col. Jasieński of the French Army.

The hectic work of training the soldiers began, with the assistance of French officers assigned for this purpose.

THE REGIMENT'S PRACTICAL TRAINING IN THE FRONTLINE ZONE

In February 1918 the regiment proceeded to a camp located in the frontline zone at Saint-Tanche, where it trained even more intensively. Courses developed on heavy machine guns, handheld machine guns, accompanying weapon, as well as a course on throwing grenades, pioneering, communications, and so on.

On 21 April 1918 the regiment was transferred to the reserve of the 4th Army of General Gouraud in Sommepuis. Their energetic stance and martial spirit earned the regiment a whole series of commendatory notices on the part of the higher French commanders who conducted a review of the regiment, namely: the chief of the French-Polish Military mission, General Archinard; the commander of 4th Army, General Gouraud; the commander of the northern army group, General Franchet d'Esperey; and the former Minister of War, Senator Doumergue.

THE REGIMENT'S BAPTISM OF FIRE AT REIMS

On the anniversary of the President of the French Republic's first decree—that is, on 4 June 1918—the First Regiment of Polish Riflemen left camp in Sommepuis due to a German attack on French units in Châteaux-Thierry and manned the first line of trenches near Reims, relieving the 142nd French Regiment during the night. The 1st Regiment manned the sector in combat groups (each half a platoon), fortified to a depth of 3 kilometers. Relieving the troops took place under constant enemy fire. The sector the regiment occupied was previously a

German position, taken not long before, full of tunnels, connecting trenches, various lines and entrenchments, which had already been destroyed by artillery fire. In this labyrinth of trenches it was difficult to get one's bearings, despite the reference tables. The terrain in the regiment's sector presented a swirling mass of chalk with barbed wire and concrete: an image that had nothing in common with the terrain shown on the map. The enemy was located at a distance of 30–100 meters. They had to familiarize themselves with every direction of fire from both handheld and heavy machine guns, as well as rifle grenades ("V. B."), according to the designated tables and a compass. Every combat group of the first line or of the reserve comprised an independent defensive unit, surrounded on all sides by wire, with the exception of the concealed passages. During the night there was no communication between companies other than with guard dogs and signal rockets.

It was under this organization of the defense and among these conditions that the regiment endured the difficult period of its first combat service. Here the soul of the soldier grew hardened to difficulties and sacrifices; here, despite the difficult conditions, the young soldier-citizen yearned for heroic combat.

ATTACKS ON THE FRONT NEAR REIMS AND THEIR CONSEQUENCES

On 18 June 1918 the regiment tried to attack the advanced German post with the goal of taking prisoners; due to lack of experience, however, the volunteer attacking unit, having found no one in the first line, retreated after 24 hours.

The Germans, having learned that the Polish Regiment was at the front, attacked its advanced posts constantly, and these attacks were repelled in heavy bayonet combat. In addition the Germans showered them with leaflets in Polish for propaganda purposes, but this had no effect on our soldiers.

After a while the regiment was relieved by French units and went to the third line in the vicinity of Sept-Saults, where they worked at night, improving fortifications of the old resistance nests and building new ones. Simultaneously reconnaissance patrols were sent out to capture prisoners, on which the French command was particularly intent at the time.

The stirring dedication of the regiment's soldiers during this period elevated the courage and honor of the Polish soldier in the eyes of the neighboring French regiments. Some soldiers paid for the nightly attacks with their lives; and others fell wounded, some heavily, some lightly. These attacks, due to a distance of several meters from the enemy, were so difficult and dangerous that the small, weary French crew manning the sector could no longer undertake them; but the Poles carried them out willingly.

The heroic death of 2nd Lt. Chwałkowski. In one of these attacks 2nd Lt. Chwałkowski, a volunteer from America, died. His soldierly virtues surrounded him with a halo of heroism in the eyes of the soldiers of the Polish Army in France and the emigrant community. The attack that he led carried out its difficult task, but the commander, heavily wounded, lost his hand by the German trenches. Pfc. Michał Mroczko carried his beloved commander back to the trenches, where he fell dead in front of the French entrenchment. 2nd Lt. Chwałkowski, carried to the ambulance, died with the words, "This is for Poland." At the proposal of the French command, before his death he was decorated, by telegraph, with the Legion of Honor by the President of the Republic of France. 2nd Lt. Chwałkowski's attack was widely discussed in the French press and beyond the sea in America.

This willingness and courage on the part of the combat patrols, this soldierly patriotism was widely recognized by the French commanders—the first decorations and honors poured in. On 18 June 1918 the Regiment received a standard from the city of Paris, delivered to the Regiment's commander by General Gouraud.

THE REGIMENT'S BATTLES AT SAINT HILAIRE LE GRAND

A German offensive began. The regiment, alerted during the night of 13–14 July, relocated to the Saint Hilaire sector. At midnight, during the march near the first line of trenches, a column of the regiment was suddenly struck by a hurricane of German artillery fire, beginning at that hour the preparation for the last great offensive. Under the artillery fire the battalions could not form up, and concealed themselves along old trenches and shelters on both sides of the highway; however toward morning they proceeded to their designated positions, fortifying the line of the 17th, 7th and 53rd Battalions of Alpine Riflemen, as well as the 20th Battalion of Infantry Riflemen. In these sectors the battalions were fighting in individual companies, even platoons, defending furiously positions in front of the German attack. The conduct of the soldiers during this period is explicitly attested by the orders of individual French commanders.

On 22 July the 1st Company in the sector of the 17th French Regiment captured "centre-Chaiton" and held it despite numerous German counterattacks. 3rd Battalion in the whole sector of the 7th Battalion of Alpine Riflemen advanced 1,200 meters in an offensive movement.

The regiment's losses on that day were very heavy, as follows: 1 officer and 33 men killed, and 312 wounded and poisoned by gas.

THE BATTLE FOR THE "BOIS DE RAQUETTE" FOREST

During the night of 24–25 July the 1st Regiment once more had the chance to take part in retaliation for the latest German offensive.

5th Company, designated for this action, under the command of the brave Capt. Krzywkowski-Woliński, with a platoon of heavy machine guns under

2nd Lt. Bartman, set out during the night from the positions it had previously held and headed along the long series of white-chalk ditches toward the enemy, located 1½ km. away. The goal of the company's attack was a little hill with a small forest called "Bois de Raquette." At 3 a.m. short and effective artillery fire began, after which the company launched its assault. The enemy, taken by surprise, abandoned the position. All their material fell into the hands of the company: ammunition, provisions, 20 heavy machine guns and 118 prisoners of war (including some Poles) from the 66th German Infantry Regiment. A battalion of the 66th German Infantry Regiment was completely wiped out by artillery fire and 5th Company's attack, and other battalions of the same regiment involved in the battle were smashed. Three powerful German counterattacks against the hill ensued, aided by powerful artillery fire. The counterattacks were repulsed, however all three officers of 5th Company perished. The last officer of the Company, a young American, 2nd Lt. Bauer, was killed at the hands of a German officer who treacherously pretended to be giving himself up. Command of the Company was taken by Sergeant Fonder, who, taking vengeance for the loss of the officers, hammered furiously with a knotted club against the foreheads of the tall "Prussians," and more than one fell with an exclamation tragic for every Pole, "Jezus Marja!" ["Jesus Mary" in Polish]. Too late!—a tragedy for every Polish soldier during the great war was the constant thought that when aiming at the breast of an enemy, he was often aiming at the breast of a brother.

The Company fought with hand grenades, struggling hand-to-hand with the attacking Germans.

The losses in killed and wounded amounted to the greater part of the company. In the latter stages, when no strength remained in the heroic defenders, the day was saved by Capt. Piekarski with the platoons of two 2nd Lieutenants, Rżewski and Wronowski. He gathered the remnants of the smashed 5th Company, already partially in retreat, and with an energetic counterblow in hand-to-hand combat won back the taken hill and held it until relieved by French units.

This heroic deed, sealed with the lives and blood of 3 officers killed and 3 wounded, 42 men killed and 77 wounded, solidified the regiment's good name among its brother French regiments as well as among their superiors. This day became a day of praise, a holy day for the regiment. A whole series of military decorations and honorable mentions in the commanders' orders spread the glory of the regiment and the Polish soldier widely throughout the world.

The commander of the 21st French Corps, in his order dated 29 July 1918, honored 5th Company as follows (5th Company was awarded the Croix de Guerre with Gold Star):

> On the night of 24–25 July 1918, after brief preparation, the 170th Division and the 14th Infantry Division, acting in close communication,

in one echelon took from the enemy a whole series of points, particularly important ones, and shifted their advance line 1,000 meters ahead of their initial positions, taking 200 prisoners.

5th Company of the 1st Regiment of Polish Riflemen, under the orders of Capt. Piekarski and Capt. Krzywkowski, after breaking the powerful German offensive of 15 July 1918, on the night of 24–25 July, after brief artillery preparation, took its designated points on the front in one leap, despite stubborn resistance on the part of the enemy, and went more than 2 km. and a distance of about 1 km. from their departure positions, in the process taking over 200 prisoners and a sizable amount of materials.

Commander, 21st Corps
(—) General Naulin

The commander of the 17th French Infantry Regiment, in order No. 970 dated 20 August 1918, singled 2nd Battalion out as follows (2nd Battalion was decorated with the Croix de Guerre with Bronze Star):

During the period 15 July to 20 August 1918, 2nd Battalion of the 1st Regiment of Polish Riflemen, under the energetic command of Major Haciski, with the assistance of Capt. Piekarski, worked together with the regiment in defense of its position, which it held in its entirety at the cost of heavy losses, despite the enemy's determined efforts.

On 25 July, along with units of the regiment, it had its way with the enemy, forcing its way into his line and taking a large number of prisoners and machine guns.

Commander of the 17th French Infantry Regiment
(—) Pean, Colonel

THE REGIMENT'S RETURN FROM CHAMPAGNE

During the 12th to the 20th of August 1918 the regiment was relieved and after a short rest departed for Arcis sur Aube for the purpose of joining up at camp Saint Tanche with the 2nd and 3rd Regiments of Polish Riflemen.

At the front the regiment did not disappoint the hopes placed in it: the soldier in blue showed the enemy and his brother soldiers that in his veins pulses the blood of the Bartoszes and Kiliński's.

General Naulin, commander of 21st Corps, said goodbye to the regiment in his order dated 17 August 1918 with the following words:

At this time when the 1st Regiment of Polish Riflemen is leaving 21st Corps, the general commanding this corps feels fortunate to be able to thank that Regiment for the aid which it provided during the military operation that recently took place. Entering into combat in unusually difficult conditions, on the eve of a very strong German attack, on 15 July,

> the Poles did their best to cover their standard in glory. Not only did they share with us the difficult times of the foe's artillery preparation and take a valiant part in the defense of our positions, but in addition they attacked the enemy's line splendidly, forcing their way deeply into it and taking numerous prisoners.
>
> The conduct of the 1st Regiment of Polish Riflemen on the fields of battle of Champagne gives the best guarantee of the future successes that await the 1st Polish Division.

The Regiment's immediate superior, the general commanding the 170th Infantry Division, said goodbye to the regiment in his order dated 10 August 1918 and honored it as follows:

> At this time when the 1st Regiment of Polish Riflemen is to leave the Saint Hilaire sector, the general in command of the 170th Infantry Division hastens to express to the regiment his congratulations on the courage and endurance which it has displayed.
>
> In a great battle, which they entered under difficult conditions, the Polish riflemen showed themselves to be fine, valiant and disciplined soldiers during the defense of the trenches entrusted to them; they have a right to the decorations which General Gouraud sent to the army fighting in Champagne.
>
> The soldiers of the 170th Division will never forget their comrades in arms. They saw with their own eyes that the Poles, like they themselves, hate the Germans.
>
> The French, who have fought for Alsace and Lorraine for four years, understand better than anyone the fervor with which the Poles fight for the freedom of their Fatherland.
>
> The General in command of the 170th Division is proud and happy to have had such soldiers under his command, wishes them success in future combat, is certain they will always distinguish themselves, and will be happy when he learns of their new feats.
>
> Commander, 170th Division
(—) Bernard, General.

THE REGIMENT IN THE 1ST DIVISION OF POLISH RIFLEMEN IN FRANCE

THE REGIMENT AT CAMP SAINT TANCHE WITH THE 1ST DIVISION

After its return from the front the regiment, greeted with enthusiasm by the civil populace, arrived at camp Saint Tanche, where the 2nd and 3rd Regiments were already being formed, and became part of the newly organized 1st Polish Division.

Command of the regiment after Col. Jasieński, who left to take command of the Divisional Infantry of the 1st Polish Division, was assumed by Col. Korszun-Osmołowski.

The first commander of the Division, decorating the soldiers and regiment, addressed the whole division, assembled for the ceremony:

> I bow my head with respect before the standards of the Polish units which are first to have the honor of forming the Polish Division, independent, on the land on which their comrades of the French Army stood victorious four years ago and, at first almost alone, faced the mighty attacks of our common foe and inflicted a bloody defeat upon him.
>
> The splendid military virtues of Poles, recently displayed so magnificently by the 1st Regiment of Polish Riflemen and the Company of Engineers, and their eternal hatred for the German which this noble people feels to a higher degree than any other, having experienced for themselves the greed and ruthless brutality of this foe, will soon allow palms to be added to their proud standards.
>
> From today, therefore, let all, whether infantryman or artilleryman, cavalryman or sapper, prepare for future success with their ardent labor.
>
> Commander of the 1st Polish Division
> (—) Ecochard, General

In camp exercises began once more, on application in the broadest measure of live fire training from half platoon to battalion in various combat situations: officers were trained in courses, preparing for new assignments at the front.

The losses suffered in Champagne were covered by the Division Training Center (reserve battalion), the so-called "C.I.D.," and the regiment's effective forces were brought up to full military strength.

THE REGIMENT IN CAMP NEAR NANCY (LORRAINE)

In September 1918 the regiment set out with the division for Bayon in Lorraine, from which it went on to camp near Nancy at the disposition of the commander of the 8th French Army. At this camp it trained along with the division's other regiments.

On 6 October 1918 the newly appointed commander of the Polish Army in France, General Józef Haller, greeted the regiment as well as the whole 1st Division, and on the standard of the 1st Regiment of Polish Riflemen swore loyalty to Poland.

THE REGIMENT AT THE FRONT IN LORRAINE

After a fairly long period of rest and reorganization, by 14 October 1918, along with the other Polish regiments of the 1st Division of Riflemen, the regiment was at the front in Lorraine at Moyen Moutier, occupying the so-called "Forain" sub-sector. The organization of centers of resistance relied on the same principles as in Champagne, with one difference, that this locality was hilly and covered with fairly thick forests. In this sector the regiment held its position in almost undisturbed peace. Life here varied only with patrols and, from time to time, attacks supported by artillery fire.

During this time, at the end of October, 7th Company carried out a sortie on a German resistance point separated from the Polish sentries only by wire.

In connection with the coalition's Supreme Commander's intended offensive against the Germans, for the purpose of compelling them to capitulate, 3 armies were grouped together: the French 8th and 10th, and the 2nd American, with a force of 30 infantry divisions. The best infantry divisions were selected for this strike, among them the 1st Division of Polish Riflemen, which was part of the 8th Army. In view of this, on 8 November 1918 the regiment was relieved and proceeded to the small town of Rembervillers, where on 11 November it was to be loaded onto vehicles which were to transport the 1st Division of Polish Riflemen to the Forêt de Parroy sector. But in view of the Germans' capitulation the loading was called off. The regiment only carried out a 4-day march in the direction of Strasbourg, for the purpose of occupying a taken part of Alsace, and then departed for Avricourt, from which it was sent back to Luneville.

That was the regiment's last action in France.

THE FORMING OF THE REGIMENT'S 4TH AND 5TH BATALLIONS FOR VOLUNTEERS ARRIVING FROM ITALY

For the purpose of receiving volunteers arriving from Italy, former prisoners of the Austrian army, the regiment proceeded to special camps in the vicinity of Nancy, where the cadres of the regiment's 4th and 5th Battalions were being prepared, into which the newcomers were to be incorporated. After the exchange among individual battalions in the regiment of newly-arrived junior officers and privates, the regiment once more worked on its training. In February the 4th and 5th Battalions were separated and formed new regiments in the Polish Division. Once more, just as the regiment had previously assigned cadres for the 2nd and 3rd Regiments of Riflemen, now it assigned some of its officers and junior officers to the regiments of the 2nd Polish Division.

THE REGIMENT'S DEPARTURE FOR POLAND

At the end of February 1919 General Haller arrived to inspect the regiment. This was a sure sign that the regiment would be leaving soon for Poland; for that reason frantic supplementation of staff and camps and issuing of uniforms, equipment and weapons were being carried out.

In the middle of this hectic organizational and training work came at last the longed-for moment of departure for Poland, to help our brothers fighting an enemy invasion.

On 15 April 1919 the regiment began its trip to Poland from the Bayon railroad station in four transports, via Mainz, Erfurt, Leipzig, Kalisz, and Warsaw, and arrived in Poland, where it was quartered in individual battalions: in Chełm 1st Battalion, supernumerary company and command of the regiment; 3rd Battalion in Kowel; and the 2nd Battalion in Włodzimierz.

THE REGIMENT'S COMBAT WORK IN POLAND

THE REGIMENT'S CONCENTRATION IN THE REGION OF CHEŁM, KOWEL, AND WŁODZIMIERZ

At the time of Poland's resurrection the whole nation put its fate in the hands of the One who had worked for years to win its independence. The Chief of State, Józef Piłsudski, took the direction of the newly formed state in his hands at the most critical time, after the Germans' retreat, and immediately had to face our ancient enemies to the east and west. The task was formidable, because it was necessary to do almost everything frantically from nothing, and only due to the iron will and experience of Józef Pilsudski, the creator of Reborn Poland's armed forces, was a National Army formed in a short time on its own territory, an Army that had to fight from the moment of its birth, because the obstinate and vengeful foe refused to accept the resurrection of Poland. From the East waves of invaders tore at the body of Poland. Heroic Lwów sealed its loyalty to the Republic with the heart's blood of its children, guarding its entrance against the Ukrainians; while the Bolshevik horde threatened to overwhelm Volhynia.

During these struggles with the enemies which threatened Poland on various sides, the gradual arrival in Poland of units of the Polish Army in France was very timely: freshly trained and well equipped, they could provide effective assistance.

After arriving in its region of concentration the regiment was taken over by Polish officers; French officers helped only as technical advisors with the regiment's and battalions' commanders.

On 1 May the regiment's forces were changed, diminishing the numbers in the riflemen's companies in order to increase the numbers in the machine gunners' companies. As a result the riflemen's companies were re-formed from 4 platoons to 3.

On 12 May 1919, after the entire regiment had concentrated in Włodzimierz, the regiment began an offensive against the Ukrainians, and subsequently against the Soviet Russian army occupying Ukraine.

THE REGIMENT'S BATTLES WITH THE UKRAINIANS

On 13 May 1919 the 1st Regiment of Infantry Riflemen charged the enemy from the region of Włodzimierz Wołyński. In a victorious march through Poryck it occupied the line of the river Styr from Targowica to Stanisławczyk (60 km.)

The enemy did not hold the field anywhere. Experience acquired in war, fervor, and ardent love for the Fatherland broke all resistance, crowning the regimental standard with new laurels. Despite attempts to offer resistance, neither at Poryck nor at Beresteczko could the Ukrainians hold back the march. The regiment's first booty in Poland: 7 heavy machine guns, 3 officers, 40 Ukrainian men.

With this concluded the combat activity against the Ukrainians, who, attacked on the east by Soviet Russian forces during the first days of June, completely yielded the foreground to the regiment. The regiment lost contact with its opponent, for the time being.

THE REGIMENT'S FIRST COMBAT WITH THE SOVIET ARMY

In order to make contact with its new opponent, the regiment sent patrols into the foreground. One of the most important and successful patrols was sent out under the command of 2nd Lt. Podoski (a platoon of 2nd Company and a platoon of light cavalrymen) for two-day reconnaissance to Wołkowyja and Edwardówka. This reconnaissance gave precise information on the movements of the larger Russian units headed in the regiment's direction. In Wołkowyja the patrol took 2 heavy machine guns and 4 Ukrainian *sotniki* (captains). Soon the regiment made contact with Russian units and continued activity only with strong patrols on the eastern bank of the river Styr.

A platoon of 7th Company under the command of 2nd Lt. Adamek at Demidówka, a distance of 8 km. from the regiment's positions, was surrounded by a crowd of the local populace in revolt, armed with rifles and heavy machine guns, and in addition was threatened by an approaching unit of Russian cavalry. After a victorious one-hour fight he took 2 heavy machine guns and withdrew, having only one man wounded. The whole time of the regiment's stay on the Styr, Soviet units with the assistance of armed bands of partisans harassed its outpost, attacking it with fairly serious strength, especially in the area of Beresteczko. Military experience, and the moral superiority that gives the knowledge that one's fight is a sacred matter, broke the momentum of the Soviet army.

THE BATTLES ON THE HORYŃ AND SŁUCZ AND REORGANIZATION OF THE REGIMENT

The regiment's combat march through Równe on the river Horyń took place almost without hindrance, because the Russians spread out before the regiment without significant combat, and attempts to put up resistance on the river Stubla near Janiewicz were swept aside by an attack of the 1st Battalion.

On 12 August the regiment passed Równe and marched on, with the goal of occupying the river Horyń in the vicinity of Hoszcza. The stop at the Horyń was for defensive work, constructing dozens of kilometers of trenches and wire obstacles, varying with sending out combat patrols on the foreground. 9th Company under the command of 1st Lt. Kozierowski made its way to Korzec, an advanced outpost in the division's sector, from which it could patrol the foreground as well as conduct reconnaissance on Zwiahel, and took it with a frontal attack; 9th Company remained in the town several hours and then returned to Korzec, bringing along a great deal of information on the enemy.

On 17 September 1919 the regiment (by Order No. 167 of the Ministry of Military Affairs) received the name "the 43rd Regiment of Eastern Frontier Infantry Riflemen." At the same time the regiment was transferred from French to Polish management. Every battalion received a national commission.

In the first days of October Zwiahel was finally taken with an attack by 3rd Battalion of the 43rd Regiment and 2nd Battalion of the 44th Infantry Regiment, and a position was taken on the river Słucz in that area.

As of 1 November 1919 command of the regiment was assumed by Major Piekarski. The regiment's ranks at the front had been thinned 80% by an outbreak of typhus. During this period began the demobilization of old volunteers and an influx of recruits from the reserve battalion, which had a rather negative effect on the regiment's state of training.

BATTLES DURING THE WINTER OF 1919-1920

The regiment spent the winter on the river Słucz, in the region of Zwiahel—Lubar—Starokonstantynów—Szepetówka, and endured the March Soviet offensive. In the meantime the regiment carefully and conscientiously organized the defense in its sector, valiantly fought off all the enemy's designs, and in victorious attacks advanced far into the foreground and nipped in the bud the Soviet units' attempts to gather for attack. In turn the regiment's battalions, redeployed transports by rail to Zwiahel, Miropol, and Starokonstantynów, and conducted sorties, often under Major Piekarski's personal command, on the sites of the enemy's larger groupings. 9th Company under the command of 1st Lt. Kozierowski, along with a cavalry brigade, took part in a successful sortie at Żytomierz, 75 km. away. In all these sorties they captured a total of 3 cannons, 4 caissons, 5 heavy machine guns, and an impressive number of prisoners and military material.

THE UKRAINE OFFENSIVE

In the spring of 1920 a reorganization of the regiment took place, increasing its forces by 3 companies of riflemen and a company of heavy machine guns (the 4th, 8th, and 12th Riflemen's Companies and the 4th Heavy Machine Gun Company).

On 25 April 1920 the regiment set out eastward from the region of Ostropol on the Słucz, taking part in the Ukraine offensive. After easily breaking through the enemy's resistance at Wojszcza and Biczowa, the regiment advanced without hindrance through Ułanów, Mały and Wielki Czerniatyn, and Samhorodek to Pohrebyszcze, which it occupied on 3 May, greeted formally by Polish, Ukrainian and Jewish delegations. In the Pohrebyszcze region the regiment had the assignment of covering the railway junction in Koziatyn by closing access along the railroad track running Tytyjów—Pohrebyszcze—Koziatyn and roads north of that track. As provided by the defensive plan of the commander of the 13th Infantry Division, the regiment set up centers of resistance: Dziunków for 1st Battalion and 4th Battery, Rozkopane for 2nd Battalion with 5th Battery, and for a time Nowochwastów for 3rd Battalion with 6th Battery. The regiment's command was in Pawłówka. The centers of resistance were built systematically, mainly with wire.

High spirits dominated in the regiment, despite the release from the ranks of the older recruits, with whom a lot of experienced soldiers departed, seasoned in combat and engulfed with martial fervor. The newly inducted soldier, despite his lack of training, now had to uphold the regiment's good name and show that he understood the spirit and tradition of the old campaigners and knew how to follow in their footsteps.

THE REGIMENT'S FIRST ENCOUNTER WITH BUDIONNY'S MOUNTED ARMY

Days of bloody and victorious combat approached. The mounted army of Budionny*, which crushed Denikin's army in southern Russia, was now on the Ukrainian front and was approaching the Polish front by quick marches from the region of Humań. A platoon of 9th Company, under the command of 1st Lt. Kozierowski, was sent through Wołodarka on the river Roś to Stawiszcze station (90 km.), to confirm that army's presence. They discovered that its main force was located in the vicinity of Zwinogródek and Humań.

From 29 May to 5 June 1920 a bloody battle played out, known under the name "the defense of Koziatyn." Budionny's whole mounted army, numbering

---

*Translator's Note: The reference is to Semion Mikhailovich Budionny, whose name also appears in English as Budienny, Budenny, Budyonny, etc.

some 17,000 swords, 5 armored trains and numerous armored vehicles, struck ferociously at the 13th Infantry Division's sector, and particularly that of the 43rd Regiment of the Eastern Frontier Riflemen. Despite an extremely critical situation—which had arisen on the eve of the actual battle as a result of the Cossacks' cutting through two battalions of the 50th Infantry Regiment with a resultant breach on the south—the enemy was unable to break the regiment's front, which stood like a wall against Budionny's hordes, even though masses of cavalry surrounded the regiment's right flank (the battle at Plisków and Annówka), seriously endangering the rear. The regiment did not yield an inch of ground to the enemy, and every local success of the enemy was balanced by bravura counterattacks that inflicted heavy losses on him.

The Battle of Dziunków. A particularly bloody battle played out at the resistance center of 1st Battalion in Dziunków, where Capt. Piątkowski commanded the Battalion, with the help of 4th Battery under the command of 1st Lt. Kowalski. Budionny's whole 11th Cavalry Division attacked this sector to no avail, and after great losses had to give up its intention of breaking this iron battalion. The 22nd of May was a bloody day for the regiment, but one of glory.

The battles were so fierce that they often came down to hand-to-hand combat. 4th Battery of the 13th Regiment of Eastern Frontier Field Artillery, the one battery in its resistance center, fired from four observation points, that is, every cannon had its own targets and direction. Capt. Piątkowski, the Battalion's commander, in order to defend against the interruption of Red cavalry attacks on the rear, threw himself into a counterattack with the company dispatch riders who comprised his last reserve. 1st Lt. Klich, the commander of 2nd Company, having split half a reserve platoon of his company for a counterstroke against the enemy's charging cavalry, fought face to face. There was no time for throwing grenades; he knocked Soviet commissar Polonskiy dead with a blow of his fist. Both officers and men, having displayed miracles of gallantry and unshakeable courage, finished these heavy struggles with a magnificent victory over an enemy with numerical superiority. How 1st Battalion defended itself in Dziunków, with a total combat force of 400 bayonets with 4 cannons, was bluntly presented by an enemy report on the situation that was found, which read as follows:

> To the Chief of Staff of the 1st Mounted Army. Copies to the commanders of the 4th, 6th, and 14th Mounted Divisions.
> Village of Dolhalevka, No. 11/III.
> Units of the entire 11th Cavalry Division were engaged in the battle at Dziunków, which lasted through the night of 29 May. The Poles held their ground very stubbornly, and when the cavalry attacked, it was met with strong rifle fire and hand grenades, of which the enemy possessed a great many. The Division charged several times, breaking through the enemy's trenches. *The number of the enemy occupying Dziunków is estimated*

at 2,000 bayonets of the regular army, splendidly armed with rifles, grenades, and with 13 cannons and a small number of cavalry. In the division losses were very high. Having tested every means and measures, the Division could not break the enemy. Exhausted by the last 24 hours, it was sent back to the rear.

Chief of Staff of the 11th Cavalry Division (—) Popov
Krzemieniec Military Commissar Vishnevetsky

And so the history of the 43rd Infantry Regiment was enriched with a glorious new page, in which alongside the heroes' names these words should be engraved with gold letters: "Courage and unshakeable valor in the defense of the beloved Fatherland makes the death of a soldier beautiful and easy."

The heroic stand of the soldiers of 13th Infantry Division was mentioned in the dispatches of the Supreme Commander (5638/III), as follows:

> The Supreme Command expresses full recognition and praise to the 13th Infantry Division, which paralyzed the blows of the enemy on an extended front in such a remarkable way.
> Announce this to all armies in Ukraine.
>
> (—) Haller, Lt. Gen.

To the dispatch of the Supreme Command, the command of 13th Infantry Division added the explanation that 43rd Regiment, under the command of Major Piekarski and Capt. Piątkowski, performed the heroic defense of Dziunków. To them, to a large extent, the division owed its holding the front.

RETREAT

On 5 June in fierce combat Budionny broke the Polish front north of the 43rd Regiment of Eastern Frontier Riflemen, in the area of Samhorodek—Ozierna—Śnieżna, and penetrated with his whole army to the Polish rear, heading for Żytomierz. The Polish 3rd Army in Kiev was cut off from the north as well. As a result of these events a retreat maneuver to the Słucz river was ordered. In the regiment's and division's sector there was no pressure from the enemy, but because of the overall situation that had been created, the 43rd Regiment of Eastern Frontier Riflemen began a retreat from the positions where it had fought so gloriously.

On 12 June 1920 the regiment, as part of 6th Army, withdrew almost without any contact with the enemy to its departure base before the Kiev offensive, that is, on the Słucz near Ostropol, where it held its position till 2 July, repulsing the enemy's attacks, especially on the flanks. The Polish Army, however, did not succeed in defeating the foe's mobile mounted forces. A further retreat ensued. As a result of the breakthrough at the front north of Miropol and the enemy's capture of Połonne, the 43rd Regiment, as ordered, headed west toward Zasław, supporting the activities of General Krajowski's 18th Infantry Division at Ostróg—Równe in order to restore communications with 3rd Army.

THE BATTLE OF BUTOWCE

During action at Zasław 3rd Battalion, in the advance guard along with the regiment's command and the Kraków staging battalion, was attacked on three sides by Kotovsky's cavalry brigade at Butowce. Thanks to assistance from 2nd Battalion, after several hours of heavy combat the regiment withdrew in the evening toward Starokonstantynów. It was here that the *Bajończyk* Capt. Mieczysław Rodzyński, commander of 3rd Battalion, died a hero's death.

After this battle the march's previous direction was changed by order of the commander of 13th Infantry Division, and they headed to Starokonstantynów under protection from 2nd Battalion, as the rear guard of 13th Division. From Starokonstantynów the regiment retreated, with almost no contact with the enemy, through Krasiłów, Bazalja, Wyszogródek, and Wisznowiec to the Horynka—Kuszlin region.

THE BATTLE OF KLITNA

During this retreat the Soviet cavalry (Prymakov's 8th Division [Vitaliy Markovich Primakov, 1897-1937]), which forced its way through to Płoskirów to the rear of 6th Army and returned north, tried at Klitna and Koszelówka to cut off 13th Division's retreat; but two attacks that day by 2nd Battalion, under the command of Capt. Wyczółkowski, with the assistance of two divisions of the 13th Regiment of the Eastern Frontier Field Artillery, forced the enemy back with losses.

THE BATTLE OF HORYNKA

On the morning of 13 July, during the course of occupying the new region near Horynka, 2nd Battalion (along with 6th Battery of the 13th Field Artillery Regiment), which due to a misunderstanding had moved prematurely to take Podhajce, encountered a superior force of Soviet cavalry and was forced to withdraw—with the loss of 2 officers and 27 men—to the forest near Horynka, where for two days it valiantly fought off further attacks by the enemy. The risk of being outflanked from the north of the sector of the 43rd Regiment of the Eastern Frontier Riflemen in the Horynka—Krzemieniec region was removed by Lt. Col. Szylling with the 44th Regiment, which on the way back from Krzemieniec (with General Krajowski's group) defeated Kotovsky's entire brigade.

COUNTERATTACK ON THE SERET RIVER

Due to the enemy's heavy pressure on 10th Infantry Brigade in Krzemieniec, the 43rd Regiment withdrew to the line of the Seret, northwest of Załoźce to Batków. On 6 August it set out to counterattack and reached the Załoźce–Podkamień highway, which it held in its possession despite efforts on the part of the Soviet army to drive it back.

BATTLES AT KRASNE AND LWÓW

At this time the Supreme Commander concentrated his main forces for the decisive battle at Warsaw. The 18th Infantry Division, along with other divisions, set out for that destination. The diminished 6th Army received the assignment of protecting eastern Little Poland and defending Lwów, which Budionny was attacking. In connection with this situation the regiment set out, in constant contact with the enemy, through Złoczów to Krasne. During this march the enemy, having shattered the staff column of the 13th Infantry Division (the Poznań staging Battalion, command of a cavalry division and an artillery platoon) at Firlejówka, cut off the regiment's retreat. In order to force the enemy out of Firlejówka and open the road to Rusinowo for the regiment, Major Grodzki, commander of 3rd Battalion, received an order to attack with three companies and two platoons of heavy machine guns under the command of 1st Lt. Antoni Szymański. From the moment of this attack the regiment came under heavy fire from the Soviet artillery. 3rd Battalion's first thrust was checked, and the enemy was thrown back only due to the presence of 12th Company's commander, 2nd Lt. Górecki. Under the protection of 3rd Battalion the regiment was able to go as far as Rostków, where it stopped for half an hour's rest. Here 12th Company captured two heavy machine guns mounted on horse-drawn *taczanki* [carts]. From Krasne a race developed between Budionny's army and the 13th Infantry Division: who would be first to Lwów? The regiment withdrew by day and by night, reached Lwów, and in the Gaje–Czyżyków region fought off attacks, after which it defended Lwów in the region of Winniki, the castle of Winniczki (9th Company) and Wólka. During the night of 22–23 August the regiment was relieved by 53rd Regiment and departed for Lwów to the Łyczaków tollgates, where it prepared for transport to another front, receiving reinforcements from guard battalions of Łódź and Łuck; several days later it moved out for action intended to corner Budionny.

THE AUGUST COUNTEROFFENSIVE

On 17 August, in the decisive battle at Warsaw, the scales of victory tipped in favor of the Poles, and a new page was opened in the history of the Polish-Soviet war. The Russians, hypnotized by their desire to capture Warsaw and blinded by their previous success, did not anticipate the blow delivered upon them by Poland's Supreme Commander, departing on 16 August from the region of Dęblin–Lublin with his 4th and 3rd Armies. The Soviet armies, active in the direction of Warsaw and circling it from the north, were doubly surprised: by the unexpected resistance of Warsaw's defenders, and by the strength of the attack by the maneuver group under the command of the Supreme Commander, Marshal Piłsudski. These four armies were shattered, and with a crumbling left flank and endangered rear, in panic and disorder they began a retreat that ended in their defeat.

Now it was the turn of Budionny, hitherto unbeaten, though badly roughed up. After unsuccessful attempts to take Lwów, on which Budionny wasted 4 whole days, he finally set out (on the emphatic order of the Soviet chief commander) toward Zamość and Lublin, to salvage the situation at Warsaw; but it was already too late. At Zamość he was forced to accept a decisive battle and was beaten, left unable even to make a planned retreat. By an amazing turn of events this utter triumph over an opponent so dangerous throughout the whole 1920 campaign fell to the lot of that same 13th Infantry Division of which the whole 43rd Regiment of Eastern Frontier Riflemen was a part, and which put up resistance in this first defeat of Budionny as effective and steadfast as at Koziatyn.

Battles at Żulice, Komarów, and Wolica Śniatycka. After unloading at Rawa Ruska and concentrating the entire division, the 43rd Regiment of Eastern Frontier Riflemen began its offensive activity with the assignment of striking a blow on the southern flank and rear of Budionny's mounted army, in action in the direction of Krasnystaw and Lublin, for the purpose of cornering that army. After successfully fighting off the lateral guards of the enemy's cavalry at Żulice, the regiment set out for Komarów in a race with the enemy, who drove by swift march to Zamość. After breaking through the rear guard's resistance, the regiment, together with the 44th Regiment of Eastern Frontier Riflemen, took Komarów on 30 August. The next day the regiment proceeded in the direction of Zamość, already under Budionny's artillery fire. At Wolica Śniatycka, with the help of artillery (the 5th, 6th , 8th and 9th Batteries of the 13th Field Artillery Regiment), the regiment shattered two attacks by a whole division of Soviet cavalry, which, after breaking the Polish cavalry's attack, rushed from the region of Cześniki toward the advancing columns of the 43rd and 44th Regiments of Eastern Frontier Riflemen.

Budionny, however, did not let himself be cornered, and fought his way northeast through units of the 2nd Division of Legion Infantrymen.

Beginning at Zamość, the regiment chased Budionny in the direction of Hrubieszów. Without resistance from the enemy, encountering traces of hasty retreat everywhere, it came to the river Huczwa in the vicinity of Honiatycze.

The enemy was in constant retreat, and his behavior clearly was that of one trying to gain time.

On 5 September the 43rd Regiment of Eastern Frontier Riflemen cooperated with the 26th Brigade in an attack at Werbkowice, easily breaking the enemy's resistance to the south of Gdeszyn. By taking Wołkowyja on the Huczwa it cut off the retreating opponent's way at Werbkowice, and with heavy machine gun fire inflicted serious losses in men and materials while the enemy was crossing the river. From there the regiment continued to pursue the enemy and without hindrance went from Werbkowice to Gródek on the Bug river (east of Hrubieszów).

THE SEPTEMBER OFFENSIVE

CROSSING THE BUG RIVER AND PURSUIT TO THE STYR

On 1 September the 1st Brigade crossed the Bug at Grodno and set up a bridgehead on the east side of the river. Holding this bridgehead cost the regiment a great deal of blood and many lives due to heavy fire from the Soviet artillery.

On 12 September, in connection with a general offensive of the 3rd Army (which included the 13th Infantry Division), the regiment attacked. Stout resistance by the enemy at Berezna and Udzin was broken with one blow. The enemy, defending himself, left behind a large number of bodies and a single cannon. The ferocity of the battle may be attested by the fact that the enemy's batteries left their positions only at the last moment, firing at 12th Company, advancing to capture them, at a distance of 200 meters.

During the course of the day strong enemy units appeared here and there, but when fired upon by artillery they scattered and retreated eastward. The regiment continued to advance, to Lasków and Zimno, with the goal of bypassing Włodzimierz on the south. In this march the enemy tried to put resistance at Oktawin, and near the village of Zimno inflicted losses on the regiment with its artillery fire. In its march toward Łuck the regiment encountered serious resistance near Torczyn at Litwa, where in a difficult attack 6th Company was held up in the swamps by heavy machine gun fire; it was only the fire of a whole artillery division and concentric attacks of the rest of 2nd Battalion that dislodged the enemy from his positions. The regiment arrived at Łuck on 13 September at 2400 hours.

BATTLE FOR ZWIAHEL AND SORTIES

From Łuck the regiment reached Równe on 19 September without any hindrance on the part of the enemy; Równe had already been taken by Gen.

Rómmel's 1st Cavalry Corps. From Równe the regiment assisted that Corp in its activities in the Korzec–Zwiahel area with separate battalions, and on 7 October established a bridgehead there on the Słucz river.

With the defense of Zwiahel, from which the enemy tried unsuccessfully to dislodge the regiment, and with sorties far to the east and northeast, the 43rd Regiment of Eastern Frontier Riflemen ended its combat activity.

Noteworthy among these sorties was the one carried out by 2nd Battalion on 5 October at Broniki and Kropiwna for the purpose of enabling the cavalry to circle and capture the enemy located in the foreground of Zwiahel, as well as that same battalion's sortie on 10 October through Gały—Niemielanka on Stara Huta, done in cooperation with the 44th Infantry Regiment. Both sorties were crowned with successful results, and in particular the latter one, during which it was necessary to break through significant resistance on the enemy's part. The enemy left in the Regiment's hands a rich military booty; in a sortie on Korosteń—in conjunction with 43rd Regiment—the Polish cavalry took 3,500 prisoners, 6 cannons and the standard of the staff of the 12th Soviet Division.

Armistice on 18 October 1920 put an end to the bloody war for the Fatherland's integrity, leaving the regiment in Zwiahel. At the 22nd hour, or two hours before the armistice took effect, 3rd Battalion under the command of Capt. Kozierowski carried out a final sortie in the direction of Broniki–Kropiwna for the purpose of taking a new advanced line of resistance, taking prisoners and military material.

* * *

After the armistice the regiment found itself in Równe and Zdołbunów. After a brief rest it set out from Zdołbunów in January 1921 to guard the Polish-Russian line of demarcation in the Korzec area. During this period the regiment underwent intensive training according to the new organization for the Polish army, based on *drużyny* [squads]. After returning from the line of demarcation the regiment conducted a final demobilization of all volunteers, French, American, and Italian; it reorganized as three battalions of three companies each and a staff battalion with a machine gun company.

In connection with the general deployment of 15 July 1921 the regiment proceeded to Dubno, where its two battalions were posted, along with its command. One battalion was assigned permanently to Brody.

At that point peacetime work began in the regiment, on educating the soldiers for the defense of Fatherland and citizens.

Every soldier of the 43rd Regiment of Eastern Frontier Riflemen can and should look with pride on his military past. It is one of beauty, unstained by cowardice.

He performed his firm soldierly duty to the Fatherland in a creditable manner, and his combat work can be appraised as equal to our past heroic deeds before and after the partitions.

He went with fervor into the battle for Poland, and with death and blood spilled generously he compensated for the faults of our fathers in the sense of the Roman principle, "It is sweet and proper to die for the Fatherland."

THE REGIMENT'S STANDARD

The regiment still possesses the standard handed over on 18 June 1918 in France as a gift from the citizens of Paris. It is a standard of durable fabric, amaranthine in color, embroidered on one side with the Polish eagle with the inscription "First Regiment of Infantry Riflemen," and on the other "The Polish Army." The standard's borders have small silver fringes.

THE REGIMENT'S HOLIDAY

Until 1924 the date of 10 January was a holiday for the regiment, as it was the anniversary of the founding of the 43rd Regiment (the 1st Regiment of Polish Riflemen), the first unit of the Polish Army organized in France.

In 1924, with the permission of the Ministry of Military Affairs, that day was transferred to 25 July, the anniversary of the illustrious battle in Champagne near Reims, because on that day the regiment upheld the traditional glory of the Polish army and won the recognition of the French commanders. By doing so it contributed to upholding the idea of President Wilson's 13th point: that is, the recognition of Poland's right to independence, with access to the sea, before the world.

LIST OF THOSE WHO FELL IN BATTLE OR DIED OF THEIR WOUNDS FROM THE 43RD REGIMENT OF EASTERN FRONTIER RIFLEMEN

Officers:

1. 2nd Lt. Bartman Antoni
2. 2nd Lt. Bauer Franciszek
3. 2nd Lt. Chwałkowski Lucjan
4. 2nd Lt. Czerwonka Ludwik
5. 2nd Lt. Czuperta Henryk
6. 1st Lt. Dąbrowski Jakób
7. Capt. Krzywkowski-Woliński
8. 2nd Lt. Martynowicz Leon
9. 1st Lt. Michniewicz Jan
10. 1st Lt. Niemiec Pawel
11. 1st Lt. Rogoziński
12. Capt. Rodzyński Mieczysław
13. 2nd Lt. Walczak Ignacy
14. 1st Lt. Walaszczyk Walenty
15. 1st Lt. Wronowski Stanisław

Men:

Translator's note: the list is given as in the original, with no attempt made to correct numbering or alphabetization.

1. Sgt. Anczak Józef
2. Pfc. Abfeld Icek
3. Pfc. Andrys Józef
4. Pfc. Adamczyk Władysław
5. Pfc. Baczyński Józef
6. Pfc. Bananiak Franciszek
7. Pfc. Bielecki Władysław
8. Pfc. Borkowski Juljan
9. Pfc. Boroń Henryk
10. Pfc. Borowiec Stefan
11. Pfc. Bożeński Wincenty
12. Pfc. Brodoliński Michał
13. Cpl. Broniszewski Władysław
14. Pfc. Brzeziński Wojciech
15. Pfc. Buba (Buda) Władysław
16. Pfc. Buhl Engelbert
17. Pfc. Baran Antoni
18. Pfc. Baran Henryk
19. Pfc. Bączkowski Konstanty
20. Sgt. Bednarz Wincenty
21. Pfc. Białek Leonard
22. Pfc. Biskupski Władysław
23. Pfc. Birnbaum Chaim
24. Pfc. Biterman Szlama
25. Pfc. Blic Dawid
26. Cpl. Borowski Piotr
27. Pfc. Bołdyga Stanisław
28. Pfc. Boluch Dodmerza
29. Pfc. Brzyski Bronisław
30. Pfc. Cebula Piotr
31. Pfc. Chmiel Teofil
32. Cpl. Chrostowski Jan
33. Pfc. Cichocki Jan
34. Pfc. Cobel Antoni Józef
35. Sgt. Chmielewski Wincenty
36. Pfc. Chnilka Jan
37. Pfc. Chuchrowski Jan
38. Pfc. Cieszak Jan
39. Pfc. Czuperek Jan
40. Master Cpl. Cynarski Ignacy

41. Pfc. Dolecki Jan
42. Pfc. Grzebalski Wacław
43. Pfc. Dudkowski Jan
44. Pfc. Dziubicki, Antoni
45. Pfc. Dardzyński Antoni
46. Pfc. Dębski Antoni
47. Pfc. Depta Stanisław
48. Pfc. Dycha Jan
49. Pfc. Dziechciarz Stanisław
50. Pfc. Dusko Wojciech
51. Pfc. Drygałek Franciszek
52. Pfc. Dobrowolski Ignacy
53. Pfc. Domański Jan
54. Pfc. Dworak Franciszek
55. Pfc. Dudek Jan
56. Pfc. Dworecki Jan
57. Pfc. Dymitr Bazyli
58. Pfc. Droshewicz Stanisław
59. Pfc. Flak Adam
60. Pfc. Gad Wawrzyniec
61. Pfc. Gawroński Jan
62. Pfc. Gawryłowicz Piotr
63. Pfc. Gistereich Emil
64. Pfc. Goldszmidt Szmul
65. Pfc. Gombala Michał
66. Pfc. Grabowski Walenty
67. Pfc. Grądziel Władysław
68. Pfc. Grajper Jan
69. Pfc. Grochulski Stanisław
70. Chief Warrant Officer Gwolecki Teodor
71. Pfc. Gaj Icek
72. Pfc. Gojas Bolesław
73. Pfc. Galart Michał
74. Lance Cpl. Gaczniak Paweł
75. Pfc. Garczyński Franciszek
76. Pfc. Grabiec Władysław
77. Pfc. Gryczka Stanisław
78. Pfc. Ganczarek Jan
79. Pfc. Grabowski Jan
80. Pfc. Glodor vel Sonder Roman
81. Pfc. Grzyb Leon
82. Pfc. Górski Jan
83. Pfc. Gołąbek Jan
84. Pfc. Głowik Wincenty
85. Pfc. Gotnajer Emil
86. Pfc. Hajduk Jan
87. Pfc. Hryniewiecki Dominik
88. Pfc. Izolski Jan
89. Pfc. Jasiński Józef
90. Pfc. Jakubozik Andrzej
91. Pfc. Jager Jan
92. Pfc. Jeziek Jan
93. Pfc. Joraszek Jacek
94. Pfc. Janicki Józef
95. Pfc. Jarecki Józef
96. Pfc. Jasiełowski Władysław
97. Pfc. Jezior Jan
98. Pfc. Jungerman Nojech
99. Pfc. Kaczmarek Józef
100. Pfc. Kalinowski Antoni
101. Pfc. Kamiński Józef
102. Pfc. Kamzelowski Michał
103. Pfc. Kanigowski Aleksander
104. Pfc. Karbowski Franciszek
105. Cpl. Kasprzak Feliks
106. Sgt. Kiedewicz Ludwik
107. Pfc. Kiersz Icek
108. Pfc. Kilmblat Lejba
109. Pfc. Kłódka Jan
110. Pfc. Kocan Jan
111. Pfc. Kochalski Ignacy
112. Pfc. Koczor Aleksander
113. Pfc. Kańczugowski Józef
114. Cpl. Koraluk Adolf
115. Lance Cpl. Koziarz Jakób
116. Pfc. Kosmalski Bronisław
117. Pfc. Kosmalski Jan
118. Pfc. Kowalczyk Walenty
119. Cpl. Kowalik Adolf
120. Pfc. Kozikowski Antoni
121. Pfc. Krasowski Franciszek

122. Sgt. Krechniak Władysław
123. Pfc. Krzemiński Piotr
124. Pfc. Kubicz Eljasz
125. Pfc. Kuchta S.
126. Pfc. Kubelski Józef
127. Pfc. Kuskielski Józef
128. Pfc. Kustyla Jan
129. Technical Sgt. Kwieczyński Józef
130. Pfc. Klokocki Adam
131. Pfc. Kościelny Ludwik
132. Pfc. Kopel Antoni
133. Pfc. Kosek Szymon
134. Pfc. Komoroszek
135. Pfc. Kaniowski Antoni
136. Pfc. Kwiecień Ludwik
137. Pfc. Kupczyński Szymon
138. Pfc. Klebeczyk
139. Pfc. Kreboszewski Józef
140. Pfc. Karp Bolesław
141. Pfc. Kula Jan
142. Pfc. Kozak Józef
143. Pfc. Kopec Wawrzyniec
144. Pfc. Kordyń Michał
145. Pfc. Kulesza Jan
146. Pfc. Kordel Stanisław
147. Pfc. Kotecki Wojciech
148. Pfc. Krykowiak Stanisław
149. Pfc. Kałuba Teodor
150. Pfc. Komorowski Bronisław
151. Pfc. Krzyszkowiak Paweł
152. Pfc. Korensztajn Jutka
153. Pfc. Kowalski Józef
154. Pfc. Kowalik Józef
155. Pfc. Kowalski Bronisław
156. Pfc. Kupka Aleksander
157. Pfc. Kania Roman
158. Pfc. Krajsmidt Dawid
159. Pfc. Kołodziej Antoni
160. Pfc. Kateleniowski Feliks
161. Cpl. Kupczyński Dyonizy
162. Pfc. Kulpa Wojciech
163. Pfc. Królski Józef
164. Cpl. Lata Franciszek
165. Pfc. Lewandowicz Walenty
166. Pfc. Lipowy Szymon
167. Pfc. Łabęcki Piotr
168. Pfc. Lubas Jan
169. Pfc. Lustman Szloma
170. Pfc. Lubijewski Czesław
171. Pfc. Lewandowski Franciszek
172. Master Cpl. Lenard Stanisław
173. Pfc. Łabęcki Piotr
174. Pfc. Łabzdyr Franciszek
174. *[sic]* Pfc. Łąkoczy Franciszek
176. Pfc. Łapniewski Ignacy
177. Pfc. Łosiecki Stanisław
178. Pfc. Mabe Icek
179. Pfc. Maciąg Roman
180. Pfc. Maciaszek Franciszek
181. Pfc. Maciejewski Jan
182. Pfc. Macioszyn Franciszek
183. Pfc. Maj Ignacy
184. Pfc. Makowski Ludwik
185. Pfc. Marchewka Jan
186. Pfc. Matejczak
187. Pfc. Mazurek Bronisław
188. Pfc. Mazurkiewicz Jan
189. Pfc. Melachma Jakób
190. Pfc. Miduch Antoni
191. Pfc. Milchman Jakób
192. Pfc. Mioduch Antoni
193. Pfc. Morawski Wincenty
194. Pfc. Macza Juljan
195. Pfc. Morawski
196. Pfc. Mikolow
197. Pfc. Morwiak
198. Pfc. Michalski Bolesław
199. Pfc. Makowski Ignacy
200. Pfc. Maciejewski Jan
201. Pfc. Małuszewski Jakób
202. Pfc. Mamrowski Stanisław
203. Pfc. Michalski Bolesław

204. Pfc. Matuszewski Stefan
205. Pfc. Michalski
206. Pfc. Moroz Lucjan
207. Pfc. Moczyróg Jan
208. Pfc. Mroczka Michał
209. Pfc. Marek Konstanty
210. Pfc. Moskwik Jan
211. Pfc. Madej Stanisław
212. Pfc. Mianowany Stanisław
213. Pfc. Marcinkowski Jan
214. Pfc. Mendelbaum Jakób
215. Pfc. Małecki Ignacy
216. Pfc. Michoń Roman
217. Pfc. Miedźwiecki Feliks
218. Pfc. Niebieski Jan
219. Pfc. Nisenweinig Haim
220. Pfc. Noga Jan
221. Pfc. Nowaczek Kazimierz
222. Pfc. Nowaszczuk Grzegorz
223. Pfc. Niedźwiecki Feliks
224. Pfc. Nosal Edward
225. Pfc. Olszewski Antoni
226. Sgt. Ordęga Józef
227. Pfc. Osiecki vel Łosiecki Stanisław
228. Pfc. Pastelski Franciszek
229. Pfc. Pater Franciszek
230. Lance Cpl. Patkowski Ludwik
231. Pfc. Pędziwiater Bolesław
232. Pfc. Ptaszynek Jan
233. Pfc. Popek Antoni
234. Pfc. Podświadek Jan
235. Pfc. Piwoński Józef
236. Pfc. Piskowski Władysław
237. Pfc. Polaczek Władysław
238. Pfc. Pułkowski Ludwik
239. Pfc. Pasiecznia Michał
240. Pfc. Parchalski Józef
241. Pfc. Podwójcik Józef
242. Pfc. Piekło Jan
243. Pfc. Pietrzak Józef
244. Pfc. Przeracki Stanisław
245. Pfc. Piotrowski Michał
246. Pfc. Post Konrad
247. Sgt. Perczak Antoni
248. Sgt. Prokop Antoni
249. Pfc. Ptak Walenty
250. Pfc. Rybowski Jan
251. Pfc. Romałowski Franciszek
252. Pfc. Rauba Józef
253. Pfc. Robankiewicz Michał
254. Pfc. Rozek Adam
255. Pfc. Rusinek Jan
256. Pfc. Ruta Antoni
257. Pfc. Rocun Aleksander
258. Pfc. Rybak Jan
259. Pfc. Szamotowski Bazyli
260. Pfc. Szymański Teofil
261. Pfc. Stoczyński Jan
262. Pfc. Saba Franciszek
263. Pfc. Sujdak Franciszek
264. Pfc. Ślusarek Czesław
265. Pfc. Silberszer Chaim
266. Sgt. Sokołowski Wincenty
267. Pfc. Solski Wacław
268. Pfc. Stefański Teofil
269. Pfc. Sielski Stanisław
270. Pfc. Sypek Jan
271. Pfc. Szczęśniak Wojciech
272. Pfc. Samaba Jan
273. Pfc. Singer Josek
274. Pfc. Strzydała Bolesław
275. Sgt. Świerkowski Paweł
276. Master Cpl. *[plut.]* Solak Franciszek
277. Pfc. Spyt Jan
278. Pfc. Siedlec Stanisław
279. Pfc. Stelnicki Jan
280. Pfc. Stasik Franciszek
281. Pfc. Szmul Piotr
282. Pfc. Sztern Iloza
283. Pfc. Sadowski Aleksander

284. Pfc. Somiński Konstanty
285. Pfc. Szerufild Maras
286. Pfc. Szczupak Eljasz
287. Pfc. Sarłocha Andrzej
288. Pfc. Sawicki Jan
289. Pfc. Schabowski Adam
290. Pfc. Sępołowicz Władysław
291. Pfc. Siadłowski Aleksander
292. Pfc. Siadłowski Stanisław
293. Pfc. Skoczeń Piotr
294. Pfc. Skoczylas Stanisław
295. Pfc. Skolbania Karol
296. Pfc. Skrzypek Jan
297. Pfc. Słowik Wincenty
298. Pfc. Sowicki Jan
299. Cpl. Spiołek Jan
300. Pfc. Stefanek Józef
301. Pfc. Stępień Władysław
302. Pfc. Strung Józef
303. Pfc. Sułek Jan
304. Pfc. Świder Wincenty
305. Pfc. Sykuła Wojciech
306. Pfc. Szadlocha Andrzej
307. Pfc. Szard Ludwik
308. Pfc. Szpiro Srul
309. Pfc. Szubert Łukasz
310. Pfc. Szulej Wiktor
311. Pfc. Szumlański Józef
312. Pfc. Szwedo Michał
313. Pfc. Szymanek Józef
314. Pfc. Saja Władysław
315. Pfc. Sienkiewicz
316. Pfc. Sokołowski Jan
317. Pfc. Taler Franciszek
318. Pfc. Teodorczyk Franciszek
319. Pfc. Terlecki Józef
320. Pfc. Turowicz Wacław
321. Pfc. Trzeciak Piotr
322. Master Cpl. Trzejański Jan
323. Pfc. Talarko Franciszek
324. Pfc. Tworek Feliks
325. Pfc. Tarłów Józef
326. Pfc. Tomczak Stanisław
327. Pfc. Turkowiak Leon
328. Pfc. Uljasz Michał
329. Pfc. Urbanek Franciszek
330. Pfc. Urbaniak Kazimierz
331. Pfc. Urbański Józef
332. Pfc. Wach Antoni
333. Pfc. Waingarten Godel
334. Pfc. Walass Jan
335. Sgt. Walczak Władysław
336. Pfc. Walewski Stanisław
337. Pfc. Waliszewski Józef
338. Pfc. Warchoł-Wardow Andrzej
339. Pfc. Wąsowski Stanisław
340. Pfc. Więcek Józef
341. Pfc. Widziński Gustaw
342. Pfc. Wieleba Józef
343. Pfc. Wiszniewski
344. Pfc. Wójcik Wawrzyniec
345. Pfc. Wojtalas Wojciech
346. Cpl. Wołek Franciszek
347. Pfc. Wrobny Franciszek
348. Pfc. Wasyl Leopan
349. Pfc. Wolsztein Judka
350. Pfc. Wacławski Michał
351. Pfc. Wójcik Michał
352. Pfc. Woliński Wacław
353. Pfc. Wandrowski
354. Sgt. Woźniak Stanisław
355. Pfc. Wasilewski Kazimierz
356. Pfc. Walkowiak Franciszek
357. Pfc. Wolski Jakób
358. Pfc. Wilucek Józef
359. Pfc. Wronowski Bolesław
360. Pfc. Wrzos Piotr
361. Pfc. Wydra Wawrzyniec
362. Pfc. Zając Michał
363. Pfc. Zalewski Stanisław
364. Pfc. Zawadzki Wacław
365. Pfc. Żelazo Jan

366. Pfc. Zięba Stanisław
367. Pfc. Zilberszeer Chaim
368. Pfc. Zubowski Łukasz
369. Pfc. Zita Bolesław
370. Pfc. Zmysłowski Władysław
370. [sic] Pfc. Zdrojewski Józef
372. Pfc. Znamiec Józef
373. Pfc. Zgórski Józef
374. Pfc. Zdziebko Jan
375. Pfc. Zalcman Szmul
376. Pfc. Złotucha Wincenty
377. Pfc. Zienkiewicz Franciszek
378. Pfc. Złótkowski Wacław
379. Pfc. Pietrusik Marcin
380. Pfc. Płazik Stanisław
381. Pfc. Pudłowski Natal
382. Pfc. Pyrz Tomasz
383. Cpl. Radek Wojciech
384. Pfc. Resman Otto
385. Pfc. Rochorczyk Paweł
386. Pfc. Rezenbaum Josek
387. Pfc. Rybnowski Jan
388. Pfc. Topolewski
389. Pfc. Flak Adam
390. Pfc. Mowak Józef
391. Pfc. Kisiel Kazimierz

In addition to those named above, the regiment numbered among the list of the fallen 162 men whose surnames it could not establish.

The number of wounded in the regiment: 29 officers, 101 junior officers, 573 men.

Poisoned by gas in France: 2 officers, 4 junior officers, 98 men.

A common grave for all those who fell on 15 July 1918 is located at Jonchery (near Souain) and at Camp Chermont, near Châlons sur Marne.

A common grave for the men of 11th Company who fell on 29 May 1920 is located at Plisków in Ukraine, and for 4th Company at Annówka in Ukraine.

In Kuszlin on the Horynka (Krzemieniec county) is a common grave of several dozen men of 2nd Battalion, and at Włodzimierz Wołyński for the staff battalion (platoon of pioneers) who fell in a group during the construction of the footbridge.

LIST OF THOSE DECORATED WITH THE SILVER CROSS OF THE ORDER "VIRTUTI MILITARI" 5TH CLASS

1. Cpl. Arend Zygmunt
2. † 2nd Lt. Bauer Franciszek
3. † 2nd Lt. Bartman Antoni
4. Pfc. Bekta Jan
5. Sgt. Białous Edward
6. Sgt. Biedka Antoni
7. † 2nd Lt. Czerwonka Ludwik
8. † 2nd Lt. Czupreta Henryk
9. † 2nd Lt. Chwałkowski Lucjan
10. Cpl. Chmielewski Wincenty
11. Pfc. Cichocki Stanisław
12. Pfc. Daniel Antoni
13. Sgt. Delikowski Stefan
14. Master Sgt. Fonder Filip
15. Cpl. Fuśniak Franciszek
16. Pfc. Gawroński Jan
17. Pfc. Gawryłowicz Piotr
18. 2nd Lt. Górecki Franciszek
19. Major Grodzki Stanisław
20. Major of the French Army Haciski Benedykt
21. † Sgt. Inglod Jan

22. Cpl. Jarmusz Stanisław
23. Col. Jasieński Juljan
24. Capt. Rev. Jaworski Józef
25. Sgt. Kaźmierczak Stanisław
26. † Capt. Krzywkowski-Woliński Jan Marjan
27. 1st Lt. Kurcz Antoni
28. 1st Lt. Klich Franciszek
29. Sgt. Kwiatkowski Jan
30. Sgt. Kosiński Stanisław
31. Capt. Kozierowski Jan
32. Sgt. Langowski Teofil
33. 2nd Lt. Lewandowski Michał
34. 1st Lt. Ledoux Jerzy
35. 2nd Lt. Łączkowski Stanisław
36. Pfc. Matejek Antoni
37. Pfc. Mazurowski Stanisław
38. † 2nd Lt. Martynowicz Leonard
39. † 1st Lt. Michniewicz Jan
40. Capt. of the French Army Moittier
41. 1st Lt. Nowak Zygmunt
42. Lt. Col. Piekarski Wacław
43. Capt. Piątkowski Zygmunt
44. 2nd Lt. Paszkowski Antoni
45. Sgt. Pawlaczek Władysław
46. 1st Lt. Polak Nikodem
47. 1st Lt. Pela Jan
48. Sgt. Ordęga Józef
49. Sgt. Reychman Kazimierz
50. Cpl. Badek Wojciech
51. † Major Rodzyński Mieczysław
52. Cpl. Siwek Sergjusz
53. 1st Lt. Rolke Bruno
54. Pfc. Sobotka Aleksander
55. Master Sgt. Skrzetuski Stefan
56. 1st Lt. Szymański Antoni
57. Pfc. Trojanowski Ludwik
58. Cpl. Trzejowski Jan
59. Pfc. Urban Jan
60. † Pfc. Walkowski Franciszek
61. Pfc. Wilkowski Józef
62. Master Sgt. Walczak Paweł
63. † 1st Lt. Walaszczyk Walenty
64. Sgt. Wesołowski Jan
65. Major Rev. Więckowski Jan
66. † Pfc. Więcek Jan
67. † Pfc. Włodarski Michał
68. 1st Lt. Wójcik Franciszek
69. † 1st Lt. Wronowski Stanisław
70. Capt. Wyczółkowski Stefan
71. Pfc. Zawiła Albin
72. † 1st Lt. Zakrzewski Ignacy
73. 2nd Lt. Zakrzewski Michał
74. Pfc. Zygdalewicz Stefan

LIST OF THOSE DECORATED WITH THE CROSS OF VALOR

Decorated with the Cross of Valor were 47 officers, 1 officer cadet, 286 men. Among that number there were 6 decorated 4 times, 5 decorated 3 times, and 16 decorated twice.

For deeds on the French front, both in combat and not, the heroes of the regiment received numerous decorations granted by President Poincaré of the Republic of France.

KNIGHTS OF THE LEGION OF HONOR

1. 1st Lt. Bukowski Emil
2. † 2nd Lt. Chwałkowski Lucjan
3. Major Haciski Benedykt
4. 1st Lt. Kozierowski Jan
5. Capt. Krasiński
6. Lt. Col. Korszyn-Osmolowski

7. Lt. Col. Piekarski Wacław
8. † Capt. Rodzyński Mieczysław
9. † Capt. Tkaczuk Józef
10. Sgt. Olszewski

3 officers and 8 men were decorated with the Military Medal (Medaille Militaire).

In addition, by orders of the commanders of 4th Division of the 21st French Corps, the 170th French Infantry Division, 17th French Infantry Regiment, the 7th and 53rd Battalions of the Alpine Riflemen, and the 20th Battalion of Infantry Riflemen of the 1st Infantry Division, the following were honored: 47 officers, 13 officer cadets, and 205 men. Of them, one, Capt. Mieczysław Rodzyński of the *Bajończyk* Legion, was honored 11 times; one was honored six times; 3 were honored five times; 2 were honored four times; 6 were honored three times; and 48 were honored twice.

Independently of individual decorations of soldiers of the regiment, due to collective heroic feats on the French front, subunits of the regiment were singled out for mention in dispatches of the abovementioned commands, entitling them to receive special badges from the French government, called the *Fanion*. The Polish Army in France received only 2 of these badges. The 43rd Regiment received both these honors, to wit:

> The Fanion of 2nd Battalion and 5th Company is a rectangular banner measuring 50 x 60 cm. On one side, held in national colors, on a field of amaranthine, a white eagle is embroidered, surrounded by the motto "Faith and Fatherland, 1918": under the eagle is pinned the Croix de Guerre. On the other side, which is red, we see the unit's emblem. The emblem's fabric is fastened to the staff, finished with a silver nail and the initials "R. F.," to which a ribbon is fastened with a knot of the colors of the Croix de Guerre. The Fanion is carried on a rifle, attached to the bayonet.

In addition the regiment received 6 commendations from the French authorities for battles in France and 2 commendations for battles in Poland.

MILITARY BOOTY

During the course of its wartime activities the regiment took: 7 cannons, 4 caissons, 55 heavy machine guns, of which 7 were *taczanki [horse-drawn carts with machine guns used by the Soviet military]*, and 334 prisoners, a great many rifles and a sizable amount of military material: and the total is increased significantly by the following, captured by General Rómmel's cavalry corps: 3,500 prisoners, 6 cannons, and the standards of the 12th Soviet Division.

Tadeusz Kwaśniewski

*Born October 29, 1892, Warszawa, Poland
Died June 1967, Chicago, Illinois, U.S.A.*

OUTLINE OF THE WARTIME HISTORY OF THE 44TH REGIMENT OF EASTERN FRONTIER RIFLEMEN

AS COMMISSIONED BY THE MILITARY HISTORICAL OFFICE

compiled by

MAJOR STANISŁAW BOBROWSKI

WARSAW

1929

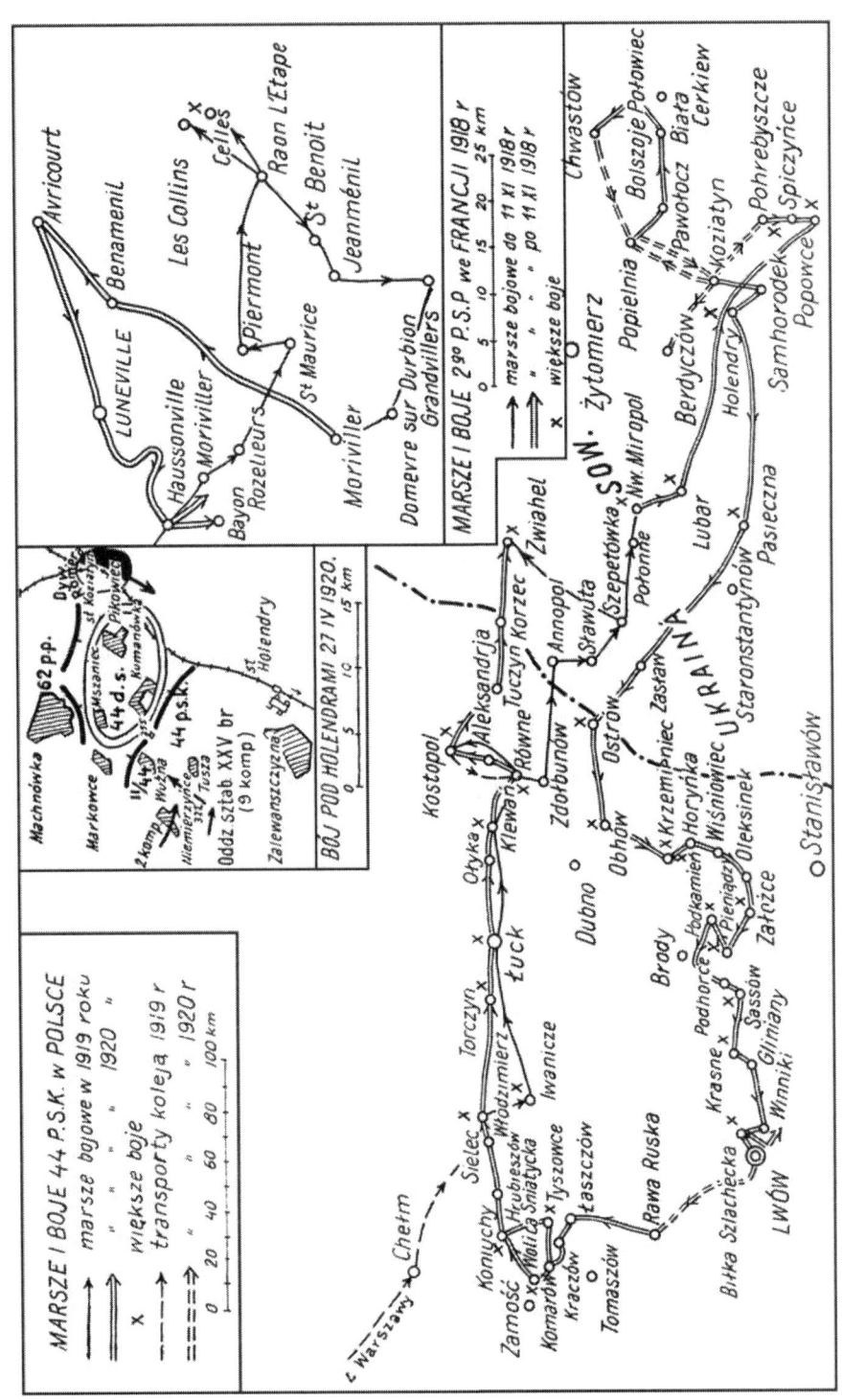

THE REGIMENT'S ORGANIZATION AND COMBAT IN FRANCE

THE POLISH ARMY IN FRANCE

The great war of the nations found not only a dense mass of our people in Poland, but also a large Polish emigrant community in the nations of Western Europe and beyond the Ocean.

Wherever Polish hearts were beating—whether in the widely scattered centers of emigration in Europe or among the compact groupings of Poles in the United States of North America, or on the lonely farms of Brazil's Paraná—the call of Polish blood stirred everywhere, striving spontaneously to organize, to create an armed force ready to go to war for the freedom and political independence of Poland. The great ideal of restoring to life a free Poland, brought before the eyes of the whole world by the martial deeds of Józef Piłsudski, was recognized by the whole anti-German coalition.

Coming soon after the declarations of other nations, the decree of the President of the Republic of France, Raymond Poincaré, on 4 June 1917 created an autonomous Polish Army in France.

That army, representing Poland in the camp of the nations allied for battle against Germany, was, like other Polish formations, proof that the Polish Nation still existed. The political direction of that army was entrusted to the National Committee, which was created later.

By virtue of the decree of 4 June 1917 a French-Polish Military Mission was formed, headed by General Archinard, and began to make recruiting plans, sending emissaries to the recruiting centers that already existed in the United States of North America, Holland, England, Brazil, and so forth. The recruiting effort was in especially full swing in the United States among the organized Polish Falcons, headed by its President, Dr. Starzyński. The Falcon volunteers would be the base, numerically speaking, and the main force of the Polish Army in France. Not uncommon were instances in which father and son reported and served in the same company.

The French-Polish Military Mission developed broad-based activity that resulted in the formation of a whole series of Polish regiments in France. It was there that, among others, the 2nd Regiment of Polish Riflemen was formed, renamed the 2nd Regiment of Infantry Riflemen, and in time given its current name of 44th Regiment of Eastern Frontier Riflemen.

2ND REGIMENT OF POLISH RIFLEMEN

Organization. Shortly after publication of the decree by the President of the Republic of France, the first officers and men arrived at Camp Sille le Guillaume, discharged from the French army. Later prisoners of war came: former German soldiers, soldiers from the Russian army (the Russian Expeditionary Corps in France and Thessaloniki), as well as Polish volunteers from the various countries of Europe. They were the first cadres, which, once trained, were divided into groups and sent to the individual camps as nuclei for battalions. The nucleus of the future 2nd Regiment of Infantry Riflemen, not yet comprising a complete regimental organizational unit, was assigned to Camps Mayenne and Mamers. They were subordinate to the camp's commander, Major Jagniątowski, at Sille le Guillaume; in these camps the arrival of volunteers from America was awaited.

The first commander of the regiment's cadres was a Pole, Major Grabiński, an officer of the French army and a descendant of an Insurrectionist (the author of *Przepisy dla powstańców 1863 roku* ["Regulations for the 1863 Insurrectionists]), a Knight of the Legion of Honor, which he received for the battle at Verdun, an ardent Polish patriot and a good organizer.

On 7 February 1918 the first transport of Poles from America arrived at Mamers; they had arrived at the port of Le Havre after boarding the Russian ship *Kursk* in the port of Halifax, undergoing a voyage of eleven days and combat with German submarines. From these volunteers, on that same day, 1st and 2nd Battalions were created. On 16 February 1st Battalion was split off from the regiment and became the nucleus of the 3rd Regiment of Infantry Riflemen (presently the 45th Regiment of Eastern Frontier Riflemen).

A second transport composed of volunteers who boarded the ship *Czar* in New York arrived at Mayenne by way of the French port of Brest on 28 February 1918.

From this transport 3rd Battalion was created, as well as the nucleus of the regiment's administrative staff. Finally on 1 March 1918 a third transport arrived, on the ship *Czaritza*, from which 1st Battalion was created anew, as well as the regiment's staff company, and 3rd Battalion was supplemented with the remaining volunteers.

At the start of March 1918 the battalions were concentrated at Mayenne. Major Grabiński took command of them, at the same time retaining command of 1st Battalion. The final formation of the regiment took place on 13 March 1918. On that day the regimental staff and headquarters were created. The regiment became organizationally and tactically independent from the camp at Sille le Guillaume, and from then on was directly subordinate to the French-Polish Military Mission in Paris and French command of the 5th territorial district.

In all the regiment numbered 66 officers (Poles and French), around 460 junior officers, and 2,500 men. Among the American volunteers many could not even speak Polish. The soldiers consisted of extremely diverse elements. Significant differences also became evident in regard to military training, which had a negative effect on the regiment's uniformity. Due to the high level of patriotic feeling and intense organizational work, all these differences were obliterated and a regimental coherence was achieved that, when later exposed to difficult labors and combat, proved to be indestructible. In terms of budget the regiment was organized as a French infantry unit. The exterior differences were decorations on the uniforms, that is: four-cornered caps, Polish eagles on the shoulder-straps, and in time also little eagles on the buttons. Every officer wore a Jagiellonian-style Polish eagle as a decoration on the breast of his jacket, and a similar little eagle on the cap. The color of the uniform was taken from that of the French army, and it was from this that the name "blue soldiers" came later.

As of 3 April 1918 command of the regiment was assumed by Col. Ryszard Edward Berecki, a French career officer, the descendant of an Insurrectionist (he is the proud possessor of the order *Virtuti militari* as an honorary legacy of his grandfather). Under Col. Berecki's command the regiment achieved a high level of training. A great aid to training efforts was the eventual issuing of the French regulations in Polish.

On 5 April 1918 the regiment proceeded to Châteauneuf sur Loire, where it was supplemented with officers and men returning from courses (on using heavy machine guns, hand machine guns, pioneers, communications, and so forth). The cadre that brought the regiment up to its full numbers was the so-called "Division Training Center" ("C.I.D." for short), which would send reinforcements as needed upon the commander's request. This center performed the function of reserve battalion.

Worthy of special attention is the cultural and educational organization in the regiment. The regiment's director of education was Rev. Wojcieszczuk, regimental chaplain, to whom the educational officers of the battalions and companies were subordinate. At places where the battalions stayed there were well-organized common rooms, set up with considerable help from the Y.M.C.A. A weekly called *Polak,* edited especially for the army, provided information on the situation in Poland.

The relationship between the local populace and the regiment's soldiers was very cordial and favorable. The people of every village where the regiment was quartered gave the riflemen a pleasant reception, which brought no small comfort to the soldiers, who were yearning for Poland.

Presentation of the standard. On 22 June 1918 in Dienville the regiment received a standard offered by the town of Verdun. The standard was presented to the regiment's commander, Col. Berecki, by the President of the Republic of France, Poincaré, in the presence of the President of the National Committee in Paris, Roman Dmowski. On 19 August 1918 the regiment came under the command of the 1st Polish Division, the staff of which was created from the reformed 63rd Division of the French Infantry. The Polish Division was incorporated into the 20th Corps, under the commander of 4th Army, General Gauroud [*sic*].

The "Parade of Nations" in Paris. On 14 July 1918 2nd Battalion had the honor of taking part in the Parade of Nations in Paris, during festivities of France's holiday. On this occasion the Battalion was the subject of a general ovation from French society. The ranks of the Polish Army paraded past the Arc de Triomphe and on the wide Champs Élysées, sprinkled with flowers. Their participation in the parade lives to this day in the memory of every soldier of the regiment, and fills him with pride. For at a time when Poland groaned in Prussian enslavement, by marching along with units of the French, English, Belgian, Italian, and American armies, the soldier of the regiment demonstrated the undeniable independence of his Fatherland.

The swearing in of General Haller. During its stay in Haussonville, on 6 October 1918, the regiment was present during the ceremonial swearing in of General Józef Haller as commander in chief of the Polish Army in France.

The appearance on the fields of Haussonville on the Moselle of General Józef Haller, who became a symbol of armed protest for Poles abroad against Prussian violence, aroused the enthusiasm and filled the hearts of the soldiers with joy. This tireless general, after leaving the Second Brigade of the Polish Legions after it was crushed by the Germans at Kaniów, crossed into Austria and sneaked through Soviet Russia and Murmansk to France, to lead the Polish army being created there into battle with the Fatherland's ancient enemy at a time when the Legions were being disbanded in Poland and the future Commander in Chief and Chief of State, Marshal Józef Piłsudski, was being taken prisoner by the Germans at Magdeburg.

BAPTISM OF FIRE IN THE VOSGES MOUNTAINS

By direct command to the army from General Józef Haller, as Commander in Chief of the Polish armed forces fighting on the side of the coalition, the regiment became part of 10th Corp of General Mangin's 7th Army. On 14 October 1918 it proceeded to Raon l'Etape, from which on 17 and 18 October 1918 the 1st and 2nd Battalions relieved the American 324th Infantry Regiment in the sub-sectors "de la Plaine" and "Croix Charpentiers" near the town of Celles. The position taken up by the regiment stretched along the forested Vosges mountains; the foreground had been cleared for the space of a kilometer and destroyed by artillery fire and mines. The German trenches were located a distance of about 500 meters from the regiment's position. The position was fortified, with observation points and concrete machine gun nests. In addition to the regiment's automatic weapons, *mitrailleuse* located in the sector remained fixed, with no change in position. The regiment's position was bordered on the north by units of the 8th French Army, on the south by the 3rd Regiment of the 1st Polish Division.

The Germans behaved passively, limiting themselves to artillery and machine gun fire, and to patrols. On the regiment's side very energetic reconnaissance was carried out. One of the patrols under the command of 1st Lt. Wiącek penetrated to the German trenches, inflicting losses on the enemy with hand grenades, and took prisoners. On this patrol Pvt. Ciszałowicz distinguished himself.

There were no particularly important events during the regiment's stay in the "de la Plaine" sub-sector. But the young soldier had the chance to become at least partially familiar with combat, and through the frequent sorties and patrols became accustomed to battle and reconnaissance. The Germans, after making attempts to incite the Poles to come over to their side, and after patrols' unsuccessful sorties, limited themselves to artillery fire. On 30 October 1918 the regiment's 1st Battalion was relieved at its position by 3rd Battalion. During the regiment's stay on the German front, in the "de la Plaine" sub-sector, the regiment lost two men killed and 11 wounded.

On 4 November 1918 the regiment was relieved at its position by units of the 60th French Infantry Division. During the change 4 men were wounded. 1st Battalion departed, relieved by 81st Battalion, and 3rd Battalion by the 223rd Battalion of the French Infantry Regiment.

THE FINAL PERIOD OF THE STAY IN FRANCE

The commander in chief of the coalition armies, Marshal Foch, wishing to defeat the German army for good, planned to break through the German front with an attack of the right flank of the French front on Metz, and by circling to the south to cut off the German army fighting in France from its homeland, thus finally destroying it. The 1st Polish Division was designated for this decisive blow as one of 30 divisions comprising the attacking hammer in the hands of the famed commander of the 8th French Army, General Mangin. The division was to attack the "General Hessler" stronghold in the area of the Metz fortress, as the second wave of the general attack, behind the color division advancing in the first wave. The regiment boarded trucks in Moriville and set out toward Metz.

On 11 November 1918 the call of trumpets announcing the armistice that meant victory for the coalition and surrender of the Germans found the regiment en route in the trucks. Turning back, the regiment was quartered in Moriville, where along with the armies of the coalition it celebrated the day of victory for the Allied armies, and thereby the day of Poland's resurrection. For on that day the Poles, taking advantage of the revolution in Germany and collapse of the army, disarmed the German garrisons. The Fatherland finally broke free of its shackles and returned to free life after a century and a half of enslavement.

From Moriville the regiment proceeded to Avricourt, where the entire 1st Polish Division was gathered with the assignment of marching to occupy Alsace. Due to cancellation of the occupation, however, the regiment proceeded to Haussonville. Here a partial reorganization of the regiment ensued; in January 1919 the regiment was assigned the 2nd Battalion of the 1st Dąbrowski Infantry Regiment, organized in Italy in Sana [sic, Santa] Maria Capua Vetere, near Naples, of men from Małopolska [Little Poland], former soldiers of the Austrian army. In exchange for the battalion the regiment assigned the same number of instructors and privates to serve as the nucleus for 2nd Division. At the same time as the arrival of the reinforcements from Italy, the regiment was reorganized in a ternary system, which decreased the number of platoons in the riflemen's companies from the existing four to three.

The regiment's final reorganization before departure for Poland was as follows: the regiment's staff—the commanding officer, Col. Grabiński, the staff company, which included special units and services—three battalions of three companies each of riflemen, and one of *mitrailleuse* (C.K.M.). The regiment, trained, organized and well-integrated, comprised a component of the 1st Polish Division, the first autonomous corps of the Polish Army in France. The French General Bernard accompanied the division to Poland.

On 13 April 1919 the regiment set out across Germany for Poland, to reinforce other units of the Polish army being created in the homeland amid battle, shielding with their youthful breasts the resurrected Poland.

THE REGIMENT'S ARRIVAL IN POLAND

THE OFFENSIVE IN VOLHYNIA

From St. Dizier, where the 1st Polish Division set out for the homeland and the regiment received a farewell ovation, the regiment traveled in loose companies, escorting provisions and ammunition for the division during the trip through Germany. By 26 April 1919 the regiment was in Chełm.

To the dispatch sent by General Haller to the Chief of State, Marshal Józef Piłsudski, on the occasion of the army's setting foot on its native soil, the Chief of State replied:

> To General Haller: It was a pleasure for me, in Wilno, newly taken, to receive from you at the western edge of Poland the dispatch on your arrival in the country. In my name please convey to the officers and soldiers under you my joy at their arrival in their Homeland, and the certainty that like every true soldier of Poland, they will defend victoriously the threatened borders of our country.
>
> Józef Piłsudski

General Haller, publishing the above dispatch in his Order No. 1, commanded at the same time that the officers and men comply with the general regulations of the country's army, and his order ended thus: "We are finally on our own soil, our Polish soil: those who were born in foreign lands; those who left an oppressed and torn Poland for work or for fortune; those who, hidden in a foreign uniform, had to go fight in it on behalf of foreign enemies' banners; Legionnaires concentrated after so much wandering in exile under the beloved standard, taken with blood; and finally those who are youngest, new recruits recently summoned to the ranks by the duty of a soldier and citizen of a Free Republic. Remember that today there are no differences, there is one Polish Soldier, whose precious blood traces the borders of the Nation. And although a different uniform may cover you, the spirit must be the same, because for us a comrade in arms or a colleague is every man belonging to the Polish Army and bearing the White Eagle as his emblem."

Organizationally the regiment changed to the extent that it received the name "2nd Regiment of Infantry Riflemen." As provided by the treaty with the French, the army of General Haller was to preserve independent organization modeled after the French example for half a year.

At that time in Poland almost all the borders of the nation, either being defended or being secured by fighting, were armed. To the west were the Czech and German fronts; to the east, on the northern sector, the Polish forces under the personal command of the Commander in Chief, Marshal Józef Piłsudski, had liberated Wilno. Lwów awaited assistance, as did all of eastern Małopolska; and Volhynia, which soon would twice be the scene of the regiment's battles, was a theater of combat for the Ukrainian army of Petlura, being pressed by Russian forces, both those of the Soviets and also those of Denikin. In these conditions the division was to set out, in the first days of May 1919, from Włodzimierz as the departure base for combat activities, with the goal of clearing out the western part of Volhynia and setting up a base on the Styr river.

THE CAPTURE OF ŁUCK

In connection with the general offensive on the southeastern front, which was assigned the task of liberating eastern Małopolska, on 12 May 1919 at

1800 hours the regiment set out in two columns. The column of the regiment's commander, Lt. Col. Grabiński, consisting of 1st Battalion, one battery of the 1st Artillery Regiment of General Haller's Army, and a platoon of divisional cavalry, was on the right, passing through Nowosiółki, Rusinowo, Zabołotowce. The left column, under the command of Capt. Prugar-Ketling, consisted of his 3rd Battalion and one battery, passing through Zimno, Bubnów, Janiewicze and Iwanicze. 2nd Battalion, under the command of Major Lawicz-Liszka, was given to General Karnicki's group, in action from Kowel to Łuck.

1st and 3rd Battalions received their baptism of fire in Poland during skirmishes in Zabołotowce and Iwanicze. The Ukrainian units facing them were too weak to put up resistance for very long. A major event in this action was the battle for Iwanicze station, which was taken by a flanking maneuver of 3rd Company. After minor skirmishes in Baranie Perytoki and Świniuchy, both columns combined to reach the Styr river and took up positions south of Łuck to Topule inclusive. During the march through Błudów the regiment spotted a sentry with a weapon who called to mind the legendary Napoleonic sentry. The Ukrainian stood there with his rifle on his shoulder, paying no attention at all to the approaching Polish army. When told to hand over his weapon, he stated that he had been posted there at an explosives magazine several days earlier, and he would not give up his weapon until another sentry replaced him—which the regiment proceeded to do.

2nd Battalion, in action with General Karnicki's group, experienced a soldier's joy at the fact that their baptism of fire on Polish soil was combined with the assignment of a frontal stroke from Krasne to Łuck and the taking of that city. Despite sturdy defense in positions favorable for the enemy, the battalion soon accomplished the assignment entrusted to them. The battalion purchased the taking of this beautiful city at the price of the death of 8 men, in whose burial the local populace participated in large numbers.

The battalion remained in Łuck as a reserve for General Karnicki's group. Taking up positions along the line of the Styr, the regiment did not encounter the enemy. The remains of the Ukrainian army, under pressure from the approaching Soviet forces, voluntarily came over to the Polish side. In connection with the departure of the 3rd Regiment of Riflemen for the German front, on 26 May 1919 the regiment took over defense of Łuck, organizing resistance points at the bridgehead with 1st and 2nd Battalions. 3rd Battalion, relieved by the 1st Regiment of Riflemen, remained in Łuck as a mobile reserve, the exploitation of which was needed for the 69-kilometer defensive sector assigned to it. 3rd Battalion returned from near Stanisławczyk, where it was active on the extreme right flank of the division in communication with the 1st Regiment of Riflemen.

By 1 June 1919 the first units of the Soviet armies, concentrated with their main forces in Równe, appeared in the foreground of Łuck in the area of Palcza and Chorłupy.

SORTIE ON RÓWNE

To prevent the Soviet armies from concentrating in Równe, a railway junction for the Kiev–Warsaw and Lwów–Wilno lines, and for the purpose of destroying the railroad equipment, the regiment conducted a sortie from Łuck with a column consisting of 2nd and 3rd Battalions, two batteries of the 1st Artillery Regiment, and one squadron of the divisional cavalry, in conjunction with the cavalry of Major Jaworski and an armored train. The sortie, conducted on the 8th and 9th of June, reached the old Russian forts of Równe after bloody combat, victorious for the regiment. At fort No. 1 (Obarów), 3 kilometers from the city, 3rd Battalion fought a heavy battle, lasting from 1120 to 1300 hours. A continual supply of new Soviet reinforcements, the battalion's using up all its ammunition, and a lack of communication with Major Jaworski's cavalry caused a retreat, which was held in perfect order, through Klewań to Łuck, without pressure on the part of the enemy. At the same time as the retreat began, the regiment's commander received the following order from division: "Enemy warned of the operation at Równe. You must retreat and take up your original positions once more." In action, and especially in the battle for fort 1, the regiment lost the following killed: 1st Lt. Urbaniak, an American citizen, 6 men; wounded, 22 men and 5 horses. The regiment captured a field cannon and 3 heavy machine guns, as well as more than a dozen prisoners. According to information gathered later, such a bloody toll for the sortie was exacted by the Russians' bringing up several transports of reinforcements in the direction of Sarny during the night of the 8th and 9th of June. At the same time as the activity in Równe, a small Polish group, which included the 1st Riflemen's Company of the 2nd Regiment, made a show of force in the direction of Dubno. In this latter action 1st Lt. Seiler was wounded.

A fairly long stay at the Łuck bridgehead was utilized for intensive patrolling and clearing the foreground of Soviet foray units. In the second half of June the French officers who had been performing the duties of technical advisers left the unit; they included 1st Lt. Jasiński, Bernard, and many others. On 21 June Col. Grabiński handed over command of the regiment to Major Antoni Szylling, who led the regiment in all battles from then on, until the armistice.

OFFENSIVE AT RÓWNE

Battle on the Stubla. In August 1919 the Commander in Chief ordered an offensive in Volhynia, in which 1st Division was to take part under the command of General Bernard. The regiment was to secure the approach to Równe, the road to which was obstructed by the river Stubla, where Soviet forces had taken up positions favorable for defense in the hills, the approach to which from the west led through narrow causeways, defended with heavy machine gun fire and artillery. The defensive junction most difficult to overcome consisted of positions in Klewań, Bielów and Żuków, blocking the Łuck-Równe highway. It was on precisely this sector that Major Szylling personally led 2nd and 3rd Battalions into the attack on 11 August 1919, supported by the fire of four batteries of the 1st Artillery Regiment. The enemy, managing his numerous and powerful artillery and taking advantage of naturally advantageous defensive positions, blocked access across the bridges, causeways and marshy meadows to Klewań and Bielów with densely spread machine guns. So the moment the first small columns of the regiment came into view, the Russians began to shell them with dense and powerful artillery fire. 2nd Battalion charged along the Równe–Łuck road, and 3rd Battalion along the Bielów–Żuków road. Artillery paved the way with concentrated fire for 5th Company, attacking in the forefront of the fighting line, with 1st Lt. Wiącek. At the moment the attack began Major Szylling appeared on the road in the forefront of the line and led the foremost squads to the assault. At the sight of their regiment commander the soldiers competed with each other to be the first to cross the causeway. The attack's tempo was so swift and decisive that the enemy could not hold his favorable defensive positions. A twofold counterattack, supported by artillery, in the area of the Klewań railroad station ended with the enemy's final collapse.

In the attack on Klewań, led personally by the regiment's commander, the Soviet positions were taken which constituted the key to the gates of Równe; the losses were comparatively minor, 5 men killed and 20 wounded. 3rd Battalion with a daredevil blow against the causeway in Bielów, losing 2 men killed and 5 wounded, mastered the crossing, decisively throwing back the Soviet infantry, which, according to aerial information, collected in Broniki and Obarów. On 12 August 1919 3rd Battalion was forced to fight a pitched battle, and in a triumphant march shed blood on the hills of Broniki.

The Taking of Równe. 1st Battalion, acting independently from Łuck through Młynów as a southern column, cleared this terrain of weak Soviet units and joined up with the regiment on 12 August in Ponebel. Toward evening 1st Battalion relieved 3rd Battalion, which had been in the first assault, and attacked the Soviet infantry, which was attempting to put up pretty strong resistance at fort No. 1 at Obarów. During several hours' fighting at night the fort's crew, which had been blocking the entrance to Równe, was wiped out, and on 13 August, without any fighting, Równe was taken. The Polish front in Volhynia was based on the Słucz and Horyń rivers. To protect Równe from the north, the regiment proceeded to the region of Aleksandrja, and subsequently occupied the "Poniatowski" sub-sector from Bereźne to Horodyszcze, in communication on the left with 3rd Regiment, and on the right with 1st Regiment, organizing resistance centers manned in Jabłonne by 2nd Battalion, in Sieliszki by 3rd Battalion, and in Kostopol by 1st Battalion.

After being driven out of Równe the Soviet armies retreated to the east, and the regiment lost contact with them. In the foreground chaos developed, and there Ukrainians appeared who, pressed on the one side by Soviet forces and soon thereafter by Denikin's on the other, turned their arms against them, while they came to an agreement with Poland. The regiment took advantage of the ferment in the foreground, and the associated standstill in combat activities, to organize defensive positions.

Before the regiment's front line the cavalry was in action, the 4th and 5th Cavalry Brigades, observing a 30-kilometer security zone (established according to the agreement with the Ukrainians). 5th Company, assigned to 4th Brigade, organized a defensive junction for the 4th Cavalry Brigade in Horodnica.

Reorganization. On 1 September 1919 the final union occurred of General Haller's Army with the national army. The regiment adopted the system of regiments of the national army in terms of administration and financing, preserving their French training. Renamed the 44th Regiment of Eastern Frontier Riflemen, the regiment was part of the 25th Infantry Brigade, belonging organizationally to the 13th Infantry Division, the former 1st Infantry Division of General Haller's army. Command of the brigade was assumed by Col. Leon Pachucki, former commander of the 3rd Regiment of Riflemen, while the previous commander of the divisional infantry, Col. Ryszard Berecki, took command of the division. The previous "Division Training Center ("C.I.D.") ceased to exist. The regiment received a reserve battalion and Siedlce county as its recruiting territory. Of the liquidated C.I.D. the regiment received a company of riflemen, which was incorporated into 1st Battalion as 4th Company. The last French officer left Kostopol, an aide to the commander of 3rd Battalion, an emigrant's son, Capt. Dr. Jan Palewski, today a renowned lawyer in Paris.

At Olewsk. On 10 September 1919 the 1st Battalion proceeded to the region of Olewsk as part of Lt. Col. Trojanowski's group, with the assignment of defending the "Olewsk" sector. Here on 19 September the Soviet infantry cunningly unleashed an attack behind the smokescreen of people traveling to a church fair from the foreground to Olewsk. The battalion succeeded in repulsing the attack, losing, however, a large number of killed and wounded. From Olewsk the battalion, relieved on 26 September by units of the 4th Infantry Division, proceeded to Równe as reserve for the Volhynia front.

THE PERIOD OF WINTER COMBAT

ON THE LINE OF THE RIVERS HORYŃ, SŁUCZ AND CHOMORA

In connection with the general advance of the front that was to ensue, with the goal of making the river Słucz its base, the regiment proceeded to Tajkury, taking over from 3rd Battalion the Buhryń–Brodów sub-sector called "Poniatowski." 5th Company, after a month and a half at a position in Horodnica advanced 30 km., and then later at Annopol, was relieved by 43rd Regiment, and proceeded along with 2nd Battalion to Zdołbunów as the regiment's reserve, and simultaneously as the town's garrison. In the deep foreground Soviet foray units appeared. The Ukrainians held in their hands the Równe–Szepetówka–Połonne railroad track. In connection with the ordered offensive in Volhynia, with a goal of setting up base against the Słucz, the regiment proceeded on 29 September 1919 from the region of Tajkury to Annopol without encountering Soviet forces.

THE CAPTURE OF ZWIAHEL

1st Battalion—as part of the operational group of Col. Machewicz, commander of 43rd Regiment—was to attack Zwiahel from the southeast. On 30 September 1919, having unloaded at Kołodzianka, it skillfully forced the bridge over the Słucz at Hulsk by a surprise attack led by 1st Lt. Solon at the head of 3rd Company. After a short but bloody battle that same company, with a decisive blow on Jurówka, defended by 500 bayonets and 5 heavy machine guns of the 392nd Soviet Regiment, drove that regiment from a strong defensive position, taking prisoner 15 men and capturing 5 heavy machine guns.

In the attack on Jurówka the battalion suffered casualties as wounded, 2nd Lt. Kozieracki and 4 of the men. The enemy, driven northward by the battalion, deflected from the regiment's attacking 43rd Battalion and finally, decimated, fled eastward, surrendering Zwiahel to the Poles. In addition to the quick tempo of the attack, one can attribute the relatively small number of casualties, despite the strong defense, to a strong snowstorm, which did not let the Soviet forces take advantage of their fire power and gave the Poles a chance to conduct a flanking maneuver, which Capt. Rafał Zieleniewski, the battalion's commander, performed with the rest of the battalion.

BATTLES ON THE SŁUCZ

On 8 November 1919 the regiment proceeded from Annopol to the Sławuta area, to occupy the line of the river Chomora as per the agreement with Petlura's forces. After the final disappearance of the Ukrainian forces, whose remnants the 43rd Regiment disarmed and received in order to save them from slavery to Moscow, 44th Regiment organized defensive positions on the Słucz for the rather long winter period, positions stretching a distance of 50 km. from Baranówka to Lubar, with the main resistance point at Miropol. Soon the regiment had before it in this sector three opponents who were fighting each other. On the left flank the Soviet forces, before the center Petlura's forces, and on the right flank Denikin's forces. The regiment reacted to the Soviet army's appearance with a whole series of sorties, which, coming as they did during the period of discharging the American volunteers and assimilating recruited soldiers, provided the young recruit lacking combat experience with a lesson in fortitude and training in how to be a soldier.

In January the regiment began to receive reinforcements in the form of marching companies from the battalion's reserve 44th Regiment. Exhibition sorties were arranged for the young soldier on purpose, to get him used to the whistle of bullets and the method of using his weapon properly, while at the same time getting acquainted with the terrain. It was precisely this period of winter battles that would determine the regiment's strength and resistance during the retreat combat in 1920 from Ukraine to Lwów.

ATTACKS ON ROMANÓW

To anticipate the Soviet attack from Romanów upon Miropol, on 23 December 1919 1st Lt. Poźniak's group, as part of 2nd and 3rd Companies, with the support of the "Postrach" armored train and a squadron of cavalry from the region of Baranówka, attacked Romanów, defended by 500 bayonets of the 395th Soviet Infantry Regiment. The Soviet forces, intoxicated with their easy victory over Petlura's small army and news of Denikin's defeat at Berdyczów, put up very stiff resistance. Since they had numerical superiority over the attacking group of 1st Battalion, they unleashed counterattacks several times. The decisive attack of 2nd Company, led by 1st Lt. Kowalczyk, broke the Soviet defense and forced the Russians to withdraw from Romanów.

During the street battle 1st Lt. Kowalczyk fell, mortally wounded. The lack of a commander for the company, and the temporary confusion and reversal of fortune that resulted for the Poles, was remedied by the commander of a platoon of 2nd Company, Sgt. Jan Tarkowski, who struck with a reserve platoon against the enemy, who was attacking once more. The Soviet infantry abandoned Romanów in a panic and in disarray, and withdrew to Cudnów and Żytomierz. One heavy machine gun was captured, and 22 hand rifles: 30 Soviet bodies were counted. The Battalion's losses: 3 privates wounded, and one volunteer from America, the late 1st Lt. Kowalczyk, was buried. After performing their assignment the sortie group returned to Miropol. The sortie at Romanów, though it may not have played any great role in the winter campaign, nonetheless had great significance for morale.

On 25 December 1919 a new sortie was undertaken against Romanów by 3rd Battalion, under the command of Capt. Prugar-Ketling. But it was not to be that this brave commander could match himself against the Muscovites in Romanów, for at the sight of the battalion's approaching columns the enemy withdrew without a fight.

THE DEFENSE OF LUBAR

Lubar, taken by units of General Sawicki's 3rd Cavalry Brigade, fell on 2 January 1920 under pressure from the Soviet infantry, supported by several thousand newly recruited from local gangs. To eliminate the resultant gap in the front line and to take Lubar back, 2nd Battalion was sent, along with 8th battery of the 13th Artillery Regiment. After liberating the town the battalion's commander, Capt. Pieslak, organized its defense, and by 6 January had to hold back powerful attacks from a mass of several thousand. Although the enemy's units did not display any great combat value, their numbers did enable the enemy to encircle and temporarily cut off 5th and 7th Companies with the 8th Battery in Lubar from 6th Company and 5th Uhlan Regiment, occupying Korostkił [sic]. Capt. Pieslak held firm against the constant attacks, renewed all day on January 6, thanks to the infantry's decisive position and the effective fire of 8th Battery, firing directly from a distance of 800 meters. 1st Lt. Mikołajczyk-Małachowski, at the head of his 7th Company, counterattacked on Karań and forced the enemy's masses beyond the Słucz. 10th Company, sent from Połonne with a platoon of heavy machine guns, brought along ammunition for artillery and infantry and arrived at Lubar, breaking the ring besieging the valiant garrison at the moment when they began to run out of ammunition. Renewed attacks on the 7th and 8th of January were finally repulsed, and the demoralized masses of newly-recruited Soviet soldiers scattered, leaving the foreground thickly covered with bodies. 35 were taken prisoner, 2 heavy machine guns and a great many hand weapons were captured. Our own losses were insignificant.

THE COMMANDER IN CHIEF IN THE REGIMENT

On 9 January 1920 Major Antoni Szylling announced news of the victorious battles of 2nd Battalion at Lubar to the Head of State and Commander in Chief, Marshal Józef Piłsudski, who had arrived at Miropol to inspect the front. The Commander in Chief personally inspected the positions manned by 1st Battalion in Miropol, and then, after a parade by 1st Battalion and after reviewing the positions of 3rd Battalion in Połonne, he honored the regiment's officer corps with his presence at a banquet given in his honor at Połonne.

OTHER BATTLES NEAR LUBAR

As a result of the continuing inflow of Soviet forces in the foreground of the 13th Infantry Division, its new commander, General Romer, arranged to conduct deep sorties along the division's front, to clear out the foreground. In a sortie on Awratyn-Bratałów, conducted on 14 and 15 January by units of the 45th Regiment of Eastern Frontier Riflemen under the command of Col. Michał Bajer, a group of 1st Lt. Wiącek's comprising one and a half companies was in action on the right flank. The enemy holding Awratyn was driven back with heavy losses, while 1st Lt. Kwaśniewski and 8 men were wounded from the 44th Regiment.

Sorties at Prywitów, Wróblewka, Kamień and the neighboring villages lying before the regiment's front line were supported by the constantly valiant crews of the armored trains "Postrach" and "General Dowbór," as well as batteries of the 13th and 7th Field Artillery Regiments accompanying the sortie groups. During one of the sorties in the direction of Cudnów the Russians struck from the northeast at Miropol, defended only by a single company of 13th Sappers Battalion. This bold Soviet maneuver was checked by the fire of heavy machine guns from the small garrison of Miropol, and the returning sortie group finally cleared the foreground of the enemy.

SORTIE AT RAJCE-DRENNIKI

On 3 February a sortie group, under the command of Major Szylling, comprised of 5 infantry companies and a company of heavy machine guns, after taking Romanów as a departure base, struck in two columns on Rajce and Wróblewka, defended by the Soviets' 418th Infantry Regiment. Due to the fierce combat that developed in Rajce, held by 300 Soviet bayonets, the regiment's commander directed to this village an additional column that was supposed to attack Wróblewka.

During the entire sortie group's activities at Rajce, when 20 Muscovites unexpectedly charged it from the flank, Major Szylling attacked them, along with one mounted dispatch rider, PFC Śledziak. With his revolver he killed two Muscovites who were shooting at him and took 11 prisoners, driving the rest away. This feat of Major Szylling, done in view of the whole sortie group, had such an effect on the regiment's soldiers that the resistance of the "Plastuns," who could meet death with cold blood and total resignation, collapsed completely. 50 bodies lay on the field of battle, and 20 prisoners were taken, along with a great many handguns. The rest of the defenders, about 200 in strength, dispersed, throwing off even their overcoats and caps along the way, to lighten their load. In the sortie at Rajce the regiment had four men wounded, including 2nd Lt. Koziarowski.

Despite the regiment's very low numbers, approaching 40 officers and 1,600 men, as a result of demobilization and an outbreak of typhus and typhoid fever, the regiment's activity in patrolling and making sorties did not cease for a moment.

THE SOVIET MARCH OFFENSIVE

The Soviet armies scattered before the division's front belonged to the 12th Soviet Army, which in the second half of March 1920 received the assignment of taking Równe. This activity was to develop parallel with the 14th Army's offensive against Płoskirów.

Strong attacks in connection with the general Soviet offensive conducted on 19, 20, and 21 March against the regiment's positions at Miropol and Czartonja *[sic, almost certainly a typo for Czartorja]*, were broken against the men, calmly defending themselves, of well organized battalion resistance centers, built during the winter. These battles are mentioned in the following communiqué of the general staff (dated 21 March 1920):

> "After very strong artillery preparation, the enemy attacked with a force of 2 infantry regiments against the outskirts of Miropol. Our units, despite the enemy's numerical superiority and strong attack, repulsed the attack victoriously, and then switching to the counterattack, drove the enemy's forces off toward the east, taking several dozen prisoners and three machine guns."

On 27 March 1920 the regiment was relieved in the Miropol sector by the 59th Wielkopolska Infantry Regiment and proceeded to Połonne.

SORTIES AT BARANÓWKA, ROMANÓW, WRÓBLÓWKA

In order to clear out the foreground in the Baranówka–Miropol sector, on 1 April 1920 Major Szylling conducted a sortie with a group consisting of 1st and 2nd Battalions of 44th Regiment, 3rd Battalion of the 43rd Regiment of Eastern Frontier Riflemen, and a squadron of cavalry of Capt. of Horse Dilenjus with divisional cavalry.

In view of the spring thaws the group set out without artillery or mobile kitchens. Unimpeded by supply columns, it made quick marches and hit-and-run attacks. At daybreak 1st Lt. Wiącek crossed the bridge over the Słucz at Baranówka and took Zaboryce, defended by units of the 518th Regiment of Soviet

Riflemen. After the sortie group crossed to the eastern bank of the Słucz Major Szylling began pursuit through Rudnia, Bubnów and Rudzisko to Romanów. The group, divided into two columns, was to unite for joint action against Romanów, where Major Szylling expected stronger resistance. The squadron of Capt. of Horse Dilenjus took Bubnów with a beautifully executed charge, spreading panic at the very appearance of the Polish cavalry, supported directly from the flanks with the infantry column's heavy machine gun. The Soviet infantry—the 518th and 519th Regiments—under strong attack, had no time to organize resistance. Individual groups saved themselves by fleeing, upon which all their heavy machine guns, supply column, and the headquarters of both regiments fell into Polish hands. The Russians did not pull themselves together till they got to Romanów, after retreating more than 30 km. And even there, resistance was limited to firing their guns, seldom hitting anything, which showed how much the enemy was upset. The long series of "Maxims" sent their shells high over the heads of 1st Battalion, which was attacking with bravado. The "Plastuns," after giving up Romanów, tried to put up fiercer resistance in Wróblówka, to which they had been driven. From Romanów 3rd Battalion of the 43rd Regiment left for Miropol through Kozary. The rest of the group attacked Wróblówka. There the influx of new reinforcements for the enemy was evident, because the resistance was much firmer; but it could not hold back the momentum acquired in the day-long pursuit. After 2nd Battalion took Wróblówka, Major Szylling ordered a withdrawal, due to approaching nightfall.

On 2 April at three o'clock the regiment crossed the outpost line of the 59th Infantry Regiment in Miropol, and thereby ended its 24-hour sortie on the foreground, having covered over 60 km. on soggy roads. The regiment sustained no losses. As booty it took: 17 heavy machine guns, the supply columns and headquarters of the 518th and 519th Soviet Infantry Regiments, 3 kitchens with food, and 60 prisoners. The enemy withdrew, having left about 100 bodies on the field of battle, and did not trouble the regiment during its return past the standing defensive line in Miropol. After a two-week stay in Połonne the regiment proceeded to the Lubar region, which constituted the regiment's departure base for the Kiev offensive.

OFFENSIVE IN UKRAINE

The Commander in Chief, having taken the offensive in Volhynia and Podolia, set himself the following goals:
Political—to liberate Ukraine from the Soviet Russian yoke, and
Strategic—to anticipate the enemy, who, according to information received, was grouping on the southern front. This information also said that the extended front was weakly manned—as he had confirmed personally during his inspection

of, among others, the 44th Regiment's sector in Miropol—and would not be strong enough to hold back inroads into the Polish positions.

Breaking the Soviet Front. The order for the offensive found the regiment in a position near Lubar and Prywalówka. The regiment was part of General Listowski's 2nd Army. In action on the left flank of the division, the regiment was to begin an offensive in communication with units of the 15th Infantry Division, in combat north of the regiment. Striking the first blow, on the evening of 24 April, was the lot of 3rd Battalion, attacking a position in front of the village of Filińcy. After a fierce two-hour battle the "Galician Sich Riflemen," fighting on the Russian side, and units of the 44th Soviet Division abandoned their position, which was partially surrounded with barbed wire, leaving 15 prisoners in the battalion's hands.

At daybreak on 25 April, 1st and 3rd Battalions, after a battle, took fortified enemy positions at Awratyn–Mały Bratałów.

Pursuit. The regiment's further offensive activities consisted of pursuit. As ordered, the regiment advanced by secure march along the axis to Krasnopol, patrolling its assigned zone of activity. Sporadically organized Soviet resistance, as at Motrunki and Mołoczki, was fought by companies of the regiment's advance guard, with support from the accompanying batteries of the 13th Eastern Frontier Field Artillery Regiment, at such a swift speed that deploying and attacking did not slow down the movement of the regiment's columns of main forces. Through Krasnopol, which companies of 2nd Battalion had taken, the regiment marched with the accompaniment of the sounds of an orchestra, which drew crowds of the inhabitants with its music. From Krasnopol it advanced as follows: 2nd Battalion as the regiment's northern column, with 9th Battery of the 13th Artillery Regiment; 2nd Company with 1st Lt. Mikuliński as a communications column, with 43rd Regiment; and the regiment's main force, with 7th and 8th Batteries, as the middle column. To speed up the pursuit and regain contact with the enemy, the columns used horses and carts requisitioned in neighboring villages. The middle unit with Major Szylling took the lead. The greatest marching effort came on 27 April 1920, when the regiment was to take and hold the localities Florjanówka and Michalin, located east of the railroad track from Koziatyn to the railroad station Holendry, more than 70 km. from Śmieła, where the regiment spent the night of 26–27 April. The middle column came under enemy fire in Wiszenka, which the enemy abandoned after a brief battle, leaving 23 prisoners, a supply column, and a heavy machine gun at the position.

The further march of the middle column took place under constant enemy fire up to Krzyżanówka, where 2 narrow-track trains with military material fell into the regiment's hands. The enemy, driven out, retreated to the northeast, there coming under the fire of Capt. Zieleniewski's northern column. The middle column, marching on Tucza and the colony Holendry, stayed ahead of the Soviet column, which stretched from Machnówka to Samhorodek. A mounted patrol, sent out with 1st Lt. Bobrowski to the Holendry railroad station, took prisoners: a staff officer of the 44th Soviet Division, and his escort, 6 men, and at the same time seized operational orders the Soviet officer had received, to evacuate the armored train from the Holendry station and to withdraw the 44th Soviet division to Samhorodek.

THE BATTLE AT HOLENDRY ON 27–28 APRIL 1920

Major Szylling, commander of the middle group, ordered the taking of old trenches straddled by companies of 1st Battalion on the Machnówka–Samhorodek road, near the colony of Holendry, with the front to the west. Doing so cut off the retreat path of the Soviet 44th Division, which was retreating to Samhorodek before the 15th Polish Infantry Division, which had taken Berdyczów. (And since Koziatyn had already been taken by a division of Gen. Romer's cavalry, the only road left for the 44th Soviet Division led to Samhorodek). The first prisoners from the cornered 44th Soviet Division, before the battle had begun, were two Soviet commissars, riding in a coach at the head of a column of 44th Division. They realized their actual situation only after having been taken prisoner. They had regarded the regiment's column as neighboring Soviet units sharing their common fate of retreat.

The first series of attacks by 1st Battalion, given around 1700 hours, on the Soviets' 44th Division, marching down the road as a deep column, forced the Soviet infantry to deploy. The enemy, surprised that its path was cut off, attacked companies of 1st and 3rd Battalions, which, despite a 70-km. forced march without rest or food, valiantly faced the enemy with bayonets. The Russian division's attack, conducted in large numbers, lasted till late at night. The bayonet combat became intense and fierce. 1st Lt. Solon with 3rd Company on the road itself stood up to the strongest pressure from the enemy masses. The fall of night only intensified the fierceness of the battle. The clash of weapons and cries of "Hurrah!", the moaning of the wounded and dying were drowned out by the booms of our own cannon and the enemy's. With one officer and 17 men, 1st Battalion's commander, Major Lawicz-Liszka, himself wounded three times and surrounded by overwhelming numbers, fought his way through each time, taking prisoners. Battle with firearms changed to hand-to-hand combat. In the Soviet ranks a desire was palpable to break through to the east at any cost. The enemy charged with loose groups of cavalrymen, as well as artilleryman on horses that had been cut free from pulling cannons and carts and harnessed. Among the mass of prisoners, there were soldiers from the Soviets' 58th Division as well, which some days before had been in the Żytomierz region. The critical moment arrived, the moment when the courage of the numerically inferior is not enough in the face of the masses' superiority. Individual nests of resistance, consisting of squads or platoons grouped around their commanders, defended themselves fiercely. Some riflemen, however, pushed back by the momentum of the charging cavalry, began to retreat individually to the artillery positions. 1st Lt. Sobieski and 2nd Lt. Zawadzki took their own lives, not wishing to be taken prisoner. Among the dead were found empty revolver magazines. Through an opening in the defensive position because of the losses incurred, Soviet units broke through and headed for Florjanówka.

Soon, however, a counterattack, led in the center of the defensive position by the regiment's commander, Major Szylling, and on the right flank by the regiment's adjutant, 1st Lt. Bobrowski, with the remnants of the men after they joined up with the defenders in the first line of combat, finally tipped the scales of victory in favor of the regiment. The appearance of the regiment's commander in extended order with a Russian rifle in his hand, taken from an enemy, lifted the defenders' spirits. On the field of battle lay 2 officers and 30 men; the bodies of the enemy numbered 123. Polish and Soviet soldiers, both stabbed with bayonets, lying as brothers in the majesty of death, still clutched their guns in their hands. The sight of their dying comrades did not overwhelm those still alive but still in danger, and did not lower their spirits. The soldier, revived by faith in victory, fighting in the dark of night, separated by more than a dozen kilometers from the rest of the Polish units, could rely only on his own strength. But faith in his moral superiority over the soldier of the Soviets' 44th Division sustained him, a faith the 44th Regiment had acquired during the winter combat at Miropol.

After driving the enemy back, companies of 1st and 2nd Battalions regrouped in a new defensive position near the settlement of Łopatyn. The enemy, driven westward by Major Szylling's column and surprised by Capt. Zieleniewski's approaching northern column, gathered in Pikowiec in a force of 3,000 bayonets, 14 cannon, and about 200 heavy machine guns. Through its representatives sent under flag of truce to the commander of 44th Regiment, it surrendered.

At dawn on 28 April Capt. Mikuliński, who had taken the station of Holendry with 2nd Company at 0200 hours, contacted the regiment, as did 2nd Battalion. Capt. Zieleniewski, the commander of that battalion, the most fortunate one in terms of quantity of booty, after the battles fought by his 2nd Battalion, could not participate in the decisive battle at Holendry. Forming the regiment's northern column, he had strong units of the Soviet infantry to deal with, stretching toward Machnówka. At 1030 hours he encountered the enemy at Jurówka; the enemy's strength was about 500 bayonets with one battery. After a battle lasting an hour and a half he defeated the Soviet infantry, capturing 4 field pieces, 3 heavy machine guns, and several dozen prisoners. This battle weakened the momentum of the advancing column, and furthermore the Russians held up the battalion, mounting counterattacks from Markowice, supported by strong artillery fire. So the battalion had to remain in the positions it had taken, and it was only by a well executed maneuver that it forced the enemy to give up two more cannons, 250 prisoners, and several heavy machine guns. Finally at 2020 hours the battalion was able to set out in the direction of the battle being fought by the regiment's main forces. After midnight, east of Wujna, the battalion encountered large numbers of Soviets, who, as it turned out later, were retreating from the colony of Holendry. Unable to mount a decisive attack due to the night's darkness, Capt. Zieleniewski limited himself to gunfire. In this battle Chief Warrant Officer Zieliński distinguished himself, marching in the battalion's advance guard.

During the skirmishes at night the mounted messengers deserve mention, as they rode with dispatches to the commander of 25th Infantry Brigade. In particular, Pvt. Józef Brzoza, sent from 2nd Battalion to the regiment but taken captive at Wujna, so skillfully misrepresented the regiment's position to the enemy that he led a whole enemy unit to be taken prisoner, 300 bayonets as well as 4 cannons and stock, by explaining to the enemy that they were surrounded on all sides and could not count on breaking through to the east. In fact there was no resistance and the Soviet units had an opportunity to surround 44th Regiment, grouped together at the settlement of Łopatyn. Private Płoski was taking dispatches to 25th Brigade when he was attacked at Tucza; he shot himself with his rifle and fell wounded from his horse. The enemy, satisfied with capturing the horse, left Private Płoski lying wounded on the ground. After regaining consciousness he crawled to the village, buried the dispatch, and toward morning reported to the regiment about the incident. The buried dispatch was found by a patrol sent out according to directions given by Private Płoski.

1st Lt. Roman Gutowski, defending the supply column with a platoon of 9th Company, was stopped by an attacking Soviet column's rifle fire at close range. He dispersed a whole Soviet infantry brigade with his platoon, thus, as it later turned out, making it easy for 43rd Regiment, attacking from the south, to capture them. After the regiment's arrival at Samhorodek the following was read to the soldiers:

M. p. 30 April 1920

Order

> The battles that lasted several days against superior enemy forces have ended with a splendid victory. On 27 April our regiment pulled ahead of our foe by a forced march and cut off the path of retreat for two Bolshevik divisions.

> We fought a battle lasting several hours, which ended in victory. Only small handfuls of our foes succeeded in breaking through our lines; the rest fell into our hands. Our regiment took over 4,000 prisoners, 14 cannons, around 200 *mitrailleuse*, an uncounted number of rifles, ammunition, and other spoils of war.
>
> Honor to those killed
>
> In the name of the service I thank all of you, officers, and men, for your courage, efforts, and heroic deeds.
>
> I commend all who deserve rewards. May the crosses of the *Virtuti militari* shine on the breasts of our heroes. In its victorious battles the 44th Regiment of Eastern Frontier Riflemen accepted the participation of 3rd Division of the 13th Eastern Frontier Field Artillery Regiment. For some time now batteries of the 3rd Division have worked along with the 44th Regiment of Eastern Frontier Riflemen, and as usual they have fulfilled their assignments splendidly. They threatened the enemy and supported our infantry.
>
> In the name of the service I thank the commander, officers and men for their work full of enthusiasm and dedication. The division commander will submit his recommendations for decorations, which I will support. The preceding order is to be read aloud in all units. Every soldier must know the glorious results of the battles we have fought.
>
> For conformity:
> (—) A. Szylling
> (—) Bobrowski   major and regiment commander
> 1st Lt. and adjutant

And General Staff communiqué No. 764 dated 1 May 1920 reads as follows:

> Our division, operating north of Winnica, with a splendid maneuver toward Kalinówka and the railroad station of Holendry cut off the retreating Bolshevik units, upon which units of one of our infantry regiments, cut off from the main forces, repelled all the enemy's counterattacks, refusing to be broken along the railroad track. The result of these battles was the utter defeat of the enemy.

62nd Infantry Regiment escorted the prisoners of war, advancing north of the regiment, while Pikowiec, where the Soviet forces regrouped after retreating from Holendry, lay within the sphere of activity of the 62nd Infantry Regiment. The 44th Regiment, as reserve for 2nd Army, proceeded to Koziatyn to secure the spoils of war. 3rd Battalion remained in the division as reserve for 25th Infantry Brigade.

Each year the regiment celebrates the memory of this difficult battle, fought victoriously on the steppes of Ukraine, as its holiday.

BATTLES WITH BUDIONNY'S MOUNTED FORCES*

(*Bellona, July 1921. Major S. G. Kurcyusz. "First meeting of the 13th Infantry Division with Budionny." *Tactical Studies*, vol. III, Captain of Horse S. G. Biernacki, "The Activity of Budionny's Mounted Forces.")

THE "NOWOCHWASTÓW" DEFENSIVE JUNCTION

After the Polish army took Kiev the Polish offensive halted. Preparation was made for defense in the position occupied.

3rd Battalion, reinforced with 12th Company, newly arrived from the reserve battalion, which at the time supplemented battalions to 4th Company, proceeded, in accordance with the order of 25th Brigade, to "form and rebuild the Nowochwastów defensive junction." In the battalion's 18-kilometer sector Capt. Bilmin organized company resistance points in Nowochwastów, Śniezna, Ozierna, and Samhorodek, and 6th Battery of 13th Artillery Regiment with 1st Lt. Ginter prepared a defensive fire plan. The rest of the regiment, after a short stay in Berdyczów, proceeded as reserve for the Ukrainian front to Pawołocza, memorable for the death there of "Jarema" Wiśniowiecki.

At the end of May, after bringing in new forces from the liquidated Denikin front, the Russians began a counteroffensive in Ukraine. The Soviet 12th Army, along with Budionny's 1st Mounted Army, was to corner the Polish 3rd Army in the Kiev area, and the weak 14th Army was to work in combination with mounted forces to tie up the Polish 6th Army. The Soviet command put great hope in victory on the mounted army, which had already contributed to final defeat of Denikin's volunteer army. The mounted army numbered 16,000 swords and was equipped with a large amount of battle gear.

First attack, 29 May. After crushing the Ukrainian insurgents Budionny approached the Polish front. On 29 May 3rd Battalion of 44th Regiment had to fight a difficult battle with the attacking 4th Soviet Cavalry Division. The battle, fought with unequal forces, ended in victory and holding the defended positions. The particularly strong attack at Nowochwastów forced 11th Company to withdraw individual combat groups temporarily. Cadet Świacki with his platoon, taking advantage of the park's good defensive position, repelled the attack directed at him and held out until the moment of the counterstroke conducted by the rest of the company. The result of this stubborn defense was holding our positions in their entirety. The first hours of the battle with cavalry had displayed the great advantages of interior regrouping and emphasized the need for skill in independent combat of the individual resistance nests.

30 May. During the course of 30 May the battalion continued to repel renewed attacks, skillfully taking advantage of fire from 6th Battery, directed at great distances, which held the enemy in check by not letting him recognize the smallness of the forces against him. Charges came to within 700 meters of the battery. Those who advanced that close, however, did not return, for the battalion's accurate heavy machine gun fire did an exemplary job of clearing the foreground. Unable to defend his whole position, Capt. Bilmin regrouped the battalion on the Śnieżna-Ozierna-Samhorodek resistance points, while 1st Battalion of 40th Infantry Regiment defended Nowochwastów. Along with its neighbor to the left, 7th Infantry Division, 4th Company of 27th Regiment arrived at Samhorodek to fortify the positions' defense, upon which the battalion itself resisted Budionny's sizable forces for two days.

31 May. On 31 May as well the battalion held up under powerful charges of the 11th Soviet Cavalry Division, freshly thrown into the battle. These strong attacks broke against the valiant breasts of the defenders. After hacking out gaps in Nowochwastów the Soviet cavalry charged the battalion's rear from the Morozówka region and pressed the command of 25th Brigade in Pohrebyszcze all day.

1 June. The battalion underwent hard times, compelled during the whole day of 1 June to repel a charge from three sides. In connection with the activity of General Sawicki's 3rd Cavalry Brigade, which had the task of eliminating the gap that had developed near Nowochwastów, on 2 June the battalion made a demonstration in the direction of that locality, cooperating in the counterattack with 1st Battalion of 19th Infantry Regiment, which had just arrived.

After the arrival at Ozierna on 4 June 1920 of six companies of 19th Regiment and one battery of 5th Field Artillery Regiment, 3rd Battalion of 44th Regiment proceeded to Pohrebyszcze, and organized the defense there. The period of battles fought by 3rd Battalion from 29 May to 4 June far from the regiment, almost always without communication with superior commanders due to its interruption by the enemy, in combat on all sides with large number of newer and newer forces of Budionny's cavalry, is one of the most illustrious pages of the battalion's combat history, under the command of Capt. Bilmin. The battalion held the sector entrusted to it, endured with superhuman efforts, and drove back an enemy immeasurably stronger than itself. The battalion's losses came to 10% of its forces.

THE COUNTERATTACK OF LT. COL. SZYLLING'S GROUP

During 3rd Battalion's victorious struggles at Nowochwastów and Ozierna, Budionny's 6th Division, after destroying two battalions of 50th Regiment, took Andruszówka, Spiczyńce and Dołżek. To eliminate this gap in the front and to attack the rear of Budionny's 6th Division, on 30 May the Regiment was transported from Chwastów to Pohrebyszcze, as Lt. Col. Antoni Szylling's sortie group, consisting of 1st and 2nd Battalions of 44th Regiment, 2nd Battalion of 40th Regiment, and 9th Battery of the 13th Artillery Regiment.

At 0600 hours on 31 May, directly after unloading on the railroad track, at the level of the village of Pedosy, the battalions attacked.

In the first echelon, 2nd Battalion of Capt. Zieleniewski attacked at Spiczyńce, supported by fire from 1st Lt. Adamczak's battery. 2nd Battalion of 40th Regiment and 1st Battalion of 44th Regiment advanced, grouped in further echelons. 2nd Battalion's bold attack was a beautiful sight. The extended orders and small columns grouped in the interior did not hold back, despite a hail of bullets and the boom of bursting cannon shells. The battalion's attack forced squadrons of the Soviets' 6th Cavalry Division to abandon Spiczyńce. After it passed through the village toward further action, the battalion's stroke was supported by 2nd Battalion of 40th Regiment. The battalions' combat with the Soviet squadrons charging in the open field, trying to reach the flank at any cost, brought the attackers complete victory. The strong will of the group's commander, the use of heavy fire from machine guns placed on dominating points, and the unusually accurate fire of 1st Lt. Adamczak's battery, supported the swiftly advancing companies. The terrain, well suited to cavalry combat, presented the enemy with the chance for a whole series of charges, always nipped in the bud, however, by the fire of the heavy machine guns and artillery. In the further attack on Dołżek and the taking of the Humań-Koziatyn railroad tracks, the Soviet resistance proved more decisive. The planned defense of the dismounted cavalry cost the valiant 2nd Battalion of 40th Regiment and the companies of 44th Regiment casualties in killed and wounded. The lightly wounded 1st Lt. Wiącek, Sosień, and Kwaśniewski all remained in the line, setting an example of devotion. (Amid the regiment's officer corps it was regarded as the highest honor to be wounded and yet remain in the line. A wounded officer received congratulations from his colleagues).

At 1700 hours Dołżek was taken. The Soviet resistance, supported in the latter period by two armored vehicles, collapsed under the blows of the infantry's steely ranks. From an order of the commander of 6th Cavalry Division that was captured in Spiczyńce the regiment's soldiers learned that the Cossacks did not recognize prisoners because they were forbidden to take any. In the further pursuit to Oczeretnia their fierceness and the tempo of their attacks increased. Toward evening on 31 May the enemy was pushed out of a gap that existed between 43rd and 45th Regiments, and he was driven back to 45th Regiment in Napadówka, where the final defeat was inflicted. Making with 43rd Regiment in Annówka and with 45th Regiment in Napadówka restored the continuity of the division's front. 9th Battery dispersed strong groups of cavalry in the Plisków region, and renewed attacks finally were broken in the infantry fire. And so the battles fought on 31 May were successful for the whole regiment. In the course of that day the regiment lost 16 men killed and 28 wounded. The enemy left 60 bodies on the field of battle.

The general position became clearer. Budionny, despite twice breaking through the division's front, was driven back to his starting positions in every instance. To restore the division's positions as of 28 May, in the general attack by 25th Infantry Brigade, the regiment attacked Andruszówka, defended by brigades of the 6th Cavalry Division. Leading the attack were 1st Battalion of 44th Regiment and 2nd Battalion of 40th Regiment. During the attack's course a charge was made against 1st Battalion's left flank, but broke against the fire of the battalion's heavy machine guns, advancing among the battalion and firing through the gaps. The cavalry's surprise attacks from the flank and the renewed attacks by dismounted cavalry did not check for a moment the frontal attack on the village. After receiving a dispatch on the enemy from an airman of the 7th Tadeusz Kościuszko Squadron, landing in the first line of attack, the squadrons were driven out of Andruszówka with an energetic blow, and they withdrew to Czerniawka, pursued by artillery fire.

The regiment's 2nd Battalion took Oczeretnia and sent 7th Company to Lipowiec to join up with 45th Regiment.

For these first victorious battles with Budionny, 13th Infantry Division was mentioned in dispatches of the Supreme Command (dated 31 May 1920, No. 5638/III): "…For 13th Infantry Division, which paralyzed the enemy's blows on an extended front so splendidly, the Commander in Chief expresses full recognition and praise. Announce this to all forces in Ukraine."

THE REGIMENT IN GENERAL KRAJOWSKI'S GROUP

Budionny broke the front between 6th and 3rd Armies. General Krajowski, the commander of 18th Infantry Division, received the assignment of attacking Ostróg and Równe from the Starokonstanynów region, for the purpose of joining up with 3rd Army.

On 2 July the 1st and 2nd Battalions and 4th Heavy Machine Gun Company, as Lt. Col. Szylling's group, came under the command of General Krajowski. 3rd Battalion remained in 13th Division. The regiment only took with it a strictly military supply column, loaded also with a supply of salt, coffee and sugar. Provisions were to be acquired by way of purchases.

On 17 July the regiment, as the advance guard of General Linde's brigade, took weakly-defended Ostróg, and thereby reached the deep rear of the enemy, who was fighting for Dubno and Równe. As per General Krajowski's order, a defensive junction was to be organized in Ostróg, and the regiment was to organize defense on the northern edge of the town, with the barracks as a base. Budionny's 14th Cavalry Division unleashed powerful cavalry charges against the regiment's position, advancing to within a grenade's throw of the defended position. The enemy prepared every attack with strong fire from machine guns and artillery brought up from near Równe. The attacks lasted till late at night. In the most critical moments of the battle Lt. Col. Szylling's personal courage and direction of the defense facilitated beating back the charge and holding the position. The regiment's spirit was not lowered by the fact that Ostróg was surrounded on all sides by the enemy.

The battle lasted till nightfall. The regiment lost 17 men killed, and among the wounded were 1st Lts. Sosień and Kwaśniewski, as well as 68 men.

At night the regiment, as the rearguard of 18th Infantry Division, withdrew from Ostróg while in contact with the enemy and proceeded to Wesołówka near Krzemieniec, fighting along the way in Piewce, Nagierany, and Lisznia. From Wesołówka on 11 July it joined 10th Infantry Brigade in Krzemieniec, which had been there without any communications with any Polish units. So General Krajowski's group continued to be suspended in space, surrounded on all sides by the Soviet cavalry.

From Wesołówka after a fierce battle the regiment proceeded to Krzemieniec, from which, by order of the commander of 6th Army, General Romer, personally given during an inspection of the front, the regiment headed south to join with 13th Infantry Division in the region of Horynka, with General Romer's orders "along the way attack anything the regiment encounters." Before starting to march away from General Krajowski's group, the regiment received 5th Battery of 18th Regiment of Eastern Frontier Field Artillery as a companion battery.

THE BATTLE AT HORYNKA

Directly southwest of Krzemieniec, in Młynowce, the regiment began a battle with Kotovsky's cavalry brigade. After all-day skirmishes on 13 July that brigade, driven back in to the forest, was finally beaten at Horynka. In the hands of the charging 2nd Battalion fell 7 cannons and the brigade's whole supply column, and 50 Polish prisoners were rescued. The regiment's losses were 1 man killed and 5 wounded. A General Staff communiqué (No. 841, dated 14 July 1920) mentions that:

> South of Krzemieniec Lt. Col. Szylling's group attacked a brigade of the enemy cavalry, reinforced by infantry on carts, and after a short battle forced it to retreat. In this retreat the enemy's units encountered our infantry battalion and retreated to the southeast, losing 7 cannons with teams, a sizable quantity of machine guns and handguns.

After fighting this battle the regiment joined with 43rd Regiment of Eastern Frontier Riflemen in Horynka, and together they fought off charges from the direction of Katerburg, conducting a forest battle with whole units and loose groups of Soviets.

From Horynka the regiment proceeded to Wiśniowiec, where it took up positions and defended for more than a dozen days, carrying out sorties on Oknin to reconnoiter.

Finally the regiment received an order to retreat on the line of the river Seret to Załoźce, from which it proceeded on 28 July to the Pieniaki sector, taking that locality after a fierce battle. From the Pieniaki region, to support the activities of 18th Infantry Division fighting at Brody, 3rd Battalion carried out successful attacks on the enemy's rear and left flank, in the direction of Ponikwa.

THE CAPTURE AND DEFENSE OF PODKAMIEŃ

To compensate for the position taken by the 13th Infantry Division, and to relieve 18th Division at Brody, on 3 August the regiment carried out concentric attacks on Podkamień, defended by Budionny's 6th Cavalry Division and three artillery batteries. 3rd Battalion attacked as a separate group from Żarków through Litowisko to eliminate the enemy grouped in front of the regiment's departure position. 1st and 2nd Battalions, under Lt. Col. Szylling's command, attacked along the Pieniaki-Podkamień road. The fierce resistance of the cavalry, supported by heavy machine gun fire from *tachanki* [horse-driven carts], delayed the regiment's advance. Two batteries of the 13th Eastern Frontier Field Artillery Regiment, supporting the regiment's attack from open positions occupied under the fire of Soviet heavy machine guns, cooperated in the attack.

Late at night Podkamień was taken. The whole regiment regrouped in the monastery, inside the walls, to avoid surprise during the night from the woods that adjoined the town. The thick, high walls encircling the monastery gave sufficient protection from rifle fire, so that the regiment, exhausted by the battles that had lasted all day, could rest during the night, guarded by alarm sentries by the entrance gates. The batteries took up firing positions on the ramparts along the walls. Before the regiment's eyes stood a living image of the defense of Częstochowa from the Swedish invasion. The monastery's prior, Father Matula, a Dominican, wandering about the monastery's courtyard in his white robe, was the personification of Father Kordecki.

The mood evoked by this environment overwhelmed all the regiment's soldiers. So it was with joy that the companies of 1st Battalion went on sorties at daybreak, to destroy the enemy, who had surrounded the monastery during the night. After fierce battles by the very walls of the monastery, and then a position taken at Palikrowy-Niemiacze-Nakwasza-Popowce, on 13 August the regiment began to retreat as ordered. In battles in the Podkamień sector the regiment lost 19 killed and 17 wounded. 3rd Company with 1st Lt. Solon distinguished itself in particular in the battle for Popowce, holding back powerful Soviet attacks advancing in four lines.

THE BATTLES AT KRASNE

After abandoning Podkamień, the regiment proceeded through Majdan and Podhorce to Sassów, where it reorganized in the position Sassów-Białykamień. In this sector the regiment held back Soviet attacks, and especially throughout the whole day of 16 August, on 2nd Battalion's positions in Sassów.

Budionny was stopped at Brody. But because 18th Infantry Division set out for Warsaw, in connection with regrouping for the decisive battle at Warsaw, Budionny, held mainly by the 18th Infantry Division, broke through the line of the Bug and drove toward Lwów. In connection with this, the 44th Regiment again had to abandon the positions it had taken at Sassów-Białykamień, and at dawn on 17 August began a battle in retreat, as ordered, withdrawing to Krasne in constant contact with the enemy. The regiment carried out the retreat in a marching column, having heavy machine guns on carts in the rear and along the sides of the column, shooting at Soviet foray units.

In Krasne the closed defensive juncture was reorganized, defended by 44th Regiment and 2nd Battalion of the 43rd Regiment of Eastern Frontier Riflemen (Capt. Wyczółkowski's). The Soviet cavalry mounted charges with lines of horses and on foot, which broke and retreated, however, pursued by artillery fire. The defense in Krasne, in view of the terrain, was difficult and unpleasant. There were incidents of casualties in the regiment among defenders of the western sector from the fire of Soviet heavy machine guns attacking from the east. In the battles at Krasne the regiment lost 10 men killed and 45 men wounded; 1st Lt. Gutkowski and 1st Lt. Szwagiel were also wounded. In the artillery duel that developed toward evening, the Polish artillery silenced the Soviet artillery.

Budionny, unable to take Krasne, which the regiment defended fiercely, went around it and headed toward Lwów. The regiment left Krasne and marched at night through Gliniany, also in the direction of Lwów.

THE BATTLE AT BIŁKA SZLACHECKA ON 18 AUGUST 1920

Per orders thrown by an airman to the regiment as it marched on the road from Glinany to Lwów, before reaching the manorial farmstead of Hermanów, the regiment turned north and took Biłka Szlachecka, from which it displaced Budionny's frontal foray units and thereby outraced the enemy's mounted army in the march to Lwów, blocking his access to the town with a victorious battle fought with Budionny's 4th and 6th Cavalry Divisions. Lt. Col. Szylling, foreseeing an influx of enemy cavalry to Lwów through Biłka Szlachecka, prepared for battle, regrouping the regiment in three echelons in the interior: 3rd Battalion took the eastern elevation in front of Biłka Szlachecka, with a base on the right flank against a small forest; 2nd Battalion organized the eastern edge of the village for defense, as the regiment's second echelon, separated from 3rd Battalion by a small river with marshy banks. 1st Battalion, as the regiment's reserve, was behind 2nd Battalion on the western edge of the village. 5th and 6th Batteries of 13th Artillery Regiment were in the center of the position, with observers advanced to the first line of the infantry.

Events unfolded along the lines foreseen by the regiment's commander.

The concentrated fire of three batteries, one of which was heavy, reinforced by the fire of machine guns on the position of 3rd Battalion, halted suddenly at 1800 hours. The enemy, obviously with full confidence of victory, decided to strike from the front, without using any flank maneuver. In the foreground, squadrons of Budionny's 4th and 6th Cavalry Divisions, regrouped in the interior, appeared in compact masses, and charged the regiment at full gallop. The batteries and heavy machine guns of the regiment began their harvest of death. The setting sun's rays shone on the Soviet swords, prepared to cut. The surging mass advanced, closely packed, at full gallop, running over those remnants of 3rd Battalion that had not been able to retreat to the woods on its right flank. After the cavalry appeared before 2nd Battalion's front, and thus in front of the village, the regrouped 20 heavy machine guns of the battalion and of the regiment's 4th Company, supported by the fire of 28 hand machine guns and infantry salvoes, stopped the charge. The batteries assigned to the regiment, with division leader Capt. De Latoun, won the hearts of the infantry with their firing efforts and the accuracy of their shots. The dense mass of cavalry almost dispersed, milled about, dwindled and returned in panic-stricken disarray to where it came from. Budionny's sizable forces (units of two divisions), caught in a crossfire, were crushed in a few minutes; demoralized, they ran away, leaving on the field of battle over 200 bodies and as many horses. 1st Battalion counterattacked; its 8 heavy machine guns aided 20 rifles in the line in their destructive work. The mass charge, at first glance so dangerous, broke, thanks to the regiment soldiers' courage and skill for battle with cavalry. The skillful use of machine guns was decisive in the victory, and thereby in saving Lwów from being taken by Budionny. The enemy, withdrawing in the direction of Kurowice, came under the fire of 45th Regiment of Eastern Frontier Riflemen, marching on the highway to Lwów. Beaten, it finally retreated to the northeast.

In the battle at Biłka Szlachecka the regiment lost 2nd Lt. Fabowski and three men killed; wounded were 2nd Lt. Zawilski and 45 men. At 2200 hours the regiment marched to Winniki, where it halted at 0200 hours on 19 August; after the incorporation of the Kraków Staging Battalion, it took positions from Czartowska Skała to Druga Wólka.

The city of Lwów presented General Stanisław Haller, commander of 13th Division, with a pennant for the division staff, as proof of gratitude for the city's deliverance.

To relieve 12th Infantry Division, fighting at Mikołajów, on 22 August the regiment attacked from Winniki along the road to Mogiła, which it took despite strong resistance, in the process losing 5 men killed and 15 wounded. The regiment, relieved in its sector by units of 5th Infantry Division, returned to Lwów, from which it traveled by rail transports to Rawa Ruska.

THE BATTLES AT ZAMOŚĆ

In connection with Budionny's march to the north, the Commander in Chief decided to have "the entire cavalry of the 6th army, along with the best division of the infantry there, set out after Budionny's mounted army." (Józef Piłsudski, *Rok 1920*, page 173.)

13th Infantry Division, thus singled out, arrived in rail transports at Rawa Ruska, the departure base for activity on Budionny's flank, who at the news of the defeat of Tukhachevsky's army at Warsaw, and after receiving a categorical order to do so, moved from near Lwów to the Sokal-Krystynopol region, with the intention of striking at Zamość and Lublin—in the rear of the Polish 3rd and 4th Armies, pursuing Tukhachevsky's castaways.

13th Infantry Division and 1st Cavalry Division formed a pursuit group under the command of General Stanisław Haller. This group's assignment was: "inasmuch as 10th, 2nd, and 7th Divisions block Budionny's paths to the west and north, to cut off his last paths, north (to Lwów) and east (to Volhynia)."

On 23 August 1920 the regiment, as part of 26th Infantry Brigade, advanced by secure march through Uhnów, Zastawie, Szczepiatyn, and Krzewica to Przewodów. In the foreground of Przewodów it encountered enemy cavalry units and fired upon them with the batteries of 13th Artillery Regiment, assigned to the regiment. From the enemy's movements it was clear the foe was advancing by flank march in relation to 13th Division toward the west. In Przewodów the regiment prepared to drive back attacks. The patrols sent out confirmed the advance of a large column of cavalry in the direction of Telatyn. To cut off its path a sortie was immediately carried out by one company, supported by artillery fire, and it brought the regiment prisoners, and took Budionny's large ammunition column as well.

Not long after, however, the regiment halted at Przewodów. On 29 August, as commanded by orders received, it advanced by swift secure march to Czartowczyk and Kraczów [*now called* Kraczew], where it was on the heels of the Soviet squadrons, among whom was Budionny himself. In Kraczów the regiment fought very fierce battles.

On 30 August the regiment, along with 43rd Regiment of Eastern Frontier Riflemen, charged at Komarów, which it took toward evening. In the course of full action at Komarów Budionny charged the regiment's rear with one brigade of cavalry. Always ready to fight, the regiment's reserves, with machine guns placed in nests covering the artillery, once again refused to be taken by surprise.

An enemy diversion weakened the Polish artillery's activity at Komarów only for a short time, because the fire had to be directed at the charging cavalry brigade. At the sight of the approaching charge, 3rd Battalion, in reserve for the regiment, instinctively bristling with their bayonets, threw themselves toward the approaching squadrons, which, decimated by heavy machine gun fire and artillery, headed back to the small forests from which they had emerged shortly before.

On the next day, 31 August, the regiment was to make contact with the garrison valiantly defending Zamość. For that purpose it set out at 0500 hours from Komarów toward hill 215, where it came under Soviet artillery fire from Ruszczyzna. On the southern slope of hill 215 the regiment formed up for an attack, which it carried out jointly with 43rd Regiment of Eastern Frontier Riflemen, and the regiment threw into the attack three battalions. Lt. Col. Szylling led 25th Brigade in the attack. On the brigade's right flank in mounted formation, General Rómmel's concentrated 1st Cavalry Division awaited the moment to take advantage of the attacking infantry, intending to wipe out the Soviet cavalry in quick pursuit.

Ruszczyzna and Wolica Śniatycka, defended by the Soviet cavalry supported by the fire of three batteries, were taken with a daring attack. After Wolica was taken fierce combat ensued, with renewed counterblows of the Soviet cavalry. Its charges broke under the fire of our infantry and artillery as well as in bloody charges carried out from the flank by 1st Polish Cavalry Division. Then the regiment advanced on Bródek, where it once more encountered strong groups of Soviet cavalry. Here it occupied advantageous defensive positions in old trenches and mounted cavalry charges of several hundred meters, and then, suddenly, opening fire from all its available resources and the artillery assigned to it, it devastated and decimated the Soviet cavalry. The charges broke and the enemy dispersed, heading east, where once more—dislodged by 1st Cavalry Division—it was compelled to run away into the woods at midnight. On this day the regiment cleared the neighboring villages of the remnants of Budionny's units and spent the night in Barchaczów.

Of the difficult struggles with Budionny, a communiqué from the General Staff dated 1 September 1920 said:

> A decisive role in the battle was played by the pursuit group of General Stanisław Haller, which for a couple of days, finding itself in Budionny's rear, followed hot on the heels of his main forces with

uncommon relentlessness and on 31 August struck toward Zamość from the east.

Budionny, seeing the danger that threatened, began a sudden retreat, everywhere encountering strong resistance from our units surrounding him. In the vicinity of Wolica Śniatycka, Miączyn, and Zawalew [*now called* Zawalów] unusually fierce battles ensued, in which individual enemy divisions, ignoring their enormous losses, several times renewed their cavalry charges. The mounted army was crushed in these battles.

The day of 1 September passed in pursuing Budionny through Wolica Śniatycka, Dub, Zubkowice [Zubowice] and Przewalew [Przewale]. The next day the regiment attacked Tyszowce, which lay on the other side of the swampy river Huczwa and was defended by a strong garrison with artillery. The open terrain between Przewalew and Tyszowce facilitated observation, which made the attack much more difficult. The attack was conducted along a causeway by the main forces, while 2nd Company conducted a maneuver on the road upon Klątwa [Klątwy]. The enemy, having seen the columns approaching along the road from far away, opened thick and accurate artillery fire upon it. Despite that, however, thanks to the unit's swift advance, casualties were relatively light, and after an attack lasting only 20 minutes the regiment crossed the river Huczwa by the bridge, defended by four heavy machine guns, and then took the town. The Soviet infantry, which retreated from Tyszowce to Lipowiec, was taken captive by a brigade of the Don Cossacks cooperating with us, which had come over to our side within the first days of Budionny's appearance on the Polish front.

Budionny tried to halt once more in the region of Hrubieszów. Only when beaten on 5 September at Werbkowice did he retreat across the Bug.

The regiment, withdrawn from Tyszowce to Zubkowice, later to Kotlice, conducted an attack from there on the strongly defended Koniuchy. In this attack the commander of 5th Company, 1st Lt. Wiącek, was badly wounded. In further pursuit through Werbkowice, Czerniszyn, and Czunów, the regiment reached the western bank of the Bug in its triumphant march; then it crossed the river as reserve for the group, went to Hrubieszów, and stayed there till 11 September, using this time to organize and prepare for the final decisive offensive.

THE OFFENSIVE BEYOND THE BUG

On 12 September 44th Regiment set out from Hrubieszów, where the regiment had stayed as reserve for 13th Infantry Division, as part of the offensive initiated by the entire 3rd Army. This activity was crowned by reaching, and in some places crossing, the current borders of Poland to the east. After crossing the Bug in Horodek, the regiment drove the enemy from its outskirts, at the same time securing passage for 9th Infantry Division, which was active on the left flank of 13th Division. Fierce resistance by two of Budionny's divisions, aided by the fire of heavy machine guns on *tachanki*, was broken in battles at Zielinów, Hoszczatyn, and Lasków. While crossing the Ług river in Sielce, the regiment lost three men killed and seven wounded. On 15 September, after a forced march interrupted by battles with the Soviets' 44th Division in Torczyn and in Litwa, late at night the regiment began an attack on Łuck. Despite the orders of the army's commander to attack Łuck no sooner than the day of 16 September, Lt. Col. Szylling, taking advantage of night and surprise, attacked the town during the night of the 15th and 16th. A foray unit of the divisional cavalry with 1st Lt. Bohdan Sawicki, using rifle fire, drove off Soviet soldiers setting the bridge on fire. On rafts hastily thrown together 11th Company with 1st Lt. Śniechowski, and then the rest of 3rd Battalion, proceeded across the Styr. Brief street battles destroyed the enemy in the town and drove the rest off toward Równe. Lt. Col. Szylling personally directed the attack by individual companies on Łuck. The surprise at night and the taking of Łuck, despite taking place at the cost of a forced march for an entire day without eating, undoubtedly preserved the regiment from high casualties. At the taking of Łuck the regiment lost one man killed and eight wounded, taking prisoners and heavy machine guns.

After the capture of Łuck cavalry pursuit ensued to Ołyka and Równe. Równe was taken by 1st Polish Cavalry Corps, and 44th Regiment took up its position there, organizing defense of the town. After clearing the Aleksandryja region north of Równe, during which the regiment defeated the Soviets' 62nd and 65th Regiments in Kamienna Góra, 44th Regiment attacked and took Tuczyn on 26 September 1920.

After clearing the region of Kostopol of Soviet forces, the regiment returned to Równe, from which it proceeded through Korzec to Zwiahel, taking the defense of the town over from 43rd Regiment of Eastern Frontier Riflemen. In the foreground of Zwiahel very intensive sorties were conducted on Kuka, Iwaszkówka, and Katerynówka, and the Soviets' 56th and 57th Infantry Regiments were crushed. In these battles, fought from 5 October to 2400 hours on 18 October, that is, until the armistice, the regiment took 85 prisoners, weapons, and the whole supply column of the Soviet 57th Infantry Division, at the cost of Capt. Bilmin and 9 men wounded.

A General Staff communiqué honored the regiment's activity (No. 914, dated 26 September 1920), saying:

> North of Równe we crushed the Soviet 19th Infantry Brigade with an energetic sortie. It was supposed to conduct a campaign for the purpose of retaking Równe.

General Staff communiqué No. 936, dated 17 October 1920, informs us that:

At Zwiahel our units repulsed fierce attacks of the enemy, who concentrated his strongest forces in this area.

In one of 3rd Battalion's sorties on Katerynówka, the battalion's commander, Capt. Bilmin was wounded, but let himself be bandaged only after having conducted the skirmish victoriously and after reviewing the wounded men.

On 18 October at 1700 hours an attack by a Soviet battalion on Czyżewka, defended by 10th Company with 1st Lt. Andruszkiewicz, was driven back by a bayonet counterstroke. This was the last large Soviet effort before the regiment's front— and this time, too, it ended with the Soviet infantry's retreat.

The regiment's last report on the situation at 2400 hours said:

> The cessation of hostilities took place without contact with the enemy. In Czyżewka the enemy retreated in panic. White rockets fired before our units signified the cessation of hostilities. It is quiet on the front, guards keep watch.

AFTER THE ARMISTICE

Throughout the whole time of peace negotiations the regiment remained in Zwiahel, which on the basis of initial negotiations was turned over to the Soviet authorities, and on 22 November 1920 the regiment proceeded to Równe. Here, too, even during peacetime, the regiment did not lose its combat readiness for a moment. As the last garrison, the one farthest east, the regiment watches and waits for when the order of the Most Illustrious Republic calls it to action, to go into battle to the sound of the regiment march *"Sambra i Moza"* ["the Sambre and Meuse," names of rivers in France and Belgium] in defense of the borders traced by the bayonets of the regiment's soldiers in 1920.

Traditionally every year when its holiday is formally celebrated, the whole regiment gathers on 27 April at evening roll call on the barracks grounds, illuminated at the corners with burning piles of logs. Amid the bang of exploding firecrackers the spirits of fallen heroes stand for ceremonial roll call, saluted by those who live and answer the call.

LIST OF THOSE WHO FELL IN BATTLE OR DIED OF THEIR WOUNDS

1. 1st Lt. Fabowski Stanisław*
2. 1st Lt. Kargol Władysław
3. 1st Lt. Kowalczyk Antoni
4. 1st Lt. Sobieski Ignacy
5. 1st Lt. Stankiewicz Michał
6. 1st Lt. Urbaniak Jan
7. 1st Lt. Zawadzki Michał**

*In the text on page 218 his rank is given as podpor., 2nd Lt.
**In the text on page 208 his rank is given as podpor., 2nd Lt.

Men:

Translator's note: the list is given as in the original, with no attempt made to correct numbering or alphabetization.

1. Pvt. Adamczyk Jan
2. Pvt. Ajzenberg Pinkus
3. Sgt. Antkowski Zygmunt
4. Pvt. Bąk Andrzej
5. Pvt. Bąkowski Józef
6. Pvt. Baran Tomasz
7. Pvt. Bartnicki Bronisław
8. Pvt. Barzycki Józef
9. Pvt. Bednarzyk Piotr
10. Pvt. Bednarek Piotr
11. Pvt. Biemkowski Władysław
12. Pvt. Bilke Edmund
13. Pvt. Birnbaum Michał
14. Pvt. Borowicz Marcin
15. Pvt. Bremol Jan
16. Pvt. Brzeziński Wojciech
17. Cpl. Czarnecki Adolf
18. Pvt. Chmiel Walenty
19. Pvt. Choda Juljan
20. Pvt. Chrząszcz Jan
21. Pvt. Cisło Władysław
22. Pvt. Czarnolewski Piotr
23. Pvt. Dąbek Tomasz
24. Pvt. Dąbrowski Stefan
25. Pvt. Dąbrowski Wacław
26. Pvt. Danielczyk Jan
27. Pvt. Domagała Józef
28. Pvt. Dubalski Władysław
29. Pvt. Duda Józef
30. Pvt. Duda Stanisław
31. Pvt. Dudziak Ignacy
32. Pvt. Dziedzic Józef
33. Pvt. Ejzenberg Pinkus
34. Pvt. Fafara Kazimierz
35. Pvt. Feć Kazimierz
36. Pvt. Figiel Chaim
37. Pvt. Filipowicz Franciszek
38. Pvt. Gacek Jakób
39. Pvt. Gałązka Bronisław
40. Pvt. Garncarz Ludwik
41. Sgt. Gawiński Konstanty
42. Pvt. Gerasimiuk Józef
43. Pvt. Giernatowicz Władysław
44. Pvt. Gliwiński Tadeusz
45. Pvt. Goldyn Wojciech
46. Pvt. Górski Józef
47. Pvt. Goździkowski Stanisław
48. Pvt. Grünblat Maks
49. Pvt. Grodzki Jan
50. Cpl. Gryczyźski Cyryl
51. Pvt. Grzesk Paweł
52. Pvt. Hein Tygeł
53. Pvt. Hering Mojżesz
54. Pvt. Holkowski Aleksander
55. Pvt. Holstein Abram
56. Cpl. Hurbol Stanisław
57. Pvt. Ickowicz Matys
58. Pvt. Jańczak Stanisław
59. PFC Jaskot Franciszek
60. Pvt. Jaskot Wojciech
61. Cpl. Kaczyński Edward
62. Pvt. Kąkol Ignacy
63. Pvt. Kamiński Jan
64. Pvt. Kamiński Kalistrat
65. Pvt. Karpiński Mikołaj
66. Pvt. Kasperek Józef
67. Pvt. Kędziorek Marjan
68. PFC Kiszewski Jan

69. Pvt. Kobecki Juljan
70. Cpl. Koclinga Władysław
71. Pvt. Kogut Szloma
72. Pvt. Kolanko Jan
73. Pvt. Kołodziej Stanisław
74. Pvt. Kordek Jan
75. Pvt. Kosecki Władysław
76. Pvt. Kościelski Aleksander
77. Pvt. Kosior Andrzej
78. Pvt. Koślacz Józef
79. Cpl. Koźlik Włodzimierz
80. PFC Krajewski Antoni
81. Pvt. Krawczyk Antoni
82. Cpl. Kruk Marcin
83. Pvt. Kubanowski Józef
84. Pvt. Kubik Józef
85. Pvt. Kuliński Karol
86. Pvt. Kulpa Jan
87. PFC Kwasiński Wojciech
88. Pvt. Kwasiłowski Wincenty
89. Pvt. Kwietniewski Jan
90. Pvt. Latkowski Józef
91. Cpl. Lawicki Ludwik
92. Pvt. Lisów Mikołaj
93. Pvt. Łaciak Jan
94. Cpl. Łaciak Franciszek
95. Pvt. Łukasiewicz Bolesław
96. Pvt. Majak Jan
97. Pvt. Majewski Franciszek
98. Pvt. Majkut Roman
99. Pvt. Maks Rudolf
100. Pvt. Malawski Ludwik
101. Pvt. Malesza Franciszek
102. Pvt. Marciniak Józef
103. Pvt. Maślarz Jan
104. Pvt. Matusiak Jan
105. Pvt. Matysiak Jan
106. Pvt. Milbaum Herszko
107. Pvt. Miśkiewicz Jan
108. Master Cpl. Morys Andrzej
109. Pvt. Motyliński Wincenty
110. Pvt. Musiał Józef
111. Pvt. Niemiec Józef
112. Cpl. Nowicki Jan
113. Pvt. Ogrodowicz Władysław
114. Cpl. Orlicki Walenty
115. Pvt. Osiał Łukasz
116. Pvt. Pakieła Franciszek
117. Pvt. Pałczyński Jan
118. Pvt. Panasiuk Paweł
119. Pvt. Pawlik Jan
120. Pvt. Palik Tomasz
121. Pvt. Pawłowski Stanisław
122. Pvt. Piasek Marcin
123. Pvt. Piechnik Piotr
124. Pvt. Piętak Antoni
125. Pvt. Pietrzyk Stanisław
126. Pvt. Piórek Teofil
127. Sgt. Pisiński Zygmunt
128. Pvt. Plewa Stanisław
129. Pvt. Pośledniak Alojzy
130. Pvt. Przybysz Franciszek
131. Pvt. Rajs Benjamin
132. Pvt. Rogaliński Bronisław
133. Pvt. Rodziński Jan
134. Pvt. Rozenbaum Hersz
135. Pvt. Rulawski Aleksander
136. Sgt. Rusiłowski Wincenty
137. Pvt. Rykaczewski Feliks
138. Pvt. Saganowski Tadeusz
139. Pvt. Serafin Jan
140. Pvt. Serafin Stanisław
141. Cpl. Skowroń Alojzy
142. Pvt. Śnieżyński Piotr
143. Pvt. Sobczak Jan
144. Pvt. Sopel Piotr
145. Pvt. Staszek Franciszek
146. Pvt. Stawiński Franciszek
147. Pvt. Świtalski Józef
148. Pvt. Szendel Mieczysław
149. Pvt. Stajer Jan
150. Pvt. Szymański Wojciech
151. Pvt. Tajtelbaum Berko
152. Pvt. Taugetman Jakób
153. Pvt. Teć Kazimierz
154. Pvt. Topf Mojżesz
155. Pvt. Trojan Marcin
156. Pvt. Turski Jan
157. Pvt. Usow Jan
158. Pvt. Walas Jan
159. Pvt. Walczak Wacław
160. Pvt. Warowny Władysław
161. Pvt. Wasiak Stefan
162. Pvt. Włodarczyk Wincenty
163. Pvt. Wójcik Jan
164. Pvt. Zaręba Andrzej
165. Pvt. Zawadzki Franciszek
166. Pvt. Zdrowiak Ludwik

167. Pvt. Żmija Jan
168. Pvt. Żurawski Jan
169. Pvt. Żymek Józef

In addition the following died of disease (primarily of typhus in Lubar and Miropol): 1 officer, 1 Chief Warrant Officer [*chorąży*, abbreviated CWO below] and 288 men. There were about 20 officers wounded (some of them twice), and 430 men.

LIST OF THOSE DECORATED WITH THE SILVER CROSS OF THE ORDER "VIRTUTI MILITARI" 5TH CLASS

1. 1st Lt. Andruszkiewicz Piotr
2. 1st Lt. Bobrowski Stanisław
3. Capt. Bilmin Stanisław
4. Pvt. Brzoza Józef
5. PFC Chruszczyk Jakób
6. PFC Ciura Stanisław
7. Cpl. Dzięgielewski Bronisław
8. CWO Glor-Godłowski Stefan
9. 1st Lt. Gorczyca Władysław
10. 1st Lt. Gutkowski Roman
11. † 1st Lt. Kargoł Władysław
12. Cpl. Komar Stanisław
13. 1st Lt. Korab-Laskowski Jan
14. Cpl. Kowalski Józef
15. 1st Lt. Kwaśniewski Tadeusz
16. CWO Laskowski Stanisław
17. † Capt. Latour Napoleon
18. Lt. Col. Lawicz-Liszka Wilhelm
19. Sgt. Lewicki Bronisław
20. 1st Lt. Łączkowski Stanisław
21. 1st Lt. Małachowski-Mikołajczak Józef
22. 1st Lt. Michno Stanisław
23. Master Cpl. Morys Andrzej
24. Pvt. Niejadlik Józef
25. Pvt. Nowicki Kazimierz
26. 1st Lt. Olszewski Witalis
27. Cpl. Parus Franciszek
28. Sgt. Pędrak Edward
29. Pvt. Pękała Józef
30. Sgt. Piekielniak Jan
31. Capt. Pieślak Mikołaj
32. CWO Piński-Piechocki Paweł
33. Cpl. Polak Władysław
34. Master Cpl. Sadowski Jan
35. Master Cpl. Sokołowski Aleksander
36. 1st Lt. Solon Stanisław
37. 1st Lt. Sosień Stanisław
38. Sgt. Straszewski Józef
39. Lt. Col. Szylling Antoni
40. Pvt. Śladowski Andrzej
41. PFC Śledź Stanisław
42. 1st Lt. Śniechowski Tadeusz
43. Pvt. Trawiński Michał
44. 1st Lt. Wiącek Antoni
45. 1st Lt. Więckus Zygmunt
46. Master Sgt. Woliński Jan or *Wierzelewski Józef*
47. Capt. Zieleniewski Rafał
48. CWO Zieliński Stanisław
49. Master Sgt. Żylak Maciej

487 were decorated with the *Cross of Valor*. Of those 61 officers, 9 Chief Warrant Officers, and 335 men received it for the first time; 31 officers, 6 Chief Warrant Officers, and 18 men received it for the second time; 16 officers, 2 Chief Warrant Officers, and 2 men received it for the third time; and 6 officers and 1 Chief Warrant Officer for the fourth time.

Lt. Col. Antoni Szylling and 1st Lt. Jan Korab-Laskowski were decorated with the French *Legion of Honor*.

9 officers received the *Medal of Victory*.

16 officers and 7 Chief Warrant Officers received the *Memorial Medal* of the Great War.

28 officers and men received the French *Croix de Guerre* for combat in France on the German front.

MILITARY BOOTY

During the military activities of 1919 and 1920, the regiment captured 4,959 prisoners, 27 cannons, 297 heavy machine guns, and rail and wheel supply columns. In addition 44th Regiment assisted 45th Regiment in the final liquidation of the Ukrainian army of *ataman* Petlura in the Chomory sector, in Lubar and Miropol. The registered booty numbers hundreds of heavy machine guns, dozens of cannons, hundreds of horses, and thousands of detainees.

Jan Kazimierz Kostrubała

*Born 2 February 1900, Zwierzyniec nad Wieprzem, Poland
Died 30 September 1958, Chicago, Illinois, U.S.A.*

OUTLINE OF THE WARTIME HISTORY OF THE 45TH INFANTRY REGIMENT OF EASTERN FRONTIER INFANTRY RIFLEMEN

AS COMMISSIONED BY THE MILITARY HISTORICAL OFFICE

compiled by

MAJOR JERZY DĄBROWSKI

WARSAW

1928

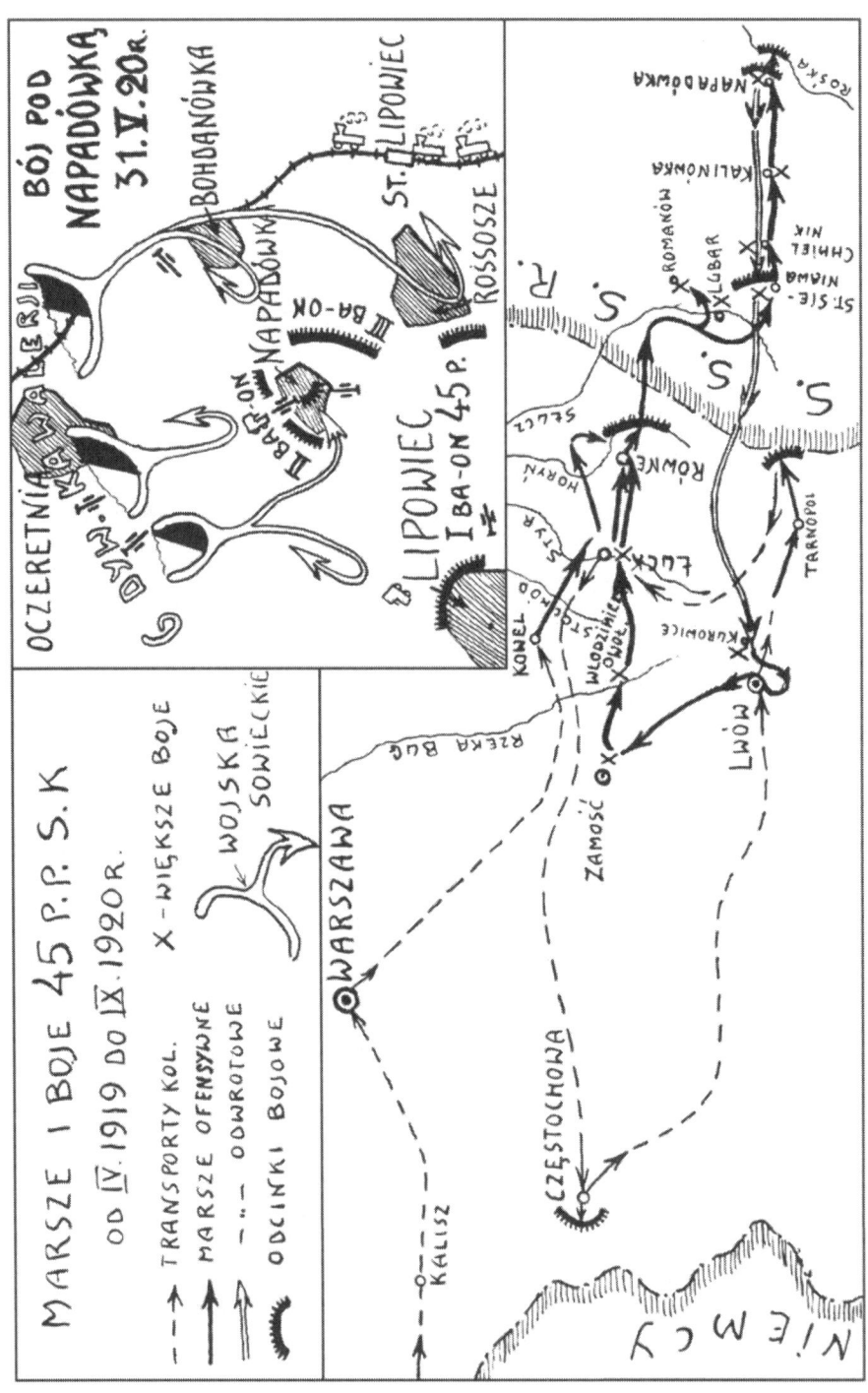

Who among the Poles does not remember the joyful and glorious, yet at the same time dangerous and uneasy days of the Fatherland's resurrection?

At Lwów the children of Poland strove to block with their heroic blood the unleashing of the Cossack horde; in the West, the Germans' iron grip on the bosom of Piast refused to loosen; while the entire East, seized by revolution, continued to burn unceasingly with hatred at everything connected with the name of Poland.

As this terrible ring of enemies tightened more and more closely around our Fatherland, the Czechs, too, rose up against Poland.

They were hard times….

But the ardent and selfless hearts of heroes at Samo-Sierry, Mozhaisk, Berezyna and San Domingo awoke from a century of sleep and called for payment for their blood and martyrdom; they cried out to France of a debt owed not to themselves but to Poland.

And behold—wanderers from all over the world, poor, tormented exiles, supported by an uncontrollable longing and carried away by the battle cry sounded in France, flung themselves in an army of blue[1] upon the enemies of Poland. All of Poland yearned for them, like a mother for her sons.

The army of defenders of the Republic came, defenders who had not lost their Polish hearts and were able to collect from all over the world that which was worthy of grafting onto their native soil.

From those cadres of wanderers, in a tradition both exceptional and beautiful, there arose a series of Polish regiments, the honor of belonging to which came to the former "3rd Regiment of Polish Riflemen," which now is the "45th Regiment of the Eastern Frontier Infantry Riflemen" [*45-y pułk piechoty strzelców kresowych*].

This regiment, like a mighty pillar, supported the base of Polish statehood in the farthest borderlands of Poland. It was with total justification and fullness of moral right that this regiment added to its title "Eastern Frontier Riflemen."

---

[1] "The Polish Army" in France wore coats, uniforms, and caps sky-blue in color.

They fought in the Eastern Borderlands, and after the war they did not leave those restless frontiers for a single day, faithfully serving as their guard.

Anyone who comes to know the history of the 45th Regiment must be struck by France's decisive influence on the regiment's origin, organization, and training.

As early as 1914 the first Polish unit in the West came into existence in France, the so-called *Bajończycy [the ones from Bayonne]*, soon to glorify the name of Poland and draw the eyes of the whole anti-German coalition.

For a long time, however, unfavorable political circumstances (above all the opposition of Russia) and the divergence of political convictions among the Poles in exile comprised an impediment to the development of a Polish army in the West.

It was not until Russia's revolution in effect crossed it off the list of the Allies that the question of an independent Polish state and independent Polish army opposing the Germans became a real possibility.

France sounded the battle cry for this, and for a long time was isolated in this view, for only the United States of North America supported France. The Italians, on the other hand, were striving for the creation of a Polish army on their territory.

The persistent efforts of the Polish "National Committee," created in Paris and supported by influential French circles favorable to Poland, did succeed, however. On 4 June 1917 a petition was sent to the President of the Republic of France from Premier Ribot, stating that it was France's moral obligation to create an independent army with a large number of Poles fighting for the freedom of the nations. Agreeing with Ribot's opinion, President Poincaré issued a decree creating an autonomous Polish army comprised of Polish volunteers and organized on the model of the French army.

In execution of this decree, the Minister of War, Paul Painlevé, appointed Major General Archinard as head (6 June 1917) of the "French-Polish Military Mission" created for this purpose.

The Polish Army in France owes a great deal to the tireless efforts of this resourceful general, for he encountered obstacles piled before him at every step.

As a result of persistent and consistent labor, however, Gen. Archinard succeeded in getting first England and Russia, and later the United States and Brazil to designate liaison officers to work with the "French-Polish Military Mission." At the same time the general created posts for conducting propaganda and recruitment in England, Holland, the United States, Canada, Brazil, and Russia.

As for France, its support, both moral and material, was enormous. Through numerous recruiting offices it soon began to bring in throngs of Polish volunteers from the French army, prisoners of war from the German army, from the

Russian expeditionary corps, and so on. At the same time Polish laborers who had escaped from Germany through Holland came in droves by way of England.

America provided the largest number of volunteers. The generosity and patriotism of America's Polish community soon created a strong recruiting organization and mobilized the Falcons; and tens of thousands of volunteers and patriots, physically well developed and sophisticated in their nationality, came to France—at first by way of Canada, but after the United States broke with Germany, directly—and filled the cadres already organized there. To better grasp the scale of the efforts of America's Polish community, it will suffice to say that in Canada even officers' and non-commissioned officers' schools were created for volunteer Poles, and several gigantic mobilization camps were set up.

While America thus produced a physically and morally healthy "food" for the newly born Polish army in the form of volunteers and privates, at the same time France forged its steel "organism," the cadres.

Shortly after the decree was issued that created the Polish army, French authorities released all Polish soldiers from their army and concentrated them in the camp at Sillé le Guillaume, along with Polish prisoners of war from the German army as well as volunteers from the Russian brigades. Inasmuch as these volunteers were comprised mainly of officers, non-commissioned officers, and experienced older soldiers, after training they actually made up the cadres of the developing Polish army.

For the purpose of providing vigorous training at the numerous drilling camps that arose, the cadres of the units being formed (so-called *détachements*) grouped themselves in the appropriate localities; all were directly subordinate to camp "Sillé le Guillaume," from which they received organizational orders from the "French-Polish Military Mission."

It was in this manner that in early 1918 the "1st Regiment of Polish Riflemen," which included the rest of the *Bajończycy*, came into existence. This was followed in turn by the formation of the 2nd and 3rd Regiments. At the end of January 1918 the main camp sent *détachements* to Mamers to form cadres of the 1st Battalion of the 2nd Regiment of Polish Riflemen. The cadres' assignments were to prepare quarters, gather weapons, uniforms and equipment, receive American transports, organize the command, and so on. The cadres consisted of: 1) officers and non-commissioned officers, Poles from the French army, in some cases even Frenchmen, 2) non-commissioned officers from the German army, 3) officers and non-commissioned officers from the Russian army, 4) a few veteran French soldiers in each company, and 5) a certain number of translators.

On 7 February 1918 the first American transport from Halifax arrived at the port of Le Havre with a total of 1,800 men, and it was directed to Mamers to fill the cadres of the 1st and 2nd Battalions of the 2nd Regiment.

On 16 February 1918 by order of the day from the commander of Camp Sillé le Guillaume the 1st Battalion of the 2nd Regiment was renamed the 1st Battalion of the 3rd Regiment of Polish Riflemen *(3 Régiment de Chasseurs Polonais)*; so the date 16 February 1918 is the day the current 45th Regiment came into existence.

Command of the battalion was entrusted to a captain of the French army, Chmielewski.

On 8 March the second transport arrived from America, which created in Laval *(département* Mayenne) the 2nd and 3rd Battalions of the 3rd Regiment of Polish Riflemen.

Command of this regiment, organized on a makeshift basis, was assumed by Major Till of the French army, who was therefore the regiment's first commander. The 1st Battalion was commanded by Captain Chmielewski; the 2nd Battalion by First Lieutenant Mackiewicz; and the 3rd Battalion by First Lieutenant Mirski. The officers' corps consisted primarily of Americans (from the officers' school in Canada); in addition to them, there were also officers of the French and Russian armies, as well as prisoners of war from the German army.

The cadre of non-commissioned officers consisted of two basic types: Americans from the Canadian schools, and prisoners of war from the German army. In addition a number of French instructors were assigned to it.

As far as privates were concerned, the overwhelming majority, 75%, were Americans, with the rest coming from former soldiers of the German and Russian armies.

This diversity of both the officers' and non-commissioned officers' corps, as well as of the privates, made the task of organizing a uniform, powerful unit from this mixture extremely difficult.

Besides the technical difficulty of training them, an even greater and more dangerous difficulty arose—creating a uniform ideal amid such a motley environment, so different in terms of descent, education, moral and intellectual level, and even language.

Only an ardent love of their Fatherland, common to all, helped make it possible to accomplish this extremely difficult task.

The lack of battle experience among the Americans was covered by the unusually rich military and combat past of the majority of seasoned veterans from almost all the armies of the world. Only the lack of functional forces could not be compensated for. Also extremely troublesome was the lack of good translators: orders were written in two languages, the original in French and a translation—often awkward—in Polish. These orders were not always properly standardized, which created a new and completely unnecessary difficulty.

So it is hardly surprising that chaos arose during the first days of the regiment's existence, a chaos that seemingly could not be overcome. The general enthusiasm and good will, however, almost without exception, conquered all, and by the end of 1918 the regiment could already boldly call itself a combat unit equal to the victorious French regiments.

On 26 March 1918 command of the regiment was assumed by Colonel Leon Pachucki (of the Russian brigade in Thessaloniki), a native Pole, which had a positive effect on the regiment's mood.

On 7 April 1918 the regiment, given a heartfelt farewell by the people, was transferred to the region of Sully-sur-Loire, where a period of intensive training strictly by French regulations began. The officers and non-commissioned officers in turn underwent various kinds of training in numerous courses created specially for this purpose. So-called *mitrailleuse* companies were formed. The total dedication of the French assigned as instructors to the regiment must be emphasized. The regiment owes an enormous debt to them.

On 27 May 1918 the regiment moved to "Camp St. Quen." This camp was a part of the enormous set of camps under the general name "Camp Mailly" and had excellent terrain for drills, of which the regiment took full advantage.

At the beginning of June, however, the German offensive on the Marne and in Champagne threatened the 4th French Army: its front retreated, and after the 1st Regiment of Polish Riflemen was summoned to the trenches, the rest of the Polish regiments were also alerted.

On 9 June the 3rd Regiment approached the front and came to a halt as a reserve for the 4th Army (of General Gourand [*sic, Gouraud?*]) in the vicinity of Trannes, where it came under combat fire and grenade assault.

It should be stressed here that at all these stops, everywhere, without exception, people said goodbye to the regiment with sorrow, and even greeted it with ovations. At every step it was met with sincere warmth and affection of the French for the Poles.

Finally on 22 June 1918 came the most solemn day in the history of the regiment, which to this day it celebrates each year as a regimental holiday: the capital of Lorraine, the city of Nancy, gave the regiment its standard, thus becoming its spiritual guardian—the regiment's godfather, as it were.

This ceremony took on even greater dimensions due to the fact that on that same day the other regiments of the 1st Polish Division[2] were given their standards. This happened on a fine summer day in the vicinity of Dienville. The presence of President Poincaré, Minister of War Dmowski, General Archinard and numerous representatives of the coalition, towns, and the generals added uncommon solemnity to this act of brotherhood of the allied armies, Polish and French. After the dedication and presentation of the standards to the regiments

---

[2] In addition to the 1st Regiment of Polish Riflemen, which received its standard at another time.

an oath of loyalty was sworn to them, expressed in the lofty words of a special oath.

At the end of July General Józef Haller arrived in France, who had been appointed commander of the Polish Army in France. This had great significance for the Polish regiments. At a review in Dienville, when the soldiers saw with their own eyes that true Pole and soldier in whose hands they might boldly place their fates, fresh spirit, confidence and faith filled the hearts of soldiers homesick for Poland.

At more or less the same time, on 4 August 1918, the 63rd French Infantry Division was reformed, and its staff, servants and camps were renamed the 1st Polish Division, part of one of the best Corps, the 20th, subordinate to the 4th Army. This division was comprised of the 1st, 2nd and 3rd Regiments of Polish Riflemen.

The Polish Division gathered in the region of L'Huitre. General Ecochard, appointed first commander of the division, greeted the Polish regiments with lofty words of an order in which he emphasized his faith in the Poles' outstanding combat abilities.

At the same time the conduct of the French counteroffensive ruled out the need for immediate use of the Polish division on the 4th Army's endangered front; instead another assignment, a very honorable one, emerged: becoming part of the 8th Army, the Polish division was to be thrown in at the decisive moment for finally breaking the German front—in a fatal direction for the enemy, toward Metz.

For this purpose on 17 September 1918 the division was transported by rail to Lorraine. The 3rd Regiment halted in the vicinity of Bayon, where it completed its final training, more than once winning the praise of the French generals for its skill. The terrain was very favorable for preparations for mobile war.

At the beginning of October General Haller was officially appointed commander-in-chief of all Polish units fighting on the side of the coalition. On 6 October 1918 a review was held of the whole division on the fields of Hausonville, where before an impressive compact square of formidable Polish ranks it swore a formal oath of allegiance to the Polish standards.

BAPTISM OF FIRE IN THE VOSGES MOUNTAINS

The French commander-in-chief, Marshal Foch, continued to delay striking the final blow in the direction of Metz. In mid-October the 1st Polish Division became part of X Corps of the 7th Army and occupied a peaceful sector, "St. Die-Nord," in the Vosges Mountains.

During the night of October 17th-18th the 3rd Regiment replaced Americans in the "Ravines" sub-sector. The regiment's combat activity dates from then.

In the forefront stood the 1st and 2nd Battalions, with the 3rd Battalion in reserve. The regiment's sector, two kilometers long, consisted of a system of points of resistance connected with continuous linking trenches and secured with strong wire entanglements and numerous lines of barbed wire. It stretched through a hilly, forested region which made movement difficult; furthermore the whole foreground was so thoroughly mined that one might have considered it completely inaccessible for both sides. So any sort of serious action was out of the question in that sector.

As a result of the proximity of the enemy, whose trenches in places were only a hand grenade throw from the Polish ones, the first days (and especially the nights) had to be anxious ones for the Polish soldier, who had not yet come under fire. The danger of the Polish positions may be attested by the fact that in some places, where the German trenches dominated over the Polish ones, they were saved from completed grenade throws only by the network of wire stretched over the riflemen's trenches. Worth emphasizing was the unusual, frankly exaggerated conscientiousness over doing difficult combat service on the part of both officers and the rank and file. Their spirits were raised by the constant, increasingly successful news from the war's main theater.

Probably fearing some sort of unpleasant changes even in this hitherto peaceful sector, the Germans conducted strong reconnaissance activity. On 21 October 1918 they attacked the 3rd Company of the 3rd Regiment and for a time even forced their way up to the trenches; but they were driven back with significant losses by an immediate bayonet counterattack. In this skirmish the regiment suffered its first losses: a private of the 3rd Company, Jan Suchomski, whom the Germans dragged from the trenches, was killed, and in addition a corporal was wounded.

In retaliation, on 25 October 1918 the 3rd Battalion of the 3rd Regiment organized a successful sortie, one for which it paid, however, with the life of 1st Lt. Roman Miller, killed before the enemy's trenches. *[Translator's Note: here Miller is said to be a por., 1st Lieutenant; in the list of casualties at the end of this booklet his rank is given as ppor., 2nd Lieutenant.]* There were also several wounded, all from the 11th Company (now the 8th).

Finally in the beginning of November the 1st Polish Division, in connection with the long-planned attack on Metz, was called up to the front line of the 8th Army. On 4 November 1918 the regiment was relieved by the French, and after a march of several days arrived at Ramberville, where the whole 1st Division was concentrated, as part of the mighty fist—consisting of 39 divisions—that was intended to settle the fate of the war at last. General Mangin arrayed his forces through Metz and Strasburg for departure toward the joining of German armies collected in Belgium, and in that way to inflict upon the Germans their final defeat.

Unfortunately, fate decreed otherwise: the time had not yet come for the final humiliation of Germany's arrogance. On 11 November 1918 at the break of a gray autumn dawn the regiment prepared to march. It was a lofty, historical moment! Dozens of vehicles waited to hasten the settling of numerous scores with the ancient enemy. Soldiers felt the solemnity of the moment, and a solemn silence dominated the ranks. Then it was interrupted by the hurried snarl of a courier's motorcycle, and after a moment the joyful news, like a stroke of lightning, flew through the ranks: "Truce!" Once more—may it be the last time—the mortal enemy had slipped from the trap set for him.

With this, actually, ends the history of the 3rd Regiment in exile, because the numerous and often wearisome marches that followed the events described—such as to Alsace and back—did not play any great role. At the beginning of December the regiment marched back to the vicinity of Bayon and there began a hopelessly long and, for morale, very burdensome period of waiting for departure home to Poland.

Only one who has been cut off from the Fatherland for a long time, who has remained in complete uncertainty and often ignorance of his fate, only he can understand what the loyal hearts of the Polish soldiers experienced then. Thousands of rumors of all kinds, often misleading and biased, raced through the ranks, sowing confusion in their minds, undermining and tormenting their spirits. But the Polish soldiers endured it all with heads held high with pride. The very few exceptions, by leaving the ranks, only served to cleanse and strengthen all the more the unified might of the Polish troops. The *"Hallerczycy"* [men of Haller's Army] lasted through and endured this difficult time, this long winter. Clenching their teeth, with Mazurian stubbornness they continued to drill so as to acquire as much military knowledge and experience as possible for the Fatherland that needed it so much.

Finally on 18 April 1919 the regiment's first transport set out for Poland.

IN POLAND

THE LIBERATION OF VOLYNIA

On 23 April 1919 the leading divisions of the 3rd Regiment of Polish Riflemen set foot on Polish soil, now free thanks to their own efforts. Much had happened in the meantime. The hands of the heroic "children of Lwów" drooped, a sixth month without change, in cold and hunger desperately defending their beloved, beautiful city. The persistent Germans tried to break the iron ring of regiments from Great Poland. In Belarus the Soviets frantically prepared to retaliate for the defeat at Wilno recently handed them by the Commander-in-Chief, Józef Piłsudski.

The 1st Polish Division was sent to the southern front, to the region of Volhynia. There the army of Soviet Russia had already torn Kiev away from the Ukrainians and tried to reach through Volhynia and Podolia to Poland itself. The division's first assignment was to take over from the weakened Ukrainian forces the fertile lands of Podolia and Volhynia, so as not to give the greedy Soviets such a rich booty. Unfortunately, however, in some places the Ukrainians, confused by some of their own politically unsophisticated leaders, resisted the Polish forces friendly to them.

On 24 April 1919 the 3rd Regiment was quartered in Kowel. After a brief and cursory reorganization (for by the treaty with France "Haller's Army" had to maintain its organization separate for the first half year), consisting of very insignificant changes—such as changing its name to "3rd Regiment of Infantry Riflemen," adapting its provisions to domestic conditions, increasing the budget for horses, editing orders in Polish, and so on—on 12 May 1919 the regiment was already in combat action with individual battalions. 1st Battalion was active in the group of Colonel Pachucki from Włodzimierz to Radomyśl; 2nd Battalion supported Gen. Karnicki's group's offensive from Kowel to Łuck; only 3rd Battalion remained in reserve.

On 15 May 1919, the 2nd Battalion, under the command of Capt. Wiktor Rusiecki, crossed the Stochód river and fought a Ukrainian armored train at Perespa station. It was the regiment's first clash on Polish soil, in which, among others, Sergeant Jan Lenard, a Frenchman, died a valiant death, paying the debt for Polish blood spilled for France by the regiment at Vosges.

On 16 May 1919, the 1st Battalion, under the command of Capt. Dzwonkowski, drove the Ukrainians out of the village of Czaruków and occupied Radomyśl.

And so without encountering significant resistance, both battalions reached the line of the river Styr, and on 21 May 1919 the 3rd Regiment set up a bridgehead on the river's east bank, before Łuck. Here the regiment remained until the end of May, wholly unmolested by the Ukrainians, whom the Russians had pushed from Kiev, so that nothing remained for them but to trust Polish generosity—which they did, *en masse,* along with their commanders, their *atamans*, surrendering to the Polish divisions. In the meantime Polish patrols anxiously watched the foreground, searching for a new enemy who was approaching: the Russians.

The tension of the situation in Polish Upper Silesia, which was being tormented by the Germans, created a need for a strong presence manning the border there. This task was entrusted to the 3rd Regiment, which was positioned on the Silesia border from 30 May to 11 July 1919. On that day the regiment was called back to the eastern front, to Małopolska [Little Poland] for the final elimination of Ukrainian units hostile to the Poles and control of the line of the river Zbrucz. This task was accomplished by the regiment on 16 July 1919.

In the meantime the Russians, threatened on the Lithuanian/Belarusian front by the victorious Polish offensive toward Minsk, began to redeploy their reserves there in large numbers. In order to hinder them in this regrouping, the Polish command decided to go on the offensive in Volhynia, and for this purpose grouped together, among others, the 1st Division of the former Haller's Army (under the command of Gen. Bernard). In execution of this task the 3rd Regiment was concentrated in Łuck till August 8th, as a reserve for the division. The group comprised of the 1st Battalion and 6 units under the command of Capt. Bronisław Grzebień, in order to cover the campaign at Równe from the north, plunged into the deep forests of Volhynian Polesie, on August 10th passing through Derażne to Paszków, where it remained until August 16th, after which it returned to Aleksandrya. The rest of the regiment was concentrated in Równe; there on 11 August it received an assignment to man and fortify the line of the river Horyń, which it succeeded in doing quite skillfully.

The regiment remained on the Horyń until January 1920, manning with its battalions the following, in turn: Ostróg, Sławuta, Szepetówka, and Zasław. Its activity was confined to clearing the neighboring forests of the Bolshevized bands threatening the area.

At that time the regiment's stay in our country had already lasted 6 months, and beginning on 1 September 1919 its reorganization on the Polish model was in full swing.[3] First of all the regiment's name was changed to the *45-y pułk piechoty strzelców kresowych*[4] *[45th Regiment of the Eastern Frontier Infantry Riflemen]* and it was incorporated, along with the 50th Regiment of the Eastern Frontier Infantry Riflemen, into the 26th Brigade of the 13th Infantry Division. Its financial system and budgets were changed; the French wagons, which were too long for Polish roads, were abandoned, horses unable to bear the Polish climate were exchanged, and to some extent the older groups of Americans were discharged. This all caused a certain amount of disorganization for a while, weakened the material force, and created ferment. Soon, however, the regiment's strong organism surmounted this crisis, and the regiment once more presented a combat unit no less strong.

WINTER CAMPAIGN 1919-1920

The winter campaign began in Volhynia. The campaign was based on a complete system of well-planned attacks, shattering the enemy's grouping and through gradual mastery of important tactical points driving the Soviet army farther and farther east from the fertile hills of southern Volhynia.

---

[3] In accordance with the decree of the Head of State dated 27 June 1919, No. 4373, and the order of the Ministry of Military Affairs L, 169/19.

[4] Abbreviated: 45 p. p. s. k.

In early December the Polish command skillfully took advantage of a unique situation: eastern Volhynia was occupied at the time by remnants of the Ukrainian army, wavering between the Russians to the east, Denikin's forces to the south, and the Poles to the west. In fact for a time this army considered itself an ally of Denikin, and so was neutral in regard to us. The defeat and retreat to the south of Denikin's forces made it clear that the uncertain Ukrainian army would have to join with the Russians. This could not be allowed, so that army had to be destroyed in time. This assignment fell on 2nd Battalion of 45th Regiment, and toward this purpose it carried out an energetic attack on Miropol under Capt. Rusiecki, disarming and taking prisoner over 8,000 Ukrainians. A commendatory order from division command emphasized the battalion's valiant behavior:

Order No. 117 dated 16 December 1919

Praise: On 7 December 1919 Miropol, which was providing a base for Ukrainian forces and loose bands, was occupied by II/45 Regiment of the Eastern Frontier Infantry Riflemen under the command of Capt. Rusiecki. In Miropol the following divisions were disarmed and taken prisoner despite stubborn resistance: a unit of the Zaporoże Corps along with its staff; Zaporoże regiments comprising part of the Zaporoże Corps—one of the best Ukrainian units; the corps staff of the army at full strength; an armored train; two artillery batteries; large stores of all kinds of military materials. This excellent outcome of the operation is due solely to the deep discipline, resilience and energy of the whole battalion along with its commander.

In the name of the service I express my sincere thanks for such outstanding conduct of the operation to Capt. Rusiecki, commander of II/45 Regiment of the Eastern Frontier Infantry Riflemen; to all officers, and particularly 1st Lt. Wisłocki, commander of 7th Company, and to all the riflemen of this battalion. I am certain that this battalion will always carry out in an equally valiant manner every task assigned to it.

Skierski, 2nd Lt. Gen.
and commander of 13th Division

In this manner the Polish army seized control of Volhynia as far as the river Słucz. There still remained in the foreground, however, many Bolshevized bands, supported also by regular Soviet units. In January 1920 the Polish command organized a series of attacks designed to clear out the foreground.

Thus on 14 and 15 January the 45th Regiment, by that time under the command of Lt. Col. Michał Bajer, carried out an attack on Lipno and Bratałów. In this attack the heaviest work fell to the 2nd Battalion, led by Capt. Rusiecki, who again carried out his task gloriously.

The attack consisted of two successive strokes: on 14 January at Lipno–Kutyszcze and on 15 January at Awratyn–Bratałów. The maneuver consisted of going around the enemy on the left flank from the northeast. Every attack was conducted by two groups: one engaged frontally from the west, the other went around attacked from the north. On both 14 and 15 January the attacking group was Captain Rusiecki's column. The 2nd Battalion was supported valiantly in this action by the 2nd Battery of the 13th Field Artillery Regiment as well as the 3rd Squadron of the 5th Regiment of Uhlans. As a result the enemy, a force of 1,500 men and one battery, was beaten and retreated to the east in disorder, leaving behind killed, wounded, prisoners of war, one cannon and several machine guns. This attack is mentioned in the General Staff communiqué dated 15 January 1920 L. 412.

At the same time the 3rd Battalion of the 45th Regiment under the command of Capt. Witold Sułkowski was in action farther north, clearing out the foreground of Zwiahel. On 15 January it carried out a successful attack on Czernica, and on the 16th took Kropiwna.

This same assignment, defeating groups of the enemy, was the purpose of an attack on Romanów on 20 January 1920. Here, too, two groups were in action: the first, Major Szylling's (44th Regiment of the Eastern Frontier Riflemen), was to engage the enemy at Romanów frontally from the west, and the second group, of Lt. Col. Bajer, was to outflank Romanów from the southeast. The main task again fell to the 2nd Battalion of the 45th Regiment, and that valiant division acquitted itself of its assignment in the best manner possible.

After concentrating on the evening of 19 January 1920 by the railway tracks near Romanów station, at 8 a.m. on 20 January the second group (composed of the 2nd Battalion of the 45th Regiment of the Eastern Frontier Riflemen, the 1st Battalion of the 50th Regiment of Eastern Frontier Riflemen, the 8th Battery of the 13th Field Artillery Regiment, and a squadron of the 5th Regiment of Uhlans) set forth, covering itself with a squadron from the east. The 1st Battalion of the 50th Regiment of Eastern Frontier Rifleman took Worobijówka after the battle, while the 2nd Battalion of the 45th Regiment executed an attack on Romanów. The enemy put up fierce opposition. The enemy artillery struck powerful blows, while that of the Poles could not effectively support the infantry due to the shape of the terrain. The terrain was completely open. The 2nd Battalion pressed forward, however, and won the day precisely because of its decisiveness and swiftness. 7th Company under the command of 1st Lt. Czesław Wisłocki went around Romanów on the southeast and captured two machine guns, flanking the 2nd Battalion. This tipped the scale toward victory for the Polish side, and the Russians, leaving several score dead and a sizable number of prisoners, withdrew in disorder to the forests northeast of Romanów.

After this attack, on 22 January 1920 the 45th Regiment was transported by rail through Szepetówka to Starokonstantynów, except for the 2nd Battalion, which untiringly covered the regrouping, having taken up a position on the river Słucz near Ostropol. The regiment remained peacefully in these localities until 17 February 1920. It carried out only one attack, on 9 February 1920, on Pilawa.

On that occasion the task was entrusted to the commander of the 3rd Battalion, Capt. Sułkowski. His attack group included: two companies each from the 1st and 3rd Battalions, and half a battery of the 15th Field Artillery Regiment.

Capt. Sułkowski's plan relied on complete encirclement of the garrison of Pilawa; due to the difficult roads, however, the encircling companies did not surround the enemy before dawn, and the light of day betrayed the maneuver, hastening the battalion's concentric attack. The enemy avoided complete encirclement, but was defeated and left in Polish hands one machine gun and 8 prisoners.

In the second half of February the Polish command decided to advance the front to the east of Starokonstantynów, to base it against the river Boh.

On 17 and 18 February 1920 the 45th Regiment, under the temporary command of Capt. Sułkowski, conducted an attack with this goal on Pilawa and Stara Sieniawa.

The guiding principle of this maneuver was to encircle Stara Sieniawa from the northeast, and by taking that locality, surround the Soviet garrison of Pilawa. The entire regiment took part in the attack. The 1st Battalion conducted the main action. Having set out from the village of Swinnoje on the evening of 17 February 1920, at 4:30 a.m. on 18 February it took Misiorówka, and at 7:30 Stara Sieniawa, from the northwest. The 2nd Battalion, after breaking through strong resistance in Adampol, also marched from Ostropol to Stara Sieniawa from the east. The 3rd Battalion under the command of Capt. Józef Rosiak took Pilawa at the same time from the west.

Toward evening on 18 February the Soviet units unleashed a strong concentric counterattack on Stara Sieniawa and for a while even forced their way to the town from the south. In a fierce street battle the regiment's executive officer, Capt. Sułkowski, died. Thanks to the resourcefulness of Capt. Grzebień, however, who quickly mastered the situation and took command of the regiment, Stara Sieniawa was retaken, with the capture of 15 prisoners and 4 machine guns.

The regiment's losses, however, were also significant. Besides Capt. Sułkowski, 4 privates were killed, and in addition 1st Lt. Wacław Ciecierski and 14 privates were injured; 8 of the privates died.

After carrying out its assignment the regiment retreated in the late evening to Pilawa. On 21 February 1920, however, it once more advanced under the newly-appointed command of Lt. Col. Bajer and occupied the line Stara Sieniawa–Misiorówka–Hreczany–Ostropol and fortified that line. The Russians however, obviously alarmed by the advance, counterattacked the new Polish defensive lines continuously. To put an end to this, Lt. Col. Bajer was ordered to carry out a strong attack on the foreground of the threatened 5th Infantry Division, in the area of Chmielnik. This attack, which lasted three days—25 to 27 February—ended successfully: for several weeks in a row the enemy left the Poles in peace.

It was not until the end of March, in connection with an attempt at a general offensive on the southern front, that the Russians also attacked the 45th Regiment several times; but each time they were repulsed with losses. Thus on 25 March 1920 the enemy attacked the positions of the 1st Battalion at the village of Charkowce, and on 26 March at Hreczana. At the same time the 2nd Battalion repelled Soviet attacks on Stara Sieniawa, and the 3rd Battalion, along with the 50th Regiment of Eastern Frontier Riflemen, did the same at Ostropol.

SPRING OFFENSIVE IN THE HEART OF UKRAINE

Along with the strong winds of spring, drying the roads and preparing them, as it were, for the marches of great armies, came the time for the battle that would decide the fate of Poland. During the winter the Soviets succeeded in stifling the Denikin reaction, no less bloody than the Revolution, and raced to get all their forces to the west so as to crush our freedom with a single mighty blow.

To anticipate the blow and cut the red colossus off from Ukraine, which fed it, and restore freedom to Ukraine, there came a bold and joyous order: "an offensive against Kiev."

Toward evening on 25 April 1920 the regiment received its departure grouping: the 1st Battalion from Stara Sieniawa took Kumanowce, the 2nd Battalion crossed over to Nowa Sieniawka. In the morning of 26 April the battalions moved to attack Chmielnik: 2nd Battalion from the front, and the 1st Battalion from midnight through Wójtowce and Wielki Mytnik. As a result of its longer road and the enemy's strong resistance, the 1st Battalion did not arrive in time and the main burden of battle against Chmielnik's heavily fortified positions,

---

[5] Thanks to Captain Rusiecki's swift maneuver to Kalinówka, a Soviet armored train, the "Tovarishch Shauman and Dzhaparydze," was cut off and captured by units of the 13th Infantry Division.

[This is one version of what happened at Kalinówka, but some of the participants told a different story. The following comment was added by Lt. Jan Kostrubała to an account of the capture of Kalinówka station given in the book *Czyn Zbrojny Wychodźtwa Polskiego w Ameryce: Zbiór dokumentów i nateriałów historycznych*, Wydawnictwo Stowarzyszenia Weteranów Armii Polskiej w Ameryce, New York and Chicago 1957 (The Polish Army Veterans' Association of America, 19 Irving Place, New York 3, N.Y.): "Kalinówka station, located on the Koziatyn-Winnica railroad line, was taken by 5th Company of the 45th Regiment, under the command of Lt. Jan Kostrubała, against the orders of Capt. Rusiecki, the commander of the 2nd Battalion. The company took Kalinówka and all the booty mentioned above, contributing substantially to the capture of the armored train 'Dżaparydz.'" — P.S.V.]

surrounded with wire, fell on the 2nd Battalion. But the daredevil attack of the Polish riflemen broke through it all; by noon Chmielnik was taken and a gap had been created in the Soviet front.

On 27 April after a 25-kilometer march the 2nd Battalion, leading the way as always, took Pawłówka and broke the opposition of an entire Soviet brigade at Kalinówka station. This was one of the finest moments in the annals of the regiment. The soldiers' mettle could not be gainsaid: the Soviet brigade's staff and an entire transport—more than 300 prisoners—were left in the hands of the 2nd Battalion.[5]

In the meantime the 3rd Battalion advanced in reserve for the division, and on 28 April also reached the vicinity of Kalinówka.

The regiment remained in those localities until 2 May 1920. This standstill was partly caused by the lateness of units in action to the right of the regiment, in the forests west of Winnica, due to which the right flank of the 13th Division, i. e., the 45th Regiment, was left hanging.

On 3 May 1920 the regiment made an enormous, 50-km. jump forward, and by that evening had cut the Koziatyn–Humań railway line south of Pohrebyszcze, concentrating itself in the vicinity of Lipowiec.

The enemy fled in panic everywhere.

Here the offensive of the 13th Infantry Division ended. It was ordered to fortify the line it had taken, which, due to its extension, was secured with the assistance of independent defensive points of resistance created on all sides and connected in certain systems as so-called "defensive knots." Every regiment formed such a knot. The 45th regiment formed four resistance points: near the village of Skitka, south of the village of Rossosze, east of Napadówka, and a reserve point in Lipowiec, connected with the advance defensive line as a sort of redoubt (between Lipowiec and Skitka).

The regiment's command was located in Lipowiec. Communications were maintained to the right with the 18th Infantry Division in Hordyjówka and to the left with the 50th Regiment in Oczytków. The regiment remained at these positions until the front was attacked by the mounted army of Budionny and our retreat connected with that attack.

BATTLE AT NAPADÓWKA ON 31 MAY 1920

In mid-May rumors began to circulate that a powerful mass of Soviet cavalry under the command of Budionny (a former dragoon cavalry sergeant), who was already known at the time in Russia as the one who defeated Denikin, was approaching by swift marches toward the front of the 13th Infantry Division, with the goal of cutting off its exit toward the rear of the 3rd Polish Army defending Kiev.

After the victories they'd won, however, the morale of our riflemen was so high and self-assured that all the menacing grumbles of the approaching storm found no echo in the soldiers' manly hearts: they felt scorn for their "Bolshevik" enemy.

So it was not terror but only surprise that ran through the ranks when suddenly one day at the end of May, as the regiment was actually preparing to advance, it was learned that there were no communications with the 50th Regiment to the north, and there were scouts of the Budionny forces in Oczytków, strongly fortified by the regiment. Then the 2nd Battalion was drawn up to Lipowiec, and undeterred by this news, the 45th Regiment prepared to jump north toward the danger.

At dawn on 31 May the situation appeared as follows: the 3rd Battalion manned a resistance point east of Napadówka; the 1st Battalion was partly in Skitka with the rest in Lipowiec, in reserve for the regiment; while the 2nd Battalion marched during the night to Napadówka and formed up for attack (but as they thought at the time, only for a march) on Oczeretnia.

The moment had arrived for the glorious battle of Napadówka, which should be engraved in letters of gold in the history not only of the 45th Regiment, but of the entire Polish infantry, for the Poles' first meeting with Budionny's dangerous and hitherto undefeated army resulted in that army's defeat: the tenacious might and courage of the riflemen of the 45th Regiment, as well as the cool blood of their commanders, caused a shameful defeat for one of the Soviets' best divisions.

At the beginning of the battle the regiment's situation was dangerous and could have become catastrophic. The units north of the 45th, startled by a large group of well-organized cavalry, were cut down virtually to a man. The whole 6th Division of Budionny's cavalry (some 6,000 swords) poured through a 17-kilometer-wide break into the regiment's rear, intoxicated by victory and sure of themselves. But having encountered unexpectedly strong resistance at Pohrebyszcze from Lt. Col. Szylling's group, it decided to break through, at any price and with all its force, toward the southeast and through Napadówka and Lipowiec to roll up the left flank of the 45th Regiment.

The Polish units knew nothing about this. The commander of the 2nd Battalion, Capt. Rusiecki, was surprised when at daybreak of the memorable 31st of May, while setting out with his battalion from Napadówka on the road to Oczeretnia, he saw strong columns of cavalry coming out of that village: squadron after squadron, battery after battery rode out on the open hills southwest of Oczeretnia. Capt. Rusiecki assessed the situation: that whole mass of enemy cavalry was obviously heading for Lipowiec toward the regiment's rear, and so he had to draw their attention to himself, to stop them. Supported by the 2nd Battery of the 13th Field Artillery Regiment at the road's opening from Napadówka to

Oczeretnia, the battalion spread out and displayed for attack. Its goal was attained: the enemy cavalry turned its front to Napadówka. The thundering Soviet ordinance sounded; the *tachanki* [horse-drawn machine-gun carts], as yet unseen by the Poles and therefore dangerous as a great surprise in the war, began to rumble; and the columns of cavalry made a frontal attack on the 2nd Battalion, "in a mass." The 45th Regiment was promptly forced to fight with a reversed front. But the enemy only littered the battlefield with dead: sure, steady salvos signaled to the Cossacks that the average Polish infantryman had not lost his head, and the charge did not terrify him.

A second attack by the enemy was supported by an armored car, which with mad courage drove up to 50 meters from the Polish battery; but it was shot at and captured. At the same time a powerful column of cavalry, circling through the woods near Uljanówka around the Polish left flank, attacked from the southwest to Napadówka.

The counterattack of the reserve, however, in which even the supply columns took part, drove them back, during which Private Kalinowski stabbed several of the enemy, including one commander of the regiment, in hand-to-hand combat.

While the 2nd Battalion was fighting so victoriously to the west of Napadówka, strewing the field with the bodies of their foes, the second column of the enemy's cavalry, supported by fire from three armored trains (from Lipowiec station), attacked the 3rd Battalion east of Napadówka; and a third, supported by an armored car, attacked from the west toward Lipowiec.

The situation became dangerous: units of the regiment were fighting now on all sides, surrounded by a mobile foe that outnumbered them. The 3rd Battalion, however, defended itself, and the armored car that attacked Lipowiec was captured by an outpost of the 3rd Company.

The enemy was driven back everywhere.

In vain new squadrons kept charging, in vain extended orders hurried to try their luck, supported by numerous *tachanki* and the battery's hurricane fire—everything broke against the iron courage of the Polish infantryman.

Toward evening the decimated Soviet regiments, leaving hundreds of dead men and horses on the field, hid in the woods northeast of the Polish lines.

Thus ended the first meeting of the Polish infantryman with the famed and supposedly unbeatable cavalry of Budionny, forcefully demonstrating yet again that for the infantryman who does not lose his head, even a tenfold superiority of the cavalry is not terrifying: always and everywhere the infantry remains the queen on the field, if only it has the will strong enough to do so.

The regiment's losses, however, were heavy: the 2nd Battalion, which bore the main burden of the battle, lost about 70 men killed and wounded, and the regiment as a whole lost 100.

A few words should be said on the meaning and consequences of this victory. Above all, a division of the Soviet cavalry sustained a defeat, and a dangerous breach in the front was patched up. Budionny's army did not succeed in making a hole in the Polish front at the appointed time and was forced to seek some other, weaker spot. The morale consequences of this battle were great. One can imagine how negatively this defeat must have influenced the spirits and certainty not only of the Cossacks, but also their leader, for whom things went wrong for the first time in his career. But the main prize of this battle was the reinforcement of the spirit of the Polish infantryman: the conviction was strengthened within him that always and everywhere, whether on foot or mounted, the Muscovite would have to flee from the Pole. This certainty never left the regiment's rank and file: even when the regiment was ordered to retreat to Lwów, the soldier was always sure that he had only to turn his face to the east and the "Bolshevik" would be humiliated. The regiment persisted in this certainty, won victories later with it, and it passed into a tradition of the regiment: "the 45th Regiment can never be defeated in open battle."

And the name of this little Ukrainian village, Napadówka, along with the date 31 May 1920, deserve to be immortalized on the regimental standard, for enchanted in those symbolic letters and numbers is the certainty of victory.

RETREAT

On the morning of the second day after the battle at Napadówka the regiment, ignoring its physical exhaustion, conducted an attack on Bohdanówka and Oczytków. Budionny's regiments, taken completely by surprise, hid deeper in the forests and disappeared from our view for a long time.

On 5 June Budionny's mounted army succeeded in breaking through to the north of the 13th Infantry Division. Despite this, the division not only did not retreat; on 6 June it even advanced on its right flank up to the line of the rivers Roś and Rośka. There was no talk of giving way to Budionny. The 45th Regiment fortified itself in the region of Żywotów and Oratów without any contact with the enemy.

Worth emphasizing was the local population's unusual civility toward the Poles: suffice it to say the Ukrainians of that area volunteered to dig trenches for us.

At the same time Budionny's army surprised the distant Polish rear at Żytomierz and Berdyczów. This forced the entire 6th Polish Army (which included the 13th Infantry Division) to begin a retreat.

In connection with this the Regiment concentrated itself in the vicinity of Lipowiec, without any contact with the enemy, and on 12 June began to retreat. For a long time it marched its long road without any information on the enemy: it passed Pryłuki, Kalinówka, Pików, Chmielnik, and finally reached its spring positions at Stara Sieniawa. There the regiment halted. The intensity of the enemy's pursuit met bloody restraint at the hands of the 1st Battalion at Tereszpol on 21 June 1920.

The regiment did an about-face: the 3rd Battalion took up positions at Stara Sieniawa, the 2nd Battalion at Misiorówka, and the 1st stood in reserve; as was its custom, the regiment immediately fortified its positions and boldly waited for the enemy. And sure enough, on 23 June the Soviet cavalry attacked Misiorówka. For two days the valiant 2nd Battalion struggled with a foe many times larger, and the mad charges of the *tachanki* were invariably broken; at critical times reserves from the 1st and 2nd Battalions supported the 2nd Battalion [sic], and the 1st Battery of the 13th Field Artillery Regiment provided extraordinarily brave assistance, more than once emerging into an exposed position.

On 30 June the enemy repeated his attack on Misiorówka, but again in vain: the bodies of 80 Soviets remained on the foreground of the 2nd Battalion.

The regiment had to stand its ground, so it did, and held out until Gen. Krajewski with the 18th Infantry Division marched through Starokonstantynów to the north, to break through Budionny's mounted forces and establish communications between the 6th and 2nd Armies.

On 6 July the whole 13th Division concentrated itself in Starokonstantynów, so as to march further in compact columns, as brigades. It had to stop at once, because its position became truly dangerous. To the north the 18th Infantry Division was breaking through in the direction of Ostróg, and communications with it were lost. Bad news had also come from the south in recent days: the 8th Soviet Cavalry Division (of Comrade Primakov [*Vitaliy Markovich Primakov, 1897-1937*]) had broken through the Polish 12th Infantry Division and attacked the 6th Army Staff at Płoskirów, temporarily taking Czarny Ostrów and operating deep behind the lines.

So on 7 July the 13th Division began to retreat through Krasiłów, with the 45th Regiment as advance guard. It was a difficult march, as the enemy was to be expected on all sides. The waiting didn't last long. At Zozulińce on 8 August [*sic, from context clearly should be 8 July*] the enemy barred the way for the 45th Regiment, but, as always, was defeated and ran off to the northeast. The retreat continued but without contact with the enemy. The regiment passed Bazalja and on 12 July manned a sector southeast of Wiśniowiec (near the village of Czajczyńce–Gnidawa), which was also fortified, as the position allowed them to hold back the enemy for some time: north of the 13th Division the Polish front gradually strengthened.

Fierce battles were fought with the enemy's advance guard. On 13 July at Kotiużyńce the Soviet cavalry made a surprise attack on the 2nd Battalion's rear guard (6th Company), causing painful losses.

The Regiment defended Wiśniowiec till 24 July, at which time it received a command to depart along the western bank of the Seret river, in connection with Budionny's continued advance toward Lwów as far as Brody. The regiment stayed in this new sector amid constant battles until 7 August, when the enemy broke through to the right of the 45th Regiment in the region of Tarnopol.

Even then, however, the regiment did not give up. Capt. Rusiecki (now in charge of a whole group in addition to 2nd Battalion: the Łódź Staging Battalion and the "General Iwaszkiewicz" armored train) turned his right flank and held back the enemy for several days with counterattacks. A pitched battle was waged from 8 to 11 August at Cebrów. The enemy never succeeded in breaking through the regiment's defensive positions. Even on 12 August Capt. Rosiak, the commander of 3rd Battalion, attacked the village of Kurowce with 9th and 12th Companies, defeating there two Soviet regiments (the 532nd and 534th), taking prisoners and 3 machine guns.

Not until 14 August, in connection with the situation of neighboring units did the regiment receive the command to retreat. On 15 and 16 August 1st and 3rd Battalions fought victoriously on the upper Strypa, at Nuszce and Iwaczów, holding back the pursuit of the Soviet cavalry.

BATTLE AT KUROWICE 18 AUGUST 1920

As a result of Budionny's breakthrough at Busk in the direction of Lwów, according to the regrouping connected with it, the 45th Regiment turned away from the enemy and went by rapid march toward Lwów, to protect that city. During the march their spirits were raised by news of the successful battles at Warsaw; every officer and soldier swore in his heart that like Tukhachevsky at Warsaw, so Budionny will never be in Lwów.

When the regiment left the hilly forests of Gołogóry, it had to fight a difficult battle with the Soviet cavalry, which was trying to catch up with it. From then on the regiment remained in close contact with the enemy, whose artillery bombarded them ceaselessly.

The regiment marched farther down the road in a column of the 26th Infantry Brigade. This was an unusual march—a race. The whole time Budionny's dark columns could be seen to the north, parallel to the path by which the 26th Brigade was also marching to Lwów. Who will be in the lead? Finally on 18 August, past the village of Kurowice, we tread upon the heels of the enemy: he had to accept a battle which looked very odd, as if it were Budionny defending Lwów.

The 2nd Battalion, in the vanguard of the brigade, tried to break directly through by the road to Lwów past Budionny's squadrons.[6]

---

[6] Probably the 11th Cavalry Division.

Right at the exit from Kurowice it came under machine gun fire, to which salvos of the Soviet battery from Hermanów were soon added. Unshaken by this, without a moment's hesitation Capt. Rusiecki took the divided formation and drove the enemy as far as Mogiła. Here powerful extended orders of speedy cavalry, supported by numerous machine guns on *tachánki* as well as the fire of two batteries, held back the leading battalion, forcing the entire 26th Brigade to accept battle, that is, to fight their way through.

Then the 2nd and 3rd Batteries of the 13th Field Artillery Regiment took up positions along the road, while the 1st Battery of the 13th Heavy Artillery Regiment actually took a position right on the highway, to begin without delay a fatal battle. The supply columns formed up on the highway in two ranks, to defend themselves from charges from beyond the carts.

At the same time as the front line was held up, a powerful column of cavalry emerged from a wide streak of dust northwest of Kurowice and without a moment's thought attacked the side of the 1st Battalions' marching column in large numbers.

Before Capt. Grzebień had drawn up his battalion for battle, Budionny's forces were already 1,000 meters from him and their daredevil charge drove forward with full momentum.

It was a dangerous and beautiful sight, such as one rarely sees in today's warfare: a long, silent double row of infantrymen, bristling with bayonets, and before them the whole field rumbles under a dark avalanche of rushing cavalry. Then only 600 meters divides the battling forces … At that point the sudden fire of all the rifles and machine guns of the whole battalion spewed hell in the faces of the daring riders. But it could not stop them: they rushed toward certain death, no longer able to break their own momentum … Only 150 meters from the unmoving infantrymen was the first mad charge of the enemy broken. The cavalry column scampered away in disorder after strewing the field with the bodies of men and horses.

Shortly after this first charge, intended only to shock, the enemy regrouped his columns and arranged 8 machine guns on his flank, and began a regular attack along the highway from Hermanów as well as farther to the right—almost directly from the north. That attack was also nipped in the bud, because it encountered a counterattack of the 1st Battalion, which, as it developed along the highway, moved forward along the whole front—like a fan heaping the enemy from the southeast along his right flank. Again we see an episode most rare in the history of war: an infantry attack on charging cavalry.

First Lt. Izydor Rozenman with a platoon of 4th Company advanced to the enemy's battery, but was wounded, and that alone kept the Poles from taking it.

In the meantime the enemy had not yet given up. Supported by units that had come up from Wyżniany (probably the 6th Cavalry Division), the enemy made a third violent charge on the 1st and 2nd Battalions from the front and both flanks. The momentum of the charge was so great that individual groups of riders, unable to stop, broke through the Polish lines and were eliminated only in hand-to-hand combat with our brave lads.

Particularly admirable were the cool heads of the officers and the combat discipline of the men. Even the sizable percentage of recruits in the ranks caused no confusion at all: every platoon, every section stood as if rooted to the spot.

Evidently it was only after this third charge that the enemy realized his helplessness against the courage of the Polish infantryman, because the attacks were not repeated, and only the fire of the batteries covered his ragged regiments' retreat to the southeast. The Polish batteries paid them back in kind, and the artillery battle lasted till 2200 hours. Night came upon a field littered with bodies, when the dead-tired 45th Regiment could once more begin its withdrawal toward Lwów, chased by no one.

After a 50-kilometer march and two battles lasting a total of some 12 hours, the regiment marched to Winniki at 0700 hours on 19 August, where it camped in the dense surrounding forests.

How significant for the defense of Lwów the battle at Kurowice was, and how valiantly the 45th Regiment acquitted itself in combat, can be best attested by the fact that at this battle 18 officers and soldiers of the regiment were decorated with the silver cross *"virtuti militari"* 5th class.

BATTLE AT ŁABUŃKI 31 AUGUST 1920

Budionny, finally convinced he would not take Lwów, obeyed his commanders' orders. His divisions stretched north to relieve the remnants of Tukhachevsky's army, crushed by the blow of the Commander-in-Chief by the river Wieprz.

In connection with this, on 22 August 1920 the 45th Regiment boarded trains and departed for Rawa Ruska, along with the entire 13th Infantry Division, so as not to lose contact with the mounted army fleeing in the direction of Zamość and to help corner it.

Although the marches along roads softened by rain strained our soldiers, the regiment's morale at the end of the retreat was just as good as at its beginning. The regiment, ignoring the generally demoralizing influence of this period, felt no drop in its spirits.

After a short rest in Ulhówek, on 27 August the regiment marched along a difficult sandy road to Radków and Lachowce *[sic, ? Łachowce, a few km. northeast of Ulhówek]*, but did not succeed in blocking Budionny's path; only the artillery of the 13th Field Artillery Regiment bombarded his squadrons' lateral guard, stretching along road from Sokal to Zamość. There was no doubt that Budionny decided to take Zamość in order to cut the Polish front into two pieces and hold in check the Polish units of 3rd Army hurrying after Tukhachevsky's beaten armies.

Without delay, therefore, the regiment set out after the Soviet mounted army heading for Zamość. This turned out to be an illustration of the old saying "The biter bit" —Budionny, trying to corner Zamość, was himself cornered.

So the regiment marched in the still fresh tracks of Budionny through Wołuczyn–Dąbrowa and on 30 August caught up with his rear guard at Krynicki Majdan [*now called Majdan Krynicki*]. The 2nd Battalion thrashed his protection, and through the forests the whole regiment approached Łabuńska Wola, where the enemy tried to offer resistance.

Without a moment's hesitation the 1st Battalion charged, supported by efficient artillery, particularly the 3rd Battery of the 13th Field Artillery Regiment. By evening the manorial farmstead and village of Łabunie were taken. The enemy retreated to the village of Łabuńki, just 7 km. away from Zamość, valiantly defended by units of the 10th Infantry Division.

Without pausing for breath, at daybreak on 31 August the 3rd Battalion attacked and took Łabuńki after a bloody, furious battle; the 1st Battalion expanded this success, taking Jatutów, located 5 km. from Zamość.

In this battle a private of the 9th Company, Baltazar Czapla, distinguished himself. The 3rd Battalion, attacking Łabuńki, had to traverse a swampy, completely open space of 400 meters. Unexpectedly the Polish extended line was halted by a canal 5 meters wide. The soldiers ran helplessly under the enemy's nearby, murderous fire, and the battalion was in danger of defeat. Then Private Czapla, without waiting for an order, threw himself into the water up to his neck and not only waded through it himself, but helped several other soldiers do so. This example galvanized the 9th Company, and behind it the whole 3rd Battalion. The enemy was beaten at a stroke.

The fate of Zamość was decided in the Poles' favor: Budionny's last risky bet was lost. As far as the eye could see one, disordered heaps of his mounted forces, beaten to the last day, were running away, each man for himself as he could; the Polish artillery routed the fleeing. Budionny's fame was extinguished in the war with the Poles.

And thus the 45th Regiment could boldly say that this Cossack headman had no luck with them: Budionny's first encounter with the regiment on 31 May, like his last one three months later on 31 August 1920, ended in an utter rout of the Soviet cavalry.

LAST OFFENSIVE IN VOLHYNIA

The commander of the 13th Infantry Division ordered energetic pursuit. On 1 September the regiment advanced once more by forced march eastward, toward

Volhynia. The 2nd Battalion, in the vanguard, broke the enemy's resistance at Wakijów. Further pursuit was taken up by the 6th Cavalry Brigade, and the 45th Regiment hurried northward, toward Hrubieszów, so that on 5 September it could rout the Soviet rear guard at Werbkowice. The ferocity of the resistance is attested by the regiment's losses—about 40 were killed that day.

That same day the regiment moved on and crossed the small river Huczwa at Werbkowice. The following days were spent in resting and preparation for the last offensive beyond the Bug river.

On 12 September the regiment set out with the goal of breaking the line on the river Bug, fiercely defended by the Soviet army. By 0730 hours the regiment had already taken Ambukowa and gone on to Cucniów. There the 1st Battalion received the assignment of taking hill "243" north of Poromów: the 45th Regiment's attack was supported on the right flank by the 1st Infantry Corps, which, having adopted Budionny's tactic, swiftly drove the Cossacks before it with numerous machine guns on carts. Poromów was taken with one rush, but there they encountered concentrated fire of unusual intensity from the Soviet artillery. Disregarding its fatigue, the regiment advanced, took Bożanka, and in pursuit reached the heavily defended Biskupiczki Małe.

The fighting with the Soviet rearguard continued till late at night; the regiment suffered significant losses that day (more than 80 men killed and wounded), but the enemy's resistance was once more broken. The defensive line of the Bug no longer existed for him, and the way to Volhynia lay open.

On the next day the regiment plunged into the gap thus created. The enemy tried once more to fight his way to the village of Sielce on the line of the very marshy river Ług. As the 2nd Battalion went around from the northwest, the 3rd Battalion, along with units of the 44th Regiment of the Eastern Border Riflemen, did not wait but attacked from the front across a 2-kilometer long dam. This was near madness. Fortunately the battalion succeeded in avoiding heavy losses, thanks only to the unusual swiftness of the attack. The enemy did not manage to pull himself together before 9th Company, headed by 1st Lt. Wojciech Stygar, wading up to their belts in the swamp, crossed the lowland and took Sielce with a daredevil attack. The enemy's counterattack was broken by Polish artillery fire.

Without pausing, at daybreak on 14 September the regiment set out in pursuit. It was known that the enemy intended to defend himself on the line of the river Styr, and for that purpose was concentrating his forces in Łuck. So what mattered was to cross the Styr quickly, without giving the Russians a chance to organize resistance. So the regiment passed Łokacze—Szelwów, and on 15 September arrived at Antonówka, where it received an assignment: to go around Łuck to the south and, crossing the Styr in Boratyn on 16 September, thwart the enemy's resistance. The regiment carried out its assignment splendidly. The last battle that the regiment fought in that war was no less glorious than the first.

Now, too, it owed its victory to the unusual self-confidence and daring of the officers and men.

Having lost all hope of holding the crossing of the Styr in his hands, the enemy set fire to the bridge; but it brought him no advantage, as Capt. Rusiak at the head of the 3rd Battalion darted through the flames onto the other side and in a few minutes organized a bridgehead there. In a daze the enemy panicked and fled. The river Styr was crossed, and the capital of Volhynia, Łuck, was in Polish hands. For this battle the valiant Capt. Rosiak was awarded the Cross *"virtuti militari,"* 5th class.

On 17 September the pursuit began once more, along with the liberation of Volhynia from the enemy's invasion. The regiment marched without coming into contact with the enemy, who was entrusted to the "care" of the cavalry.

On 19 September at 1400 hours the 45th Regiment entered Równo from the direction of Obarów, no more to leave that post, lying in wait on the border of Volhynia.

Here the regiment experienced the glorious day of victorious armistice.

AFTER THE WAR

After twice liberating the lands of Volhynia from the Russian yoke, exhausted by four months of victorious struggle with Budionny, the 45th Regiment of Eastern Border Riflemen remained on watch over the borderland.

For a long time, till February 1921, the regiment stood as the border guard and without resting performed heavy service that differed little from combat, since the ferocious eastern elements awakened by war and revolution did not wish to enter into the framework of normal life.

But even later, when finally barracked in Równe, the regiment began arduous peacetime labor, and knew no rest: it constantly had to be on guard and remain in readiness, to protect the Fatherland with their own breast at any moment from the foe's designs.

For a long time masses of Bolshevized so-called *dywersanty [partisans]* running loose on what were truly the "wild steppes" of the eastern borderland would not let them have a moment's peace.

And this watchful readiness entered the blood of the regiment. "To watch over the peace of the Fatherland" became the regiment's main watchword.

Their peacetime work in these conditions was extremely difficult, for every so often training gear and materials had to be exchanged for those of combat. Systematic training, education, and maintaining discipline in such conditions was made very difficult.

So if all these valuable peacetime virtues of the regiment were maintained at a fittingly high level without loss of constant battle readiness, that can only be attributed to the unusually self-sacrificing and committed work, full of tact and dedication, of the officers' and non-commissioned officers' corps.

The splendid combat history of their commander for long years, Col. Kazimierz Rybicki, and of many officers and non-commissioned officers of the regiment guarantees that the sacrifices of the heroes at Napadówka, Lwów and Zamość were not in vain.

The memory of their deeds will live on in the heart of the Polish infantryman, strengthening love of Fatherland and will for victory in the ranks of the 45th Regiment of Eastern Border Riflemen.

LIST OF THOSE WHO FELL IN BATTLE OR DIED OF THEIR WOUNDS

Officers:
1. Officer cadet Grodecki Teodor
2. 2nd Lt. Miller Roman
3. Capt. Sułkowski Witold

Men:

1. Pvt. Abraszek Jan
2. Pvt. Baczewski Mieczysław
3. Pvt. Borowy Konstanty
4. Pvt. Brodzik Jan
5. Pvt. Buczak Władysław
6. Pvt. Chudziński Michał
7. Pvt. Cichocki Antoni
8. Pvt. Czajkowski Bronisław
9. Pvt. Drab Stanisław
10. Pvt. Drzymała Stanisław
11. Pvt. Flis Adam
12. Pvt. Forejak Franciszek
13. Pvt. Fuks Bernard
14. Pvt. Garbowski Stanisław
15. Pvt. Gleba Stanisław
16. Pvt. Głodowski Edward
17. Pvt. Gordyjasz Ignacy
18. Pvt. Gródka Szymon
19. Pvt. Grzymała Stanisław
20. Pvt. Gurałtowski Juljan
21. Pvt. Guzek Stanisław
22. Pvt. Hojna Leon
23. Pvt. Jakubson Abusz
24. Pvt. Juszkiewicz Bolesław
25. Pvt. Kacpura Władysław
26. Pvt. Karczmarz Józef
27. Pvt. Karwański Józef
28. Pvt. Kaspura Władysław
29. Pvt. Kędziora Michał
30. Pvt. Keler Jan
31. Pvt. Kierzkowski Feliks
32. Pvt. Kieszkowski Tadeusz
33. Pvt. Klonowski Henryk
34. Pvt. Kłubiec Stanisław
35. Pvt. Knieja Józef
36. Pvt. Kohn Nathan
37. Pvt. Kolszewski Baruch (Stanisł.)
38. Pvt. Korpała Jan
39. Pvt. Kostrubiec Stanisław
40. PFC Kotczak Franciszek
41. Pvt. Kowalski Antoni
42. Pvt. Kowalski Michał
43. Pvt. Kozioł Stanisław
44. Pvt. Kraus Kauma
45. Pvt. Krzemieniewicz Marjan
46. Pvt. Kuc Józef
47. Pvt. Kuć Józef
48. Pvt. Kurczab Jakób
49. Pvt. Kuryłek Wacław
50. Pvt. Lejzerowicz Samuel
52. Sgt. Lenard Jan (Frenchman)
53. Pvt. Ligenza Bolesław
54. Pvt. Lipiec Franciszek
55. Cpl. Lipiec Józef
56. Pvt. Lipiński Władysław
57. Pvt. Łapiński Jan (Aleksander)
58. Pvt. Machowicz Stefan
59. Cpl. Majewski Aleksander

HISTORY OF THE 45TH REGIMENT – 257

60. Cpl. Malczewski Stanisław
61. Pvt. Malec Andrzej
62. Pvt. Małocha Piotr
63. Pvt. Małolepszy Stanisław
64. Pvt. Marchewka Faustyn
65. Pvt. Migoń Stefan
66. Pvt. Mirko Jan
67. Pvt. Miszczuk Andrzej
68. Pvt. Modzelewski St.
69. Pvt. Mozolewski Antoni
70. Pvt. Mścichowski Stanisąaw
71. PFC Muszyński Antoni
72. Pvt. Niebrzygowski Aleksander
73. Pvt. Nowojerski Józef
74. Sgt. Nyczka Franciszek
75. Cpl. Oleszczuk Stan. (Andrzej)
76. Pvt. Organiszczak Władysław
77. Pvt. Ostrzyniec Romuald
78. Pvt. Pakaluk Aleksander
79. Master Cpl. Paluszkiewiez Wacław
80. Pvt. Pawełczuk Józef
81. PFC Pińczyński Mieczysław
82. PFC Plizga Michał
83. Pvt. Płotyniak Adam
84. Pvt. Protyniak Adam
85. Pvt. Pruchniewicz Sylwester
86. PFC Pruszyński Stanisław
87. Pvt. Przystaś Ignacy
88. Pvt. Ruch Leon
89. Pvt. Sejborski Stanisław
90. Pvt. Sejda Antoni
91. Pvt. Siledec Grzegorz
92. Pvt. Ślepko Józef
93. Pvt. Słomski Aron
94. Pvt. Smolis Bolesław
95. Pvt. Sobczak Kazimierz
96. Pvt. Stolec Jan
97. Pvt. Suchowski Jan (the regiment's first casualty)
98. Pvt. Świderski Józef
99. Pvt. Świtalski Stanisław
100. Pvt. Szot Franciszek
101. Pvt. Szpilski Antoni
102. Pvt. Sztolc Jan
103. Pvt. Szymborski Stanisław
104. Pvt. Terciak Franciszek
105. Pvt. Trojan Ignacy
106. Pvt. Trop Stanisław
107. Pvt. Wagner Stanisław
108. Pvt. Warakowski Paweł
109. Pvt. Wasiak Bronisław
110. Pvt. Waszak Bronisław
111. Pvt. Wątroba Andrzej
112. Pvt. Wegner Stanisław
113. PFC Wertman Salomon
114. Pvt. Wnuk Antoni
115. Cpl. Wojciechowski Józef
116. Pvt. Wójcik Juljan
117. Cpl. Woźniak Andrzej
118. PFC Woźniak Stefan
119. Pvt. Wszoła Franciszek
120. Pvt. Wyszyński Tomasz
121. Pvt. Załęski Feliks
122. Master Sgt. Zamojski
123. Cpl. Zaorski Franciszek
124. Pvt. Zdrodowski Bolesław
125. Pvt. Zdunek Władysław
126. Sgt. Żebrowski Stanisław
127. Pvt. Zięba Antoni
128. Pvt. Ziebroń Piotr
129. Pvt. Żuzik Tadeusz
130. Pvt. Żyła Józef

In addition the following died of disease (primarily typhus) at the front: officers 2, men 192. Wounded (approximately): officers 14, men 350.

LIST OF THOSE DECORATED WITH THE SILVER CROSS OF THE ORDER "VIRTUTI MILITARI" 5TH CLASS

1. Lt. Col. Michał Bajer
2. Master Cpl. Józef Bajorek
3. Sgt. Tomasz Borowicz
4. PFC Jan Brzuszkiewicz
5. Master Cpl. Jan Cencek
6. Cpl. Józef Chachaj
7. 1st Lt. Wacław Ciecierski
8. Pvt. Baltazar Czapla
9. Lt. Sylwester Drączkowski
10. 2nd Lt. Tymoteusz Fuczyła
11. Pvt. Jan Gromek
12. Master Sgt. Szczepan Gruza
13. Capt. Bronisław Grzebień
14. Sgt. Wacław Klemczak

15. Sgt. Alojzy Kurtok
16. Cpl. Edward Kuta
17. Capt. Konstany Lubicz-Kośmiński
18. Cpl. Stefan Małoga
19. Lt. Antoni Mieczkowski
20. Master Sgt. Jan Mikuła
21. Pvt. Szczepan Mizio
22. Sgt. Józef Nowak
23. Pvt. Kazimierz Nowak
24. Col. Leon Pachucki
25. Pvt. Franciszek Panicz
26. Master Cpl. Józef Paprocki
27. 1st Lt. Józef Perzan
28. 1st Lt. Jan Pospuła
29. Master Cpl. Franciszek Ratajczak
30. Capt. Józef Rosiak
31. Capt. Wiktor Rusiecki
32. Sgt. Paweł Rychlik
33. Master Cpl. Stefan Simiński
34. 1st Lt. Wacław Smakosz
35. Master Sgt. Paweł Stefaniak
36. Master Cpl. Damazy Święcicki
37. Sgt. Antoni Szymański
38. 1st Lt. Czesław Wisłocki

Awarded the *Krzyż walecznych* [Cross of Valor] were: 36 officers and 168 men. In addition the French Cross "De la Victoire" was awarded to 14 officers and 70 men.

THE REGIMENT'S BOOTY

Around 9,000 prisoners of war (1 army staff, 1 division staff, 2 brigade staffs as well as several regimental staffs), several hundred horses, one armored train, two armored cars, 7 cannons (1 active in battle), 100 medium machine-guns (17 active in battle), several thousand rifles, 5 locomotives, 460 wagons (including dozens with ammunition) and a Ukrainian army strongbox.

The caption says, "Gen. Haller surrounded by Hallerczycy *departing for America, 19 January 1921." Often regarded as the last troop transport of the Polish Army in France, the* President Grant *departed Danzig January 19, 1921 and arrived in New York City on February 16, 1921. It has been discovered that additional ships brought back* Hallerczycy *in smaller groups as late as 1923 with some ships bringing back men with their families from Poland, and other ships bringing the wounded home after extended hospitalizations in France and Poland.*

In this photo, General Haller, with his distinctive goatee, is pictured slightly right of center. 1st Lt. Jan Kostrubała is seen in the forefront, standing fourth from the left.

Helena and Stanisław Nastał.

*Stanisław Nastał: Born February 5, 1899, Stara Wieś, Brzozów, Galicia (Poland)
Died September 6, 1947, Milwaukee, Wisconsin, U.S.A.*

Stanisław I. Nastał
Staff Captain, 13th Division

THE BLUE DIVISION

CLEVELAND, OHIO

PUBLISHED BY THE POLISH ARMY VETERANS' ASSOCIATION IN AMERICA

7146 Broadway

1922

FOREWORD

Soldier of the "Steel Division" in America! Mindful of the blood of your comrades who fell on the fields of Champagne and Lorraine; mindful of the blood of comrades who died with a smile on their lips in their Fatherland, returning to it the Eastern Borderlands; mindful of the heroic death of the 7th Battery at Żywotów; mindful of the fatal battles at Holendry, Dziónków, Lipów, Zamość—raise your head high and be proud of your deeds. Defend the honor of your land, for which you shed blood in various countries; defend your soldierly honor, for which the entire 7th Battery died, and your comrades!

Be a soldier! Forget personal grudges, for you are a soldier, above personal interests! Blue soldier, often forgotten, history will praise your services!

As for the vestiges of your blue uniform, take them with you to the grave.

I dedicate this work to the Polish soldier from America, and to those who supported that soldier.

Author

POLONIA-JUTRZENKA PUBL. CO., 7007-9 BROADWAY, CLEVELAND, O.

At the camp in Niagara on the Lake, new units of volunteers kept arriving, dressed all different ways, with a red-white band on the left sleeve that said "Volunteer to Polish Army in France." Word that an autonomous Polish Army was being formed in France, one that was to fight for Poland alongside the Allies, awakened the everyday laborer in the steelworks and the mines from his lethargy. The emigrant community in America realized that the time had come for action. With few exceptions they all worked in the same direction: either in the ranks or for the ranks. The worker abandoned his previous occupation and set forth with broad chest and wrinkled hands to "kill Germans."

After "warm scenes" which those staying behind provided the volunteer, he set out for the mobilization camp amid the enthusiastic cries of those saying goodbye. "Come back healthy and victorious," was the cry sent after the departing trains.

Camp Niagara, later called Camp Kościuszko, had a military look: hundreds of tents covered the fields by Lake Ontario. The volunteers arrived with traces of warm goodbyes: flowers, ribbons, flags and banners. The camp looked colorful and animated. Poland in America was waking up!

Among the crowd of volunteers, miners from Pennsylvania with bushy mustaches and stern faces, newly created officers in red coats from the Canadian school were bustling, imposing structure and a more or less military order on the crowds that looked around at everything good-naturedly. Worth emphasizing is the unusual harmony that ruled between the red-coated representatives of the military and the broad-shouldered, mustached volunteer.

And no wonder—after all, it was in service to the Fatherland!

Each of the volunteers received an assignment to "board" in a tent, where he met seven more of his comrades, who sketched out his "room" on the floor with chalk. The volunteer put his things (a towel and, if he had one, a blanket) in the designated section of the tent's circular platform, and he sat down on these precious items to spend the evening chatting with his comrades about bygone days, about Poland.

Lying down to rest had already become a military activity and demanded technical experience. The men sharing a single tent stood all around the pole that supported it and on command stretched out on the floor, each in his section, along the borders marked out in chalk. Giants from Pennsylvania had to pull in their legs somewhat, since their heads touched the tent walls and they stretched to the pole standing in the middle of the tent. And so, forming almost a single body, the tent fell asleep, dreaming of future battles, of lady loves left behind. At the reveille signal all got up together, as there was no way to manage any further sleeping; the tent's modest platform did not have room for so many "number-12" shoes in motion.

The cold fall days required one to dress quickly. The "redcoats" were already walking along the line of tents, giving directions and orders.

The washrooms were in the fields and some distance from the tents. "Quick, on the run," each encouraged the other as they ran toward the washrooms in hopes of staving off that most difficult operation: washing with cold water … The red-coated officers are already here, too, and again they lead: "A gentleman shaves every day, and a soldier must." In the face of such a logical statement, it was better to be a gentleman and shave voluntarily. But that was a difficult operation, because the razors, two to a platoon, purchased with joint money, were nicked, and soap froze on the chin. Two towels per platoon were also common property, and forced the less patient who could not wait their turn to wipe themselves off on the more hygienic sections of their shirts.

"Old women don't serve in the army," they encouraged each other; and this same operation was repeated every morning.

Breakfast. In line for the kitchen with mess kit in hand; those who lost their own spoons or knives borrowed them from their comrades or did without these implements—after all, you had to eat, and there wasn't that much and it was all in one piece. "Not enough bread," some grumbled.

After breakfast the "redcoats" already on the field gave the signal for assembly. Then the work of combining began: arranging, comparing, picking—at last one of the freshly minted officers begins to explain in detail the posture "Attention!" Military training was mixed with calisthenics and sports games. Among the most interesting and most hard-fought games were those of football. This game demanded a certain sophistication, so at the beginning there were many surprises and humorous scenes. Here a heavy miner throws himself toward the slender football as it falls from above; he aims his blow and kicks, but since he's doing it for the first time in his life, he misses the ball and kicks the air. Another, aiming lower, kicks the earth—the earth groans, and he, unfortunately, falls over.

Beginnings are always hard. In the course of time both the military training and the various other sports, practiced for the sake of physical skill, went better. Even though the lads lost weight, they felt more compact in their bones.

New volunteers kept arriving at the camp. Their seniors offered them help with advice and experience. Despite the common misery, and even though camp life did not turn out to be as picturesque as it had been portrayed at meetings, the volunteer in camp persevered, conquered everything, struggled with the misery so that with his dedication, and in the future with his blood, he could advance Poland's cause into the arena of history.

After 150 years of enslavement the support and sympathy of foreign nations had to be purchased with blood and dedication.

The rallies, rich in words, were complemented calmly amid discomfort by the volunteer in the camp, and there he made a soldier's vow to himself. The newly-made officers spent whole evenings chatting with soldiers, and there they raised spirits and strengthened the weak.

The winter of 1917 was very hard. The poorly dressed volunteer had to sleep in tents despite snow and hard frost. He was comforted by the thought of the imminent departure for France. The volunteers pressed forward, one past the other, toward the transports being formed so as to depart as soon as possible.

Finally that longed-for time came. The first transport, consisting of 600 volunteers, left by trains from St. John, Ontario for New York, to sail from there to France.

In port the small, modest French ship *Niagara* waited. The port was sleepy, due to the winter season and the German submarines which were such a threat at the time. A modest handful of volunteers passed quietly along the creaking gangway and disappeared into the ship's hull. Several of the port's coal merchants accompanied them with an indifferent glance. At 6 o'clock in the evening the ship's siren howled dismally, the anchor made a grinding sound, machines began to rattle, and the ship left port. The lads instinctively ran out onto the deck; they were solemn, their eyes glittered in the light, and some glistened with tears. In time to the initial movement of the machines, instinctively, involuntarily the hymn sounded from every breast, *"Boże coś Polskę."* The moment was so solemn and extremely moving that even today as I write this, tears come to my eyes. The dull quiet of the port, the piers flickering in the waves of light, the calm faces of the ship's crew, the ship's suppressed lights, the noise of the machines, entangled with the echo *"Ojczyznę, Wolność racz nam wrócić Panie"* [Lord, deign to return to us our Fatherland and Freedom]—it moved not only those who were leaving rich America to fight somewhere for their Fatherland's liberty, but even the foreigners who were on the ship. Several of the French senior officers, spontaneously repeating the hymn's melody, furtively wiped away tears.

The ship had already passed the Statue of Liberty, the port's lights had disappeared in the darkness, and the passengers of the ship *Niagara* still stood on the deck without a word.

The time for abstraction passed. The next day the sun cast some wintry rays through the clouds, illuminating the sea's waves and our smallish ship, heading toward France.

Day after day passed, our ship climbed through wave after wave, alone, like a fly on a dome. Humor returned—the volunteers took up exercise so as to shorten the days of the voyage. It was difficult to maintain the stance of "attention," so this exercise was limited to sporting games.

On the ship exemplary structure and order prevailed. The passengers were divided into groups for the lifeboats in order to avoid panic and chaos in case of need.

Christmas was spent on the ship. Who does not remember that Christmas Eve, those mutual Christmas wishes?

On the last night the ship was threatened by two German submarines, but thanks to Providence and the shrewdness of the ship's captain we avoided catastrophe.

On 28 December 1917 our ship weighed anchor in the French port of Bordeaux.

On the shore stood an army company in blue uniforms with rifles, in the forefront several Polish faces in four-cornered caps—these were the *Bajończycy* ["the ones from Bayonne," Polish volunteers who served in the French Foreign Legion] who came to greet the volunteers from America.

The gangway was lowered. On shore horns played Dąbrowski's mazurka, and the company presented arms. Our lads walked along the gangway solemnly, joyfully greeting the hospitable French soil. Then the battalion of volunteers stood in military order, and Col. Mokiejewski spoke to them in the name of the Polish soldiers in France. The official greeting ended, and now there were sincere greetings from the heart: survivors of the heroes at Arras and Verdun in horned caps threw themselves on the battalion of miners, woodcutters and smiths with the cry, "Greetings, brothers! Greetings, comrades from overseas!"

A miner from Pennsylvania burst out crying in the embrace of a *Bajończyk* comrade with a wooden leg. These greeting scenes were extremely moving. The surging battalion, adorned with blue uniforms and four-cornered hats, with an honor company of the Foreign Legion in the fore, trailed slowly through the streets of Bordeaux. The port's inhabitants were lavish with cries from the heart. "Vive la Pologne" flew along the streets, and "Vive la France" yelled the Bajończyk soldiers in the horned caps, and the volunteer bowed with a smile, while supporting by the shoulder a comrade who was a cripple, wearing the four-cornered cap with decorations on his chest.

This stirring parade headed for the barracks past the town, where the volunteers were received in a soldierly way, with warm wine. On the next day French trains took us to the region of Le Mans, which was designated for the formation of the Polish Army.

The first transport of volunteers from America traveled to Laval, where the first regiment was to be formed. Several days passed and our lads received blue uniforms and gear. Due to their prior military training, they looked spry and very impressive. Those who had not yet been able to acquire outfits because they were "too narrow in the shoulder" looked at their comrades with envy. Acquaintances were even made, for the French, garrulous by nature, stopped the giants on the street, trying to make themselves understood at any cost. Little dictionaries were in use, and pretty French women were an incentive.

In a few weeks a second transport arrived, and then a third.

On 10 January 1918 Gen. Archinard, Chief of the French-Polish Military Mission which was forming the Polish Army, handed over to Col. Jasiński the regiment formed from the first American transports, calling it "The 1st Regiment of Polish Riflemen." The ceremony was held in modest fashion in the "Shneider" barracks in the town of Laval.

Col. Jasiński, the grandson of a participant in the 1831 Uprising and a career French army officer, was regarded as the best officer of his rank. In several days the colonel's work was evident. The regiment was divided into battalions and companies according to the French Army's rules and regulations. Military training began at full speed.

Here it should be stressed the enormous amount of work to which the officers coming from America had to dedicate themselves. The French rules and regulations were foreign to them, so they had to work whole evenings and nights, after their usual all-day pursuits, to master the regulations. The superior officers, beginning with the company commander, came from the French Army and usually spoke Polish poorly. The whole work of instruction fell upon the officers from America. Thanks to their iron will and desire, they themselves mastered the regulations superbly in a short time, passing it on to the junior officers and soldiers. The work went full-steam and the soldiers made great progress.

Col. Jasiński did his utmost to place the instruction on the highest level. Military discipline gradually became tighter, and one felt that he was in an army and at war. The French soldier was allowed 300 gm of bread a day and that was his ration—our stomach was not content with this. Constant confidential complaints drew a military commission, which stated that the stomach of the Polish soldier needed more—and bread was added. Every soldier could have a piece of bread in the morning with black coffee, if one of his comrades had not eaten it during the night. Our soldier was characterized by an energetic face and by song. Whether going to or from training, there was always a song. This pleased the French so much that they hummed our soldier's songs.

The regiment's organization was completely finished, and the regiment was equipped with everything provided by the rules and regulations of the field army.

At the beginning of March 1918 the first regiment was redeployed to the so-called army zone for the purpose of completing its combat training. The military camp of St. Tanche was designated for us. Every one of the regiments headed for the front had to undergo training in this camp. There the soldier was finally acquainted with total war. The spring marshes of Champagne cut us to the quick. The sticky chalk along with the marshes made all kinds of training enormously harder. After passing through this camp a soldier had to be ready for the trenches. That work, too, was done there. Reveille was at 5 a.m. Afternoon exercises were from 1 to 5. At night there were all kinds of alarms and night marches. In the camp there the world did not exist for the soldier, because he had to devote all his mind and energy to military training. After roll call, to put your head on the pallet was to know true bliss. Night passed like lightning, and once more it was reveille. The whole camp had to be on its feet in five minutes.

The spring of 1918 was difficult for the Allies' armies. In April the Germans broke through the front at Somme. The situation was so critical that the French threw everything to the front to stop the German advance. The French armies, conveyed by vehicles, went immediately from the vehicles to the attack, organizing their positions on craters from shells.

Even though the regiment was undergoing the "bloody dysentery" that was raging at the time, Col. Jasiński, our regiment's commander, saw how critical the situation was and reported to the French command that the regiment was fully trained and could go to the front to help the French armies fighting bloody battles.

On 5 May 1918 the 1st Regiment of Polish Riflemen set out for the Champagne front. The march was difficult. Some soldiers, having just gotten over their illness, weakened on the road; but they went. We halted on the front line in the vicinity of Chalonne sur Marne.

Here again the officers from America had to give a lot, really beyond their power. The danger at the front is mutual, and orders must be carried out as meticulously as possible. The inexperienced soldier awaited these orders at every step. The officer who was with the soldier in every situation, the section commander, was an officer from America. Often this officer, just as inexperienced in war as the soldier, did not eat or sleep, watching over everyone and for everyone, probing the mysteries of the situation, the mysteries of war. His unsophisticated military conscience constantly raised questions of responsibility and regulations. He was the commander of a given sector in direct contact with the enemy, he was responsible for the position entrusted to him, the soldier awaited orders from him on what to do at a critical moment—and it was at him the cry of the falling soldier was directed, "Lieutenant, I am wounded!" Amid the hurricane fire of enemy artillery, having protected the whole section to the underground, he stood at the threshold, listening to hear "Are they attacking?" and he heard whether or not a wounded sentry was moaning. Until he got accustomed to all this and his military conscience was formed, he underwent a great deal.

On 15 July the Germans attacked on the whole front. A veritable hell on earth was created. Senior French officers who experienced the entire war, all the events at Verdun, say that they never saw such raging fire. This fire lasted only a few days.

Thanks only to our young commanders—that they could support our soldiers at the same time—the regiment, despite its losses, was able to occupy its sector. When the German offensive turned into a French counteroffensive on 21 July, the regiment advanced, taking German positions and capturing prisoners.

The 1st Regiment of Polish Riflemen, having 60% losses on the Champagne front, was withdrawn from the front to reorganize.

With its behavior on the front in Champagne it bought the whole French opinion for the cause of Poland.

Meanwhile volunteers kept arriving from America. Two new regiments were formed: the 2nd and 3rd Regiments of Polish Riflemen. The 2nd was commanded by Col. Berecki of the French Army; the 3rd by Col. Pachucki, a very upright Pole, a former officer of the Russian Army at Thessaloniki.

In August General Haller arrived in France, the leader of the Legions' 2nd "Iron Brigade," who after the battle with Germany at Kaniów made his way through Murmansk to France in order to provide valuable assistance to the Fatherland.

Providence sends us people in great moments.—General Haller arrived at just the right time. On behalf of the National Committee he immediately took the helm of the Army and without delay visited all the Polish camps, and the soldiers gave their Commander a hearty greeting. The heart swelled within the soldier from America, for the Polish Army in France had grown, becoming powerful, and was taking on the seal of its nation.

In September 1918 the three regiments of lads from America, with their own artillery and cavalry, comprising the First Division, occupied the front in Lorraine. This sector was among the quiet ones, so the division was posted there, as was every newly created one, so that the soldier could gain experience in the trenches without great casualties.

The division remained at the front in Lorraine until the armistice, that is, until 11 November 1918. After the armistice it advanced to occupy territory on the Rhine, as provided by the treaties. The division turned back when ordered and halted in Lorraine, to prepare for departure to Poland.

Oh, what joy that was! A soldier could not sleep.

Preparations for the departure lasted for some time. The question of transit became a difficult and complicated problem. Finally after a long wait a decision was made and officially agreed upon between the Allies and Germany.

The first transports with the blue army set out in the first half of April 1919. Train after train tore along through Germany to the homeland, to Poland. The heart swelled at the fact that we would soon be on native soil and that our dreams, the culmination of our desires as soldiers, were becoming a reality.

In the forefront was the 1st Division with its vanguard, the 1st Regiment.

The passage through Germany was very formal. The German soldiers standing guard at the stations scowled at us, and having met the ignoring glance of our "Majek," turned their haughty faces away. The civilian population approached to ask for bread; our good soldiers had mercy on them.

With every hour as we approached our Fatherland's borders, our hearts began to beat more loudly.

In the forest stood an outpost, and alongside it waved our homeland's standard. Who was not moved at that moment? The train stopped, soldiers from beyond the sea in blue uniforms ran off the train to kiss the soil of Free Poland. As a crowd of pilgrims falls when it reaches a place of miracles, humbling themselves before the cross and with their whole soul before God, so the blue soldier from beyond the sea, having gotten off the train, hugged our Mother, the Polish soil, in ecstasy.

The miner from Pennsylvania prayed, and tears flowed from him: "Oh my Fatherland, I have come running from beyond the sea, fighting in faraway lands, to free You. I greet You, my Fatherland! I am happy to see You! With my French bayonet I fought to defend You, my native land!" Sobbing he whispered more quietly, "Do not forget about my comrades who were hastening to You but fell on the fields of Champagne, o my native land!"

The locomotive's whistle signaled that we were journeying onward. The exiled soldiers rose heavily from the ground and climbed into the train's cars. The Polish spring smiled on the returning eagles; the freshly tilled fields, already turning green, riveted the exiled soldiers to the windows.

At the first Polish station, Kąkolewo, an honor company of the Poznań Army greeted us. The citizens received us with bread and salt.

After the exchange of military honors, the train went on. Gray-haired villagers came running from nearby villages to the train to see the "Blue Army." Our boys, touched by the sight, threw through the train's windows fragments of cigarettes and tobacco, and provisions—for this was Poland, and there were Polish children going hungry. This was during the Easter holidays. At Ostrów in Poznań province our train was held up; ladies came to the cars and treated the soldiers to Easter meals. Oh, how cordially Poznań province greeted us!

On the second day of Eastertide we arrived in Warsaw. The capital—the train stopped at the Dworzec Kowelski [Kowel station]. The exiled soldier from beyond the sea waited in vain for some warmth in the capital of Poland.

At 3 p.m. dinner was served and the train set out for Chełm—to the front.

The 1st Division, under the command of General Bernard, disembarked in Chełm, Kowel and Włodzimierz Wołyński. These were times when there was no regular army in Poland. Unattached units conducted partisan battles in the Eastern Frontierlands. The best soldier and the whole military force of the young nation defended Lwów.

The Ukrainians were coming closer every day to taking the city.

The unloading of 1st Division in this area gave them a lot to think about. Our preparations for an offensive lasted only a few days. The division began its offensive on 13 May 1919, moving out in three columns from Włodzimierz Wołyński. The Ukrainians were driven back beyond the river Styr. The Chief Command of the Polish Army issued a first modest communiqué: "The blue riflemen of Gen. Bernard have driven the Ukrainians beyond the Styr, taking the town of Łuck. In Łuck 3,000 Ukrainian prisoners were taken, and 12 cannons."

The Division remained on the Styr for three months, fighting first with the Ukrainians, and later with the Bolsheviks.

In the second half of August 1918 the division moved forward. After large battles at Diatkowce, Filipowicze and Klewań, on 13 August we took the city of Równe, the largest railway junction in Volhynia. After taking Równe, the division halted at the river Horyń and held that line, fortifying it strongly.

Here the division was renumbered the 13th, and received the name of Eastern Frontier Riflemen. At more or less this same time the Commander in Chief organized the Polish Armies' *ordre de bataille*.

On 31 [sic] November 1919 the 13th Division of Eastern Frontier Riflemen took the town of Zwiahel, occupying the line of the river Słucz. The division held the line of the Słucz up until the Kiev offensive. In January 1920 the 13th Division, holding 162 km. of front, held back the Bolshevik offensive. Battles along the division's entire front lasted two months. The division, having before it three Bolshevik divisions (the 44th, 47th and 58th of the Soviet Infantry), not only held the entire front, but succeeded in mounting local counterattacks, defeating divisions of the enemy.

The Bolsheviks knew the 13th Division as the "American Division"—the peasants knew it as the division *"kotoraya delayet poryadok"* (which brings order).

The 13th Division of Eastern Frontier Riflemen's Battles and Race with Budionny's Mounted Army

As early as the beginning of 1920 the Polish Armies' High Command had information, from its own reconnaissance bureau as well as from prisoners of war, that the Bolsheviks were organizing a select mounted army consisting mainly of Cossacks and Kirghiz, commanded by a former cavalry sergeant of the Russian Army, Budionny. This army was supposedly used recently against

Denikin, and had acquitted itself well, for in several months it completely wiped out Denikin's counterrevolutionary army.

General Karnicki, chief of the Polish mission with Denikin's command, confirmed this information upon returning to Poland after the destruction of his army. The Polish Armies' High Command sensed that the Bolsheviks, having dealt with Denikin's army to the south, would strike with all their force on the Polish front. Wanting to take the initiative from the enemy, it decided to anticipate his intentions by beginning the Kiev offensive.

The Kiev offensive not only augmented the glory of the Polish soldier's arms, but brought great material benefits as well. The Polish forces, advancing with great speed under the total personal command of the Chief of State, took the enemy by surprise to such an extent that the enemy could not manage to take away the spoils of war collected for the projected offensive.

The goal of the offensive was attained as the Chief had wished, and as planned by the High Command: Kiev was taken on the fifth day of the offensive—the richest part of Ukraine was in our armies' hands. With the agreement of the Ukrainian commander, the part of Ukraine taken by a new offensive was to feed the Polish forces.

Our victorious armies, having attained the goals of the offensive completely, did not rest on their laurels. Immediately after arriving at the specified lines, on the command of the Commander, who personally visited the new positions, they proceeded to organize them, building trenches and fortifications by means of the newest techniques.

Our watchful position at Kiev was clear for every soldier; so this soldier worked day and night, scheming to advance the work as far as possible and prepare the strongest line where he could receive the enemy at an advantage.

The tactical goal of our offensive at Kiev was equally clear to the soldier. He saw that advancing would paralyze the enemy's boldness, and take the initiative from him—by behaving aggressively he would compel the foe to change his plans daily. The soldier knew that he would move against the enemy so as to strike the first blow on his native soil, to hinder his movements subsequently and shift the danger of war as far as possible away from the Fatherland.

The soldier at Kiev foresaw great battles, for at the first outposts "Grandfather" *[Translator—apparently a nickname for Piłsudski]* unexpectedly appeared. He measured with his steps that freshly burrowed ground, didn't say much, looked at the soldier's thin face, at the rest of his dress and shoes, stood for a while and directed his eagle eye to the east as if he was looking at something. The soldiers said among themselves, "It will be hot going, we'll be giving the Bolsheviks a thrashing, because Grandfather is here."

They didn't have to wait long—our mounted foray units reported that the Bolsheviks had started, and the vanguard of Budionny's Mounted Army was a day's ride away. Along the towns and hamlets the Jews began to get up earlier and run energetically along the streets with beaming faces, while the Ukrainian peasant gathered his horses and took to the forests. Flocks of crows croaked fearfully. Yes! The Bolsheviks—having spread among the crowds false and erroneous words such as "The Poles intend to conquer all Russia, from Kiev they will go to Moscow"—came in a dark wave such as only Russia, with its inexhaustible supply of people, could summon up.

At the head of these hordes composed of peoples of various tribes and ethnicities came the mounted army, dazzled by its recent victories over Denikin—it was the flower and idol of these hordes.

The mounted army rode, sure of itself, young men made into a team in past battles with Yudenich, Kolchak, and recently Denikin, warmed with vodka, they rode boldly with a great strategic plan: to capture Kiev from the southwest and cut off our forces occupying Kiev and the Kiev bridgehead; then they intended to storm our rear, paralyze it, and cut off our retreat.

The reports coming from all sectors of our front did not make our Commander hesitate. The impatient soldier finally heard the opinion of "Grandfather," which was at the same time an order: "Hold back the first momentum of the enemy as long as possible in the occupied positions. If overwhelmed, retreat in jumps, if possible without contact with the enemy, to new positions defensive in nature. Fortify yourselves in the new positions and take an offensive stand. Defend our native soil and the honor of the Polish soldier."

Budionny's mounted army, spreading out loose Ukrainian units which were sympathetic to us and were active in our foreground—struck on his right flank against the cavalry corps of Gen. Karnicki, operating in the vicinities of Biała Cerkiew and Fastów, and on his left flank against the 13th Infantry Division, formerly Gen. Haller's 1st Division.

The soldier had an inkling that "it will be hot going." Terrible battles began on the whole southern sector of the Kiev front. Our cavalry's encounter with part of the mounted army in the vicinity of Biała Cerkiew was positively medieval in terms of momentum and ferocity, and at the same time terrible in its consequences. It was truly a battle of the steppes of cavalry against cavalry.

Twelve of our regiments fought against four Cossack divisions. Our cavalry attacked with the courage of lions, again and again charging the Cossacks—who exploited this, using a stratagem tested against Yudenich, Kolchak, and Denikin. This stratagem consisted of the Cossack regiments' appearing to receive our cavalry's charges; but when our cavalry drew near, their mounted bands scampered off to the side, leaving the so-called *tachanki* they had been concealing and armored vehicles, which struck our charging regiments unbearably.

The first and great battle of the cavalries turned out unfavorably for us. This battle proved that the Cossacks were splendidly organized, had a tested manner of fighting, and that in order to resist them effectively, we needed to change our tactics and arm our combat units in a technically suitable manner.

That part of the mounted army that fought the battle at Biała Cerkiew and, one can say, defeated our cavalry corps, forced its way into our rear and actually began to paralyze it. Some of these units reached as far as Berdyczów and Żytomierz, cutting down the garrison and command there to a man. These units, half wild, drunk, intoxicated by their temporary victory, did not even spare our wounded in the hospitals or the civilian populace. They were concerned with creating as much panic as possible; so these frenzied gangs, rushing around the country like a whirlwind, left behind corpses and smoldering ruins.

The activity of the mounted army's left flank was not so successful, for it was defeated outright in battles with 13th Infantry Division. The division, sufficiently fortified, gave Budionny's cavalry a suitable reception. It was a terrible clash. The Cossacks struck with their whole wave, and the fight raged in every sector. The enemy, having sensed the weak spot of our badly manned front, kept pushing at it with more and more new columns renewing the attack. The soldier of the blue division fought day and night, hanging the wild riders on barbed wire ten paces in front of his own trench. The rabid mass attacks of the Cossacks had a demoralizing effect, frankly, but the soldier of the Steel Division did not lose heart—he met the gangs of Cossacks with a bullet, and when they advanced on the machine guns with swords, he waited calmly with a grenade in hand to receive them at the moment when, sure of their momentum, they rose in their saddles to cut him down.

13th Division, formerly the 1st of Haller's Army, was called "Steel," and these were the lads from America.

The gangs of the mounted army came flying at the Steel Division from everywhere. The situation changed so rapidly that counterattacks were conducted on carts to wipe out the Cossack units, which from all sides forced their way into the heart of our front. Ten times the Cossacks broke through the front, and ten times the Steel Division repaired the front. Such places as Dziónków, Pohrebyszcze, Lipowiec, and Nowożytów will be inscribed in honor, not only in the history of 13th Division, but also in the history of Polish war.

At Dziónków the cooks fought with teeth, fists, and knives—the artillery fired grapeshot. "Defend your honor," said the Commander; and the 7th Battery of the Steel Division did so, for beset by Cossacks at Nowo-Żywotów it perished, along with its commander, 1st Lt. Szymbarski from America. Those who didn't die at the hand of the enemy found death in captivity. (Proof of the abovementioned facts attesting the great heroism of the 7th Battery of the 13th Field Artillery Regiment is in the archives of 13th Division.)

13th Division, on the line Skwira to Dziónków to Lipowiec, took vows with the mounted army, a vow of lust for battle to death or victory. It held and finally was the first to break the furious momentum of the mounted army, paralyzing its initial success.

"Pull back upon your commander's order," the Commander said. The High Command, taking advantage of having held the enemy for the time being along the entire Kiev front, and seeing that it would be difficult to hold on this line, gave the order to fall back to the line of the river Słucz.

He who saw our forces withdrawing from Kiev—the soldier who fought all day and changed positions at night, the soldier whose rifle had not left his hand for several weeks, who was living on greens, that common soldier with a face emaciated and lashed by winds and frost, that soldier without shoes, in torn pants, those valiant 18-year-old boys who had recently stepped forward as volunteers, the soldier who with a song on his lips repulsed all the raids of the enemy cavalry—he saw the best army in the world. The soldier, withdrawing, did not lose heart, believing that he was conducting a tactical retreat, and that this retreat would lead to final victory.

3rd Division of the Legions holding the bridgehead at Kiev was completely cut off, and had to fight its way through masses of the enemy barring its way. This division did fight its way through, complete with artillery and supply columns.

Our forces, having reached their newly assigned positions based against the river Słucz, prepared for immediate defense, to hold back the pressing enemy.

On the second day after we reached our new positions the Bolshevik armies—without supply columns because supply columns were unknown to that mob, since they lived on whatever they found in the area, particularly Budionny's cavalry—attacked along the whole front. In places the combat was so fierce that there were reports of clashes in the water where both drowned.

Our forces held back the enemy's attacks along the Słucz for almost two weeks. Our soldier, having been at these positions for a fairly long time before the Kiev offensive, regarded them as the borders of the Republic; so he defended them with a lion's ferocity. The sorties conducted in the foreground proved the great courage and personal valor of the soldier, as well as his initiative. Our sortie battalions did wonders, wiping out and shattering entire divisions of the Bolsheviks.

The Steel Division became famous in these battles. The Commander decorated 60% of the soldiers and officers with crosses.

After battles in the vicinity of Biała Cerkiew, Fastów, and Koziatyn the mounted army headed northeast to Zwiahel, striking against the right flank of the Słucz Group. In vain were the superhuman efforts, in vain the courage of our soldier. The wide and weakly manned front was hard to hold. Again and again new Bolshevik gangs, sensing the weak spots, pushed ahead with whole columns, cutting off our units as they stubbornly defended their positions. Victory tilted toward the enemy and the Słucz Group had to abandon its positions on the Słucz.

The Steel Division, on the left flank of Gen. Romer's 6th Army, still held its Słucz positions. Well surrounded with wire, the soldier could not be budged from the spot. Due to the Słucz Group's withdrawal to the river Korczyk, the division's left flank was completely cut off, or rather exposed, which forced the divisions to bend their left flank from Ostropol on the Słucz through Korżówka, Marjanówka, to Brażyńce and Kupczyńce, so as to give its flank some cover and try to maintain tactical communication with Gen. Szymański's brigade, operating on the right flank of the Słucz Group and located on the river Korczyk.

Communications were established temporarily, thanks to the courage of our lads; but Gen. Szymański's brigade, strongly pressed, had to withdraw once more to Szepetówka, which forced 13th Division to bend its left flank again, from Ostropol to Rajki, Macewicze, Chryców. The division's center and right flank continued to hold the Słucz and its old positions.

The blue division found itself in a critical situation, as the Bolshevik masses—the mounted brigade of Commander Kotovsky and the 44th Soviet Infantry Division, which had created a gap that resulted from the withdrawal of Gen. Szymański's brigade to Szepetówka—threatened its left flank and rear. The situation was so critical that the orderlies, cooks and clerks stayed in their positions.

Gen. Romer, our 6th Army's commander, played his last card. Considering the Słucz Group's lack of success to be temporary, despite the scandalously endangered situation of the 13th Division—that is to say, his army's left flank—he ordered them to stay in their old positions, risking everything—so that as soon as Słucz Group could set up a base and hold back the Bolshevik march, he would throw 13th Division on the enemy's flank and rear, propping up Słucz Group and aligning our front along the Słucz river.

In the meantime the Słucz Group's situation had not improved at all. It was pushed back to the Horyń river. 13th Division fought deadly battles, but held the entire front. The commander of the 12th Soviet Army ordered that 13th Division be destroyed at all costs, so that he could align his front and advance with all his units on a level height.

Gen. Romer was still taking risks and trying to improve his own situation. Even though battle was raging on his army's entire front, he ordered them to hold the flanks at all costs, while he pulled 18th Division out of its central sector and sent it to the left flank of his army with this assignment: "Strike northward, clear all enemy units out of the way, reach our units and establish communications with them. After establishing communications go on the counteroffensive and align our front."

The 18th Division's assignment was very difficult. The last card was played. Either we would stop the enemy's frenzied march, or we would be in an extremely dangerous situation. The front held by 18th Division was covered by the 13th and 12th Divisions despite frantic attacks. We considered the line of the Słucz to be the borders of the Republic. The Commander had said "Defend your native soil"; so the soldier of the Steel Division defended his position on the Słucz. He held onto his positions by his teeth while waiting for whatever the "last card" would bring, whatever 18th Division's maneuver would do.

The 18th Division went into the Bolshevik masses and fought great battles, advancing northward to Szepetówka-Zasław, and then in the direction of Ostróg on the Horyń river, where Gen. Szymański's brigade was still defending itself.

In vain the command of 6th Army waited for news of success from the north. The 18th division passed through the Bolshevik waves, which then once more poured over the entire foreground, renewing their constant attacks on the Steel Division's flank. The 6th Army's front, even more thinned out by the pulling out of the 18th Division, had already been holding back and resisting the enemy's frenzied attacks only with difficulty. The Bolshevik hordes, urged on by Jewish commissars, broke through 6th Army's front in the 12th Divisions sector at Deraźnia. Gen. Romer personally led the battalions into the attack, wiping out enemy units that had penetrated as far as Proskurów, where 6th Army's command was staying.

The 44th Soviet Infantry Division and Commander Kotovsky's mounted brigade, marching southeast from Miropol and Połonne, went around 13th Division on the west. The Bolshevik mounted units, which fought their way through at Deraźnia, attacked our rear as far as Czarny Ostróg, cutting down the staff of the railway supply columns, cutting down the wounded in the trains, burning and destroying provisions and ammunition.

The enemy's ring tightened, and the Steel Division's situation worsened every hour. The left flank fought deadly battles continually. These battles, like that at Butowce on hill 337, 7 km. northwest of Starokonstantynów, fought by the 13th Division's 43rd Regiment of Eastern Frontier Riflemen, are among the fiercest in the history of Poland. In this battle Capt. Rodzyński died, a former officer of the French Army and the Polish Army.

13th Division, surrounded on all sides, still stood and defended its position on the Słucz, awaiting orders. An airman, Col. Fount le Roy, an American, brought Gen. Romer's order for the whole 6th Army to retreat. The divisions, each on its own, assembled, fought their way through the enemy, and as soon as possible extended the Słucz Group's right flank along the river Ikwa, taking Krzemieniec, Goryńka, Maniew, Wyszgorodek, and based themselves farther south against the Zbrucz.

13th Division's regrouping was incredibly difficult, since the enemy was still attacking strongly on its heels. The division regrouped in Starokonstantynów and on the night of 6 July, covered and firing in all directions, it set out to the west through Kuźmin-Krasiłów for Bazalia. This night persists in memory. The boom of cannons shook the air. The glow of villages burning from the shells lit up the whole vicinity, the bang of bridges and ammunition stores being blown up, hand weapons of the rearguard, vanguard and lateral guards, gave the beautiful Ukrainian night a solemn and memorable nature. What soldier of the Steel Division does not remember that night? The whole division marched together, the soldier felt its strength, and although surrounded on all sides, walked firmly. Sadness was painted on all faces because they had to abandon the soil they had once purchased with the blood of their comrades. That night was filled with episodes, and they were terrible ones: a unit of 25 of our beaten soldiers, having sought shelter in the village of Chmielewka, was attacked by the local Ukrainian peasants and put to the sword. The lateral guards reported this information to the staff. This news spread like lightning among the soldiers, and each soldier turned white with anger. The command ordered the village burned and the inhabitants punished. At midnight the village was set on fire.

In the river valley at the sources of the Słucz the 13th Division stood, grave and mighty, among the surrounding glow. With the flames of the burning village it spit in the face of the surrounding enemy and stood, awaiting the break of day to begin the attack.

The morning chill pierced to the bone, and our units went on the attack to break through the enemy's ring or die with honor. The battle lasted from early morning to evening, and ended well for our side, as the routed enemy moved aside. The division took the villages of Zozulincy, Klitna, and Koszelewka. After bloody combat the soldier rested for a few hours during the night, and in the morning advanced.

The enemy did not give up yet; only our packs moved, and the enemy's mounted brigade of Kotovsky attacked our column's head from the village of Mecherzyńce. The attack was wiped out utterly by our artillery, firing from open positions. The Bolsheviks headed for the forest, leaving on the field many bodies and wounded. The victory he'd won raised the soldier's spirits and fired his imagination.

The ring of surrounding enemies was broken. The division moved on in the direction of Bazalia and Wyszgorodek, where it took up positions on the next day. The new positions were immediately fortified. The soldiers showed a lot of their own initiative, pulling barbed wire lying on the fields here and there so as to wire their trenches. The fortifications arose surprisingly quickly. Tactical and telephone communication was established and once again a more or less solid front was formed.

New attacks began, and once again clashes at Goryńka, Wyszgorodek, and Krzemieniec were entered in the bloody history of war. The divisions held these positions for two weeks; compelled, however, by the situation of our 2nd Army, it had to withdraw, along with the entire 6th Army, to the river Seret and its tributary the river Grabarka. In these positions the 13th Division once more held back the enemy's frenzied attacks for two weeks.

After taking Dubno and Krzemieniec, Budionny's Mounted Army, Golikov's mounted group, and the 44th Soviet Infantry Division set out to the southeast toward Brody and Lwów.

Our 18th Division and the right flank of 2nd Army, operating in the vicinity of Brody and Beresteczko on the Styr, were driven back several times, but repaired the situation once more, leveling the front. These efforts lasted nearly two weeks, until finally Budionny's mounted army took Brody, driving 18th Division in the direction of Krasne, and Golikov's mounted group took Beresteczko, headed for Kamionka-Strumiłowa.

In the meantime our situation on the northern front grew worse each day. The Bolsheviks advanced with great speed and were threatening Warsaw. From the enemy's entire maneuver it was obvious that the Mounted Army, striking through Brody on Lwów, aimed to cut the whole 6th Army off from Poland. General Iwaszkiewicz, who at that time was in command of the Army, was planning to hold up the march of the Mounted Army by striking with 13th Division on the left flank in the vicinity of Busk and Poburzany, and decided to do so. The 6th Army's command gave the order to pull the entire 13th Division from the line running Zborów-Kotłów-Sasów-Białykamień to Krasne. At the same time the Command of 6th Army broke up the permanent front, creating operational groups that were to act on their own. This was the plan for further military activity.

In carrying out this order from the Commander of 6th Army, the Commander of 13th Division, Gen. Stanisław Haller, former Chief of Staff to the High Command, ordered one regiment to patrol the vicinity of Zborów-Złoczów on its own, and the rest of 13th Division's regiments would assemble in Krasne to carry out the Army Commander's plan.

This order was extremely difficult to carry out, because it required passing right under the enemy's nose, with our flank to him, which is very dangerous and exposes one to casualties. Nonetheless the swiftness of activity required it, and our forces began to execute it. One brigade, along the Division Command, made it to Krasne after extremely heavy fighting. The enemy, taking advantage of our position, struck powerfully and cut off 26th Brigade from the rest of the Division.

After departing to Krasne, Division Command explained that the situation had become significantly worse, namely: some units of the mounted army, marching with frenzied speed, were already at Lwów. The Division Command received this order: "Give up on executing the first plan, march as quickly as possible with the whole division to Lwów—defend Lwów. Mounted units at Lwów."

In view of the above it was necessary to take off immediately with the whole division for Lwów. This order had to be sent to our Brigade that had been cut off. The order was sent three times by officers' forays, but the attempts were in vain, the enemy surrounded us on all sides.

One of our brigades, along with Division Command, shut itself up in Krasne, fighting off attacks the whole day. Our units took the town and station. The artillery battle came to a peak, the cannons sounded all day, and the Bolsheviks covered the entire town with shells. The soldier of the Steel Division fought off attack after attack, charge after charge, till twilight. During the night the Commander of Gen. Haller's Division ordered a retreat to Lwów. Disengaging from the enemy was very difficult, the rearguards were fighting with hand weapons. One can boldly state that if not for the courage and great combat experience of the Steel Division soldier, that brigade would have been buried in Krasne. This should also be ascribed to the soldier's understanding of the situation.

Marching all night, the brigade halted on the Lwów-Złoczów road in Kurowice, from which Division Command once more sent an order to 26th Brigade, cut off by the enemy, to march by the shortest road to Lwów. This order was carried by 1st Lt. Szewc of the artillery brigade, and forcing his way through forests and over hills south of the Lwów-Złoczów highway, he reached Gołogóry, where he met the brigade and delivered the order. The brigade immediately changed direction for Lwów.

While in Kurowice the commander of Gen. Haller's Division sent Staff 1st Lt. Nastał to the commander of the city of Lwów to ascertain what steps were being taken for the defense of the city.

The city made an impression of unusual calm and solemnity. On the streets traffic was normal, in the suburbs old men were digging trenches and putting up barbed wire of their own accord. The city's commander was Col. Jasiński, who, when he learned that the 13th Division had halted near Lwów, asked, overjoyed, "We are defending Lwów?" "We are," was the answer. The Colonel commander of the city of Lwów outlined the plans that had been made, emphasizing that Lwów was counting on its inhabitants, since the military contingent was not large. On paper it numbered 1,125 bayonets, but these were students and military schools. It was decided to defend the city, however, even with such forces, to the end.

Our column marching from Kurowice on the road to Lwów halted at the river Kabanówka, and there the General decided to wait for the 26th Brigade, marching from Gołogóry.

At 4 p.m. that evening enemy mounted foray units appeared from the northeast.

Budionny, having realized at Krasne that our brigade had slipped out, sent his 11th Division by the Krasne-Gliniany-Kurowice road with the assignment of crushing it; and with the further plan of attacking Lwów from the south,

Budionny sent his 6th Cavalry Division from Krasne along the Krasne-Lwów railroad track, with the assignment of attacking Lwów from the northeast. He himself along with the 4th Division and the so-called "Ace Brigade" became the reserve, in order to attack the city from the east if the 11th and 6th Divisions succeeded in going around Lwów.

Budionny had no luck with the Steel Division. The 6th Cavalry Division, going toward Lwów along the railroad track, came upon our 25th Brigade, halted on the river Kabanówka, and at Biłka Szlachecka suffered a terrible defeat. The course of the battle went as follows. Cossacks regrouping in the woods a kilometer east of the village charged the 44th Regiment of Eastern Frontier Riflemen from behind a hill. As soon as the enemy's charging regiments approached and came under the fire of our artillery, their ranks were badly thinned; there was also an airplane of ours sent from Lwów that dropped several bombs on the charging masses. The attack was so fierce, however, that the scattered Cossacks not exposed to artillery fire fell under the fire of our machine guns, but these charges did not break either, and the Cossacks sped forward with their sabers. The heroic soldier of the 44th Regiment held and broke the attack, throwing himself with his bayonet on the speeding Cossacks.

The enemy fled past the hill to the forest, leaving behind heaps of human bodies and horses; but before half an hour had passed, he reorganized and attacked once more. The greatest momentum of this attack was directed at the spot where it had penetrated the farthest in the previous one.

Col. Szylling, the commander of 44th Regiment, experienced in combat with the Bolsheviks, foresaw the site of the strongest blow and placed 12 machine guns there. This time our artillery let the Cossacks come very close before opening fire along with the machine guns. The result was so terrible that the attacking Cossacks, as if struck by lightning, began to turn back from the spot, got confused, their commanders lost their heads—and the artillery and our machine guns played on. The Cossacks' horses bolted and ran together into a mass, trampling on each other. Our artillery shot so accurately that every shell brought a new death, new devastation in the ranks of the enemy—new heaps of human bodies were blown up. The battery commanders kept thundering, "Sweep to the right, sweep to the left."

The bewildered Cossacks hurled themselves into flight in a panic, letting the horses run wherever they wished. To get out of view and escape the accurate artillery fire, the majority of those fleeing hurried toward a green meadow of the river Kabanówka, overgrown with bushes, and they drowned in the marshes there. The defeat was so terrible that Budionny's 6th Division was withdrawn to the rear to reorganize.

On this day the Steel Division fought with great success. Budionny's 11th Division, marching from Krasne through Gliniany to Kurowice, met with our

26th Brigade, headed for Lwów, and there, too, suffered a fatal defeat. The battle at Kurowice lasted more or less the same amount of time as the one at Biłka Szlachecka, and was similar in character.

Our plans, which had not been coordinated by the joint command, came together wonderfully, as the brigades, each fighting on its own, assisted each other.

In this way the first momentum toward Lwów for the purpose of taking the city was broken by 13th Division. The city of Lwów was whole thanks to 13th Division—the lads from America.

After both brigades joined up, the Division withdrew, as per the plan to defend Lwów on the line of old trenches, that is, hill 288, Podhorce, Czartowska Skała, Winniki (exclusively), hill 388 and Fort Sichów. In these positions the Division was to await a repeated attack on Lwów. 13th Division's radio station intercepted coded dispatches Budionny sent to the commander of the 12th Soviet Army, in which he assured the commander of 12th Army that he would take Lwów in one day, and then head for Zamość-Lublin.

The Mounted Army's *"nachal'nik"* [*Russian for "head, commander"*] was mistaken, for one day passed after another, but the Iron Division continued to defend Lwów, and defended it effectively. Nothing came of the probing attacks, nothing came of going around Fort Sichów—Lwów was untouched. In vain were all the efforts of the wild horde, there was no pillaging.

A few days later 13th Division's radio station once more intercepted coded dispatches to the *nachal'nik* of the Mounted Army, signed by Trotsky. In this dispatch Trotsky ordered Budionny to break off the siege of Lwów immediately and head in the direction of Lublin, to support Bolshevik victories at Warsaw.

The loot of the city of Lwów was so near for the Bolsheviks, yet so far. The commander of 6th Army, in view of the enemy's passiveness and the intercepted dispatches, ordered 13th Division as well as 5th and 6th Divisions, operating in the vicinity of Kulików, to take the offensive and attack the enemy. The divisions advanced, driving the Mounted Army back on the line Mikołajów-Mogiła-Laszki Królewskie-Zadworze. Here our reconnaissance reported that the Mounted Army was headed through Kamionka Strumiłowa-Krystynopol in the direction of Zamość-Lublin, as ordered by Trotsky.

In view of this, the command of 6th Army withdrew 13th Division from the Lwów front and redeployed it by rail from Lwów to Rawa Ruska, in order to begin action from those areas, with the goal of striking the Mounted Army's flank or rear.

After 13th Division unloaded in Rawa Ruska and after clarification as to the enemy's situation in the vicinity of Bełz and Sokal, the command of 6th Army placed under Gen. Stanisław Haller, the commander of 13th Division, Col. Rommel's 1st Cavalry Division, thus forming the Gen. Haller Operational

Group, and gave it this assignment: "Acting on your own, disrupt the Mounted Army."

In this position the Gen. Haller Group restricted itself to offensive skirmishes with Budionny's guards and exchanging artillery fire.

Gen. Haller's plan was not to reveal to the enemy his whole strength, but to hamper the enemy's flank and rear with deception, using the position and terrain to fight a concrete, decisive battle. By coincidence units were in action here, together and under a single command, that had fought the first battles with the Mounted Army at Kiev when it appeared on the Polish front. These units, despite their initial ordeals, had vowed to crush the Mounted Army or else die themselves.

The Mounted Army's main forces were rushing from Sokal through Waręż to Tyszowce. The innumerable columns of bandits went proudly, wreaking havoc and conflagration as they went. Their Jewish commissars encouraged them to march with vodka, future plunder, and music. "To Warsaw, comrades!" went the cry. The Mounted Army went, sure of itself, disregarding the terrain, driving before it the right flank of our 3rd Army, of Gen. Sikorski.

The Gen. Haller Group watched in silence from the hills, counting the endless columns. "Forward," ordered Gen. Haller. The Steel Division and the 1st Cavalry Division rushed at the rear of the Mounted Army, tearing at it at Tyszowce, Łaszczów, and Czartowo.

Budionny, confident of victory ahead and of his own swift advance, rushed ahead, ignoring the disadvantages of the terrain for cavalry. He stepped among the marshes of the tributaries of the Huczwa and the river Łabuńka, aiming to destroy the garrison at Zamość and take the city as quickly as possible.

After crossing the river Huczwa at Łaszczów Gen. Haller sent the Steel Division at the rear and left flank of the Mounted Army, and sent his cavalry divisions through Tyszowce-Perespa-Dub, in order to paralyze any retreat by the enemy.

Gen. Haller's whole group stayed in close contact with the enemy, hampering his movements. Advancing, Gen. Haller sensed the moment had come, and striking the flank, cut off the Mounted Army's supply column, along with its ammunition.

Budionny believed in his star, believed that he would take Zamość easily, that the 13th Infantry Division's infantry could not keep up with him, and the cavalry division could not withstand his forces. Budionny sensed that he was surrounded, but reckoned that by attacking our rear he would create panic, and he could always get out of the situation with his cavalry. Knowing the situation of Soviet forces on the northern front and at Warsaw, he wanted to strike with all his might at the right flank of our 3rd Army, shatter it, reach Lublin, base himself on the Soviet armies operating there, and take action deep in our rear.

The *nachal'nik* of the Mounted Army miscalculated, for the infantry of 13th Division not only kept up with him step for step, but managed to go around his left flank, striking with one brigade along the Wołuczyn-Antonówka axis, and then along the Tomaszów road to Łabunie. The marshes of the river Huczwa delayed Budionny and forced him to try to capture Zamość. 25th Brigade of 13th Division and the 1st Cavalry Division moved along the Siemierz-Komarów axis, closing off the Mounted Army's retreat.

On the evening of 29 August 1920 a great battle began. The boom of artillery fire and bang of machine guns shook the air. Gen. Haller's Group began a general attack. Two infantry brigades struck, one, under the command of Col. Bajer, at Łabunie, the other under the command of Col. Szylling at Komarów. The bellow of cannons, fire, smoke, turned the vicinity into a hell. General Haller stood amid enemy artillery fire on a mound created in 1912 to commemorate the anniversary of the 3rd of May, and personally directed the battle. The mound's high position made for excellent observation. The General, observing the whole theater of the battle, kept issuing commands, maneuvering with battalions in various directions. The General's calm spread to the commanders and soldiers. None of them worried about his life—the high point of their dreams and desires as soldiers was to smash the Mounted Army to smithereens.

Evening approached, and the battle still raged on. Breathless couriers kept bringing new reports that the whole Group was in mortal combat. The cannon flashes lit up the whole vicinity, and the General continued to stand there, by the mound, and issue new orders. His dark figure could be seen from afar amid bursting shrapnel. The General listened with his practiced ear to the echo of shots, trying to draw a conclusion as to which side would gain the victory. He saw flashes of fire, looked off toward Zamość, and regarded the flash of cannon shots. The General cried in a single breath "Zamość is defending itself, thank God" and issued orders to fight with hand weapons, regardless of the night.

The experienced soldier trembled with excitement, noting thirteen flashes of fire from Zamość, because now he was sure the historic old city was defending itself, and that Budionny was closed in on the west. The soldier cried with joy that he had achieved his goal in time, that he had not gone through the difficulties of the chase in vain, those marches day and night in bogs up to his belt and in rain. In view of such important certainty, he forgot about his empty stomach and the remnants of muddy bread in his bag. This news spread like lightning, encouraging the soldier of the Steel Division, raising his spirits—the soldier rushed with his bayonet at the enemy. The artillerymen fired from their cannons according to their map, aiming by the flash of an exploding grenade.

Utter darkness fell on the combatants. The shots subsided to a certain extent. This day's battle had turned out favorably: Łabunie and Komarów were taken.

Despite exhaustion the soldier of Gen. Haller's Group did not sleep that night. The commanders studied the terrain on a map; the infantryman with bayonet in hand, the artilleryman at his cannon, and the cavalryman in his saddle with his sword, all watched to make sure the enemy did not slip away in the dark of night.

The General studied our positions all night and made plans for the next day.

Zamość still did not sleep—cannons continued to flash, showing that the fortress was being defended. Amid the darkness of night every so often one could hear the echo of fighting by the reconnaissance patrols—the enemy was not sleeping, either. The soldiers of both camps understood the seriousness of the situation, and, gathering their last reserves, prepared the field for the next day's battle.

The night passed without serious incident.

At daybreak on 30 August the roar of cannons combined with the clatter of machine guns began again. The battle had begun. On green fields chains of extended orders appeared, groups of riders raced among the little hills, and orderlies sped on frothing horses. Our artillerymen got to work zealously, pounding away at the cannons with rolled up sleeves. The orders of the battery's commanders rang out; "Sweep to the right, sweep to the left." The regiments of our cavalrymen with drawn swords and raised lances pulled up stealthily to their positions. Their reflexive restraining of the horses' snorting gave proof of nervous tension: a moment, and the spurs will strike as one, there will be a swishing in the ears, swords will shine in the sun, lances will lower, horses will snort and stretch their necks—and in a mad rush cavalry will strike against cavalry.

General Haller stood calmly on the mound by the cross, taking in the view of the field of mortal combat, and even though this high position was covered with the enemy's frenzied artillery fire, he did not leave it, because he wished to observe and direct the battle personally.

25th Brigade struck through Wolica Śniatycka toward the southwest, and the 26th struck with one regiment from Łabunie along the road to Łabuńki, with another at Ruszów-Wierzba. The cavalry division struck at Śniatycze, then directed itself westward past hill 236 toward the forests between Bródek and Barchaczew *[now called Barchaczów]* and Cześniki, closing off the Mounted Army's retreat on that side. To the north the marshes of the Łabuńka river, impossible for cavalry to cross, cut off the Mounted Army on that side; they were also to be defended by the 2nd Division of the Legions, operating in the vicinity Hrubieszów-Werbkowice and Horyszów Ruski. The fortress at Zamość, located in a wedge between the river Łabuńka and its tributary, repulsed attacks very effectively, cutting off the Mounted Army from the west.

Budionny was surrounded.

The iron ring of our armies created confusion in the ranks of our foe. Budionny believed in the wild fantasy of his young men, and having assembled his whole army between Barchaczew and Cześniki, he carefully followed the movements of our forces, picking a spot where he might be able to break through.

At 10 o'clock in the morning a hurricane of artillery fire, ours and the enemy's, drowned out the echoes of other weapons. The whole Mounted Army burst out of the woods in a frenzied dash. At an extended trot it flashed across a small clearing north of Wolica Śniatycka, headed for Steel Division's 25th Brigade. The concentrated fire of our batteries did not terrify the Cossacks. With broadswords flashing in the sun they tore forward to a little forest located east of the village of Brudek *[? Bródek]*, where the 25th Brigade had occupied positions. The first ranks of the Cossacks rushed helter-skelter at full speed, the next as a line of squadrons in intervals, and so on for a distance into the depths—the rear line of the squadrons.

The General, still constantly under fire by the cross, watched in silence, every so often giving orders, sending battalions of the 45th Regiment toward the main fighting to help out. Riders sped off with his orders, carrying them on all sides. The General constantly monitored the little glade—suddenly there was confusion there. The forward ranks of the Cossacks, encountering heavy fire from our machine guns, had turned to flee, breaking their own rear ranks. Our artillery continued to beat them, decimating the enemy's ranks. The whole Cossack swarm turned to flee back toward the forest from which it had emerged to attack.

The first attack was broken.

Our cannons continued to pursue them as they fled; the machine guns smoked; the soldier settled in his position, seeing that this was not over yet.

There hadn't yet been enough time to water and resaddle the horses before the Cossacks once more charged in two masses. One hurtled again at the 25th Brigade, and the second dashed off in a more easterly direction, where our cavalry division stood beyond a hill. This time the masses of combatants fought hand-to-hand; the Cossacks' attack was broken on the bayonet of the infantryman and the lance of the cavalryman. Our cavalry division fought with fists, teeth and hooves. The fighting was so intense that riders and horses rolled around on the field in a deadly embrace.

Once more the survivors returned to their former positions.

This time the reorganization in Budionny's ranks took longer. Neither the dead nor the wounded were pulled off the field. The whole glade turned color from blood. The constant boom of the cannons drowned out the moans of the wounded. Every so often a rider or horse would jump up from the battlefield in mortal agony, bleeding, would run a few steps, and then would fall down and die. The wounded horses, as if possessed, darted all over the field, trampling wounded people with their hooves. Wounded commanders in the grip of approaching death still kept giving some sort of military signals.

The General formed new positions in case the 25th Brigade's line was broken.

Once more the Cossacks burst out of the woods. This time they sped in a mass as if mad. The ranks were closed up and the fighting was hand-to-hand. In vain the General strained his eyes, impatiently waiting for the ranks of the enemy to break. The ferocious fighting continued. The "ace brigade" in red caps flew across the glade, and at its head with a sword in his hand was Budionny himself. Clearly this was the decisive attack.

The General leaned against the cross and looking on the new idol said, "God, maybe they won't repulse them. But after all, that is the 1st Haller Division." This warmed the souls of the officers around him—this was the first Haller Division fighting, and the Commander in Chief's former chief of staff, his right-hand man, he knew this often nameless Blue Division.

The personal courage of Budionny did not help, nor did this new unexpected charge. The soldier of the Steel Division took it; dying with a bayonet in the horse's belly, he pulled the trigger to bring down the rider. Our commanders paid no attention to their own lives; running along the lines, they seized the machine guns from the dead men and fired them themselves. Col. Rommel never doubted in our victory, even though the dead bodies of 12 of his best officers lay on the battlefield, and just as many fainted on their horses from their wounds.

Our artillerymen paid no attention to their faces blackened with smoke, to their bursting guns. It was a moment when a soldier, seeing the blood of his comrades, would die, but would not leave his place.

The third Cossack attack was broken as well. The broken ranks fled. The soldier, encouraged by having driven off such a furious attack, took heart. The artillerymen ignored the shells—he'll die here, but he won't withdraw—and with the last shell bursts his cannon, blowing himself up along with pieces of iron. The cavalry division commenced surrounding Budionny with its right flank.

Seeing the danger of the situation, the Cossacks threw themselves once more into an attack. At the head of the attacking regiments were red standards. The commissars bustled about, exhorting them to have courage.

The red rags and red watchwords did no good. The demoralized Cossacks did not even get as far as halfway across the glade, then in a moment they turned and hurried back to the forest. The last attempt came to nothing.

Budionny chose another plan. He decided to fight his way with the remnants of his forces to the north, through the marshes. He rushed to Cześniki through Miąszyń and Horyszów Ruski. The line of the Łabuńka river's marshes and those localities were defended by the Legions' 2nd Division. This division, not knowing Budionny's tactics very well, manned the village and elevations with battalions, creating separate combat groups. Budionny took advantage of this, sweeping away battalion after battalion, and defeated one whole brigade of the Legion division. Having crossed the marshes of the Huczwa river at Werbkowice, he attacked Hrubieszów, took the town, and captured 500 prisoners of war of 2nd Division. In vain was 2nd Division's courage; the Cossacks' system of outflanking small combat units gave them the upper hand.

Budionny, having slipped away with the remnants of his forces, took advantage of the river Huczwa's swamps, organizing defense on them. A temporary rest was essential to put his army back in order.

After the battle at Zamość Gen. Haller's Group set out immediately, without rest, to continue chasing the Mounted Army, heading for Werbkowice, where the Huczwa's marshes were narrowest, with the intention of crossing the river in that place. The cavalry division went through Tyszowce.

Despite powerful resistance by the Mounted Army on the Huczwa, Gen. Haller's Group crossed the river in one day in both places and drove it back beyond the Bug. Stopping at the Bug, the Group held up for several days, to give the men and horses some rest, put the front back in order, and establish communications with our forces and the army command. The river Bug, difficult to cross, also demanded certain preparations for a further offensive.

On those lines Gen. Stanisław Haller, promoted by the High Command to commander of the 6th Army, took his leave of our Division and Group. With tears in his eyes the soldier of the Steel Division said goodbye to his beloved commander. "General, if you someday read my report for the Emigrant Community in America, written with a soldier's direct hand, remember that the soldier from America, comprising more than three-quarters of your division, worships you for your soldierly simplicity, and for the laurels the Division encountered through you, your genius, your example in battle."

A further offensive was prepared by the army's commanders very quickly, so as not to give the enemy a chance to fortify himself strongly.

Our forces' crossing the Bug was difficult, because the enemy, having excellent positions on the eastern bank, which is higher than the western, covered the crossing army with lethal artillery fire.

From the line of the Bug the enemy retreated to the river Ługa, defending against cutting off Włodzimierz Wołyński. 13th Division advanced from Zimne to Sielec to cross the river there. The Bolsheviks defending against the crossing set the bridge on fire. Our lads charged so courageously that some companies swam across to the other side, and others plunged into the water, extinguishing the burning bridge. This crossing cost a lot of lives, for many soldiers drowned, and many were wounded by the enemy's artillery fire.

From the line of the Ługa river, the Mounted Army retreated to Łuck. The Steel Division, making 70 km. a day, constantly followed them, tearing at them.

At 11 o'clock on the night of the 15th–17th of July [sic], the 25th Brigade of the Steel Division attacked Łuck. The Bolsheviks destroyed all the bridges on the Styr, leaving only one footbridge of planks. The 25th Brigade's attack was so unexpected to the enemy that he did not succeed in breaking up the footbridge, for the soldiers of the 44th Regiment, like ghosts, were on the footbridge throwing the Bolsheviks into the water with their bayonets. Like lightning our lads found themselves in the city, cutting down the Cossack guards and soldiers sleeping in the houses. Such a panic developed among the Cossacks in the town that they ran into the fields undressed, in the greatest disorder. The bayonet attack was magnificent—the whole city was captured.

In the morning the enemy began to shell the town with artillery, but sorties were sent out and chased the batteries from their positions.

13th Division, losing no time, set out after the Mounted Army along the road to Równe. From the Styr our cavalry corps attacked one column through Ołyka to Klewań, and a second through Młynów to Równe. The left column fought a great battle at Klewań, and the right column cut off the Mounted Army's supply column at Młynów.

Równe was taken on 19 September 1920. The soldier of the 13th Division demolished with his bayonet the freshly adorned gates set up by the Jews for Trotsky's drive. After taking Równe our forces halted for a short time at the river Horyń. The cavalry division moved forward, catching Cossacks of the Mounted Army scattered along the forests.

The High Command ordered the taking of the Słucz river. 13th Division, along with a cavalry corps, advanced, taking the town of Zwiahel. In the battle at Zwiahel we captured great military booty.

Budionny vanished from the line of the Słucz, heading to Kiev with the survivors of his once mighty Mounted Army, in order to reorganize. The credit for destroying the Mounted Army should be ascribed to the Battle at Zamość. If Budionny had won there and joined up with the Soviet army operating near Warsaw, who knows whether the fortunes of our country would have turned out so successfully?

The history of the Mounted Army ended sadly. The vow the 13th Division made at Kiev was fulfilled.

The armistice found the Steel Division on the Słucz river. As ordered, it withdrew to the Korczyk river, according to the conditions of the armistice, and remains there to this day, guarding the Polish Eastern Frontier lands.

The demobilization of our lads from America took place as ordered by the Ministry of Military Affairs after the armistice, on the Korczyk river.

Dear soldier of the "Eastern Frontier Division," still standing guard on the eastern borders of Poland, may God give you good fortune in your further soldierly work for the Fatherland! Preserve the traditions of the "Steel Division"!

INDEX OF POLISH, UKRAINIAN, AND RUSSIAN NAMES OF PLACES MENTIONED IN THE REGIMENTAL HISTORIES

The names of places in Poland and Ukraine are given as follows:

1) if they have well-known English versions, those versions are used, e. g., Warsaw, Kiev;
2) otherwise, for places that were in Poland during the period covered by the text, the Polish versions are used, as in the original text;
3) places that were formerly within territory ruled by Poland, but now are in Ukraine, are given with their Polish names, as in the text. For those who are familiar with Ukrainian and wish to establish the Ukrainian names, those are given below, both in Cyrillic forms and English phonetic renderings. For larger towns it was possible to establish the Russian version of the name; in such cases the Russian names are also given in Cyrillic and Roman-alphabet forms.

The whole idea is to facilitate finding these places in various reference works, as English-language works on them may be hard to come by. For many of these places it may be possible to find them only on maps or in gazetteers in Polish, Russian, or Ukrainian; so it would help a lot to have their names in those languages available.

It's important to recognize that the Polish name forms given in the text are not always reliable, possibly due to human error, but possibly also because the names have changed. For instance, the village one author calls *Zabołotowce* is apparently the one that shows up in gazetteers as *Zabołotce*; *Topule* is apparently *Topyle*. Several of the older names of Polish villages near Hrubieszów vary from their current forms: clearly *Zubkowice* is the place now called *Zubowice*, *Przewalew* is now *Przewale*, and *Klątwa* is *Klątwy*. Variations of this sort are normal, and researchers must always take pains to identify place names correctly.

Another factor that makes it particularly difficult to establish the correct name of smaller villages is the fact many places have the same names, or very similar ones. There are numerous localities in Ukraine called *Pavlivka*, for instance; establishing with certainty which one corresponds to the place called *Poryck* in the text is not so easy. Information from 19th-century maps and from the 19th-century Polish gazetteer *Słownik geograficzny Królestwa Polskiego* was compared with modern maps of Ukraine to determine the correct name, insofar as that was possible. In many cases, however, there simply was not enough information available to be certain every place was identified accurately.

When a Polish name is followed by a Ukrainian name without a question mark, that means the identification is reasonably certain; the reference is to a town or village large enough to be found on maps and verified as a likely match. When a question mark precedes the Ukrainian name, the identification is less certain; there is a place with that Ukrainian name in the area indicated, and the Ukrainian form corresponds fairly well to the Polish name given in the text. But treat these cases with skepticism, until your research verifies them.

In a word: be careful when dealing with place names!

As of this writing a good 19th-century map of Galicia, with Polish names of places, is available online at **http://lazarus.elte.hu/hun/digkonyv/topo/3felmeres.htm**. Note that the master map at that site gives names in their Hungarian forms; but they are usually not too hard to recognize. The individual maps show places by their Polish names, which can then be compared with modern Polish and Ukrainian maps.

Adampol – *Ukr.* Адампіль, *Adampil'*
Aleksandrya – *Ukr.* Олександрія, *Oleksandriya*
Ambukowa – *Ukr.* Амбуків, *Ambukiv*
Andruszówka – *Ukr.* Андрушівка, *Andrushivka*
Annopol – *Ukr.* Аннопіль, *Annopil'*
Annówka—*Ukr.* Аннівка, *Annivka*
Antonówka – *Ukr.* Антонівка *[Antonivka]*
Awratyn – *Ukr.* Авратин, *Avratyn*
Baranie Peretoki – *Ukr.* Барані Перетоки, *Barani Peretoky*
Baranówka – *Ukr.* Баранівка, *Baranivka*
Batków – *Ukr.* Батьків, *Bat'kiv*
Bazalja – *Ukr.* Бвзвлія, *Bazaliya*
Berdyczów – *Ukr.* Бердичів, *Berdychiv, Russ.* Бердичев, *Berdichev*
Beresteczko – *Ukr. and Russ.* Берестечко, *Berestechko*
Berezna – *Ukr.* Березна, *Berezna*
Bereźne – *Ukr.* Березне, *Berezne*
Białykamień – *Ukr.* Білий Камінь, *Bilyi Kamin'*
Biczowa – *Ukr.* Бичева, *Bycheva*
Bielów – ? *Ukr.* Білів, *Biliv*
Biłka Szlachecka – *Ukr.* Білка Шляхетська, *Bilka Shliakhets'ka*
Błudów – ? *Ukr.* Блудів, *Bludiv*
Bohdanówka – *Ukr.* Богданівка, *Bohdanivka*
Boratyn – *Ukr.* Боратин, *Boratyn*
Bożanka – *Ukr.* Бужанка, *Buzhanka*
Bratałów – *presumably Ukr.* Великий Браталів, *Velykyi Brataliv,* or Малий Браталів, *Malyi Brataliv*, both in the area west-southwest of Zhytomyr
Brodów – *Ukr.* Бродів, *Brodiv*
Brody – *Ukr.* Броди, *Brody, Russ.* Броды, *Brody*

Broniki – *Ukr.* Броники, *Bronyky*
Bubnów – *Ukr.* Бубнів, *Bubniv*
Buhryń – *Ukr.* Бугрин, *Buhryn*
Busk – *Ukr.* Буськ, *Bus'k, Russ.* Буск, *Busk*
Butowce – *Ukr.* Бутівці, *Butivtsi*
Cebrów – *Ukr.* Цебрів, *Tsebriv*
Charkowce – *Ukr.* Харківці, *Kharkivtsi*
Chmielnik – *Ukr.* Хмільник, *Khmil'nyk*
Chorłupy – *Ukr.* Хорлупи, *Khorlupy*
Chwastów – ? *Ukr.* Фастів, *Fastiv*
Cucniów – *Ukr.* Цуцнів, *Tsutsniv, apparently now called* Петрове, *Petrove*
Cudnów – *Ukr.* Чуднів, *Chudniv*
Czajczyńce – *Ukr.* Чайчинці, *Chaichyntsi*
Czarny Ostrów – *Ukr.* Чорний Острів, *Chornyi Ostriv*
Czartonja – *almost certainly a typo for* Czartorja, *Ukr.* Чортория, *Chortoryia* = Нова Чортория, *Nova Chortoryia,* and Стара Чортория, *Stara Chortoryia*
Czartowska Skała – *(per the gazetteer Słownik geograficzny Królestwa Polskiego this is the name of a mountain near Winniki)*
Czaruków – *Ukr.* Чаруків, *Charukiv, Russ.* Чаруков, *Charukov*
Czerniawka – *Ukr.* Чернявка, *Cherniavka*
Czernica – *Ukr.* Черниця, *Chernytsia*
Czyżyków – *Ukr.* Чижиків, *Chyzhykiv*
Demidówka – *Ukr.* Демидівка, *Demydivka*
Deraźne – *Ukr.* Деражне, *Derazhne*
Dolhalevka – *Ukr.* Догвалівка, *Dovhalivka*
Dołżek – ? *Ukr.* Довжок, *Dovzhok*
Dubno – *Ukr.* Дубно, *Dubno*
Dziunków – *Ukr.* Дзюньків, *Dziun'kiv*
Filińcy – *Ukr.* Филинці, *Fylyntsi*
Firlejówka – *now Ukr.* Андріївка, *Andriyivka, Russ.* Андреевка, *Andreyevka*
Florjanówka – *Ukr.* Флоріанівка, *Florianivka, Russ.* Флориановка, *Florianovka*
Gaje – *Ukr.* Гаї, *Hayi*
Gliniany – *Ukr.* Гліняни, *Hlyniany*
Gnidawa – *Ukr.* Гнидава, *Hnydava*
Gołogóry – *Ukr.* Гологори, *Holohory*
Hermanów – ? *Ukr.* Германів, *Hermaniv*
Holendry – *Ukr.* Голендри, *Holendry*
Hordyjówka – *Ukr.* Гордіївка, *Hordiyivka*
Horodnica – *Ukr.* Городниця, *Horodnytsia*
Horodyszcze – *Ukr.* Городище, *Horodyshche*
Horynka – *Ukr.* Горинка, *Horynka*
Hoszcza – *Ukr.* Гоща, *Hoshcha*
Hreczana – *Ukr.* Нречана, *Hrechana*
Hreczany – *Ukr.* Нречани, *Hrechany*
Hulsk – *Ukr.* Гульськ, *Hul's'k*

Index of Place Names – 293

Humań – *Ukr. and Russ.* Умань, *Uman'*
Iwaczów – *Ukr.* Івачів, *Ivachiv*
Iwanicze – *Ukr.* Іваничі, *Ivanychi*
Iwaszkówka – *Ukr.* Івашівка, *Ivashkivka*
Jabłonne – *Ukr.* Яблунне, *Yablunne*
Janiewicze – *Ukr.* Яневичі, *Yanevychi* (*apparently now* Іванівка, *Ivanivka*)
Jurówka – *Ukr.* Юрівка, *Yurivka*
Kalinówka – *Ukr.* Калинівка, *Kalynivka*
Kamień – *Ukr.* Камінь, *Kamin'*
Kamienna Góra – *Ukr.* Кам'яна Гора, *Kam'iana Hora*
Karań – ? *Ukr.* Карань, *Karan'*
Katerburg – *apparently now* Катеринівка, *Katerynivka*
Katerynówka – *Ukr.* Катеринівка, *Katerynivka*
Kiev – *Polish* Kijów, *Russ.* Киев, *Kiyev*, *Ukr.* Київ, *Kyiv*
Klewań – *Ukr.* Клівань, *Klivan'*
Klitna – *Ukr.* Клітня, *Klitnia*
Kołodzianka – *Ukr.* Колодянка, *Kolodianka*
Korosteń – *Ukr.* Коростень, *Korosten'*
Korostkił – *almost certainly a typo for* "Korostki" = *Ukr.* Коростки, *Korostky*
Korzec – *Ukr.* Корець, *Korets'*, *Russ.* Корец, *Korets*
Kostopol – *Ukr.* Костопіль, *Kostopil'*
Koszelówka – *Ukr.* Кошелівка, *Koshelivka*
Kotiużyńce – *Ukr.* Котюжинці, *Kotiuzhyntsi*
Kowel – *Ukr.* Ковіль, *Kovil'*, *Russ.* Ковель, *Kovel'*
Kozary – ? *Ukr.* Козари, *Kozary*
Koziatyn – *Ukr.* Козятин, *Koziatyn*, *Russ.* Казатин, *Kazatin*
Krasiłów – *Ukr.* Красилів, *Krasyliv*, *Russ.* Красилов, *Krasilov*
Krasne – *Ukr.* Красне, *Krasne*
Krasnopol – *Ukr.* Краснопіль, *Krasnopil'*
Kresy: literally "borderlands," term used by Poles to refer to the territory that was at one time the eastern part of the Commonwealth of Poland and Lithuania (till 1772), much of which was again ruled by Poland 1921-1939. Now these lands lie primarily within the independent nations of Belarus and Ukraine.
Kropiwna – *Ukr.* Кропивня, *Kropyvnia*
Krynicki Majdan – village in Poland, now called *Majdan Krynicki*
Krystynopol – *Ukr.* Кристинопіль, *Krystynopil'*, *apparently now* Червоноград, *Chervonohrad*
Krzemieniec – *Ukr.* Кременець, *Kremenets'*, *Russ.* Кременец, *Kremenets*
Krzyżanówka – *Ukr.* Крижанівка, *Kryzhanivka*
Kuka – ? *Ukr.* Кука, *Kuka*
Kumanowce – *Ukr.* Куманівці, *Kumanivtsi*
Kurowce – *Ukr.* Курівці, *Kurivtsi*
Kurowice – *Ukr.* Куровичі, *Kurovychi*
Kuszlin – *Ukr.* Кушлин, *Kushlyn*
Kutyszcze – *Ukr.* Кутище, *Kutyshche*

Łabunie – village in Poland
Łabuńki – village 7 km. from Zamość
Lachowce – ? Łachowce, a few km. northeast of Ulhówek
Lasków – ? *Ukr.* Ласків, *Laskiv*
Łasków – *Ukr.* Ласків, *Laskiv*
Lipno – *Ukr.* Липне, *Lypne*
Lipowiec – *Ukr.* Липовець, *Lypovets'*
Lisznia – *Ukr.* Лішня, *Lishnia*
Litowisko – ? *Ukr.* Літовище, *Litovyshche*
Litwa – ? Ukr. Литва, *Lytva*, or Літва, *Litva*
Łokacze – *Ukr.* Локачі *[Lokachi]*
Łopatyn – *Ukr.* Лопатин, *Lopatyn*
Lubar – *Ukr.* Любарь, *Liubar*
Łuck – *Ukr.* Луцьк, *Luts'k, Russ.* Луцк, *Lutsk*
Lwów – *Ukr.* Львів, *L'viv, Russ.* Львов, *L'vov*
Macheryńce Dubowe – *Ukr.* Дубові Махаринці, *Dubovi Makharyntsi, Russ.* Дубовые Махаринцы, *Dubovye Makharintsy*
Machnówka – ? *Ukr.* Махнівка, *Makhnivka*
Małopolska – "Little Poland" (historically the region now comprising southcentral to southeastern Poland; "eastern Małopolska" would extend into what is now western Ukraine)
Mały Czerniatyn – *Ukr.* Малий Чернятин, *Malyi Cherniatyn*
Markowce – *Ukr.* Марківці, *Markivtsi*
Michalin – *Ukr.* Михайлин, *Mykhailyn*
Mikołajów – *Ukr.* Миколаїв, *Mykolayiv*
Miropol – *Ukr.* Миропідь, *Myropil'*
Misiorówka – *Ukr.* Мисюрівка, *Mysiurivka*
Młynów – *Ukr.* Млинів, *Mlyniv*
Młynowce – *Ukr.* Млинівці, *Mlynivtsi*
Mogiła – ? *Ukr.* Могила, *Mohyla*
Mołoczki – *Ukr.* Молочки, *Molochky*
Morozówka – *Ukr.* Морозівка, *Morozivka*
Motrunki – *Ukr.* Мотрунки, *Motrunky*
Nagierany – ? *Ukr.* Нагіряни, *Nahiriany*
Nakwasza – *Ukr.* Накваша, *Nakvasha*
Napadówka – *Ukr.* Нападівка, *Napadivka*
Niemiacze – *Ukr.* Нем'яч, *Nem'iach*
Niemielanka – *Russ.* Немелянка, *Nemelianka*
Nowa Sieniawka – *Ukr.* Нова Синявка, *Nova Syniavka*
Nowochwastów – ? *Ukr.* Новофастів, *Novofastiv*
Nowosiółki – *Ukr.* Новосілки, *Novosilky*
Nuszce –? *Ukr.* Нище, *Nyshche*
Obarów – *Ukr.* Обарів, *Obariv*
Oczeretnia – *Ukr.* Очеретня, *Ocheretnia*
Oczytków – *Ukr.* Очитків, *Ochytkiv*

Oknin – ? *Ukr.* Великі Вікнини, *Velyki Viknyny and* Малі Вікнини, *Mali Viknyny*
Oktawin – *Ukr.* Октавин, *Oktavyn*
Olewsk – *Ukr.* Олевськ, *Olevs'k*
Ołyka – *Ukr.* Олика, *Olyka*
Oratów – *Ukr.* Оратів, *Orativ*
Ostróg – *Ukr.* Острог, *Ostroh, Russ.* Острог, *Ostrog*
Ostropol – *Ukr.* Старий Остропідь, *Staryi Ostropil'*
Ozierna – *Ukr.* Озерна, *Ozerna*
Palcza – *Ukr.* Пальче, *Pal'che*
Palikrowy – *Ukr.* Паликорови, *Palykorovy*
Pasieczna – *Ukr.* Пасічна, *Pasichna*
Paszków – ? *Ukr.* Пасхів, *Pashkiv*
Pawłówka – *Ukr.* Павлівка, *Pavlivka*
Pedosy – *Ukr.* Педоси, *Pedosy*
Perespa – *Ukr. and Russ.* Переспа, *Perespa*
Perytoki – Ukr. Перетоки, *Peretoky*
Pieniaki – *Ukr.* Пеняки, *Peniaky*
Piewce – *Ukr.* Півці, *Pivtsi*
Pików – *Ukr.* Пиків, *Pykiv*
Pikowiec – *Ukr.* Пиковець, *Pykovets'*
Pilawa – *Ukr.* Пилява [*Pyliava*]
Plisków – *Ukr.* Плисків, *Plyskiv*
Płoskirów – *till 1954 Ukr.* Проскурів, *Proskuriv, Russ.* Проскуров, *Proskurov; since 1954 Ukr.* Хмельницький, *Khmel'nyts'kyi, Russ.* Хмельницкий, *Khmel'nitskiy*
Podhajce – *Ukr.* Підгайці, *Pidhaitsi*
Podkamień – *Ukr.* Підкамінь, *Pidkamin'*
Pohrebyszcze – *Ukr.* Погребище, *Pohrebyshche*
Połonne – *Ukr.* Полонне, *Polonne, Russ.* Полонное, *Polonnoe*
Ponebel – *Ukr.* Понебель, *Ponebel'*
Ponikwa – *Ukr.* Пониква, *Ponykva*
Popowce – *Ukr.* Попівці, *Popivtsi*
Poromów – *Ukr.* Поромів, *Poromiv*
Poryck – *Ukr.* Порицьк, *Poryts'k, now* Павлівка, *Pavlivka, Russ.* Павловка, *Pavlovka*
Pryłuki – *Ukr.* Прилуки, *Pryluky, Russ.* Прилуки, *Priluki*
Prywalówka – *Ukr.* Провалівка, *Provalivka*
Prywitów – *Ukr.* Привітів, *Pryvitiv*
Radków – village in Poland
Radomyśl – *Ukr.* Радомишль, *Russ.* Радомышль, *Radomyshl'*
Rajce – ? *Ukr.* Райци, *Raitsy*
Rawa Ruska – *Ukr.* Рава-Руська, *Rava-Rus'ka, Russ.* Рава-Русская, *Rava-Russkaia*
Romanów – *Ukr.* Романів, *Romaniv*
Rossosze – *Ukr.* Росоша, *Rososha*
Równe – *Ukr.* Рівне, *Rivne, Russ.* Ровно, *Rovno*
Rozkopane – *Ukr.* Розкопане, *Rozkopane*
Rudnia – *Ukr.* Рудня, *Rudnia*

Rusinowo – ? *Ukr.* Руснів, *Rusniv*
Samhorodek – *Ukr.* Самгородок, *Samhorodok*
Sarny – *Ukr.* Сарни, *Sarny*
Sassów – *Ukr.* Сасів, *Sasiv*
Sielce – *Ukr.* Селець, *Selets'*
Sieliszki – ? *Ukr.* Селіски, *Selisky*
Skała – *Ukr.* Скала, *Skala*
Skitka – *Ukr.* Скитка, *Skytka*
Sławuta – *Ukr. and Russ.* Славута, *Slavuta*
Słucz river – *Ukr. and Russ.* Случь, *Sluch'*
Śmieła – ? *Ukr.* Сміла, *Smila*
Śnieżna – *Ukr.* Сніжна, *Snizhna*
Sokal – *Ukr.* Сокаль, *Sokal'*
Spiczyńce – *Ukr.* Спичинці, *Spychyntsi*
Stanisławczyk – *Ukr.* Станіславчик, *Stanislavchyk*
Stara Huta – *Ukr.* Стара Гута, *Stara Huta*
Stara Sieniawa – *Ukr.* Стара Синява, *Stara Syniava*
Starokonstantynów – *Ukr.* Старокостянтинів, *Starokostiantyniv*, *Russ.* Староконстантинов, *Starokonstantinov*
Stawiszcze – *Ukr.* Ставище, *Stavyshche*
Stochód river – *Ukr.* Стохід, *Stokhid*, *Russ.* Стоход, *Stokhod*
Świniuchy – ? *Ukr.* Свинюхи, *Sviniukhy*
Swinnoje – ? *Ukr.* Свинне, *Svynne*
Szelwów – *Ukr.* Шельвів, *Shel'viv*
Szepetówka – *Ukr.* Шепетівка, *Shepetivka*, *Russ.* Шепетовка, *Shepetovka*
Tajkury – *Ukr.* Тайкури, *Taikury*
Targowica – *Ukr.* Торговиця, *Torhovytsia*
Tarnopol – *Ukr.* Тернопіль, *Ternopil'*, *Russ.* Тернополь, *Ternopol'*
Tereszpol – *Ukr.* Терешпиль, *Tereshpil'*
Topule – ? *Ukr.* Топілля, *Topillia*
Torczyn – *Ukr.* Торчин, *Torchyn*
Tucza – *Ukr.* Туча, *Tucha*
Tytyjów – ? *Ukr.* Тетиїв, *Tetyiv*
Udzin – ? *Ukr.* Лудин, *Ludyn*
Uhnów – *Ukr.* Угнів, *Uhniv*
Ułanów – *Ukr.* Уланів, *Ulaniv*
Ulhówek – village in Poland
Uljanówka – *Ukr.* Улянівка, *Ulianivka*
Volhynia – a region of what is now northwestern Ukraine, but 1921-1939 it was part of eastern Poland; called in Polish *Wołyń*, in Russian Волынь, *Volyn'*, in Ukrainian Волинь, *Volyn'*
Wajików – village in Poland
Werbkowice – village in Poland, southwest of Hrubieszów
Wesołówka – *Ukr.* Веселівка, *Veselivka*
Wielki Czerniatyn – *Ukr.* Великий Чернятин, *Velykyi Cherniatyn*

Wielki Mytnik – *Ukr.* Великий Митник, *Velykyi Mytnyk*
Wilno – now Vilnius, Lithuania, *Russ.* Вильна, *Vil'na*, or Вильно, *Vil'no*
Winnica – *Ukr.* Вінниця, *Vinnytsia*, *Russ.* Винница, *Vinnitsa*
Winniczki – *Ukr.* Виннички, *Vynnychky*
Winniki – *Ukr.* Винники, *Vynnyky*, *Russ.* Винники, *Vinniki*
Wiśniowiec – *Ukr.* Вишнівець, *Vyshnivets'*
Wiszenka – *Ukr.* Вишенька, *Vyshen'ka*
Wisznowiec – *Ukr.* Вишнівець, *Vyshnivets'*
Włodzimierz – *Ukr.* Володиимир-Волинський, *Volodymyr-Volyn's'kyi*, *Russ.* Владимир-Волынский, *Vladimir-Volynskiy*
Wójtowce – *Ukr.* Війтівці, *Viytivtsi*
Wólka – ? *Ukr.* Вулька, *Vul'ka*
Wołkowyja – ? *Ukr.* Вовковий, *Vovkovyi*
Wołodarka – *Ukr.* Володарка, *Volodarka*
Worobijówka – *Ukr.* Воробіївка, *Vorobiyivka*
Wożuczyn – village in Poland
Wróblewka – *Ukr.* Врублівка, *Vrublivka*
Wujna – *apparently now called* Перемога, *Peremoha*
Wyszogródek – *Ukr.* Вишгородек, *Vishhorodek*
Wyżniany – *Ukr.* Вижняни, *Vyzhniany*
Zabołotowce – ? *Ukr.* Заболотівці, *Zabolotivtsi (probably a mistake for* Zabołotce, *Ukr.* Заболотці, *Zabolotsi)*
Zaboryce – ? *Ukr.* Забороче, *Zaboroche*
Załoźce – *Ukr.* Заложці, *Zalozhtsi*
Zamość – a city in southeastern Poland, near the border with Ukraine
Zaporoże – *Ukr.* Запоріжжя, *Zaporizhzhya*, *Russ.* Запорожье, *Zaporozh'ye*
Żarków – *Ukr.* Жарків, *Zharkiv*
Zasław – *Ukr.* Ізяслав, *Izyaslav*, *Russ.* Изяслав, *Izyaslav*
Zazulińce – *Ukr.* Зозулинці, *Zozulyntsi*, *Russ.* Зозулинцы, *Zozulintsy*
Zbrucz river – *Ukr. and Russ.* Збруч, *Zbruch*
Zdołbunów – *Ukr.* Здолбунів, *Zdolbuniv*
Zielinów – *Ukr.* Зелинів, *Zelyniv*
Zimno – *Ukr.* Зимне, *Zymne*
Złoczów – *Ukr.* Золочів, *Zolochiv*, *Russ.* Золочев, *Zolochev*
Zozulińce – *Ukr.* Зозулинці, *Zozulyntsi*, *Russ.* Зозулинцы, *Zozulintsy*
Żuków – *Ukr.* Жуків, *Zhukiv*
Zwiahel – *Ukr.* Звягель, *Zviahel'*, *Russ.* Звягель, *Zviagel'*, *now* Новоград-Волинський, *Novohrad-Volyns'kyi*
Zwinogródek – *Ukr.* Звенигородка, *Zvenyhorodka*, *Russ.* Звенигродка, *Zvenigrodka*
Żytomierz – *Ukr.* Житомир, *Zhytomyr*, *Russ.* Житомир, *Zhitomir*
Żywotów – *apparently* = *Ukr.* Старий Животів, *Staryi Zhyvotiv*, *now called* Новоживотів, *Novozhyvotiv]*

General Józef de Hallenburg Haller
Born August 13, 1873 in Jurczyce, Poland
Died June 4, 1960 in London, England

General Joseph de Hallenburg Haller

by Regina M. Kasaczun

As presented to attendees at the Banquet in Honor of Gen. Joseph Haller, Commander of Polish Armies in France, Tuesday January 2, 1934 at the Mallow-Sterling Hotel, Wilkes-Barre, Pennsylvania

Poland is fortunate in having had, during her critical period, General Joseph Haller. A great son, a great patriot! He has served his country and his God well, and has earned and always will find a warm place in the hearts of his country men. He, in his own characteristic way, conceived the independence of Poland as his main purpose of life, and devoted his great talents to achieve that object. The name Haller is so closely connected with the World War that one cannot be mentioned without recalling the other. It is not an easy task to present to the reader an accurate, and life-like image of this extraordinary man, and to disengage his personality from the mass of details which surrounds his life. Yet, each detail is of great importance and cannot be omitted. This writing, however, of a single personage, cannot supply the materials of an adequate, or even a nearly adequate account of the life of this renowned man.

Joseph Haller was born on August 13, 1873 in Jurczyce, near the city of age-old reverence and culture, picturesque Kraków, in Poland. The ancestors of Haller were natives of Tyrol, and belonged to the nobility of the ancient Republic of Poland, but in the 14th century they migrated to Kraków. Many of his ancestors held high positions in public, and private life. His grandfather Joseph, was President of the Senate of the free Krakow State; the silver coin, known as "Little Hallers" was the last money issued by him in the free Poland. Another noted member of the Haller family was Caesar, an insurgent in the years 1848 and 1863, who fought for Poland's freedom. He was also a member of the national government, and later a representative to the Galician Senate and to the Austrian Parliament. One of the first printing establishments in Poland belonged to the Haller family. Emperor Leopold confirmed the nobility of the Hallers, and presented them with their own coat of arms and the title "de Hallenburg."

His mother, Olga Treter, was a daughter of Wiktor Treter de Szreniawa of Lubomirz, a captain of the Polish Army of 1831, and of the Baronesse La Sollay de Malescot, from whom he inherited French blood.

The early boyhood days of Joseph were spent in Kraków until 1882, when his parents migrated to Lwów, where his father, Henry, was engaged as director of a Credit and Loan Bank. Here in Lwów, Joseph began his higher education. In 1886, he was transferred to the school of Koszyce, where, together with his Polish schoolmates, he organized the "Klub Polski."

Ten years later, after the death of his father, in 1888, he continued his education in Hranice which he finished in 1892.

Ever since his childhood, Joseph was attracted to military life up to the moment when he flashed across the vision of the world as one of the greatest generals of his time.

A better opportunity for training later was presented when at the age of 19, he was enrolled as a cadet in the Military Academy of Vienna, where he came under the influence of men of fine culture and intelligence. This change marked the approach of manhood, yet did not deeply affect his character, but it developed quickly and strongly his potential genius. He confined himself to military history with intense earnestness; became one of the most learned of soldiers, and especially pored for laborious hours over military maps and plans for fortresses, tasks that laid a strong foundation for his future career. After graduating from the Academy in 1895, he passed the officer's examination. He won his lieutenancy and then entered to active service as an officer in the Artillery Corps.

Such was the environment of his boyhood. There was wholesome, strenuous, useful work to be done, yet, education was the essential. This was the typical Pole's life at the time, and it produced strong men for the period of the crisis.

In 1906 he married Miss Alexandra Sala, daughter of the Marshal of the County of Brody. Three years later Joseph Haller was advanced to the rank of Captain, and in 1910 he left the active service in the Austrian Army, in order to study agriculture. The next step of the aspiring leader was to try to organize cooperative unions, and he assigned himself to the task with untiring energy, and with admirable adroitness and persuasive skill. Later, he led the Scout movement, the Falcons, and in 1912 he trained them in military tactics. Through his zealous efforts and interests, the first convention and maneuvers of the Falcons was held at Lwów, to commemorate the 50th anniversary of the Insurrection of Poland.

In 1914, the World War began. General Haller was at this time preparing young Falcons for military service. Since he was a pensioned Austrian officer, he was bound to first consider her rights and interests, yet, he sincerely wished to gain Poland's independence. Automatically, as it seemed, Haller was called by the Ministry of War to active service. Due to political influences he was able to relieve himself of the Austrian service in order to form a volunteer Polish army.

At this time, from the representatives of the parties of Poland's independence, a General National Committee was formed in Kraków as the only polish [sic] authority. From the eastern section of this National Committee, General Haller received official authorization to organize the 2nd Eastern Brigade of the Legions, while Joseph Piłsudski had been organizing the first brigade.

As commander of the Eastern brigade, Joseph Haller recognized the Eastern Section of the Polish National Committee as his supreme power, and because of this he fell in discord with the Austrian authorities, who from the beginning distrusted the Polish Army. Later, after the Legions had left Lwów, Colonel Fijałkowski was assigned commander of the brigade by the Austrian authorities, while Haller was left in command of the 1st Regiment.

Ever since the birth of the 2nd Brigade, Joseph Haller stood firmly, because he thought it was a Polish Army and that it had taken an oath to the Polish nation and not to the Emperor of Austria. He believed that this army would fight only for Poland's independence. However, he soon discovered that this was impossible, as the 1st Brigade had already taken the Austrian oath. Soon the parties in the Eastern Section of the Polish National Committee, under the influence of Roman Dmowski, began to seriously doubt whether the 2nd Brigade, according to the demand of Austria, agreed in general with the standards of the Polish nation. Joseph Haller was faced with a serious problem. The further upkeep of the brigade placed him in conflict with national sentiment, while the disarming of the brigade would compel thousands of under officers to join the active service of the foreign Austrian Army. Haller extricated himself from this delicate situation with military skill. He disbanded the 2nd Brigade and within the regiment he organized a 2nd Iron Brigade.

He went to the front of the 3rd Regiment of the famous 2nd Brigade, and rose from the rank of Major to that of Lieutenant Colonel. Haller justly merited this title. Then followed many battles against the Russians. In the battle of Rafajłowo in November 1914, Lieutenant Colonel Haller was wounded and while being carried off the battle field he warned the soldiers saying: "Do not give up boys," and "As soon as my wounds are dressed, I shall return to you." In spite of the great loss of blood and crude medical treatment he returned to the battle and by a series of brilliant maneuvers he checked the retreat of his army and broke the Russian attack.

Throughout his military life a marked feature of his record in the many commands he held was the confidence and trust placed in him by all who served under him, and the cheerful and prompt obedience that his orders received. The importance of this feeling among troops he well understood, and at this period and after, he always sought to inspire and maintain it. In this manner he was beloved by all his soldiers.

Haller's Regiment, as a fighting unit, was kept under continuous fire at Rafajłowo and Zielona in the Carpathian Mountains until the attack of the Austrians on January 31, 1915.

After these grueling battles, Haller and his regiment rested in Kołomyja and here on March 15, 1915, he was advanced to the rank of Colonel by the Austrians. Now, he decided to have an understanding with the proper authorities on behalf of his regiment, but mainly, on behalf of Poland. First, he traveled to Budapest, then to Vienna, then to the quarters of the commander of the Austrian armies of Cieszyn, and finally to the headquarters of the Legion of Piotrków. After a conference with the Commander in Chief, General Durski, Colonel Haller, accompanied by Major Sikorski, journeyed to Kielce for an understanding with Joseph Piłsudski. While traveling, Haller had an accident and broke his leg. The bone was improperly set at the German Hospital at Częstochowa and complications developed. For a long time Joseph Haller fought with death. Through his political influence he was transferred to Vienna, where under the constant care of his wife, he slowly recuperated.

From Vienna, through Kraków, Colonel Haller continued to the Wołyń front, where Joseph Piłsudski commanded the 1st Brigade; Colonel Kuettner, a Hungarian, the 2nd; and General Grzesicki, an Austrian, the 3rd.

At this time, Colonel Haller had no command, but during one of the serious battles of the Styr River near Stochód, he hurriedly organized a column of his own and surrounded Stobychwa at Czeremoszne, where on the same day, July 15, 1916, he was made a brigadier-general and commander of the 2nd Brigade to succeed Colonel Kuettner.

The appointment of Brigadier-General Haller in the place of the Hungarian Colonel was the recognition of the Polish cause by the Austrians, but it did not prevent the dissatisfaction growing amongst the Legionaires. Now, more than ever, they strongly demanded the decision on behalf of the Polish cause and above all, the acknowledgement of the Polish National Army.

General Puchalski's position as commander of all three brigades became more and more difficult. He was soon replaced by Colonel Stanislaus Szeptycki. In the meantime, Piłsudski also lost command of the 1st Brigade.

Now, in reality, began the agitation among the Legionaires to dissolve the Legions and to place their resignations. At the end of November, 1916, the 1st Brigade was transferred to Warsaw, and Joseph Piłsudski became a member of the Council of State. The Legionaires who refused to take the notorious oath approved by the Council State, were disarmed and imprisoned at Szczypiorna by the German occupational authorities. The 2nd Brigade, at the initiative of

Joseph Haller, refused allegiance to the Germans and therefore, was transferred to Przemyśl as a Polish Aid Corps, this title being suggested by Brigadier-General Haller in a famous memorial of the Councils of Colonels.

From Przemyśl, the Polish Aid Corps, or Haller's Brigade, was led to the Bukowinski front at Rarańcza, where after a certain time, Brigadier-General Haller received the news of the creation of the Regent Council at Warsaw by the "will of the monarchs." Upon receiving this news, which he read at the front, he immediately wrote to the Council, stating that his army recognized it as the temporary commanding authority of the Independent Government of Poland.

On February 9, 1918, Bolshevik-Russia signed a secret peace treaty with the Austro-Germans at Brześć, where the three hostile forces again provoked the Republic of Poland. They intended to separate Chełmszczyzna from Poland and offer it to the newly formed Ukrainia. This caused much indignation in the ranks of the 2nd Brigade, as it became evident that the occupants, contrary to their promises and proclamations, with reference to the independence of Poland, prepared to perpetrate her fourth division. It was the general opinion, that the continuance of the Legions under the Central Powers did not cohere with the dignity of the Polish Nation.

Brigadier-General Joseph Haller then decided upon a daring exploit, an act which indicated that a Pole in war for the independence of his country fears no power no matter how great, and therefore, he did not fear the power of the Germans. So on February 15, 1918, Brigadier-General Haller, after discarding all his German and Austrian decorations, declared open war upon these two powers. After the battle with the Austrians at Rarańcza, General Haller led a part of his 2nd Brigade across the trench line to the east in order to join other Polish formations. Part of his Brigade was cut off by the Austrians, and therefore, could not follow their commander. Those who could not break through, were imprisoned by the Austrians, and the famous case at Marmaros-Sziget concluded the period of the Legions' battles for the independence of Poland, at the side of the Central Powers.

"Brigadier-General Haller attacked the Austrian front and saved the Legions' honor", wrote Division General Sikorski, who was later to become famous for his heroic wartime deeds, "and his future battles with German Armies at Kaniów tended to confirm, in the eyes of the world, a feat more perceptible than at present, that the Polish Legions in 1914 marched upon the historically alleged Russian Front for the purpose of uniting independent Poland."

On the day that the 2nd Brigade broke through the Austrian lines on Russian Territory, Brigadier General Haller issued a proclamation to the Polish nation vowing, in the spirit of Kosciuszko's address, that the banner of combat to secure the independence of Poland would not be withdrawn by the Polish soldier, until such freedom had been obtained. In a separate letter to the Austrian Emperor, he openly denounced the ignominious treachery of Austria and Germany towards Poland.

Lacking food and money, Haller and his Brigade encountered many difficulties while in Ukrainia. The addition of men and materials hampered their advancement for a short while but, on the other hand, increased their strength.

Out of the chaos which now reigned in Russia and the Ukrainia, the polish [sic] soldiers organized themselves into two divisions: the first corps under the command of General Dowbór-Muśnicki at Minszczyzna; the second corps under General Stankiewicz at Soroka, while General Michaelis began to organize a third Corps at Antoniny. The nearest corps was that of General Stankiewicz, which after a few weeks of aimless wandering, in the middle of March, 1918, was joined by Haller's brigade. After reorganizing the corps and reintroducing strict discipline, Haller took over the realms of his 5th Division with the rank of General. Shortly afterward, on April 10, 1918, general Stankiewicz retired, leaving the entire 2nd Division under the command of General Joseph Haller.

After taking charge of the 2nd Corps, General Haller issued an order to march at midnight, occupying in turn the towns of Maksymowka and Human. He intended to unite with the 1st Corps under General Dowbór-Muśnicki. Although the further march of the 2nd Brigade was not approved by the German Marshal Eichhorn—(who threatening to use force demanded that they check it,)—nevertheless, General Haller moved on through Olhopol and Winohrady to Bogusław.

This was now a march through the territory occupied by the Prussians in Ukrainia, therefore, it required much caution to avoid hidden German troops. Following the heroic five-day battle at Kaniów in May, 1918, Haller hacked his way through the overwhelming superior German forces. In the meantime, agreements were made through the Regent Council at Warsaw, which resulted in the Germans guarantee of neutrality to the 2nd Corps. No one suspected that in Germany's promise was hidden deep treachery. On May 10 and 11, 1918, the German Army attacked the neighboring villages occupied by General Haller's troops. There followed a bloody battle. In spite of the Germans 15,000 men, not considering the artillery and cavalry, 250 were killed and 800 wounded, while out of Haller's army of 3,000 only 100 were killed and 200 wounded.

As the situation was unsolvable and further shedding of blood useless, General Haller agreed to the proposed armistice. Taking advantage of this delayed inactivity of the enemy, he dissolved his Corps, divided them into smaller groups, and scattered them over Russian territory with instruction to keep up the fight for their cause.

This occured [sic] about the same time that the Germans were launching the last attack upon the French Front. In order to put over this great final drive, Hindenburg needed all his reserves from Ukrainia, but could not withdraw them because he believed Haller commanded a great force. By engaging the attention of the Germans in Russia, thus preventing them from joining in the attack on the French front, Haller's army was instrumental in the Allied victory.

After the battle of Kaniów and the sending of Polish armies to places of security, General Haller was forced to disguise himself before the Germans, who were anxious for his capture. On May 20, 1918, while hidden in the home of Hulanick and Bogusław, he received word from the Polish military organization and the Inter-Party Circle that he was intrusted with the command of all the Polish Armies outside of the territory occupied by the Austro-Prussians.

From Wasyłków, General Haller marched to Kijów and from there to Moscow, organizing, on his way, Polish armies. In Moscow, he formed a military commission with Colonel Michael Żymierski as leader, and placed Colonel Żeligowski in command of the army on Russian territory appointing him General.

On July 4, 1918, General Haller sailed, with a few officers of the 2nd Brigade on the English Steamer "City of Marseilles" that he might reach France through England. On July 12, he arrived at Havre and the following day he was greeted by Roman Dmowski in Paris. Immediately, they visited Premier Clemenceau who said, "My whole ministry is at your command General." Haller was at once admitted as a member of the Polish National Committee at Paris, and later elevated to the rank of Commander-in-Chief of the Polish Armies on the side of the Allies. Now began the strenuous and painstaking work for enlarging the Polish Army, part of which was already in France, organized by the Poles in the United States. The 1st division of this army was commanded by Colonel Jasiński. He, under the command of General Gouraud, was engaged in a spirited encounter at Champagne. General Haller accepted the command of the first Division of Polish Infantry at Alsace, and immediately began organizing Polish armies.

Thousands of volunteers were drawn from all parts of the world. America sent 24,000, Italy 35,000, France 15,000, England a few thousand, and even Brazil contributed. The general of the Polish Armies now had under his command more than 100,000 men divided into seven divisions comprising artillery, cavalry, a fleet of supply automobiles, camp wagons and first aid corps and soldiers animated with the highest spirit of patriotism and readiness for supreme sacrifice for their country. This army of which a part was engaged in many battles with the Germans on the coalition front up to the time of the complete rout of the German troops, made it possible for Poland to enter the Peace Conference at Versailles.

Unfortunately, the Polish army could not return at once to Poland through Danzig after its victory over the Germans, because in Poland as in France, the elements, sympathizing with the socialistic revolutionists of Germany exercised their influence. Being afraid of the "White Guard," the Germans, with the aid of England, took advantage of these sympathies and refused to allow Haller's army to pass through Danzig. In view of such a situation, the tedious and trying deliberations between the Polish National Committee and Marshall Piłsudski, between Paris and Warsaw, were extended from day to day, from week to week.

Foreseeing danger in this delay for the newly gained independence of Poland, Ignacy Jan Paderewski left America for Poland. A patriot and a statesman could not be resisted even by opponents, and so after seeing the enthusiastic reception which Poland prepared for Paderewski, Marshall Piłsudski decided to intrust to Paderewski the Presidency of the Polish Cabinet and the office of Secretary of Foreign Affairs. This turn in the state of affairs enabled Haller's Army to return immediately from France.

Much depended on this hasty return. When in April 1919, General Haller arrived with his army to the reborn Republic of Poland, the conflagration of war spread over the entire eastern front. Now the whole Polish nation turned to Haller's army with full confidence and this confidence was not betrayed.

On May 8, 1919, General Haller took command of the Russian Front from Pinsk to Karpaty, and with a few concerted attacks defeated the enemy forces and defended the town of Lwów. Then he delivered "Małopolska" from the hands of the Ukrainian rebels who were led by the German officers.

After the defeat of the Ukrainians, General Haller left for the Silesian front. In 1920, he captured Pomerania; on January 21, Toruń; and on February 10, Puck. When he reached the Polish boundary line on the shores of the Baltic, he and his men gathered on the bank overlooking the sea. Here, in the presence of all, he took off his ring and threw it into the calm water. By this simple action, which signified a marriage, so to speak, he united Poland with the Baltic forever.

In Pomerania, Silesia and other captured cities, he introduced Polish administrative authorities. Then with renewed vigor he proceeded to attack the Germans, but in the midst of this evidently beneficial drive, he was recalled to Poland.

In the beginning of April 1920, General Haller left on a much needed furlough to Zakopane, because he declined to assume the responsibility of the apparent war with Russia, for which Poland was not prepared. Meanwhile, there followed the disastrous retreat of the Polish Army from that ill-fated expedition of Joseph Piłsudski at Kijów to obtain the sceptre for the Ukrainian leader, Petlura. The news of this great catastrophe at Kijów spread like a forest fire, and immediately the Bolsheviks began to march against Poland pressing their advances on Warsaw. General Haller was at once called to this point where he was given orders to organize the Polish volunteer army and take command of the defense of Warsaw. The territory under his command comprised the land between Deblin and Prussia.

On July 23, 1920, General Haller took charge of the armies on the northeastern front where he fought two victorious battles on the Bug, making it possible for an easy return of the Polish Army to Warsaw. Later he gained another victory called, "The Miracle of the Vistula", *Cud nad Wisłą*. The three outstanding battles at this time were fought at Radzymin, Nasielsk and Ossów, where the chaplain, Rev. Father John Skorupka met his heroic death.

In 1921 General Haller was named chairman of the Supreme Military Commission, general inspector of the artillery and later a member of the Council of War. These positions were honorary and well merited because of his heroic deeds to gain Poland's Independence.

General Joseph Haller, as long as he lives, will always spread his activities in national and social affairs. At present, he works untiringly as president of the Red Cross Organization, Polish Scouts and Veterans' Organizations for the invalids. For his valor and deeds he was decorated with the following orders: White Eagle; Virtuti Militari; Cross of Valor—four times; The High Commandor [sic] of the French Honorary Legion; The French Military Cross with a palm, Commandor [sic] of the Italian Crown; and with the American Orders: "Distinguished Service"; and the "Cincinnatus" with the inscription, *"omnia reliquit servare rem publicam"* [He left all behind to preserve the republic], which order he placed in the museum of the Polish Army at Warsaw in memory of the comradeship of the Polish and American Armies.

General Haller will always remain, to the Polish nation, the most honorable example of a pure, sacrificing and unselfish son of Poland. No man ever gained more enduring fame. No character in Polish history who owed less to his own ambition or design has ever achieved such a supreme success.

A striking feature in the General's character, and one that has contributed to his success, was the intensity and earnestness with which he devoted himself to whatever duty might be before him.

As a soldier, General Haller possessed to an eminent degree the qualities that are indispensable in a commander who is called on to lead troops in battle, and who has the right to expect success and victory. He has shown the ability to think and act promptly and energetically, and secure cooperation and support for whatever responsibilities his demands have required. He has demonstrated unmistakable power to impress his will and personal influence upon all who were under his command.

After the World War and after Poland had gained her independence, a peaceful future seemed inevitable for this great man, but he continues to devote his great energy and patriotism to Poland's progress and influence as a world power.

COL. A. D. LEPAN,
Camp Commandant

Polish Army Camp

(By Col. A.D. LePan)

(As printed in *Niagara Historical Society* #35, 1923. Published by the Niagara Historical Society)

Col. A.D. LePan has very kindly sent us his official report to the Chief of the Staff at Ottawa, which is herewith published with the permission of National Defence Headquarters. This will be a very valuable addition to what precedes it and will give a complete record of a most remarkable event in the history of Niagara. My prosaic account, "The Real Polish Touch" of Major Young, given with poetic vigor, the humanitarian paper of Mrs. E.C. Ascher, and now the official account giving much heretofore unknown to the general public. Col. A.D. LePan and Major Young have both received the decoration of the Cross of Commander of "Polonia Restituta" from the Polish Government.

Polish Army Camp

Niagara-on-the-Lake, Ont., March 26th

From: The Commandant
        Polish Army Camp

(Confidential)

To: The Chief of the General Staff
    Militia and Defence
        Ottawa, Canada

Sir,

On the closing of the Polish Army Camp at Niagara-on-the-Lake, Ont. I have the honour to submit the following report: -

On authority under Militia telegram 2424 confidential (sp) of date Sept. 22nd, 1917 the staff of the School of Infantry M.D. No. 2 with the Polish Probationers then in training at Camp Borden moved to Niagara-on-the-Lake to establish a Polish camp there. We arrived there early on the morning of Sept. 28th.

The association of this staff with the Polish cause dates back to January 3rd, 1917 when 23 Polish men were sent to the School of Infantry M.D. No. 2 in Toronto to be qualified as officers. Classes grew in size till in the summer of 1917 at Camp Borden we had 150 Polish Probationers.

Accommodation

Billets

As practically no winter accommodation was available at Niagara Camp, it was necessary almost immediately on arrival that this matter should be given attention. On October 25th, 1917 work was started on four huts, Major Barry taking charge of this work and the labour being entirely supplied by men of the Polish Army. These were completed about December 1st when the last man was moved from canvas to billet. These huts holding a total of 1,200 did not provide sufficient accommodation and about Dec. 1st 1917, 15 other billets in town in the form of disused hotels, unoccupied residences, old canning factories. Town Hall, etc., were occupied by Polish troops. These were obtained free of all cost from citizens of the town. On this date our camp strength all ranks was 3,078. These billets in town were repaired and made fit for winter occupation. This accommodation while not ideal either from a physical or administrative standpoint at least enabled us to carry on. In addition to this work water mains had to be lowered and sewers constructed.

Numbers

The total number of Polish troops received in this camp and their disposition was as under:—

Total number of recruits received		22395
Sent on draft to France	20720	
(a) Discharged (Physically Unfit)	1004	
(Compassionate Grounds)	129	
(Subject to U.S. S.S. Law)	193	
(Undesirable)	5	
(Other causes)	91	
(c.) Died	41	
(b) Deserters	212	
Total	22395	22395

Of this amount about 221 or slightly less than 1% were enlistments from Canada, the balance all coming from the United States. The majority of the men gave their nationality as "Russian Poles who formed approximately 62% of the total enlistments, with Austrian Poles approximately 31.5 per cent. German Poles approximately 3% and miscellaneous 3.5%.

Our maximum camp strength occurred on November 21st 1917 when we had 4,279 men.

With the exception of 1,573 Polish troops all ranks who sailed from Halifax, all Polish troops embarked at New York for shipment to France.

Organization

With the instructions for the opening of this camp no information could be obtained as to numbers or possible duration, so that our organization had to be developed as new conditions arose. Our early organization consisted of a Headquarters, with its services and departments and three depot battalions. These battalions were divided into companies of 150 to 200 men, the number of companies varying constantly with the number of men in camp. The 1st Depot Battalion was moved to St. John's Quebec late in November 1917 and with the closing of that depot on February 20th, 1918 this unit was disbanded and only the 2nd and 3rd Depot Battalions were maintained during the balance of the camp. We also organized and maintained the School of Infantry Polish Army, where all Polish officers were trained before being commissioned and proceeding overseas.

The staff of these battalions consisted of four Canadian officers a Canadian sub-staff varying from two to four, and acting Polish officers according to strength.

The staff of the School of Infantry, Polish Army consisted of a Canadian O.C., an acting Polish Officer as Adjutant and one or two Canadian sub-staff instructors with lectures and special work given by the staff of the School of Infantry, M.D. No. 2 attached Polish Army.

Staff Officers

The Canadian officer Staff on November 25th, 1917 after organization had been completed was as follows:

Headquarters Officers

Rank	Name	Unit	Duty
Lt. Col	LePan, A.D.	COTC I C.M.D. No. 2	Camp Commandant
Major	Young, C.R.	COTC	Camp Adjutant
Capt.	Harris, J.	109th Regt.	Asst. Camp Adjutant

Capt.	Parr, C.H.	36th Regt.	Camp Quartermaster
Lieut.	Richards, J.	C.O.C.	Ordnance Officer
Lieut.	Ross, E.H.	C.A.S.C.	A.D. of S.& T.
Lieut.	Kerr, H.M.	C.A.S.C.	Transport Officer
Capt.	Smuck, J.W.	C.A.M.C.	Camp Medical Officer
Lieut.	Graydon, W.L.	C.A.M.C.	Asst. Medical Officer
Capt.	Fowler, C.H.	C.A.D.C.	Camp Dental Officer
Capt.	Stethem, H.	R.C.D.	D.A.P.M.
Capt.	Hamilton, W.G.	109th Regt.	Camp Paymaster

First Depot Battalion, Polish Army

Major	Madill, H.H.	C.O.T.C. I. C.M.D. No. 2	Commanding Officer
Capt.	Smith A.G. (MC)	37th Regt.	Adjutant
Capt.	Wright, E.B.	109th Regt.	Quartermaster
Lieut.	Johnson, B.K.	Cob. H. Batty	Asst. Adjutant

Second Depot Battalion, Polish Army

Major	Kirk, W.F.	C.S.C.I.	Commanding Officer
Capt.	Pembroke, H.E.	31st Regt.	Adjutant
Lieut.	Dickie, E.	48th Regt.	Asst. Adjutant
Capt.	Ferguson, R.J.	13th Regt.	Quartermaster

Third Depot Battalion, Polish Army

Major	Kenrick, F.B.	C.O.T.C.	Commanding officer
Capt.	Nash, C.R.	C.A.S.C.	Adjutant
Lieut.	Brown, N.H.C.	48th Regt.	Asst. Adjutant
Capt.	Marriott, W.G.	91st Regt.	Quartermaster

Probationers' Detail or School of Infantry, Polish Army

Capt.	Lewis, J.L.	9th M.H.	Commanding Officer

If this camp has had any success it is due in large measure to the excellence of the Canadian officers, N.C.O.'s and men. All ranks Canadian have at all times shown an efficiency and devotion to duty that has overcome many difficult situation. The Canadian officers whom it has been my privilege and good fortune to have on the staff of this camp, have by their tact and good judgment and devotion to duty made a success of what was, on account of the number of interests involved and the difficulty of different languages and races, a difficult problem. They are all worthy of special mention and I hope it is appreciated the part they have contributed in enabling the Canadian Government to discharge creditably its obligation to a foreign power.

Training

During the early part of the camp and until the middle of the summer of 1918, all instruction was given in British drill with English and Polish commands, and all Polish officers qualified at the School of Infantry, Polish Army, took the regular course as laid down in Canadian regulations. At this time a change was made and instruction in French Drill started at the School of Infantry and in the units. As practically none of the men speak French, this was given in English and Polish.

The bulk of the training was carried out by acting Polish officers and N.C.Os. under the supervision of Canadian officers and was rather restricted to physical training and Squad and Section Drill with enough Company and Battalion Drill for the practical movement of the battalions and drafts.

N.C.O. classes were continually kept going in the depot units and passed a unit examination both oral and practical and assisted very materially in the training.

No Musketry instruction was given except to the Probationers at the School of Infantry, and no Rifle Drill to any except the School of Infantry and the necessary camp guards.

Training was of necessity limited on account of the short period a great many of the men were in camp.

Three bands (two brass and one bugle) were trained in the camp and proceeded overseas as units.

School of Infantry

Just prior to our movement to Niagara the Probationers at the School of Infantry, M.D. No. 2 had been almost entirely Polish, so that this unit with the changed staff already noted was converted into the School of Infantry, Polish Army. It did I think very excellent work and in all in both schools 295 Probationers were qualified. It filled a very necessary place in our organization, because the Canadian Staff was far too small to actually do all training and the acting Polish officers from this school deserve great credit for the progress in training made by the men during their stay here. Occasional lectures were given in the school by French and Polish officers at various times attached to the camp. Examinations were held in both English and Polish depending on the probationer.

Appointments Polish Army

All appointments in the Polish Army here were made in every case in French Orders almost always after qualification and recommendation here.

St. Johns, Que. Depot

In the latter part of November 1917 with over 4,000 men in camp and provided with winter accommodation for only 1,200 we were badly crowded and it was decided to open up a depot at St. Johns, Que. This depot was placed under Major Madill of this staff and a detail from this camp, and in the period from November 1917 when it was opened until February 1918 when it was closed, 2,400 men passed through this depot, all having passed through our camp. The accommodation provided here was far from being ideal.

Fort Niagara N.Y. Depot

Early in December when the camp strength was over 3,000, additional accommodation had to be provided and instructions were received to open a depot at Fort Niagara, New York. Canadian officers did not take charge of this depot, but matters, such as Pay, were attended to by Canadian officers visiting this depot. The first troops were sent here on December 13th, 1917 and the last Polish troops proceeded overseas from this depot on February 18th, 1918. During this time 1722 Polish troops were sent to this depot. All from Niagara-on-the-Lake.

Responsibility to Government

As a Canadian Staff operating on Canadian soil we were of course responsible to the Canadian Government. The services and departments were supplied by Canadian forces on repayment by the French Government. The regular Canadian issue was supplied to the men in nearly every case with the exception of clothing in which the Polish troops were supplied almost entirely with old militia uniforms. Regular debits against the French Government for materials supplied and services rendered were prepared, checked and certified to each month.

Fortunately in the handling of this scheme which presented many features entirely different from those in purely Canadian service, we were given a large degree of freedom by District and Militia Headquarters. They fortunately for the scheme and for us, recognized that it presented peculiar and complicated problems that only those who under stood the Poles and who were in touch with the different interests involved could handle successfully. The thanks of those interested in this camp are due District and Militia Headquarters for the sympathetic manner in which our requests were received and for the material and moral support given.

Our responsibility to the Polish Military Commission was due to the fact that they were responsible for recruiting the Polish Army in America and all questions of enlistment and discharge were dealt with by them. As the scheme was one of voluntary enlistment, the conditions under which the men lived and their treatment in camp were closely allied to recruiting and our relations with this body were very intimate. We have tried at all times to get the Polish viewpoint and I feel that the smoothness of our relationship in this connection is an indication that in a large measure we were successful.

We also had a very distinct responsibility to the French Government represented by the French High Commission in Washington and New York. Colonel James Martin of the French Army attached to the French High Commission in Washington was the senior officer with whom we dealt and practically all our correspondence and arrangements were with him.

It is only fair to say that we did not always agree. It is perhaps difficult for a foreign officer, not young, from a country where armies are not raised by voluntary enlistment to entirely appreciate the problems of enlistment, of a volunteer army, in a country where men have been used to a very great freedom and where money has an entirely different value; but after all, our differences were minor ones and were always adjusted. I feel sure that if we did not always agree it was always appreciated that our one endeavor at all times was to further the interests of the Polish Army.

Our responsibility to the United States Government consisted in the fact that only certain men were eligible. Latterly lists of all recruits arriving in camp, giving detailed information in regard to them were prepared here and transmitted through the French High Commission of the American authorities.

We also came into direct contact with American Army officers during the maintenance of a depot at Fort Niagara, N.Y., and our relationships at all times were the most cordial.

Intimate associations were also formed with the United States Customs and Immigration authorities with the most satisfactory results.

Health of the Troops

Immediately on arrival all recruits were medically examined by officers of the Canadian Medical staff along lines laid down by the French Medical services. If a man was found to be physically unfit he was immediately discharged and provided with transportation back to the place of enlistment. Men found to be suffering from venereal disorder on arrival or on subsequent examination were also immediately discharged in the same way. In general the health of the troops in camp was very good, the men being of a rugged strong type.

Like others we suffered from an outbreak of Influenza starting about September 13th and running about six weeks. During this outbreak out of a maximum camp strength of 2,500 men we had a total of 24 deaths. This was a very trying period and was added to by the fact that we were continually receiving recruits from infected areas in the United States. To have stopped recruiting absolutely, would have been a very serious blow to the Polish Army in America. On January 2nd, 1919 Captain E. B. Wright, a Canadian officer who had excellent service here, died with pneumonia complicating Influenza. During this period the Medical personnel under Captain J. L. Robinson responded splendidly and it is due to their very excellent work that our death rate was not higher.

We had a slight recurrence of this epidemic about the middle of February 1919 but with less serious results. Our total deaths during the period of the camp were 2 Canadians and 41 Polish troops.

All deaths in the Polish Army were recorded with the Polish Military Commission and the bodies either sent to their homes or buried here. The men buried here were all buried in the same plot in the Roman Catholic cemetery here, each grave indicated by a stone marker and the plot by a large cross. Arrangements are being made for the maintenance of this plot.

Pay

The men received pay at the rate of .05c per day. Sergeants received pay at the rate of 20c per day and acting officers at the rate of $1.22 per day. In addition each man was entitled to a premium of $150.00 per year of which we paid here $10.00 per month to each officer, N.C.O. and man.

The money for these payments came to me direct from Controller Johannet, French High Commission, 65 Broadway, New York City and statements with supporting vouchers were rendered to him each month.

Discipline

With the institution of the camp, no one could be quite sure as to the question of discipline and law and order. Fortunately our most happy prediction came true and discipline among the men was splendid. The Canadian staff during this association have developed the greatest admiration for these splendid men and have the highest regard for their patriotism and devotion to their country

The townspeople were much agitated when the establishment of a Polish Camp was announced. With the arrival of the men they were at first skeptical, but they now speak with enthusiasm of these men. Never they say has there been such an orderly camp or a better behaved lot of men.

Relations with the Townspeople

Our association with the townspeople was I think in almost every case entirely satisfactory. They were very kind in their treatment of both Canadian and

Polish troops. A great deal of the accommodation occupied by the troops was provided gratis by the townspeople during the first winter and at a nominal rental during the second winter, while free light and water was supplied by the municipality. To show that in some measure at least these kindly feelings were reciprocated by the people of the town, I am appending below an extract from the *Niagara Advance* on the Polish Camp.

The Closing of the Polish Camp

It is hard to realize that after nearly eighteen months of military activity, old Niagara and the historic camp ground to the east of us is once more deserted, so far as the military is concerned.

When the news reached us early in September 1917, that we were to have a Polish Camp, the prevailing opinion seemed to be that we were in for a pretty rough time and that it would be well to provide accordingly.

How agreeably we were disappointed, we now know, and our regret is that the Polish boys could not stay with us indefinitely. Both from a financial and social point of view, we have benefited greatly but it goes without saying that we regret the departure of our Polish friends, more because they were our friends than because their sojourn here was of financial benefit.

Never in the history of Niagara as a military centre, have we had a more orderly camp, a more soldierly lot of boys, or a more congenial and efficient staff than during the Polish occupation of the reservation, and while we are pleased and thankful that the wind up of the world's greatest war obviates the necessity for the continuance of the camp, our regret at parting is keen, not only because of our long and pleasant association with such a magnificent lot of men, but because they were, first and always, soldiers and above everything gentlemen.

Y.M.C.A.

Almost with the institution of the camp the Canadian Y.M.C.A. offered its service which were gratefully accepted. I cannot speak too highly of the work done by this association. Its secretaries readily adapted themselves to the peculiar conditions of the camp and were of the greatest assistance in keeping the men happy and contented.

They co-operated with the Canadian Staff to the fullest extent in arranging sports and entertainments.

American Red Cross

Early in the camp came the American Red Cross represented by the Niagara Falls Chapter of Niagara Falls, N.Y. To each soldier leaving this camp they made a presentation of a comfort kit, soap, socks, and tobacco. They also established in this camp a Service Station for the use of relatives visiting camp. Facilities were also offered here, whereby enlisted men through Red Cross channels were able to communicate with relatives in enemy countries. This association also helped materially in supplying assistance during the Influenza epidemic. Too much cannot be said for their very successful and helpful efforts.

Customs and Immigration

On account of the large traffic both in men and material across the border we had considerable dealings with the Customs and Immigration officials of both the United States and Canada and I cannot let this opportunity pass without testifying to their sympathetic co-operation and unfailing courtesy.

Attached Officers

At different times and for different periods, French officers were stationed in this camp. We found them a delightful lot of men and our association with them was in every case most pleasant.

Visitors

At different times this camp was honoured by visits from H.R.H. Prince Arthur of Connaught; The Duke of Devonshire, Mr. Ignace Jan Paderewski and other prominent visitors.

Tribute

On March 3rd and 4th, 1919 the Canadian officers and their wives were the guests of the National Polish Department in Buffalo, when everything possible was done by these kind people to show their appreciation for our small efforts.

Canteen

The Y.M.C.A. very generously agreed not to open a Canteen in connection with their activities so that the only Canteen was that operated by the camp authorities for the benefit of the Poles. During the period of our existence the total sales in this canteen amounted to roughly $122,500.00 yielding net profits of approximately $19,250.00 which were expended for the benefits of the men on the Polish Army in camp here.

Closing of Camp

With the discharge of 3 Poles, medically unfit, from hospital on March 11th, 1919 and their return to their homes, no more Polish troops were left in camp, and every effort was made to close the camp with the least possible delay. By this time the Canadian personnel had been very much reduced, and simply enough kept for the physical closing of the camp and accounting to the French and Canadian Governments.

On March 24th our accounting with Ordnance was completed and March 25th Lieut. Labat of the French High Commission visited the camp, audited the accounts of money advance directly from the French High Commission and found them correct.

On March 26th, the balance of the staff moved to Toronto and opened an office at the University of Toronto till a final clearance of Ordnance and Canteen accounts could be obtained.

I feel that I cannot close this report without respectfully expressing the debt owing to Major-General W. G. Gwatkin, C.B., C.M.G. for his sympathetic interest and assistance during the whole period of the Polish Army in Canada. Without his practical sympathy, our existence would have been I am afraid a difficult, if not an impossible one.

I have the honour to be, Sir

Your obedient servant,

        A.D. LePan
           Lieut.-Colonel
    Commander, Polish Army Camp
      Niagara-on-the-Lake, Ont

MAJOR C. R. YOUNG,
Camp Adjutant.

The Polish Force in Niagara

by Major C. R. Young

[The version printed here is the one published in the *Niagara Advance* ca. March 1919. The same article also appeared in *Niagara Historical Society* #35, 1923, published by the Niagara Historical Society; that version, however, has a number of spelling errors, so that this one seemed the better one to reprint here.]

Seventeen months ago there began at Old Niagara perhaps the most unique chapter of all in its history. Of fighting, these plains had seen a plenty, and the tramp of alien soldiery was not entirely unknown; but never before had this place become a part of Slavdom, where the customs were those of Central Europe and where there was heard a language as foreign to Canadian ears as Hindustani.

There was much that was distinctive in the life of the Polish Army in camp. It was unnecessary to remind an observing visitor that he had left Canada and was now in Little Poland.

A casual glance across the parade ground might have given the impression of a Canadian training camp before the war, for here passed and repassed the scarlets and dark blues and rifle greens of the old militia. But yonder from a staff flew an unknown twin-striped red and white service flag, and from the end of the hut vigorously rose a white eagle from its amaranth field. Then here was seen the square-topped head dress of the Polish soldier—the czapka—and down the breeze from a band that lightened the drudgery of drill floated the March of the Falcons. These too could not be Canadians who spent their hard-earned rest period in dancing the mazur and the polka on the green. Besides, the young men who swung by at a hundred and twenty to the minute were shorter, bigger-chested, sturdier and more stolid than Canadians of the same age.

To those who had been accustomed to see men jump to the explosive "Squad, 'SHUN'," it was perhaps unexpected that anything should happen when there rang out over the field "Zastep, Bacz-NOSC". Yet for a year and a half one might have heard at almost any hour of the day the sharp staccato of drill instruction in Polish. Soon, too, officers who in civil life would have sputtered at Beauchamp or Cholmondeley might be seen nodding with ill-concealed understanding and self-approbation at such a sequence as this:–

> Cieszczyk
> Grzeszczuk
> Kolodziejczyk
> Krzyzanowski
> Przybylowicz

It was in music that the spirit of the Pole, that variable mingling of light-heartedness and melancholy, had its most compelling expression. That which might well have brought "Tears, Idle Tears" to Tennyson, floated across Niagara plain on many a soft summer night. Those who heard it, will never forget the haunting charm of that song of happy youth with its foreboding of sorrow to come, "Jak Szybko Mijaja chwile (How Fast the Moments Fly)." Then there was the tripping care-free march of the victorious legions of Dombrowski, "Jeszcze Polska nie Zginela" (All is not yet over with Poland) and the somber "Boze cos Polske," (O God, Protector of Poland), by common consent regarded in this camp as the National Hymn of Poland. Men and women who have heard all that is most impressive in music have often stood with tear-filled eyes as a thousand Poles poured forth in this sublime hymn, the pent-up emotion of a hundred and fifty years of persecution.

Time may dim the impression of those who here witnessed the events of the past seventeen months, but there is at least one lasting momento [sic] of the Polish occupation. Beneath a cross in the cemetery of St. Vincent de Paul [Niagara-on-the-Lake] there rest twenty-four young men who, as wrote the good Father Rydlewski in the inscription, "Gave their lives for Poland."

[These last two paragraphs appeared in the version published in *Niagara Historical Society* #35, 1923:]

Extract from a letter written by Father Rydlewski on the eve of his departure from France for Poland, with the 4th division of the Polish Army:

> "It will no doubt be a pleasure to you and all our other friends at Niagara-on-the-Lake to learn that, although the French are naturally tired of soldiers in general, having seen so many of them in the past four years, yet I heard wherever I went in Bretagne, Normandie and Lorraine, regrets that our Polish boys are leaving. So they have kept up the fine reputation they got at Niagara and I am proud of it. God will bless such soldiers wherever they may be sent and I hope there will be little fighting needed to chase our enemies from within the boundaries of Poland, because "If God is with us, who'll dare be against us"?

The Polish Army in Niagara

(By Janet Carnochan)

(As printed in *Niagara Historical Society* #35, 1923. Published by the Niagara Historical Society)

Many have been the Military forces seen in Niagara and its vicinity, Regiments with the picturesque dress of the Gael marching to the music of the bag pipe, the pipers swinging their tartans so proudly, across the river the blue of the French regiments assisted by the Indians, meeting the scarlet coats of British regiments also assisted by many of the Six Nation Indians, 150 years ago, again in 1812 British regiments combining with Canadian Militia, many of them the U.E. Loyalists who had given up homes of plenty to be true to their king and live on British soil, fighting to drive back the invading U.S. army with their different uniform. Again in peaceful days the regular training camp of twelve days on Niagara Plains and again on days that we remember our own boys, sons and brothers and friends preparing for stern battles to be fought in France and Belgium to free the oppressed and drive back the brutal invader, also of many who returned not, but never has such a unique sight been seen as that of September, 1917 when appeared aliens drilling on Canadian soil coming from the neighboring republic paid by France, offered by Canadians hoping to free their country taken by force 123 years ago by three grasping enemies, Russia, Prussia, Austria. These patriotic people without a country we may say, still the patriotic fire burning and though living thousands of miles distant now give up prosperous homes to give their lives so that they might again feel that they had a country and that they were free from Russian or Austrian or German yokes. It was wonderful, yes, there were so many remarkable things connected with it, the visits of Prince Poniowtoski *[sic]*, of Paderewski and Madame Paderewski, giving up his fame as an artist spending his fortune like water to help the Poles his country men, the unfurling of the Polish flag, the white eagle, the story of the flag, the hunting up in the library of the history of Poland, of the works of Sienkewitz [sic], the officers who drilled them, some of them professors from college halls, others were veterans with medals and clasps from the Boer War, the Rev. Rydlewski who gave up his comfortable parish, in Pittsburgh to comfort and help the recruits, lonely, away from home and with the thought of death before them, the visits from ladies of Buffalo, Niagara Falls, N.Y., bringing farewell soldiers' kits before their departure from the town, the contact arrival of fresh recruits, arriving in their civilian clothing, sometimes two or three groups in a day, the departure by train of the same, dressed sometimes in discarded scarlet coats of our troops, the crowds to see them off mid cheers, and the good conduct of the men. At first there was some fear of what we had been accustomed to call Polaks, but never were seen so well behaved soldiers, quiet, rather stolid, heavier than our more active looking recruits, never had officers so little trouble in drilling troops. Niagara has the most pleasant recollections of officers and men of the Polish force and we are glad to know that they have pleasant recollections of our town. Many public buildings were given up for their use, some of them unoccupied, but several citizens gave up the use of houses free of charge, the Y.M.C.A. did all that could be done for their comfort, for their amusement and the most wonderful sight of all was the parade on Armistice Day, wholly performed by the Poles and Canadian officers, cannons, flags, cages for the Kaiser and the most unique disguises, marching through the town, across the common from Fort George and then to Fort Mississauga.

And literature was not neglected: addresses were given, Polish songs were given by noted singers, the Public library was thrown open for their use, many of us recalled Campbell's "Lines on the downfall of Poland", and "Freedom shrieked when Kosciusko fell," and there was sadness too in the camp when the Spanish Flu, which prevalent in the armies in Europe reached the United States and was brought to our town. At first confined to the Polish Camp at Fort George. Our own recruits at Butler's Barracks were free for some time and then several were attacked in the town and some died, but of the Polish force forty died and are buried in St. Vincent's cemetery, one from Jamaica buried in St. Mark's. The article written by Major Young, published in our local called "The Polish Touch" is as fine a piece of literature as can be seen and the account given by Father Rydlewski to the reporter of the *Montreal Standard* must also in part be quoted.

> On expressing my admiration to Father Rydlewski, of the Polish National Hymn he was kind enough to give me a translation of it as well as the words in Polish. When I said it is very solemn and sad he said "You know it is a prayer."
>
> "God who has been our Ruler through the ages,

Thou who hast brought us victory and might
Sending Thine aid when tyrants would oppress us
Shielding us from harm and guiding us aright.
Before Thine Altars humbly are we kneeling
Grant us we pray Thee Fatherland and Freedom."

This is a fair translation of the Polish words given below:

Boize cos Polske pezez tak liczne wieki*
Otaczal blaskiem potzgi i chawly
Cos jz raslanial tarcza Swej Opicki
Od nieszezesc ktore pnzguebic za miaty
Puzed Twe Oltavze zanosim blaganic
Ojezyzne, Wolnosc raez nam wrocie Panie

Z Rydlewski, C.S. Sp.
Chaplain at Niagara Camp

And there was doubt in the minds of some of us: Are the Poles fitted to govern their country? After a hundred and fifty years of oppression have they developed the qualities to form a stable government? At the children of Israel, after their years of servitude in Egypt, required forty years to strengthen them in body and mind to fit them to go in and possess the land, will the Poles have to go through a process of education in will power, in wise training, to enable them to govern wisely and well? And is Paderewski, a specialist in music, fitted for a military leader, or a statesman, or a diplomatist of the highest order? And how reconcile the various factions, the views of the nobles who despise the common people with those who wish a democracy, or with the views of autocracy or monarchy. And when we saw that the Poles intoxicated with their first success, seized territory beyond that allotted to them and were driven back, we felt doubtful, still more when the reports came, no doubt exaggerated of their treatment of the Jews, we paused in dismay. But by degrees the Poles are showing ability and we hope for them a happy home in a well governed country, those who have had no country as it were, "sitting under "their own vine and fig tree none daring to make them afraid," with their beloved white eagle flag over their heads flying in the breeze. In a lecture given by Major Young, a Professor of Applied Science in Toronto University, a sketch was given of Polish literature.

**Translator's Note:* We have reproduced the lyrics as printed, but the reader should know that this version is full of misspellings! It should read: "Boże, coś Polskę przez tak liczne wieki | Otaczał blaskiem potęgi i chwały, | Coś ją osłaniał tarczą swej opieki | Od nieszczęść, które przygnębić ją miały! | Przed Twe ołtarze zanosim błaganie: | Ojczyznę wolną racz nam wrócić, Panie!"

Frequently from visitors and from our own people was heard the phrase, "Foreigners drilling in Canada, why did they not drill in the United States where they lived" and the explanation was. The United States was at peace with Germany it would have amounted to a declaration of war, if the Poles were allowed to drill there to attack Germany and so Canada opened her doors and even when in 1917 war was declared the Poles were not allowed to drill in the United States and still came to our plains to help France and eventually reach Poland till 16,000 had passed under the instruction of Canadian officers.

How to explain the Polish army drilling in Niagara 1917-1918 requires dipping into the records of several countries and above all to understand the intense patriotism in the hearts of thousands of foreigners living in the United States hopes long repressed from what seemed impossible, the thought of a Free Poland, of their land restored to them.

The idea of a National Polish Army was considered early in the war but did not bear fruit till on the 4th June 1917 the declaration of the French President Monsieur Poincare creating an autonomous Polish Army, not a legion. The French government guaranteed the expenses of recruiting, equipping and maintaining it. The Canadian government supplied the necessary camp sites, the Canadian staff equipment, etc. They also supplied the clothing and food to equip and feed this army on repayment by the French Government. The payment of the men themselves is made from money which comes direct to camp from the French Mission in New York. The men it must be understood enlisted voluntarily, are paid at the French rate of pay of five cents per day, receiving in addition from the French Government a bonus of $150 a year, this making their pay about forty-five cents a day, contrast this with the pay received by our Canadian volunteers. To provide additional quarters for so many in winter for what had been chiefly a summer camp, the work was chiefly done by the Polish troops themselves, buildings made water tight and wind proof and water mains lowered below the frost line, buildings erected, all done under the superintendence of Canadian Engineers and all done it is said with cheerfulness by the Poles though often suffering in the early and severe winter.

There might be seen Polish officers, French officers, American officers, and Canadian officers. At no time during the period of the camp, did the Canadian staff exceed twenty-eight. It had sometimes been asked by whose influence did Canada provide the help thus given to the Poles. It is now admitted that the high officer called the "Godfather of the Polish Army" was Major General W.G. Gwatkin, C.E.C.M.G., Chief of the General Staff at Ottawa, the good friend referred to. The question often asked also was how were officers provided to drill so large a force, officers able to make themselves understood. It was not generally known that the School of Infantry, M.D. No. 2 had been at Camp Borden for some time training 150 Polish probationers. These arrived with Canadian staff at Niagara, Sept. 28th, 1917 at 4 a.m. and acted as advance party, laid out the camp, erected tents and on Oct. 3 recruits began to arrive and soon a camp of over 4000 was hard at work drilling. From that time groups arrived and after two months training a number were sent on to St. John's, Quebec, for a short time before embarking for France. At different times, troops when the camp became crowded 500 were transferred to Fort Niagara or to Quebec. News soon came of the arrival of the force in France where they received an ovation. From this time might be seen constant arrivals and departures at all hours of the day and night, on one occasion in a blizzard head quarters to be found in the middle of the night for a wearied group.

The chief officers were — Col. Le Pan, Camp Commandant; Major Young, Camp Adjutant; Major Madill, Major Kerk, Major Kendrick. Captain Harris, Pembroke, Parr, Hamilton, Pugh, Fowler, Lewis, Smith, Ferguson, Nash, Wright, Peart, Dr. Thomson, and Dr. Geddes. I attempt not to give the names of Polish Officers, but one chaplain must be mentioned beloved by all, Zy. Rydlewski, who went with them to Poland and has frequently written from there describing the losses, gains, and hardships of the forces.

A word must be said of the Polish Flag with the White Eagle on dark red on one side and the picture of Our Lady Czestochowa on white field on the other side, the historical flag of the days of Poland's glory. Its origin is this, the legendary forefather of the Poles, Lech found a nest of white eagles on the spot where he built his castle and a city called Ginezno [sic, should be Gniezno] from the word Guiazdo, west [sic, should be gniazdo, which means "nest"].

Many of the officers had occupied important positions previously, Col. Le Pan was joint superintendent of Toronto University and served as instructor to the C.O.T.C. of 1914. Major Young, a civil engineer held a position in the University as professor in the school of Applied Science also instructor in the C.O.T.C. Major Madill was lecturer on Architecture in the University. Capt. Harris served in South Africa and Capt. Pembroke had fought at Ypres and Vimy Ridge. It was interesting to notice the different uniforms, our own khaki so familiar, the light blue of the French officers and afterwards of the Polish soldiers when they had put off the scarlet coats and dark blue uniform of our militia, the gorgeous dress on occasion of Capt. Lewis and the picturesque Highland dress of Lieut. Dickie worn so proudly. The uniform of Major Wagner a veteran of France with the cross of the Legion of Honour. There were many functions when the Y.M.C.A. or ladies from Buffalo and Niagara Falls, N.Y. brought down presents for a detachment leaving chocolate, socks, soap, towels, cigarettes, kits.

Father Rydlewski the Polish Chaplain in conversation with a reporter pays a high tribute to Canadians and gives a statement which goes back to an earlier date than September, 1917 of the first steps to form a Polish Army. He was pastor of a church at Pittsburg, PA and the first chaplain to enlist said "I have spent six months in the Polish Camp at Niagara-on-the-Lake and have learned to love and admire the Canadians and especially the Canadian Officers Staff in charge of our camp.

We resolved to organize a Polish Army. But no army is possible without officers. We started twenty-three trustworthy young Polish men at the school of Infantry, Military District No. 2, Toronto. There they soon endeared themselves to their instructors. In May these young cadets were ready to help as instructors in the military schools for Polish boys which the Polish Falcon's Allowance [*sic*, Alliance?] opened on the 19th of March at Cambridge Springs, Pa., with 250 pupils.

The United States having declared war Mr. Ignace J. Paderewski offered to form a Polish Army but the United States Congress did not allow any special legions and on the 4th of June, France decrees that a Polish Army is to be formed, Canada opens its arms and the best young men are selected from among those of the training school at Cambridge Springs and sent to Camp Borden where Col. Le Pan with his excellent staff Majors Young, Madell, Kirk, and Kenrick who had taught from the first 23 young men at Toronto devoted themselves with zeal and love to make of them good officers and with them Col. LePan went to Niagara Camp, in October 1917 to receive three thousand volunteers and train them. Who was instrumental in getting that sacred historical spot Fort George and Fort Mississauga could not be learned and those who knew would not tell. I only know there is in Canada a certain high officer who likes to be called the "Godfather of the Polish Army" who obtains from the Canadian Government all the favors and privileges for the Polish Army. On 4th November I witnessed the touching scene when after 125 years of persecution the "White Eagle, Polish banner was unfurled and on the spot where Canadians had shed their blood in defence of their country, a hundred years ago. The banners were given that day to three thousand men who had only been four weeks or less in the camp and Canadian officers were giving the commands in Polish who had no idea about Polish till they met our boys. The water and light is furnished to our camp by the town free of charge. What we admire is that Canada furnishes the whole staff of officers, the hospital, the camp with all its implements.

The Canadian Y.M.C.A. furnishes a recreation tent, a large hall for divine worship on Sundays and entertainment on work days, writes letters, makes their wills, helps in many ways. My words are too feeble too indolent to express adequately the Polish Army's gratitude for all that is being done by Canada for us.

MRS. E. C. ASCHER

Polish Relief Work at Niagara
(By Elizabeth C. Ascher)

(As printed in *Niagara Historical Society* #35, 1923. Published by the Niagara Historical Society)

> O, Polish Mother, kneel thou before the image of the mother of sorrows
> And gaze upon the sword that has transfixed her bleeding heart,
> With a like blow the foe shall pierce thy bosom,
> Because, though all the world shall bloom in peace,
> Though nations, rulers, minds shall be as one,
> Thy son is called to battle without glory,
> To martyrdom without a resurrection.

This quotation from Mickiewicz's poem "The Polish Mother", was used by Madame Helena Paderewski as she was pleading for help for the suffering, homeless people of Poland, her native land, before an immense assemblage at the Polish Army Camp (or the Camp of Kosciuszko as it was known in Polish circles), at Niagara-on-the-Lake on the afternoon of July 27, 1918, her last visit to the troops in training for service in France. She had come on from New York for a dual purpose to say farewell and bid God speed to a number of her personal friends who were on the eve of departure for France and to assist at the ceremonies in connection with the opening of an American Red Cross service tent, or station at the camp, destined to fill a great part in the recreation plans during the closing months of this unique training centre. Members of the Niagara Falls Chapter of the American Red Cross, of the Polish White Cross (a society that owed its organization to Madame Paderewski who was its first and only president), prominent Red Cross workers from both side [sic] of the border and many leading Poles from Buffalo and elsewhere were present at these ceremonies and watched with interest the review of the Polish troops, and the presentation of field comforts which were a part of the day's programme. Before the gathering dispersed, Madame Paderewski made a brief speech in English during which she thanked the friends of the Polish Army for their many kindnesses and then pleaded for help for the starving, homeless people of Poland. In speaking with the Madame and with other prominent Poles, from New York and Buffalo to whom I was introduced by Father Rydlewski and Mr. Beckett of the Y.M.C.A. I learned of the great distress in Poland and heard the wish expressed that some one would do something in the way of relief work in Niagara and its immediate vicinity. But, believing that our Red Cross workers and others who had more friends than I in the rank and file of the Polish Army, would take the matter up, I did not think of offering to do anything just then, nor did I offer to help till the good Father Rydlewski broached the subject and asked me to take the matter up. I could not decide till a few days later when a letter came to me from Mr. Nowak of Buffalo, saying how much help was needed and that with my news papers connection I was in a better position to make an appeal than anyone else and urged me to begin my work. So I commenced with an appeal for money only as that seemed to be most urgently needed. Money could be sent into Poland while anything else could not because of the fact that Prussia's Army was in occupation of the country and that enemies surrounded Poland on every side. It is rather interesting to note that the first contribution came from a wee two year old girl, little Margaret Masters, who gave the contents of her "gift box" for the Polish babies. This was the sum of $2.05 and was supplemented by a further contribution from her parents, both given on August 6th, 1918. Between that time and Aug. 8th quite a sum was collected and I was able to tell Father Rydlewski, as I said good-bye to him on his departure for France, that my work was begun and would no doubt be as successful as he hoped. On Aug. 28th, I sent in to Mr. M.M. Nowak of Buffalo the sum of $52.45, to be forwarded to White Cross head quarters at New York. On Sept. 25th I sent in a second contribution of $51.00. Then to save expense and also because Mr. Nowak was leaving on a long business trip, I decided to send further contributions direct to the Polish White Cross head quarters. Early in September I received a letter from Madam Ivanowski, vice-president of the White Cross Society in which she conveyed to me on behalf of Madame Paderewski, the thanks of the Society for taking up this work and asking me to accept a membership later on, the gold badge of membership, also a very handsome certificate, signed by Madame Paderewski, who sent to me a proof of their appreciation.

In October I sent away $30.00, on Nov. 6th, $32.00 and in December $45.00. Collections from that time till March were small, only $11.00 being sent away but in April the sum of $60.00 was sent, $50.00 of which was contributed by our Women's Institute. Just at that time the White Cross people wrote me with a request that clothing, hospital supplies, etc. be collected in addition to money and said that with the war over, it was possible to transport things of this kind to

Poland where thousands of homeless and destitute people were in the greatest need. And so I began appealing for clothing. It was just at spring house-cleaning time when all good housekeepers were turning out the contents of clothes-closets, trunks, dressers, etc., with a view to clearing out what was not to be kept any longer. With the wonderful way our people had given clothing to the Belgian and other Relief collectors in war time, I did not expect to be able to gather any great quantity together, but the result of my first appeals surprised me, they were so generous and so varied. On April 29th in addition to sending away a cheque to New York for $60.00, I also sent a large package of splendid clothing to New York and followed it in the first week in May with two more, one of which consisted of pillow slips, sheets, towels, hospital supplies, and soap. In acknowledging receipt of these gifts, the director of the White Cross depot said: "what wonderful kind hearts of the people of Niagara-on-the-Lake. After doing so much for the comfort of our soldiers in training, they are now helping relieve the martyred people of our devastated land. Your own splendid work has been an inspiration to us; we think "when a woman who is not of Polish blood can do so much, surely, we who are Polish should try to do more". May God forever bless you and the other kind people of your town".

On July 7th, 1919, I sent in another cash contribution of $12.75, in August, $15.00 and later sent $65.00, $56.00 of which was contributed by the Girl's Service Battalion, who also gave a large quantity of excellent clothing. Between April and the end of August 1919, I sent 15 bales of clothing and 2 of hospital supplies to the White Cross headquarters in New York. Then early in September when the Polish Women's Relief organization began work, at the request of Mr. Witkowski and others in New York, I changed my shipments to Buffalo and sent everything afterwards to that city except some of the soap recently collected.

Early in 1919 some recognition of my relief work was being made by Polish folk. One of the first evidences of appreciation came to me in the shape of an invitation to a reception and banquet that was to be given in Buffalo, on March 4th by the Polish Citizens' Committee to the "Canadian friends of the Polish Army." The Canadian officers from the Polish Army Camp and their wives, members of the National Polish Committee from various parts of the United States and Canada, Sir Willoughby Gwatkin, of Ottawa, (Known among the Poles as the Godfather of the Polish Army), Mayor Macphee of this place, and James W. Mercer of the Military Y.M.C.A. were among the guests of this very charming event which took place in the hotel Iroquois in Buffalo.

Early in May, 1919, the President and several members of the Polish Citizens' Committee came down from Buffalo to arrange for holding a service in memory of the soldiers who were laid to rest in St. Vincent de Paul's graveyard and who had "died for Poland" in France and on other fields of glory; while here they came to see me and in the name of the Polish Women of Buffalo, presented me with a very beautiful armlet of crimson, moire silk, on which the white eagle of Poland and a motto were embroidered in silver thread. In placing this badge on my arm, Father Krzyzan asked me to accept it as a token of sincere appreciation of my relief work. At the same time I was requested to convey to the people of Niagara the gratitude and appreciation of the Polish people of their wholehearted generosity and their sympathy for the suffering people of Poland. This I was very glad to do through the medium of my column in the Standard. On the American Decoration Day, (May 31st) a large party of Poles from the American and Canadian sides held this memorial service in the little plot in St. Vincent de Paul's where 26 men of the "Army of Kosciuszko" are sleeping their last sleep. At the close of the service, the Rev. Fathers Pitass, Krzyzan, and Ostaszewski thanked the people of Niagara for their many kindnesses.

All through the summer of 1919, though I was unusually busy and at times not very well, I continued my collections of clothing and about every fortnight sent away at least one large package filled with many useful things. At times it was difficult to find the time necessary for listing, packing, and shipping these things but I managed it, encouraged by the knowledge of the necessities of those for whom I was working. Proof that at least some of my shipments were reaching Poland came to me in the shape of letters from relief workers in Warsaw who found my address in the package while proof that there was great suffering came in letters from Father Rydlewski, Mr. Bernacki and other friends who arrived in Poland from France early in May, 1919. One extract from a letter written to me by Father Rydlewski soon after his arrival contains a volume; it said "my poor people, what they are suffering and how brave is their endurance! We reached Poland in the midst of a blinding snow storm (This in May too), and while it looked as if the Almighty was showering His flowers those brave heroes who had helped win freedom for their country, I could not keep the tear back as my eyes beheld the frail, ill-clad forms of the women and little children who, with no shoes on their poor feet and little to protect them from the bitter cold, were still rejoicing because "Poland lives again". What have my people suffered and how has God repaid them for what they have endured, Poland is once again restored to her place among free nations. Dear friends, you need not doubt that your work is needed, may God bless it and give you strength to go on till it is completed". I was feeling rather discouraged and was debating whether to go on or give up my relief work, but this letter made me feel that I should "carry on" for a while longer at least. As I received the generous contributions and sent them on, I marveled at the way our people were giving and was more than pleased at the frequent expressions of grateful appreciation that were coming to me.

In October, 1919, I asked to attend a meeting of the Polish Council of Canada in St. Catharines and to bring a report of what I had done in the way of relief work. I accepted the invitation and met prominent Poles from all parts of Canada. Here again were expressions of gratitude for the generosity of my townspeople and I was told that Niagara-on-the-Lake, "The home of the Polish Army: as it is known to Polish folk, had exceeded any other place in Canada with the exception of Montreal, in the help it had given to the Polish Relief. I was very much pleased at hearing this, as may be suposed [sic]. I was asked to make an appeal on behalf of Polish Relief to the women's organizations, in St. Catharines and did so in November, "St. Catharines women could not do anything just then", wrote Mrs. Malcolmson in reply to my appeal, "because they were too busy getting ready for Christmas." They forgot that the Polish people by sending an army to re-inforce the French Army at the most critical period had turned the tide that was setting strongly against us, made victory possible and so enabled us to enjoy Christmas and they also forgot that in Poland there would be no Christmas celebrations because of the havoc and suffering caused by the war. A second appeal was ignored and so far as I know nothing was done by Polish residents and except for several generous donations made a few months ago by a kind-hearted lady who will not let her name be known.

In November, 1919, a great gathering of Poles was held in Buffalo, the 2nd annual convention of the Poles in America when Poles from all parts of Canada and the United States met together to discuss plans for the relief of Poland and to tell of what had already been done. There were hundreds of delegates, women as well as men and I was given a special invitation and was also down for a speech. As I could not be away from home for very long I asked my Polish friends in Buffalo to let me know what days would be most interesting for me and I was told to come on the 10th to hear Mr. Herbert Hoover speak on relief work in Poland. So I went to Buffalo early that day and was met by a deputation who told me first to register and leave my bag at the Lafayette Hotel and then on to Dom Polski the big Polish hall on the corner of Broadway and Fillmore Avenue. As we motored down Broadway we passed under arches and festoons of Polish and American flags, thousands of which were to be seen everywhere, while the main entrance to the hall was hidden by decorations in which the Amaranth and White colors of Poland predominated. Arrived at Dom Polski, I was given a delegate's badge (a very beautiful ribbon in the Polish colors, with a suitable inscription thereon and with a medal attached on which was a fine likeness of Mr. Paderewski. (Just then the idol of his people). I was given a seat on the platform among the guests of honor and had a splendid opportunity of hearing all that was said and done. Mr. Hoover was speaking when our party came into the hall and it was so quiet you could have heard a pin drop. He told some wonderful things regarding the work of his organization among the people of Poland and other war torn countries; part of his speech was in Polish but he spoke chiefly in his own language. It was a very interesting address and so were those that followed.

At recess, nearly everyone left the hall and went out for luncheon, the lady delegates being guests of the Polish women of the city. At my table were Madam Newman, acting president of the White Cross, Madam Andrejewski, head of the Polish Women's Alliance, (both from Chicago), Miss Jean Newman, of Brooklyn; Mrs. Haiman and other relief workers from Buffalo, whom I was very glad to meet. We discussed relief work and all the ladies had something nice to say about what was being done in Niagara. As the ladies were most anxious that I should see the reception to Prince Casimir Lubomirski (The first Polish Ambassador to the United States) and his wife, we did not prolong our luncheon but hastened back to Dom Polski and got there just in time to see the arrival of the distinguished party. It was a very wonderful sight. We Niagara folk were witnesses of the raising of Poland's banner on Nov. 4th, 1917 at this place and of the emotion displayed by the Poles on that occasion but it was nothing compared to what took place on Nov. 10, 1919, in Buffalo. When Prince Lubomirski and his party arrived at Dom Polski, they were greeted by thousands of their country men with wildest enthusiasm, children and older folk sang the national songs of Poland and cheer after cheer rent the air. Pictures were taken outside the hall and then the guests of honor escorted by the delegates streamed up the stairs and into the large assembly room. Prince Lubomirski was carried to the platform on the shoulders of his people and one heard everywhere a glad hymn of thanksgiving because here was actual proof that Poland was restored to her place among the nations and that the sacrifices of her people had not been in vain. Had any one wished for a lesson in patriotism he would have found it here.

During the reading of a financial report our town's givings in cash were read among others and later on what had been given in the way of clothing, etc., was also read aloud. I was interested to learning this report, that over $6000 had been raised at the Polish Camp in 1918 towards the million dollar fund for providing insurance for the Polish soldiers. I may say that my own first cash contribution towards any Polish fund was made to this one in May, 1918, to Father Rydlewski who was in charge of collections here. The Canadian officers at the camp, Messrs. Beckett and Henry of the Y.M.C.A. and one or two other civilians contributed towards this fund and later on we all received a very beautiful certificate as a membership of this "golden deed."

I had to stand up before this assemblage of Poles and receive their thanks for my own work and hear an expression of their appreciation of all the people of Niagara had done, on behalf of the Polish Army and the poor sufferers in Poland. I was expected to make a speech but had a violent attack of stage fright" and had to go back to my seat all I could manage to say was "thank you." Dr. Syski, the chairman said afterwards that he thought all newspaper folk were fluent public speakers but now he had found one that wasn't. I was only glad that I had gone to the convention because I had learned that there was great suffering and need of help in Poland and that the Poles are a grateful and appreciative people and so I was encouraged to continue my work. As a result of this gathering, the National Polish Relief Committee was organized and I was enrolled as a member of the Women's Section and later received a gold membership badge. As you may all remember, the winter of 1919-1920 was unusually severe, yet about every two weeks I sent away at least one package of clothing and my brother, Mr. Arthur Masters, made many trips through the ice across the river to get things safely away. One very wonderful gift from the Polish relief, of which special mention must be made was that given by the Women's Institute, of which details are given further on. Every one, with few exceptions, wanted to do something for a less fortunate people and so the work went on. The Girl's Service Battalion gave me the balance of their funds early in the spring of 1920 and to this was added $9.00 given by other friends, making this remittance $65.00. Early in June when the Polish women began a drive for funds for Child Relief work in Poland, I had sufficient funds in hand to send in a contribution of $25.00.

In the autumn of 1920, the Niagara Bowling Club held a Scotch Doubles Bowling Tournament in aid of the Polish Relief and besides having a lot of sport raised $26.00 which I sent in together with $4.00 given by other friends. In all, the cash contributions amounted to $600.20, the most of which was sent to Relief Headquarters. Small sums were at times sent to Father Rydlewski and others serving in the Polish Army in France and Poland, together with packages of field comforts.

During the early spring of 1920 some of the ladies of the Virgil Women's Institute became interested in my Polish Relief work and sent in several small cash contributions also a number of packages of splendid clothing. They told me of the work they had been doing in their branch for the Red Cross, for Belgium and other relief work during the war and that they were continually working for the Children's Shelter of St. Catharines or they would do more for the Poles. I was sure they were willing to do what they could and was grateful indeed for the kind assistance given.

Again in May, 1920, did the Polish people come here and hold a service of requiem and remembrance over the last resting place of the Polish Soldiers and the visitors were greatly pleased because some of our young ladies had decorated the graves and the little plot with beautiful flowers for the occasion. Grateful appreciation of Niagara's great work for the Poles was once more expressed by representative speakers. On June 23rd the Consul general, of Poland, Mr. Josef Okolowicz came to Niagara and called on me to express the thanks of the Government of Poland for my relief work and to ask me to convey to the people of my town the gratitude and appreciation of that Government for the generous help given in time of need. With Consul-General were members of the Consular staff and of the Polish Council of Canada most of whom I had met before. By their request I accompanied them to the little burial plot and placed a wreath of beautiful flowers on the cross, afterwards taking part in a brief memorial service, conducted by Father Ostaszewski, of St. Catharines, (since deceased) and Rev. Dr. Tarasink, of Hamilton. We posed for a group picture, then made a motor trip around the camp ground where I was able to point out places of special interest to the party.

Soon after this I met a lady from Toronto, who became greatly interested in my work and made a large contribution of children's sweaters, wool, etc. and also gave me some cash with which to meet shipping expenses. At this time I was paying shipping charges myself so the help was very welcome. The following are the totals of the contents of the 60 relief packages that were sent forward between April, 1919 and December 31st, 1920, when my work ended.

Men's Garments – 29 suits underwear, 32 combination suits, 32 pairs shoes, 15 pairs slippers, 20 sweater coats, 20 pairs trousers, 37 pairs vests, 8 suits, 310 pairs socks, 3 pairs overshoes, 10 mufflers, 10 pairs suspenders, 20 pairs gloves, 11 pairs mitts, 10 pairs wristlets, 37 overcoats, 22 collars, 15 ties, 17 caps, 21 packages shoelaces, 25 cakes shaving soap, 29 coats, 3 razors, 4 strops, 17 pairs pajamas.

Women's Garments, etc. – 11 cloth suits, 142 skirts, 45 print skirts, 29 long coats, 43 short coats, 10 sweaters, 4 sets furs, 5 muffs, 2 fur coats, 6 hats, 21 Tams, 18 pairs gloves, 19 aprons, 68 pairs stockings, 54 pairs shoes, 14 shawls, 10 scarves, 85 waists, 57 dresses, 17 kimonas [sic], 20 pairs slippers, 19 wrappers, 23 capes, 10 flannel petticoats, 5 pairs rubbers, 325 pieces of underwear, 48 cotton and flannelette petticoats, 78 blouses, 2 feather boas, as well as pins, belts, handerchiefs [sic], safety pins, soap, etc.

Baby's clothing - 826 pieces some of which was finest flannel or lawn and all was whole, warm and serviceable.

Girl's wear – 78 dresses, 51 petticoats, 17 Tams, 42 blouses, 39 coats, 48 pairs of shoes, 15 pairs slippers, 5 pairs sandals, 7 pairs rubbers, 72 pairs stockings, 21 pairs gloves, 7 pairs mitts, 22 suits, 39 middies, 9 fur sets, 11 hoods, 10 scarves, 35 sweaters, 2 hats, 91 sets of underwear, 23 night dresses, as well as ties, handkerchiefs and other necessary clothing.

Boy's wear – 38 suits, 15 coats, 19 overcoats, 37 pairs trousers, 17 pairs shoes, 31 pairs stocking, 5 pairs short socks, 10 pairs gloves, 18 pairs mittens, 14 pairs wristlets, 3 pairs rubbers, 41 shirts, 46 blouses, 29 toboggan caps, 49 suits underwear, shoe laces, belts, etc.

Bed Clothing, Hospital, Supplies, etc. – 17 pairs sheets, 23 pairs pillow slips, 69 towels, 27 wash rags, 5 quilts, 4 baby blankets, and 5 squares, 2 rubber sheets, 28 tins condensed coffee, 27 tins condensed milk, and 17 of cocoa, 826 cakes soap, 40 packages cigarettes and 10 of tobacco, 26 yards hospital gauzes, absorbent cotton, antiseptic dressings, bed socks and hospital jackets, talcum powder and vaseline, boracic acid, Copenhagen snuff, listerine, rolls of old linen and many other supplies for hospital use. Special mention must be made, in this connection of the splendid gift of the emergency bag belonging to the Women's Institute who, having no further use for it, gave it to me to send to some hospital in Poland. To the bag was added a quantity of lovely baby clothing by several of the individual members. This splendid package was sent away on Feb. 3rd, 1919 to the Polish Women's Relief Society in Buffalo with a request that it be sent as soon as possible to some hospital in Poland where such articles were most urgently needed. In acknowledging the receipt of this and two other packages shipped at the same time, the secretary of the Society said "your splendid consignment of relief packages arived [sic] safely just in time to be included in a shipment we were making up for Poland in New York. The relief ship is now in port and will sail on Tuesday next for Gdausk (Dantzig) [sic] with packages of clothing and other supplies as well as quantities of drugs, food stuffs, machinery, etc., all destined for relief head quarters at Warsaw from whence all relief is distributed. The request made by your ladies will be complied with, we will arrange that. Please thank the ladies of the Women's Institute and our many other kind and generous friends in your town for this fresh proof of their sympathy for a stricken people. "Bog Zaplac", the Polish expression of gratitude meaning: May God reward you for your kindness". Among other gifts that deserve special mention are the many pairs of children's new shoes given by E.P. Healey, the soap and cases of condensed coffee and Copenhagen stuff [sic], given by A.J. Coyne, the many suits of men's combinations, children's underwear, men's gloves, hospital gauze, wool, packing paper, etc., (as well as money), given by Thos. Mulholland, the many pairs of warm socks (28 in all), knitted by Miss Carnochan, the children's lovely warm sweaters knitted by Mrs. McPhedran, of Toronto, the sweater, socks and bed socks knitted by Miss Alma, Mrs. William Ryan, Mrs. Charles Brown, and Mr. Arthur Masters must not be overlooked because it was always given cheerfully and willingly and was most helpful. The members of the Women's Institute also deserve special thanks because they did so much towards making this work successful.

[Some idea of the extent of the work done to help the distress in Poland may be gathered from these figures. The whole may be summed up thus: Clothing for men and boys consisting of underwear, coats, trousers, suits, sweaters, shoes, gloves, waists, caps, collars, socks, etc. - 1034 articles. Of clothing for women and girls, suits, skirts, coats, sweaters, shawls, kimonas [sic]*, scarves, capes, hats, gloves, shoes, furs, stockings, etc. - 1082 articles; baby clothing - 826 articles; bedding, quilts, sheets, pillow slips, towels, 144; soap, 876 cakes; boxes of cigarettes and tobacco, 50; and innumerable other articles as muffs, wristlets, toilet articles, handkerchiefs, hospital requirements, too numerous to mention, making 4682 without the latter not mentioned or numbered. - Editor.]*

The last phase of the Polish Relief work the "Soap Shower", was like all previous effects attended with great success and the result exceeded all expectations. Over 500 cakes of soap were contributed, all of excellent quality. One box containing 70 cakes went to the Polish Government Relief Bureau in New York but for economical motives the remainder was packed in with bales of clothing and thus sent away. The Polish people of Buffalo were surprised at this fresh gift for their suffering countrymen and in the leading Polish papers of that city there were lengthy articles telling all about it, while one of the largest Polish papers in Chicago had an article entitled "Our Friends in Canada" referring to the generosity of Niagara people to the Poles and to the "diligent efforts of Mrs. Ascher on behalf of Polish Relief and the Polish cause". This article was translated and sent to me and was reprinted a few days later in the Standard in order that everyone might learn of the grateful appreciation of the Polish people for what was being done here. I may say here that at the time during its progress had I any thought of deriving any personal credit for its success; nevertheless it was very pleasant to know that my efforts are appreciated but still more so to realize that it has really been of use. It has not always been easy to find time to carry on the work but somehow I managed it and at the same time kept up with my many other duties.

Someone has said that he could not understand why Niagara folk have such a sympathy for the Poles. I think this query can be answered by an extract from a letter written by Colonel A.D. LePan, (formerly commander of the Polish Army Camp), in which he says, "All of us who formed Polish Associations during the period of that unique camp developed the greatest admiration of those people. I am quite sure none of us will ever forget the debt we owe your splendid old town and its citizens on the part it was able to play in this unique undertaking. The Poles are people of different nationality but of the same ideals as ourselves". Had we not had the sons of Poland set down in our midst to be trained to stand beside Allied soldiers on the battlefield of France and learned something of their patriotism and true worth, perhaps we too would have turned an indifferent ear to the tales of suffering that came later to us from their native, desolated land. But we had.

> "Lived to see thee, sword in hand
> Uprise again, immortal Polish land.
> Whose flag brings more than chivalry to mind.
> Majestic men, whose deeds have dazzled faith,
> Ah yet your fate's suspense arrests our breath."

And perhaps because of the fact that the presence of the Polish Army in our midst has linked us and our town with the future history of emancipated Poland we have and will always have, a greater sympathy with her people; and so we have given again and yet again in order that those who suffered with us and for us in the closing days of the bitter war, may be clothed and fed and put in better condition to help reconstruct their ruined homes and re-build the fortunes of a martyred country. It would have stirred your hearts and repaid you for anything you have done, had you heard, as I did, the applause that went up from hundreds of Poles at the memorable convention in Buffalo in the autumn of 1919 when the name of your town and the list of its gifts to Polish Relief was read out. To hear that our little town occupied such a prominent place in the "Book of Golden Deeds", a volume compiled by a leading Polish writer was pleasant indeed and I rejoiced that it was so. We have been generous towards these unfortunate people but if we have we were only following, I truly believe that Golden Rule which bids us "Do ye unto others, as ye would they should do unto you." In closing this little record, this extract from a letter, which came to me a few days ago from the Consul-General of Poland in Canada, might be interesting; he says "I have just returned from a trip to various Polish centres in this country and the United States and find that the name of your town, (Niagara-on-the-Lake) is known and loved because of its association with our army and also because of the beneficence of your people to ours, while your own name and work in the cause of Polish Relief and in the defence of our country is equally well known and esteemed wherever there are Poles, the name of Niagara and the fame of its generous people are known and your town will forever be indissolubly linked with my native land." Other prominent Poles have expressed similar grateful appreciation which is some reward for the time and energy spent in this relief work, a work that could not have been carried on so long and so successfully had it not been for the generous kindness, the wonderfully sympathetic hearts of our people. Our help has been an inspiration to Polish Relief workers every where and has often spurred them to a greater effort. Poland lives again after more than a century of suffering and oppression but needs the help of her friends for a little time during reconstruction days. It has been a great privilege to us that we have been able to give or help at a time when it was most urgently needed.

One or two interesting items will show how the Polish folk and Niagara are linked together. The first is that almost the first contingent of Polish troops from Niagara camp crossed the Atlantic to France on the steamship Niagara, this ship being used extensively as a transport in closing of the war; second that a part of the relief supplies sent from Niagara were taken across the ocean on this same steamer; third, that in Plowaret, Potigny, Constance, Lille [sic, Sille?] le Guilliaume and the other places in France where Polish troops were encamped, each camp had an avenue named after Niagara-on-the-Lake; fourth, on high days and holidays Polish soldiers who met together for a social time never separated without first drinking a toast to "Niagara and our good friends in Canada," whether the meeting and celebration was in France or Poland.

"Niagara's name shines like a ray of golden sunlight across the fair pages of the history of re-born Poland", said a Polish speaker at a great gathering not long ago, "because it was there, on the ancient and historic camp ground, our army was trained and our flag was once more flung to heaven's breezes; while the names of her golden hearted generous people, those who have done so much to relieve the distress of the martyred people of our native land, will live in our hearts forever, may God reward them for their kindness". And so this relief work has been of some use and has been, you will all concede, well worth while.

Article from the Polish Daily telegram of Buffalo, of Oct. 28th, 1922
(Translated)

At Niagara-on-the-Lake to-day, Oct. 27th, 1922, was closed one of what may be the last chapters of the short, important and beautiful episodal history of the Polish Army. When the Republic of Poland gave public thanks to one who has so willingly worked on behalf of the State and of its Army and who, though foreign born, worked like a true and sincere Polish woman for the restoration of Poland. The evidence of sincere friendship and sympathy shown the Polish folk on that day will live long in our memories; as long as will stand the massive cross of granite, with its inscription "Died for Poland," in the small cemetery plot set apart for the last rest of our Polish Soldiers. It happened to-day that the ceremonies were begun by paying homage to the dead heroes when Consul-General, Straszewski, together with many Poles from Buffalo and other places, placed a large and beautiful wreath on the cross and joined in praying for the repose of their souls May they rest in peace, secure us the knowledge that so long as the beautiful Niagara flows, a grateful Poland will not forget them.

From the cemetery the party went over to St. Mark's hall where the ladies of the Newark Chapter, I.O.D.E. had called a meeting for the occasion and who, after greeting all the Polish guests with cordial welcome, gave them front seats beside Mrs. Ascher, whose fellow members and friends filled the building to capacity. After the singing of the Canadian and the Polish National hymns. The meeting was opened by Mrs. W. E. Hunter Vice-Regent of the Chapter after which the Consul-General, of Poland, Dr. Michal Straszewski, came forward, made an address in which he referred to Mrs. Ascher's great service to the Polish cause during which he pinned on her breast the beautiful cross of the Order of Polonia Restituta in the name of the Government of Poland and congratulated her first on her investiture. Mrs. Ascher was warmly applauded, the Poles sitting near her voicing their hearty congratulations to this big hearted Canadian woman on her well-deserved honor.

Mrs. Dr. Borowiak, in the name of the Polish Women's Relief Auxiliary of Buffalo, presented a golden fountain pen and sheaf of beautiful roses together with their best felicitations while the Rev. C. Krzyzan, in the name of the Polish Citizens Committee presented a large box of roses and ferns and said he hoped that long after the flowers had faded, the fragrance of the memory of this very happy occasion would remain with her and with all present. Little Miss Betty Hunter then came forward with a bouquet of creamy white Mums, from the Newark Chapter and other friends presented flowers and gifts and living congratulations.

Secretary Kaleuski of the Polish Consulate, of Buffalo read a telegram of congratulations from Dr. Z. E. Fronczak welcoming Mrs. Ascher into the Order while Mrs. Hunter read letters of regret from Major C. R. Young and others (who were unable to be present), all saying "Nobody among Canadians served better or more willingly on behalf of the Polish cause than Mrs. Ascher or more greatly deserves reward." Captain Charles K. Masters, of St. Mary's thanked the Polish Government and its representatives on behalf of his sister for the decoration and for the honor shown by the Poles in their presence in such numbers on this occasion while speeches of congratulation were made by ex-mayor Jas. Macphee, Rev. Canon Garrett, Miss Janet Carnochan. (Mrs. Ascher's old school teacher and friend), all saying that the Polish Boys were liked and admired for their sturdy patriotism by all Niagara and that it was only a pleasure to help them. Other speakers included Rev. A. J. O'Brien, now pastor of St. Vincent de Paul's church but formerly in charge of the parish of St. Stanislaus Polish Church in Toronto, Rev. Cesary Krzyzan, of Buffalo: Major Henry Burgoyne, of St. Catharines and Lieut. Rycozutci, who with three other young officers were sent to convey the congratulations of the veterans of the Polish Army. The speeches were marked with great sincerity - "We Poles were greatly pleased with the landatory remarks of the Canadians about our Polish soldiers," "They were true gentlemen, patriots all" said ex-mayor Macphee and the hearty applause that followed proved that all agreed with him. There was a brief program and later all were hospitably entertained at tea by the ladies of the Chapter who are very pleasant hostesses, Mrs. Ascher, the decorated lady, received and was congratulated again and again, Canadians rivaling Polish friends in showering congratulations on her well deserved honor. The Polish folk left on their return to Buffalo about 5:30 p.m. only leaving early because of other engagements but taking with them the most pleasant memories of our good and noble Canadian friends. We hope that to-day's happy incidents will strengthen our friendship. We hope that Mrs. Ascher and the good citizens of Niagara, who helped Poland when she was in need, will also remember her in her better days and that the traditions of this friendship will out live us.

The Poles on this happy and unique occasion were represented by many officials and private citizens. Present were Consul-General Straszewski, from Montreal; Consul Manduk, of Buffalo and Mrs. Manduk; Mr. Edmund Kalewskis, secretary of the Consulate at Buffalo; Mr. And Mrs.

Borowiak, Mrs. F.E. Fronczak, Mrs. Hodkiewicz, Mrs. Andrzejewski, Mrs. Schunike and Mrs. Noryskiewrcz [sic], representing the Polish Women's Relief Auxiliary; Mr. And Mrs. Tallyn and son, Mr. and Mrs. M. Haiman, Mr. Jelmski, Mr. And Mrs. K. Urban, Mr. and Mrs. Frank Andrejewski, Rev. C. Krzyzan, Mr. and Mrs. C. Zawadsky, representing the Polish Citizen's Committee, Chicago, the Polish Catholic Union was represented by Mr. and Mrs. Andreas Kazunerski, The Polish White Cross by Father Glapurski and Mr. Bezerski; The Buffalo Chapter of the Polish Veterans Union was represented by Lieuts. Zawadzski and Reszutci and the Veterans Association by Lieut. Krob and Sergt. Czechowski the one from Cleveland, the other from Detroit. No Polish organization in America failed to send a delegate to do honor to Mrs. Ascher.

We went home with the best impressions of the hospitality of our Canadian friends in our minds and hearts and were glad, that we were able to have the privilege of witnessing the occasion when Poland paid her debt of thanks and appreciation to Mrs. Ascher for her noble work extending over many years. Our thanks to her and to our Niagara friends for the help they have given us in our time of need.

"Long live Canada and her people."

M. Haiman, Editor

Y.M.C.A.

A word should be given in connection with the assistance given by the Y.M.C.A. When the Poles arrived they found already on the ground a large tent with the usual equipment in charge of Mr. Ross L. Beckett, J.M. Mercer, and L.J. Henry. In the town was a large recreation hall and reading room. In three centres were moving picture machines, also a branch post office and a room for banking business. The recreation halls were used as chapels on Sunday, the sacred vessels being loaned by Rev. Father Sweeny, of St. Vincent de Paul's Church. All arrangements are made in the buildings and grounds for amusements, for entertainments. The signs in the buildings are all in Polish. The chaplains working in harmony with the Y.M.C.A. and on arrival advised the recruits to place their money in their hands and $240,000 was in the hands of the Y.M.C.A., in sums large and small till the banking system was introduced. Athletic exercises were encouraged, all kinds of games, concerts were given by visiting choirs and ladies of the town. The library consisted mostly of the Polish language and many books were sent with them when leaving. Frequent visits were paid to the hospital to cheer the inmates and write letters for them. The help given to the Polish Camp by the Y.M.C.A. has been of incalculable value.

[YMCA] With the Polish Autonomous Army

Excerpted from Service With Fighting Men, *Association Press 1922*

Among the most interesting of the minor units fighting in the Allied cause was the Polish Legion, recruited largely from Polish Americans before the United States entered the war and later including those Poles in the United States who wanted to fight for a liberated Poland but who were not eligible to military service in American armies. This force, originally about 60,000 strong, became known as the Polish Autonomous Army, and was later increased to 75,000 by additions in France of former Austro-German war prisoners of Polish birth. With this force the Association served, first through the Foyers du Soldat, and later under purely American direction. When this army under General Haller returned in triumph to Poland, secretaries accompanied it by express request of the commander and were able to inaugurate work there.

Y M C A work was commenced with the Polish Autonomous Army in France under the auspices of the Foyers du Soldat in January, 1918. A request for Y M C A aid was made to Mr. Carter by a Polish soldier who came with other Polish troops on a ship from New York, on which Y M C A secretaries, both men and women, served the troops. Walter S. Schutz, who had an indefinite appointment in the Foyers, was sent to Laval in the department of Mayenne by D. A. Davis in response to this request.

The first hut was opened on January 31st at Laval for the benefit of the First Regiment of Polish Chasseurs. A canteen was also opened here and a few weeks later two American women went to Laval to operate this canteen. A little later, small huts or foyers were opened in other training camps of Polish troops at Mayenne, Sille-le-Guillaume, and Mamers.

The work spread rapidly as new contingents of the Army arrived from America and were sent to French training camps in the Departments of Mayenne, Sarthe, Calvados, La Manche, and along the Loire. In all about fifty men and women secretaries served with these Polish soldiers in France, following the regiments from one training area to another. On March 1, 1918, the two pioneer secretaries accompanied the 1st Regiment of Polish chasseurs into the Champagne area and opened their canteen at Sainte-Tanche in the Mailly district. In early June the first regiment went into the lines between Chalons and Rheims with General Gouraud's French Army, and gave an excellent account of themselves. The Y followed them in camionettes. Later the First Division, composed of the 1st, 2d, and 3d Regiments, held the lines in the Vosges sector first occupied by the United States Army. Here there were huts between the first and second line trenches whose service also reached out to the men in the outposts. One of the secretaries was decorated with the Croix de Guerre for his bravery under fire. After the Armistice, the First Division continued in the Nancy area preparatory to its departure for Poland, secretaries serving them in the various camps and towns where they were billeted.

As about 80 per cent of the soldiers composing the Polish Army were recruited in and came from America, their needs and preferences were American rather than French, although they were equipped and rationed by the French military authorities. It was decided, therefore, to transfer the Polish Army Work from the Foyers du Soldat to the American Y M C A. This had been suggested as early as June, 1918, and the transfer was effected as of August 1, 1918. From that time the work was entirely under the auspices of the American Y M C A. Secretaries were privileged to participate in three epoch-making events in the history of the Polish Army in France; May 3, 1918, the anniversary of the adoption of the Constitution of 1791 (corresponding to our Fourth of July); June 22, 1918, the presentation of the Polish flags to the 1st, 2d and 3d Regiments by President Poincare near Brienne-le-Chateau—this was the first time that an independent Polish Army had fought under its own colors in more than a hundred years; and October 6, 1918, when General Joseph Haller, the Polish patriot, assumed command of the entire Polish Army in France, near Nancy in Lorraine.

In March, 1918, General Haller officially requested the Y M C A to accompany his army to Poland, and promised it every facility possible in carrying on its work, which he said had become almost a necessity to his men. Five secretaries accompanied General Haller's staff to Poland, leaving Paris on April 16, 1919, and reaching Warsaw on April 21st. On April 29th, these secretaries were present at the meeting between General Haller and the Chief of State, Josef Pilsudski, on his return from the recapture of Vilna; and they also shared in the magnificently impressive celebration of the 3d of May-- the first since Poland became free and independent. While the Y M C A went to Poland at the invitation of General Haller and with only sufficient equipment to serve his Army, Commander in Chief Pilsudski and his officers urged the extension of its work to all the Polish troops and especially the young, new recruits. The Ministry of War officially requested the Y M C A to serve the Polish Army, promising full cooperation.

- - - - - - -

Poland

On the invitation of General Haller, Commanding the Polish Legion in France, five American Y secretaries, accompanying the second section of the Polish General Staff, arrived in Warsaw April 21, 1919. Planning to work with the first three divisions of the Polish Army, they opened the first hut at Lublin, May 18, 1919, General Haller and staff attending. A second hut was opened at Modlin on Memorial Day; and following the exercises, the first American baseball game on Polish soil was played, Ambassador Gibson pitching the first ball. By July there were thirteen centers in operation with a personnel of seventeen Americans and many more Polish workers. An official request had been received from the Vice-Minister of War that the service should be extended to the entire Polish forces. A budget had been prepared calling for $150,000 for the second half of 1919, all to be supplied by the American Association. D. A. Davis, Senior Secretary for Europe, wrote:

> "Work ought to be carried on till at least the first of July, 1920. The dangers that threaten Poland from the Germans on the one side and from the Bolsheviks on the other, make it extremely improbable that the Army will be greatly reduced during the coming year."

When July came, the Association was at the height of its activity, operating at 40 points, with eight rolling canteens serving mobile troops.

Although the aim was to make canteen service secondary, more than was intended proved necessary. In many places soldiers were scantily fed, especially near the front. They went without food for days, because of lack of organization and transport. The wholesome drinks and food that the Y canteens furnished at low prices went far to supplement the insufficient rations, and thereby made a basic contribution to morale. But in the city huts, the canteen was conducted rather as a social feature and aid in building character and citizenship. Through the theater and concert, effort was made to acquaint the men with the best works by Polish authors and composers, and to let them hear their own language spoken in its purity by trained actors and singers. The printing of simple programs, containing in brief the story of the play and the lessons the author sought to teach, with a sketch of his life, developed, because of the interest shown, into a sort of periodical with a circulation of 10,000 weekly. Great interest also was taken in mass singing, and in some huts choirs of trained singers were formed. Educational work included teaching of illiterates, in which the Y cooperated closely with the Education Department of the new government, classes in English and French languages, and in Polish history and literature. A newspaper exchange, by which papers from different localities were circulated throughout the country, facilitated a truly national interchange of information and understanding of local conditions and points of view, a thing impossible while the nation was divided under three alien dominations. By the end of the first year some 20,000 library books were in circulation and half a million booklets had been distributed, many of them translations especially made, on moral, patriotic and social subjects calculated to inform and stimulate soldiers as to cleanliness, order, good living and good citizenship. The cinema was used not only for entertainment but for educational purposes, especially to help in the anti-typhus campaign—a method particularly useful among a people with a high rate of illiteracy.*

The physical recreation program met with enthusiastic response among soldiers, students, and women. In April, 1920, 40,000 participants in athletic events were recorded. The work was varied, including reconstruction exercises for convalescent wounded, drills and mass games for recruits, boy scout training and games, and exercises for women mobilized as guards for railroad and public property.

Evidently the work demanded a much larger personnel than could be furnished from America. This coincided with the Association policy which aimed to transplant American welfare ideas into Poland and make them indigenous. Some were ambitious to establish training courses, and a summer school was conducted for a few weeks at Modlin, followed in January by a short course in physical training for officers. Caution and tact were necessary, however, and the method of gradual practical training of selected assistants in the huts, though slower, was deemed wise under existing conditions. The atmosphere in which Association work was carried on is indicated in a report of A. S. Taylor, Senior Secretary, in May, 1920:

"To understand clearly what progress has been made, it is necessary to bear in mind the conditions under which, from the start, the work was carried on. When a year ago the Association commenced activities, it was entirely unknown in the country, except to the Haller troops, with whom they had come from France. Poland at that time was in a very disorganized state. Living conditions and transportation facilities were very bad. The people on the whole were very suspicious of foreigners, as a result of their experience with them in the past, and the deep-rooted feelings on political, social and religious matters and the intense passion shown for everything Polish, made it necessary to work with the greatest tact and care, so as to avoid the mistakes which might easily ruin any future chances of success. The people were also suffering, as they still are, from lack of food and clothing; they were ravaged by disease and continually threatened, as a result of these conditions and the work of agitators, with an

---

*See *Typhus and Doughboys: The American-Polish Typhus Relief Expedition 1919-1921*, Alfred E. Cornebise, 1982.

outbreak of Bolshevism within their borders. At the same time they have been fighting all along this enemy without. As a result the country has been on a war footing, which has made the work which we are doing especially difficult, due to the continual movement of troops and changes in plans. These conditions, in fact, do not improve with time. Of late they have even become worse as a result of the fighting along the front, and many of our important points have had to be closed and new points quickly opened up. Notwithstanding these conditions, as can be seen from the foregoing reports, the activities have not only been kept up, but have spread over the country until today we are operating in more than forty places, and had we the means and personnel, it would be very easy to operate in forty more, for invitations come to us almost daily to start work in new places.

"Speaking generally, the chief aim during the first year has been to conduct our activities in such a way as to bring the Association into the confidence of the whole Polish people. That we have succeeded in doing this is shown, not only by the expressions of opinion coming to us from various quarters and the number of newspaper articles written about us, though no effort has been made by ourselves to have this done, but also by the number of requests that are coming to us to take up civilian work."

No problem was more difficult than that of religious activities. On one side were Roman Catholics, naturally suspicious of any Protestant organization; on the other were the Socialists, frankly anti-religious. Both types were watchful and ready to protest against the first sign of proselyting propaganda. The solution as embodied in a "Spiritual Betterment Department," may best be stated by a further extract from Mr. Taylor's report:

> "So far we have had no definite religious program, though from time to time addresses have been delivered in our buildings by priests and Protestant pastors and other inspirational speakers. Yet it is evident that if the Y M C A is to justify its existence in Poland it must have a definite contribution to make along Christian lines. What should that contribution be? To attempt to proselytize by turning Roman Catholics into Protestants, or to endeavor to root out old ideals, sucked in as it were with their mothers' milk, or to change practices that have been the custom of centuries is certainly not the work of the Association. For this organization there is a far greater task. The Roman Catholic churches filled to the doors on Sundays and Holy Days show the strong hold that religion has on these people. To come to know them and to read their literature also convinces one that they are great idealists, even though it is true that up to the present their idealism has been chiefly of a national character. Yet the fact that they are capable of such idealism and of suffering to the utmost for it as they have done indicates that they have the capacity for a higher idealism still. If, therefore, by working along the lines of this religious temperament and idealistic tendency we can point them to the highest ideal of all — the

Christ ideal as it is symbolized in the cross, to the sign of which they are so strongly attached, and show how it is meant to affect the whole life of the individual, and how through this same ideal their own national idealism can find its highest expression, we should be pointing out to them a way which, as a result of their national characteristics and training they should not only be prepared to tread but in which they may even be a guide to others. In other words, not to proselytize but to vitalize should be the work of the Y M C A."

The wisdom both of the policy and its execution appeared in the fall of 1920 when an Officers' Club was inaugurated amid much enthusiasm at Krakow. Some of the priests of the city were much concerned at the numbers and character of the audience, and at the reception given an address by the Senior Secretary outlining the Christian character of the Association. A few days later one of the secretaries began a special course of lectures on the philosophy and psychology of the Y M C A, at the express request of the University. In the discussions following the lectures, charges of proselyting were made. They were met by the voluntary declarations of women workers in the Y huts, themselves Catholics and members of families of high standing, that no proselyting word had been spoken in the huts, to them or in their hearing. "I have never," said one, "felt such a good Roman Catholic as I do now when working for our soldiers and for our people."

Later, at an ecclesiastical conference on the subject at the Palace of the Prince Bishop of Krakow, the discussion was concluded by the Bishop, who remarked that he had observed the work of the Y M C A and that the Church saw no reason to oppose it but every reason to let it continue its work without interference.

That Premier Witos, a Socialist, should at about the same time have sent an official letter expressing the appreciation of the Government, which he confirmed in a personal interview, was satisfying evidence that the work had spoken for itself with no uncertain voice.

Meanwhile a serious interruption had occurred. It is not the function of this history to pass judgement on the territorial ambitions of Poles, but a glance at the map will show that in pressing into the Ukraine as far as Kiev, in the spring of 1920, they far exceeded the boundaries assigned by the Treaty of Versailles. Although cooperating with the Ukrainians, their operations gave the Soviet Government an obvious excuse for a counter attack. So successful was this undertaking that not only was Kiev taken, but the Poles retreated until Warsaw was on the point of falling into the hands of the Russians.

The Association workers had accompanied the Polish advance and were carrying on a full program in Kiev, having opened a fine building in the center of the town, which had become the rendezvous of all the Poles stationed there. When the troops entered Minsk, a droshky driver conducted the Y men to the hut abandoned by Y workers in Russia, February, 1918, when the Germans advanced into Russia. This now became headquarters for work extending along the fighting line. The story of the next two months was one of desperate endeavors. The retreat of the Poles was rapid, and the Y men spent themselves to the utmost, serving bread and hot drinks to the hungry and tired soldiers. At point after point, service was continued until evacuation was completed, the Y stores being loaded ready for removal only an hour or two before the Russians entered the town. Railroad cars not being always available, the secretary secured farmers' wagons and drove with the marching troops, distributing food at every pause for rest. Canteens were run day and night. Learning that a battalion north of Minsk had been without food for six days, 36 wagons were sent out to find them, literally saving them from starvation. The reports of this period are full of memorable experiences of secretaries. At Borysov, for example, the little white house where Napoleon slept the night before his defeat on the Berezina, became a Y canteen for a few days until the Russians crossed the river and made it untenable.

In the meantime the Y headquarters was a very busy place. The breaking up of so many centers and the opening of new ones caused a great rush of work. At this period the general impression was that Warsaw would fall. All the foreign legations moved out, as well as private citizens who had the means. In order to safeguard its supplies the Y emptied its warehouse, the bulk of the material being moved to Danzig, whither women secretaries and the wives of American secretaries were sent for safety. The business department removed to Lodz with all important papers. However, activities in Warsaw were extended rather than decreased. New canteens were opened and considerable hospital work was carried on, as the hospitals were overflowing with wounded men who, for lack of adequate medical staff and supplies, were receiving scant attention. By this time Warsaw was in the very center of the front line operations. At one railway junction east of Warsaw the Chief Secretary reported that over a considerable period upwards of 60,000 men were served daily by the Association. At this time there were 25 rolling canteens serving the Polish Army along the lines at the front. The most critical days of the summer were the 13th and 14th of August when everyone expected to see Warsaw fall. The Y secretaries had taken every precaution to meet this emergency if it arose. Fortunately, however, the Bolshevik advance was suddenly held up fifteen kilometers from Warsaw. Once again the Y had to reorganize its work and again go forward with the Poles as in the spring advance into the Ukraine. As they reached towns where they had previously been operating they reopened the old buildings.

During the summer a second training school for Y workers was opened at Modlin with 45 students, but its work was naturally curtailed by the military situation. After the crisis was past another training course was started at Lodz.

During July a center for students which had been running over six months with success had to be closed, all the students being called to the front. While the experience of these two months entirely upset plans and caused the loss of many buildings, on the whole it helped rather than hindered the work of the Association. It brought the Association to the attention of many people who had not previously heard of it. One prominent Pole said that the Bolshevik advance had tested the mettle of the Y and he was generous enough to add that it had won its spurs.

In spite of the difficulties and strain resulting from the experiences of the summer the Association went ahead increasing its work and becoming better known and more appreciated in Poland. The Army even had a marching song about the Y, spoken of affectionately as a kindly relative from America.

By October, 1920, activities began coming back to normal after the changes of the previous months. But a new discouragement fell upon the work of the Y in Poland. As a result of the necessary reduction in the budget for 1921 the work in Poland was cut down by more than half. Work in small centers, canteens in general and all entertainment activities entailing expense were entirely stopped and the work and personnel in the larger centers reduced to a minimum. Eleven secretaries left in November, fifteen in December, and the Y work was reduced to five localities with several centers in Warsaw and Krakow still under the leadership of A. S. Taylor.

It is deeply to be regretted that financial conditions forced the major withdrawal of American support at this time. The confidence of the Polish people and authorities had been won, and the practical benefits of Association work had made them eager for its continuance. The demonstration of American efficiency in quick organization under difficulties and in adaptation of unfavorable resources, had made a deep impression, as shown by numerous exhortations by officers and others to the people to learn from the Association achievements how to solve their own problems. Into an atmosphere of factional strife had been injected an example of friendly, disinterested cooperation, and among the pressing demands of every day living the ideals of character, patriotism and service had been kept bright. Beyond the ministry of material things to needy men and women, itself no small or unnecessary service, there was an increasing contribution to good citizenship and constructive national spirit. How far Poland will be able to carry forward the work thus begun is problematical, on account of lack both of leadership and funds. But the record shows clearly the kind of service that all Central Europe needs in the coming years, and points the way to America's opportunity.

Interview
With
Walter S. Schutz

* * *

At Hartford, Connecticut,

February 4th 1920.

Q. Did you ever have anything to do with the Y before you went overseas?
A. I had been simply interested in connection with Sunday meetings here.

Q. Just for local Y.M.C.A. work?
A. Yes

Q. When did you get over there in the first place?
A. December, 1917, I got to London on the last day of the year and then went over to Paris the first of January.

Q. What were you assigned to at the time?
A. I was somewhat in doubt, having gone over as a result really of a cablegram which Dr. Mott read at the meeting in Boston from General, later Marshal Petain, that they wanted to start work in the French Army, having seen the work in the American Army and others and as a child I had been over there two years and had a knowledge of French and they wanted me to go over and help the French and while I was waiting around in Paris for assignment with the French Army—it took five or six weeks to get passage. I believe I was to be sent to somewhere in

the Vosges and I asked Mr. Davis who was then assigned to the Foyer to give me something to do. He had a letter which had come from Mr. Carter from one of these Polish-American boys who had come over on a French liner in December and there were various Y workers, men and women, on that boat and arrived in Western France at one of these camps where the Polish Army, which had been trained at Niagara on the Lake in Canada and then went to France and was distributed to the various leave areas, he wrote Mr. Carter and said he had been over in France a month and hadn't seen anything of the Y.M.C.A. and wanted some help.

Mr. Davis said: "Here is the letter, you go down to Laval in the Province of Mayenne," which is practically in Brittany, just East of Brittany, where the first regiment of Polish soldiers was then located. Count Orlowski, who married a Miss Stevens of Hoboken and spoke English perfectly and who had in some way or other gotten in touch with the Y over there said: "He was going to Laval" and offered to introduce me. I went down there early in January—I think it was the twelfth or thirteenth of January—and I remember arriving on a Sunday morning. We went out to the barracks, the old French barracks in this small provincial French town, very ancient and very particularly French. In fact, I think I was the first man in khaki uniform, the first American to arrive in that town, and I remember going through the streets that the children rushed out to get me and said: "Look at the American."

I went out to this barracks with the Count and there these boys began to swarm around me and were dressed in most non-descript uniform. Some had French uniforms on, others had red breeches and long black coats of the Canadian Militia and they swarmed about me and began talking in English and I asked them where they were from. They all said: "From America." I said: "Where" and they answered, "From Chicago, Buffalo, Detroit, Pittsburgh, New Britain, Conn. and other places." I was at once introduced to the Chaplain of the 1st Regiment whose name was Jaworski, and who was, of course, familiar with the Y and I think had cooperated a good deal with them in Pittsburgh where he came from. He was very glad indeed and said: "These men have been over here, they are receiving French pay, they get French food and they are awfully home-sick and lonesome and they want the help of the Y.M.C.A." I can remember these men rubbing my coat and saying: "I wish I was in khaki, we are from America."

That spirit was the same throughout all the work over there. They welcomed you as a connecting link. The Y.M.C.A. was, I think, with that Army the direct link that connected them with America. They were then being trained and instructed entirely by French officers, most of them of Polish decent who had served in the French Army. The Colonel was really a French Army officer who had served in the Colonies and he didn't understand the Y.M.C.A. It was an entirely new idea to him that the soldiers should be treated any differently than soldiers had always been treated. He was courteous at all time with me but he believed these fellows needed above everything else to learn to obey and the discipline was the one thing he complained of. I went back to Paris and made my report.

Q. While you are there, Mr. Schutz, I want to interrupt you, if I may, with this question: Your contacts with the Polish interests there must have given you a great deal more knowledge of the back ground of that Polish work than the ordinary person would have. Won't you just briefly indicate something about the Poles in this country and their attitude toward the war and the part they played so that we will get that related to the United States? How many Poles are there here and where are they located chiefly? What can you say about them?
A. I never was in contact with them in the slightest in the States before going over.

Q. Did you pick up any of that from contact over there?
A. Oh, yes. These figures are subject to verification; I know that upwards of two hundred thousand of the Poles served in the American Army and then in addition there were about a total of 60,000 who were not eligible for the American Army, not being American citizens or too old for the service who joined this Polish Army, autonomous army, and went to France.

Q. What is the history of that autonomous army from its early beginning?
A. They began to recruit before America went into the war.

Q. Do you know who took the initiative in that thing?
A. Mr. Paderewski was very actively interested in it. If you care to get that information, though, his son-in-law, Mr. Gorwski, whose office is in the Aeolian Building, New York, can give you the whole history.

Q. Do you know of any published sources of general information about the Polish situation?
A. No, he would be the one. It became known afterward as the Haller Army because General Haller commanded it and took it into Poland.

Q. They drifted across the border into Canada?
A. No, the government authorized them to recruit an army, both Canadian and the United States, but they were trained at Niagara on the Lake, in Canada and shipped from there in detachments and went by the French Line. The French Government contributed the equipment and the maintenance of this army; I think the Americans made a loan for the purpose also.

Q. Where were they located for training purpose chiefly in France?

A. The first place they went to was Lepuys in Haute Marne, and that later became a leave area, and that was the first place. Then they were spread out all through the Province of Mayenne and put into these various barracks and trained in groups of a thousand or so. Then they were also up at Caen in Normandy, the capital of Normandy. They were also through sections of Brittany, trained there first. As soon as these barracks were vacated by the Frenchmen that had been trained they were put in there at these different places, but primarily Laval. I have put in a good many reports to Davis.

Q. If you will just give me the principal places we won't go into detail.

A. I want to spell them so I have to have them before me.

The recruiting center or the business center was the little known town of Casille-le-Guillaume in the Province of Mayenne. Then also in the Province of Manche and parts of Brittany. They were later, the 2nd and 3rd regiments, located near Orionotloire. Those divisions gradually, as they passed the preliminary training, were advanced toward the East and later, in fact Mr. Johnson and I—Carl H. Johnson, an old Y secretary of Jackson, Michigan, who was the first athletic director that went with the troops—went with me. He stayed with them until he became regional athletic secretary in charge of the Mailly district.

Q. When was that Army finally organized?

A. It was organized into a separate Army when General Haller took command. The first formal recognition as a separate army was when President Poincare presented the flags to the first four regiments near Brienne-le-Chateau on June 22nd, 1918.

Q. And in the meantime this training process was going on?

A. Yes, and the 1st regiment had been brigaded with General Gourad's army and they participated in the defense of Chalons and in the engagement around Rheims in the early part of June. Then, later, on October 6th, 1918, near Nancy, General George Joseph Haller took formal command of the entire army.

Q. How many men, about, did they have there at that time?

A. They had then about 50,000 men.

Q. Then in addition to that particular army, there were some 200,000 men in American troops?

A. Yes.

Q. I suppose they came in through the usual process of the draft, etc?
A. Yes, and volunteers. And they made a very good record.

Q. Was there any effort made to select them along lines of nationality or were they simply mixed in?
A. Mixed in absolutely.

Q. Was there any effort made to serve those men as Poles in the American Army?
A. I don't think so.

Q. They got just the usual treatment?
A. Yes.

Q. So that your special connection with the Poles was with this Army?
A. Yes, we were at one of the great camps, Sain-te-Tanche, I got there on the first of March, 1918, having left the troops at Laval when they entrained. The French Colonel said: "He didn't know what my relationship was to the Army. He would like to have me come but he didn't feel that he could transport me as a military man because he didn't have the proper papers," so I went to Paris to get authority, etc., and overtook the troops and really got to the camp just as soon as they did and there went with them on this training in camp.

Q. Lets go back to Paris when you made your original report.
A. I told Davis that these able men were Americans and certainly needed just what the Y.M.C.A. could give and that the officers and the men, especially those that came from America, including the Chaplains were very solicitous and anxious, that the men had no books, they had no comforts whatever except the regular French Army places. So I made quite an elaborate report.

Q. Did you make that report in writing?
A. Yes.

Q. Have you a copy of it here?
A. I don't believe I have. Still I will try and find it.

Q. I would like to copy all your reports, as I might have trouble in assembling them.
A. They were all made. I did later make a report to Mr. Carter.

Q. Then you were specifically assigned?

A. Yes, they said: "It is up to you, Schutz, to organize the work for the Polish Army."

Q. Had you picked up any knowledge of Polish here?
A. No. I never hear but very little Polish and only learned a very little Polish. My knowledge of French helped me with the French officers. And then later when I was in Germany I was quite helped by that.

Q. Then you went back to Laval?
A. Yes, and organized the first Y.M.C.A. hut for this Polish Army in this Caserbe in Laval and we decorated this room and got what athletic supplies we could and started them in. We had the formal opening and the first celebration on the twelfth of February which is Lincoln's and Kosciusko's [sic] birthday. And at that time I remember that some ladies had been sent to help us out and a Mrs. Hering and Miss Stinson were sent down there by the Women's Department to look the field over and they were present at that opening and helped open the hut and stayed with us all through the time up to the twenty-sixth of February. And then they tried to go out into the camps and that is a later story. They did later join us and I think they were the first American women to go into a regular French camp.

Q. Did you establish huts later?
A. Yes, we established huts at towns of Mayenne, Sealigeon *(?)*, Mamers and later at Domfront.

Q. How many did you have altogether?
A. You mean counting those later on?

Q. In this particular locality.
A. Then we had at Brieuc and at Quantin—we had in all about ten different localities in that particular neighborhood.

Q. Then did you get over to open the same work in Leprey?
A. No. There was one started there for the prisoners. That is an interesting item. In addition to these men that came from America, there were in all I should say about probably as high as 6,000 who had been in the Germany Army, Poles in the German Army, that were captured by the French. In fact they were not at all reluctant to be captured, and they were located at Leprey and other places and they were given their opportunity as to whether they would prefer to continue as war prisoners or to join a Polish Legion and a great many of them, some six or eight thousand of them, joined the Foreign Legion, the Polish Le-

gion, and then served in Morocco and then came back and joined this Army. And there were a great many that came from Austria and so that the Army ultimately including the prisoners captured by the British, French and Italians amounted to about 75,000 men.

The prison camp was at Leprey and we sent a secretary down there and maintained a good work for them.

Then later, as soon as these various units were co-ordinated and formed into regiments and then into a division they advanced into the region of the Army and I joined them at Mayenne and they were also at various places in the Vosges, and not far from Chaumont.

Q. Was the whole group kept together as a unit from that time?
A. No, they were only at Mossup until really the time that General Haller took command; they were spread out in a good many different places. They were brigaded with the French whenever used in the French lines.

Q. To what extent were you able to follow them up in your service?
A. There were four of us at the Camp in Mayenne and the other camps adjourning [sic, adjoining?].

Q. How many Polish troops were there?
A. There were in all about 5,000 men there. We had the French help us and you see we were in contact with the American Y at Mayenne. Then it very soon became apparent that these boys who had come from America liked American methods and disliked French methods to a large extent. Then they wouldn't smoke a French cigarette if they could get anything else. They wanted to get the privileges of the American Y and the A.E.F.Y, and at Mayenne, under Ches Lee, he was very sympathetic and he came out repeatedly to them and I was able to secure everything through him at Mayenne. And the Americans came out there and they were, of course, very musical. That is one very important part of their distinct nationality that they are so musical. They will sing, and a great many of them play. We encouraged it in every possible way. The organization of a band and orchestra was all done in the Y hut. We furnished some of the instruments and some they had themselves.

Then, we had dramatic entertainments and, etc., which they put on for themselves and we got all the Americans. They were above all, anxious to hear American entertainers and several of them came out there from Mayenne. Fred B. Smith came out and spoke to them, and I remember a remark he made to me. He said: "Walter, if America was only as good a place as these Poles think it is, we would never have to apologize for it." And they were perfectly delighted and that is one of the things that impressed itself upon me. You saw the foreign-born

American and you saw his idealism of America and realized what a wonderful country we belonged to.

Q. Were you under Davis administratively?
A. I was up to the first of July, and then as I said, because they were so anxious to have the American side of the thing, the boys, I laid the matter before Davis and Carter and it was agreed to take it over as of the first of August and I was asked to organize. I had been out there with this first regiment. I was asked to come into Paris and to organize the work for the entire Polish Army and then it was put under the American Y entirely.

You see, they had been attending to the leave area. Some of them went down to Nice, etc., and the question came up as to whether they were eligible to come into the American Y, etc., and it was finally decided and a letter was sent out by Mr. Carter that they were to be treated just as other American soldiers were.

Q. They were in French uniforms?
A. Yes, except that they wore always a fatigue cap, a Chapka *[czapka]*, which is the four-cornered distinctly Polish hat, but otherwise they were in French blue.

Q. When you opened up these headquarters in Paris, the various Polish divisions were in the line?
A. The 1st, 2nd, and 3rd Regiments were in the line. As I said, the 1st Regiment was, and the other regiments went into the Vosges, and practically took up some of the positions that some of our American boys vacated after they got into the more active part of the line.

By that time the work had expanded very materially. We had work in practically all the training areas and then were with them and we had about ten secretaries that actually were attached to these regiments and they followed them wherever they went.

Q. Your idea was to have one secretary with each regiment?
A. Yes, one or more with each regiment. McAdams and Modre had at that time huts in the Vosges in the very advanced areas, between the 1st and 2nd line of trenches. McAdams and Modre were given the Croix de Guerre.

Then, the athletic contribution was a very important part. The Poles in their own country know nothing of modern sport. In this country they are not naturally athletic, but the officers were very much impressed by the importance of this and they encouraged it in every way, the boxing and baseball and football, so that they became a very important part of their work. The French Army officers, at least particularly the Colonel of the 1st Regiment, didn't definitely assign certain hours for training the way the American Army did. The under-officers were very keen for it. And every Sunday, however, was given up particularly to athletic sport and entertainments of one kind or another.

While they were at Mayenne the American teams from the different American camps came over there and played and we had a very delightful relationship, entirely due to the Y.M.C.A. bringing them together. And so far as appreciation was concerned, there was absolutely no fault to find except that we couldn't do more.

Q. What were the outstanding impressions in your mind as to the Poles as a race?

A. They are very tremendously patriotic, idealistic, individualistic and that was the one thing that we tried above everything else to make them work together in every way as a unit, to train them in team work.

Q. That is the characteristic that is very apparent in the early history of the root, the root of their national difficulties.

A. Yes, and it is the only thing that I worry about now. If they can't develop team work—and they seem to be—they will not succeed.

I personally with Mr. Antoin Potoski and Colonel Francis E. Fronsak—who is health commissioner in Buffalo—he was appointed Major and later a Colonel in the American Army, attached to this Polish Army, and he can give you, by the way, good information. He could give you in English a good and full account of the inception of it. I will make it a point to write to him.

Q. Did these fellows fight?

A. They made very good fighters. They were commanded by French trained officers and as a matter of fact, with the exception of the 1st and 2nd Regiments, they didn't see much of hard fighting. You see, it was on account when the full army was organized and they were put into the Vosges Mountains and had just been withdrawn preparatory to an additional intensive training to be advanced into a more active section when the armistice came. And then during all of this time, they began to call me "Schutsinski" and Johnson was "Johnsinski" and they always were asking us: "Are you going with us to Poland" and we said: "Surely, if you fellows take us," and not only the men themselves but finally the General, when he reviewed the first Regiment. He had the most remarkable history. He was captured by the Russians and escaped to England and came to France and was put in command of the Army. He was one of the most enthusiastic men over the Y.M.C.A. I have a letter that he gave me finally as I left, which I think possibly it might be well to publish.

Q. I would like to have it.

A. I confered with him after the armistice as soon as their plans were made to go to Poland and he said: "We want the Y.M.C.A. to go with us", and he made a formal request in writing to Mr. Carter to let the Y accompany him and his Army into Poland and said to me: "I want you to go with me when I go" and the five of us, including four men and one woman, who was a Miss Jorkiewies, who was of Polish extraction but never lived in Poland, went with the second division and his staff when they started for Poland and went through Germany.

Q. Do you recall under what auspices they went; was it by arrangement of the French Government?

A. Yes, it was under the terms of the armistice. The troops were to be allowed to be sent to maintain order in independent Poland and the great question was how they should go. It was stated they should go through Danzig and the Germans opposed it and Foch said: "They will go through Danzig or some other way as you suggest." And the Germans suggested they go through Germany. A great many of the cars were the rolling stock of what had been given up by the Germans, and 380 trains in all went through Germany starting by two loops from Coblenz either by way of Frankfort and Leipsiz or to Emmonshalle and in that way through Germany, taking about forty hours to cross Germany. I went with the 2nd Division of his staff. We left near Noce and went straight through Germany via Coblenz. It was very interesting and quite a thrilling trip. They were entirely under Allied convoy and two Allied officers went with each train and made stops every six hours going through Germany, outside the stations. The public was not allowed to come into the station, except the German guards and the Allied guards there. We had no armed guards on our train at all and then General Haller arrived on Polish soil on Easter Day, 1919, and they had a great reception at Lods [Łódź].

Q. Where did they mobilize in Poland?

A. Warsaw was their first headquarters. Then they were sent out to the Eastern front and I followed just as soon as I could, by the last of April, and joined this 1st regiment. And they were very, very enthusiastic and there we at once began to organize for them, but they moved around so very rapidly that no sooner we sent secretaries out to a different division it was very hard to keep up with them. Of course, the supplies we finally got through with the help of the Red Cross who arrived six weeks after we got there.

But the work was started and the first hut was opened at Lublin which was then the headquarters of General Haller's Army, which is about 150 miles southeast of Warsaw. Then for the second hut, that was opened on Decoration Day on the Modlin, the large Russian fortress, 25 miles south of Warsaw on the

Vistula. Mr. Hugh Gibson the first American minister to Poland was present at this opening and delivered an address to the men and then opened the first American baseball match and he pitched the game and the French General, General Petit de Mange was the commander of the fortress and of the soldiers there and he welcomed the Y.M.C.A. with very great enthusiasm and the work was continued there ever since and during the Summer they have had a training school.

Very soon the Ministry of War desired the Y.M.C.A. service for all of the Polish troops. You understand, the other was a separate army but Pilsudski, who is the chief-of staff of the state and was the dictator who took over from the Germans the control of Poland on the tenth day of November desired the Y for all. He granted me an audience and discussed the Y.M.C.A. for half an hour with me and turned me over to his chief-of-staff saying: "We want you to do everything you can for these men. We need their assistance and particularly the young men who are coming from the country, that have just been mobilized." I was only there two months in Poland but I came away with a letter from the Minister of War directed to Dr. Mott urging us to continue and develop the work in every possible way and promising every assistance on the part of the Army.

Q. That interview is the sort of thing that Dr. Miller, our present editor in chief, is very keen on. What were the circumstances of that?

A. I had met in Paris through a prominent Polish citizen of Paris, Dr. Mots, the Minister of the Interior, who was in Paris, and I expressed to him a request to meet the head of the state, and very soon a letter came that he would be glad to see me at the Belvedere, his palace, which had just a few months before been occupied by the German general who had control of Warsaw.

I went there at noon and was at once ushered into his presence and found him most democratic and a most cordial man. I spoke with him in French. I don't think he speaks any English. At that time Mr. Paderewski was the Premier, and Pilsudski was the President, the head of the state. He undoubtedly will be the first President of the republic.

I outlined to him the purpose and plans of the Y.M.C.A., and he had already heard of it through Mr. Rose. I told him one thing that our organization opposed was alcohol, and he said: "That is a very excellent thing". In fact, I said to him: "After the first of July (this interview was on the 19th of May)"—my diary says he said: "That is a most interesting experiment and I have already signed your papers." I didn't know that, but that was giving me absolute freedom and putting us on a military basis and agreeing to furnish us military transportation and everything that we had in France.

When I told him that after the first of July there was to be no liquor in America, he said: "They will have wine and beer, won't they?" I said: "No, they won't have that either." He said: "They will send over to France and England, won't they?" I said: "They can't do that." He said: "That is a very interesting experiment." I said: "You are trying an interesting experiment and I wish you success." He said: "I wish your experiment success." He was a man who had come through tremendous effort. He was seven years exiled in Siberia. He had been the second time banished to Russia. He was three years banished from the country. He had been a year in prison by the Germans when he escaped and got to Warsaw just before the armistice.

He emphasized particularly the value of the development of the young men in Poland. He said: "They are not accustomed to sports and games such as you know them, and I welcome it very heartily and beg you to tell the authorities that we should be glad to do anything we possibly can to help and count on you." And later before I left, in fact, I attended a conference with the Minister of War and the Minister of Military Education and he said: "Send us an athletic director and we will put the whole programme of athletics and physical development of the army into the hands of the Y.M.C.A.

And they did. They carried on this school for hundreds of selected men from the army, and they have been developing in that line ever since. We sent out for a package of cigarettes and he said: "Won't you let me offer you a cigarette?" I had some Hartford Club cigarettes and offered him a box and he said: "I see you are not altogether angels in America. You still smoke."

He has been the figure in Poland and is the man on whom the future of the country depends more than any other. He was head of the Socialist Party before the war, and organized all these secret athletic organizations, sokal [sic], they call it, and had been absolutely determined that he should live and see the independence of Poland.

I told him that we were non-sectarian and in fact, between ourselves, he is a Protestant, but, of course, the country is Roman Catholic, and it was distinctly understood there should be no proselyting [sic]. But there was really nothing said about it. He didn't, of course, know of the work from first-hand experience at all, not as General Haller did and his officials. But he gave me a letter and his chief-of-staff told me to take it up with the various department heads. The only thing is that you need plenty of patience. Most of those people make an appointment for 11 and make you wait until 12. They are polite afterwards, but they are eastern in the sense of putting things off, and we really did get on very well indeed.

Another thing he said—"Tell your people anything in the way of clothing and supplies and food is what we need," because his own army had been fighting all through that winter with practically no shoes and socks, and were in a very bad condition.

Q. How large an army did they have at that time?

A. The Polish army, his army, numbered 200,000 men, I guess, at any rate, and it has been increasing since.

Q. Were they doing much active fighting at that time?

A. He just returned when I saw him from the capture of Vilna in Lithuania. They had some very active fighting there against the Bolshevists and the Ukrainians.

Then I went down after that to Lemberg, and in Polish it is Lwow. That was the capital of Galicia, and there had been very active fighting. There the women had even armed themselves and driven out the Ukrainians. But most of the fighting was in small groups, wherever they would find a concentration of the Ukrainians or Bolshevists. Then they would pursue them and have engagements with them.

And, of course, very soon after that—it was the time that Germany had to make up her mind whether she would sign the treaty or not, and they were supposed to be massed on the Silesian border; and I went down there because General Haller's troops were moved to that section with headquarters at Cracow. And there we began at once to have particularly huts with writing materials and hot chocolate and coffee, anything they could get. We had a very interesting picture of the first cup of tea served in the hut. General Haller received it and gave his very hearty thanks to the workers there for undertaking it; and it has developed ever since then very successfully.

I really feel that apart from the war work, that there is much opportunity in Poland because the people want just such an organization, and I hope the permanent civilian work may continue there as well.

Q. Did the frontier lines as demarcated by the treaty include practically all the Poles?

A. Well, that was one of the difficulties. I went south of Cracow with General Haller. There in the Carpathians the boundary line is very much in dispute. Some of the land which was country that is 80 percent Polish was included in the Czecho-Slovak boundary and Teschen. For instance, except one or two of the cities very predominantly Polish, not German or Austrian—that is where the difficulties may come; and that is one of the reasons why the League of Nations is necessary to settle these disputes.

Q. What really became of these around the boundaries?

A. As a matter of fact, the secretaries advanced into a certain section beyond the line that was laid out for them, the tentative line, at least, established by the War Council of Paris.

Q. Was that on the theory that their own people were on the other side of the line?

A. I can believe the Poles that they were after the mines, and Silesia has the mines, and they said they must have them; but the ethnological boundary would give that to Poland.

Q. How about the Bolsheviki?

A. So far as I could judge, the Bolsheviki, so-called, when I was there in April, May and June, hadn't made any real advance in Poland itself, among the Poles, because their one idea from the top to the bottom, except the Jews, was to establish an independent Polish country. The Bolsheviki was in Russia and, of course, extended into Russian Poland, which is the old kingdom of Poland, which has all been under the dominion of Russia.

I saw, for instance, on May 1st in Warsaw a procession of the Socialist Party which carried banners through the streets, which I think were more or less of a Socialist character, but absolutely orderly. There was no rioting and just as quiet as can be, much more quiet in Warsaw than it was in Waterbury, Connecticut, at that time. And on the 3rd of May, which is their great independence day, the national holiday of Poland, I was present there at the first celebration of independent Poland and all the military, all the civilian organizations, everybody marched through the streets; such tremendous impressive patriotic demonstrations, you never imagined anything more impressive. It lasted all day long.

In the citadel, where Pilsudski had been a prisoner, where the Russians and then the Germans had been in control, they had this great celebration, the school children and all the patriotic organizations bringing out banners that had never been allowed to be displayed in public in all these years and planted three trees to commemorate the union of the three parts of Poland—the Russian, Austrian, and German. Pilsudski was, of course, the chief figure at that gathering.

When you come to see that they have established a nation, when everything was against them—the Russians wouldn't even allow them to wear a Polish eagle on their watch-charm; that was a sign of revolution. For instance, all the street names in Warsaw were written in Russian above and Polish beneath, and later they painted out the Polish.

Q. Were they permitted to speak the Russian *[Polish??]* language?

A. They could, but they had to instruct in Russian. In some of the schools the Russian emissaries would go about and if they thought the school teacher too zealous in teaching Polish, they would curtail her right to teach, cut out mathematics the following year, or geography, or something of that kind; just simply to try to stamp out the language. But that is the one thing, they are absolutely persistent; they wouldn't forget their language. And that was the wonderful thing that these men coming from all parts of the world can immediately speak their own language.

Q. Were they allowed to distribute books and their Polish literature?
A. Yes, and Austria was very much more liberal than any of the others. In Austria and Poland they practically had an autonomous state but, of course, under Austrian supervision.

Q. What seemed to be the economic condition in Poland as far as you could observe?
A. The great curse that the Germans imposed on the country was to absolutely commandeer and take away every bit of metal they possibly could. Not a single manufacturing plant in all the section of Poland I was in was intact. They would take out the machinery and take off the roof, and even in the private houses they would take every brass knob or bit of metal off the door; and their one crying need is some kind of machinery and implements to go ahead with.

Then, of course, the crops had been so very much reduced on account of the fighting, and most of that country had had at least three armies living on it—first the Russian and then the Austrian and then the German. So that the general economic condition was very distressing.

Q. Had the men been drafted by these armies?
A. There was compulsory service in all branches. So that they had all served. But, for instance, I talked to a number that had been with the German army on the front, officers, said: "We are here and will do what we have to do, but we won't do any more." In the Austrian army they were more liberal to them than they were in the German army.

But they had all had military training. Of course, they had had compulsory military training.

The Jewish question is one that I don't want to go into. I will say for my own observation, the great majority of these stories of persecution are absolutely deliberate exaggerations or misrepresentations. I think the figures show that some 233 Jews were killed during these trials, during this condition; but at that time certainly more Christians were killed. There was rioting.

So far as my observation goes, the Jew has no loyalty for Poland, he wanted to be a Jew. He wanted to be an international, and he didn't want Poland to be established. In fact, they were caught red-handed dealing and trafficking with the Ukrainians and Bolshevists. I was in Cracow the day there was quite a riot there. These troops found that the Jews were extorting awful prices from the Polish women, and went into the chief square and rough-housed some of the Jewish stores. There was only one person killed, and it was purely accidental.

I spoke of it to General Haller, and he said: "You know that all of these stories are absolutely false." And I also spoke to Mr. Paderewski afterwards. I saw him later in Paris.

Q. Tell us about that.
A. I had known Mr. Paderewski personally. At least, he knew my family very well. His wife saw me soon after I got there. He was in France when I first went to Poland, and he was only a very short time in Warsaw while I happened to be there. But his wife had said "that he certainly must see you before you go back to America."

I saw him in Paris when I came back in June, 1919. He had then practically carried out his programme with the peace conference, and I think history will show that he did more than any other individual to establish the rights of Poland in connection with the general European situation at the peace conference. He took both my hands and said: "I want to thank you most heartily for what America and the Y.M.C.A. have done for my country. I sometimes don't feel that we deserve all that we are getting." I said: "You certainly have been fighting and struggling for it, and I am tremendously impressed by the conditions, the calm and sane and definite conditions that seem to be established in Poland.

Of course, we spoke English. He had heard all about the work of the Y and the Red Cross, and begged me in coming to America to urge them to continue in every way their work.

Q. Did he comment on any special phases of the Y work?
A. No, he didn't. He was very brief because he was absolutely filled up with engagements.

The K. of C. never did anything for the Polish autonomous army in France. The Red Cross and the hospitals helped and in some of the canteens where they had their regular canteens the Poles were admitted. But the Y.M.C.A. was the only American organization that had a particular work for the Poles.

Q. The only one that went to Poland?
A. Yes, except the Red Cross had gone there, but not in army work at all. When I got there, Colonel Bailey was in charge of the Red Cross work among civilians and they only did work east of the Bug River to fight typhus.

Q. How many Y men had gotten into Poland up until the time you left?
A. 30.

Q. And they were with the various divisions?
A. Yes.

Q. You were giving the ordinary type of Y service as conditions permitted?

A. Yes, more the foyer type. We didn't attempt to carry on any dry canteen. That was distinctly understood that we wouldn't attempt to take tobacco. The American Y sold to the Polish Haller army, gave them six months credit for $50,000 worth of tobacco, which was sold to that army and most of it hadn't reached Poland when I left. I hope it got there, but we didn't have anything to do with it. We weren't in the grocery business, but tea and coffee and chocolate, the wet canteen stuff, and the complete moving picture outfits.

Through all these huts we had moving pictures, American, and they must have the American films.

Q. Did the American lecturers or otherwise address the boys much?

A. Yes. Whenever it was possible we had them.

Q. Was there any specific propaganda being put over by you?

A. No. Pututsky was head of the Polish propaganda, and I went with him and spoke in many of the camps.

Q. The Polish propaganda people availed themselves of the Y huts to address the troops?

A. Yes, and were particularly interested in all kinds of American magazines and wanted to model their work and plans for the future.

Q. What problems do you feel that the Polish republic is confronted with internally, from the standpoint of democracy?

A. The greatest difficulty of Poland today is that it practically has no natural boundary. They are hemmed in by enemies on all sides. On the east is Russia with a tremendous flat desert, plain, and simply an imaginary line to separate them. On the southeast are the Ukrainians, so-called. I am not going to comment on Ukrainia, but I think it is Russia. It is a state of mind, and I think they have practically given up any idea of independence of the Ukrainians. Then on the south are the Czecho-Slovaks, who are of the same general race, but are not sympathetic. As the Poles, they are Slavs, but they are for the most part Protestants; at least, they are not as distinctly Roman Catholic. And the Poles always say they have been under German and Austrian influence so long that they are Boche. So at present the feeling is quite intense between the Czechs and the Poles.

Q. There is no natural boundary there, is there?

A. No, except the Carpathians in one section, and that is only partially a boundary. Then on the west is, of course, Posen, which is Poland but has been German, and there is no demarcation between that and the main part of Germany or Prussia.

Then, of course, there is East Prussia, which is a sore and probably always will be, almost in the heart of northern Poland. Danzig is to be a free port probably under Polish control.

Q. That is practically synonymous with the word "free-fight".
A. I am told that the Germans tried to make out there would be a terrible calamity, that the people of Danzig wouldn't live under Polish control. But it is going to be one of the great ports of the world, and I think that if the German influence can be kept out long enough simply to establish the business of the port, I think it will succeed and will be a very important branch of commerce of the East.

Q. What is racially the basis of East Prussia?
A. Almost entirely German.

Q. Is that due to colonization?
A. Yes, as I understand it. It was formerly Pole or Estonian, but it has been occupied by Prussian inhabitants for a good many year.

Then Lithuania on the north is a real disappointment. They are practically the same as Poles. Their history and connection has been intimate and practically the same, but they have gotten the bee of independence in their bonnet and they want to be independent.

Now Vilna is the capital of Lithuania and Pilsudski took command there from the Bolshevists, the Russians, and he in no way attempted to subjugate it and make it a part of Poland; gave them the opportunity to be independent or ally themselves with the Poles, and it is hoped that will result; but I don't know.

Q. How about the old aristocratic disposition of the Poles?
A. For instance, the new constitution that they have adopted—they have re-adopted the old constitution of, I think, 1793, which was for that day a very democratic constitution. But it was a constitution of the privileged class and not of the populace. For instance, the king was chosen from the nobles and it wasn't a life tenor [sic, tenure?]. It was subject to election. Of course, the great struggle there will be between the Socialists so-called, the proletariat, and these great proprietors of land. For instance, Samowski [sic, Zamojski?], he and his family own a whole province practically. Samow [sic, Zamość?] is the capital of it; and these estates have to be divided up. In fact, when I was in Poland they had passed by a very narrow margin a law that no man should be allowed to hold over 1000 square kilometers of land.

So that that will be a difficult proposition. But at present, it seems to me—at least it seems to me then—that for the most part the aristocracy was deliberately trying to help the government and to co-operate and to work for a unified Poland.

Q. Turning in team-work and in such principles of organization as we are familiar with, it is a great thing on any event.

A. Yes. For instance, we found the great difficulty in Warsaw—they began all sorts of relief work for the soldiers. Every rich woman or group of them, and especially if she was a countess somebody or something or other, had organized a hut, or what they call *Ognisko*, for the soldiers. In one hospital that I went to, there were seven different organizations carrying on huts in that hospital. They couldn't work together. They hadn't learned how to work together. And that is what the Y.M.C.A. an outside organization, was doing. I was particularly that they should send some of the best trained Y women up there to get these other women to work with them, but I couldn't get Davis at that time to send American women there.

The country, of course, has been fought over and fought over, but if the German intrigue can be kept out, if they can have enough of an army and the Allies will absolutely see that their boundaries are preserved long enough for them to get on their feet, I believe that their ardent patriotism, their determination to make a go of it, I believe will succeed if anything can.

I was impressed with talking to older people there who would say: "We used to dream that our children's children would live to see an independent Poland, and it seems a miracle that we should live ourselves to see it."

Q. What is Ross doing there?
A. He had been sent over by Dr. Mott in connection with the student's voluntary movement, and was captured in the Protestant Poland, and he got out during the war and brought the message of the conditions there to Paris and then to America. Of course, his desire is, and there was a very distinct opportunity for distinct religious work of a Protestant character, particularly in modern Poland. And I saw it in the army. The young men resent the very antiquated formula and religious programme; that is, living in the past rather than in the present. I know the boys used to complain. They had mass and they didn't object to going to mass but didn't feel as though that the church should be over-emphasized.

Q. How about the Papal influence?
A. I couldn't judge of that, although I believe there would be a possibility of an independent Polish church of Roman form but without the Papal influence. I don't think they are very strong.

Q. The Pope was pretty Boche, you know, and I don't think they are very keen.

A. I went to the national shrine of Poland. Here is this wonderful picture of the Virgin and her child, which was stolen when the Swedes made an invasion of Poland. This picture was carried off by a Swedish soldier and suddenly he was struck down from Heaven; and the picture has a most marvelous curative power, and they have these pilgrimages there, and we have a Y.M.C.A. establishment there which has a great chance. I think the name of the place is Csestochowa. [Częstochowa].

Q. When you came back, did you have an opportunity to talk these matters over with Dr. Mott?

A. No.

Q. Whom did you report to in New York?

A. I reported to Hibbard and to some extent to Dr. Mott, and to Davis, of course.

Q. Did you file a final report in New York?

A. I filed a report in Paris and sent a copy to Dr. Mott.

I want to say this, that I think the work for the Polish troops was in every way more than worthwhile. I think that the appeal which the organization made to the men is something that they reflected in their letters home, and that their relationship to the Y in America will be very much stronger for this, and especially for those who have seen it in Poland and have written back, because they felt that it was and is their direct link between America and their own country; and, frankly, America is the one country that they really believe is their friend in Poland. They think every other country has some ulterior motive in dealing with them, and they have been fleeced by almost every nation under the sun, and they have reason to be suspicious. But they have no reason to believe that there is any ulterior motive.

Q. There is a great field for trade there, isn't there?

A. Yes, if we can only give them the credit which they have. Of course, the Polish mark is at the lowest ebb, and the worst danger I feel is—while they don't want to trade with Germany, Germany is right beside them. They will give them any credit they want for the sake of getting in there, and they will gradually get control of the entire business and financial ground-work of Poland, because the Pole is an agriculturist. He isn't a businessman. Their aristocracy has never gone into business. They are trying their best to do so now.

I came in contact with the electric light company that the Poles had taken over. Still, they are so close to the Germans. You saw German cameras and German films that were sold very cheap, and the Jew is the man who will be the liaison man. They hate him for about the same reason that in Palestine they hated the tax-collector because he has been the representative of the outsider to get their money from them.

Q. The high-class Poles are a very highly-strung, nervous, temperamental bunch, aren't they?
A. Yes. They are sentimental and they are artistic to a degree. For instance, their country, the physical conditions of Poland were a tremendous disappointment to me. It is almost entirely, all the section from Warsaw east and south-east is a great big sandy plain with stretches of fertile soil and then great patches of pine forests and marshes. There is absolutely nothing picturesque from the standpoint of an American who is accustomed to a variety of scenery. And, still, they idealize it and you see the pictures and the wonderful colors, and their costumes are very gay, which is so idealistic that I am afraid they are rather impractical and that their danger may lie in just that—that they aren't able to deal with the best advantages they have got.

They all said to me: "You must go to Sakopane [*sic,* Zakopane?], which is right in the foot-hills of the Carpathian Mountains." I did go there. It is an all-day trip from Cracow, and there these mountains rise right out of the plain to a height of about 10,000 feet, very impressive, and it is the Switzerland of Poland. It is a fine place for a leave area, and everybody goes down there that can.

But the rest of the country, as far as I saw it, was very discouraging, because the peasant, except in Posen, lives in log huts covered with plaster, if they are fairly rich, and with tile if they are really rich. Otherwise, it is a thatched roof. They have a few cows and get their existence off the soil, which raises wheat and other grains and potatoes. It is like the wilds of western Canada, most of it. And when you think that Galicia is the most thickly-settled part of Europe as a whole and how little they gain in life, you don't wonder how it is to come to a new country.

For instance, there all the natives were dressed in their home-spun costumes, and Captain Chambers, who was with me, who was a chaplain in the Canadian army but who had been educated in Poland and is a great friend of Mr. Ross and was a very good man. He made an address in Polish, and to see an American and Englishman come and address them in their own language, is a wonderful thing.

And I asked them how many had relatives in America, and I think one-third of them held up their hands. Now I hear the stories of about a lot of Poles going back. They will go back and stay there about one year and spend their money, and then come back to America and go at it again.

1921 YMCA Women's Letter from Poland

Warsaw, 12th of March, 1921.

We Polish women, workers of the Mission in the Young Men's Christian Association (Y.M.C.A.) gathered in conference for the first time to the number of 46 in view of the many objections raised against the Y.M.C.A. and us personally, hereby declare that working in the Association for nearly two years we have found here a work that was started for the noblest ends, viz., to bring moral and physical advantage to our young men.

In the very numerous Y.M.C.A. huts there can be found an eloquent proof of our words. The soldier finds there during the rainy autumn days and the dull winter weather a warm, clean room, a cup of cocoa, a wholesome entertainment, useful books, educational courses. During spring and summer time all kind of games in the open air develop him physically and guard him from waste of time and unhealthy influence.

Our huts are open to everybody who desires to visit them. The books in our libraries can always be inspected, it is easy to become acquainted with our courses and the spirit of our lectures. There is no secrecy in the work; all that we do is openly and frankly done, and the results prove this.

During the two years stay in Poland the Y.M.C.A. activities have developed wonderfully. Starting by excursions in the vicinity and flying concerts for Warsaw garrison we passed to the work at the front when the Y.M.C.A. canteens accompanied the vanguard of our army. Later, during the August days the popular "Auntie YMCA" distributed cigarettes to the soldiers in the trenches almost within reach of the Bolsheviks guns.

To-day when the soldier is returning home exhausted and without occupation the Y.M.C.A. is starting a number of courses which will help him to earn his living, as for instance, bookbinding, weaving drawing, typewriting, shorthand, etc. Model colonies are even to be established in Eastern Poland for the demobilized and invalids.

The Y.M.C.A. does not forget the wounded and sick soldier, visiting him in the hospitals with cigarettes, writing paper, chocolate, books, etc.

The Y.M.C.A. desires to elevate the ethics of our officer and for this purpose has opened two Officers' Clubs—one in Warsaw and another in Krakow, where our officers spend their leisure hours out of reach of alcoholic drinks and gambling. They take great interest in sports, start artistic and literary circles, attend to lectures, concerts, etc. Remembering our homeless officers the Y.M.C.A. has opened for them two dormitories in Warsaw.

In cooperation with the World Students' Christian Federation the Y.M.C.A. is helping our students clubs with scientifical libraries and understanding the hard food and living conditions is opening a dormitory and is providing dinners for the students.

Our heroic school-boy soldier is also not forgotten; a dormitory is being planned for him in Warsaw.

These facts need no arguing; the high ethics and noble aims prevailing in Y.M.C.A. institutions are evident to anyone.

The administration of the Mission in Poland until now composed only of Americans is most favorably disposed towards the Polish personnel. We appreciate endlessly the influence of the leadership and the directions it gives us workers so quite untrained in any social work. Though among the numerous American workers there appeared individuals who were not up to the high standard necessary, they were released immediately. We can but witness that in general we have met with the greatest tact from all the members of the Red Triangle Mission, in everything concerning our religious and national ideals. Our feelings as Poles and Catholics were never met with either an unkindly thought or sharp words. On the contrary we certify that the American have given every possible support and have shown the greatest consideration for all religious practices, remembering our free mornings on Sunday and holidays in order to let us attend the Holy Mass. They are always mindful of the dedicating by a priest of every new building; they are careful to have a sacred picture in every Hut; they are observing Lent, forbid dancing in the Huts during Advent and Lent time. They also respect our national holidays doing their best to get a nearer knowledge of our traditions and customs. They read the works of our thinkers so as to know better the mind of our nation; they study our language in order to understand better our needs.

The libraries, courses and lectures are exclusively in Polish hands. We select books, secure lecturers and teach the soldiers. There is absolutely no foundation for any objection that the members of the Mission have a harmful influence on our soldiers. First their slight knowledge of our language does not permit of this. Second there is no Y.M.C.A. Hut where in the personnel the Poles are not in the majority. Enclosed history of the Women's Department will furnish details about the work of the Polish women and their part in the Y.M.C.A. Huts. We want to emphasize here briefly that the motive underlying our whole work done under Y.M.C.A. leadership has been love to our country.

All that we do is in full harmony with the principles of our faith. In our acts there is not a single thought which could not be publicly known. On the contrary we Polish women are proud of these two years of long service with the Y.M.C.A. since being able to know better this Association we have learned to respect it as our social agency. As Poles we are deeply thankful for all it has done for our heroic brothers, sons, and husbands.

We find no proofs which would cast a shadow on the Y.M.C.A. or justify suspicions of proselytizing.

We affirm that we have met no propaganda of this kind for in general the Americans never touch the question of dogmas.

Neither anyone of us nor any soldier in our Huts has ceased to be a loyal Child of the Holy Church. Indeed all argument is superfluous in view of the words spoken here in Warsaw by the General Secretary of the International Y.M.C.A. Dr. Mott who stated several times that the Y.M.C.A. accepts always the spirit of the prevailing Christian faith and therefore here in Poland must be Catholic.

In summing up we repeat once more that we have no reasons to suspect that Y.M.C.A. has secret ambitions.

No one who casts suspicions of any kind on the Y.M.C.A. can furnish proofs compromising the Association.

We call upon the whole Polish public to make closer acquaintance with the work of the Y.M.C.A. and to cease giving expression to unconsidered opinions.

We do believe that this will help to clear away all misunderstandings and the Y.M.C.A. will meet with fully deserved recognition and gratitude.

Wherefore: we Polish women workers of the Y.M.C.A. are resolved to work on under Y.M.C.A. leadership; believing that this service brings help to our fellow-men, and is in accord with the holy traditions of our nations as well as in harmony with the teaching and principles of our Holy Church; mindful that Polish women have ever in the course of our history striven for all that is noble and that brings glory to the immortal spirit of their nation:

Signatures:
    M.R. Dobrowolska (Chief Directress Women's Dept.)
    H. Evert (Secretary Women's Dept.)
    M. Alberg (Directress Library Section)
    B. Mercere (Directress of Artistic Section)
    W. Mlynarska (Directress Students Hut)
    Z. Jarosinska (Directress Hut for Invalids)

H. Brochocka
A. Baczynska
Z. Cywinska
H. Czecz
Z. Czecz
W. Domaniewska
W. Dziewonska
A. Domaniewska
H. Detloff
E. Frankenstein
H. Grudzinska
M. Gorny
W. Kazimierska
J. Kaska
H. Kakolewska
K. Jasienska
M. Licuori
I. Harajewicz
Z. Mieszkowska

A. Moszynska
M. Maurizio
I. Mlynarska
N. Missuna
M. Ostrowska
J. Ropalewska
H. Szwedzinska
J. Siedlecka
J. Strzembosz
T. von Schafnagel
H. Sokolowska
H. Powierza
J. Tanska
K. Wankowicz
H. Tomaszewska
Z. Link
K. Zapalowicz
J. Zaleska
Z. Antonowicz

[Editor—Names are listed as in the original text, with no attempt to alphabetize them or check their spelling.]

1921 Y.M.C.A. Women's Letter from Poland – **381**

Where the Poles Now Dwell

The sections in color (gray) [the original map was in pink] roughly outline the territory now occupied by Poles. In East Prussia, their increase has continued in spite of ruthless measures taken by the German Government. On the Russian side, also, there is a large percentage of Poles in the territory contiguous to Poland proper. The precise boundaries of resurrected Poland have not yet been determined.

AN INDEPENDENT POLAND

Why and How the Ancient Democratic Nation Should Be Resurrected for the Thirty-Five Million Poles Now Under Oppressive Foreign Rule

By

IGNACE JAN PADEREWSKI
(Plenipotentiary of the Polish National Committee in America)

[*Reprinted from* The World's Work, *published by Doubleday, Page and Company, December 1918*]

Although President Wilson has spoken emphatically for an independent and reunited Poland, I think it must be difficult for Americans to understand how deeply his utterances have touched Polish hearts, how profoundly they have stirred our gratitude. You have been free so long I fear you have come to take your freedom somewhat for granted. Can you, who for a century and a half have exercised the elective franchise, realize the unquenchable thirst for liberty that during a century and a half has consumed Poland?

I want to present Poland's democratic claims to your attention before I undertake a narrative of the steps by which she was dismembered: three acts of imperial banditry which, so any historian will tell you, are the blackest on the long criminal calendar of European diplomacy. We have been painted as an unstable and bellicose nation, bordering upon anarchy when left to our own devices; your textbooks, drawn partly from German sources, have depicted us as always spoiling for a fight. And it is true that Poland has done much fighting. She has fought a hundred wars, but not one for conquest. All have been in self-defense, or in defense of justice, of Christianity. In 1241, at the Battle of Lignica, she threw back the Tartar invaders. In 1683, John Sobieski saved Europe from Ottoman dominion. Through five centuries Poland bore the brunt of Turkish arms, until she won the appellation of "the Buckler of Christendom." She has warred often for the liberty of others; and among the illustrious generals who fought for the independence of your own country, the only one who possessed no slaves was a Polish nobleman, Tadeusz Kosciuszko.

Poland has been the cradle of the world's liberalism. She concluded, in 1413, a political union with Lithuania, an act of free union, proclaiming for the first time, in a document of almost evangelical beauty, the brotherhood of man. Two centuries and a half before England achieved a Habeas Corpus Act, three centuries and a half before the French Declaration of the Rights of Man, Poland introduced, in 1430, her famous law, *Neminem captivabimus nisi jure victim**; she was first to provide that no man should be imprisoned unless legally convicted. Her Constitution of 1505 was the world's primary application of a democratic parliamentary system. In 1573, she inaugurated a virtual republic, its chief magistrate elected for life and called a king, but forbidden to lead the militia across the frontier except with the consent of the Senate. And in that very same year, the year, you remember, of St. Bartholomew's Night, the Polish Senate provided freedom for all creeds, the right of every man within its jurisdiction to worship as he chose.

In those days Poland was what America is to-day, a refuge for all men oppressed and persecuted. Your country is a political descendant of the nation which, in 1208, first applied the elective franchise, and, in 1347, established the first complete civil code of Christian Europe.

Poland's enemies have had much to say about the excesses committed by our nobility. There is no need to discuss this at any length, but I may say that with the exception of a few almost feudal families, the Polish nobility was not an aristocratic class, but simply a privileged democracy. The Polish nobility was a vast body of men enjoying all civic and political rights, even some rather mediaeval privileges won by their ancestors or by themselves on battlefields or in other public service. They were electors, voters. Everybody who distinguished himself in war, in statesmanship, in science, or even in art could become a nobleman, a voter. How democratically this was applied some facts and figures will attest: In 1847, in France, at the time of Louis Philippe, out of a nation of twenty-eight millions, there were but 150,000 voters; whereas two hundred years before that, in 1647, Poland had nearly 300,000 voters in a nation of less than eleven millions. In England, before the famous Reform Bill of 1832, 2 per cent. only of the population enjoyed all political rights, while in 1732, 12 per cent. of the Polish population was in complete possession of those rights. And it may be said

---

*This Latin sentence means literally "We will take no one captive unless convicted by law."

further to the credit of our nobility that in the middle of the Eighteenth Century, our landowners of their own initiative began the emancipation of peasants from conditions of serfdom.

This war has been fought to make the world safe for democracy. The cause of Poland's partition lay in her democratic and progressive premiership. The causes cannot be found in any inherent anarchic predilection. There is always a tendency toward anarchy in accomplishing the overthrow of autocratic establishments; but Poland's momentous reforms were accomplished without revolution, without bloodshed, by unanimous vote, in quiet and dignity.

The Polish executives, the kings, were limited in their power by an excessively liberal Constitution, and so were lacking in authority; the nation deprived of a permanent standing army, was an easy prey to predacious neighbors; and her fertile plains, known in ancient times as the granary of Europe, afforded an added temptation to them. But the primary reason was her democratic temper, which aroused the suspicion and fear of near-by feudal despots.

POLAND NOT A SMALL NATION

Notwithstanding the fact that in this war nearly three million Polish-speaking soldiers have been forced into fratricidal combat, driven into battle by German and Austrian and Russian conscription, to fight their cousins and brothers, many persons seem to believe Poland a small nation. They forget the magnitude of its historic domain and the numbers of its people. The Kingdom of Boleslaus the Great (992-1025) stretched from the Baltic Sea to the Carpathians. It included part of Saxony, the whole of Silesia, and stretched almost to Berlin. In 1772, when came the first dismemberment, Poland covered 300,000 square miles, almost 100,000 miles more than the German Empire of to-day. Its population was eleven and a half millions. It ranks, indeed, with Italy as the fifth European nation. Before the outbreak of this war there was a compact mass of 35,000,000 people in Europe speaking the Polish language; and whatever ruler might claim dominion over them, they were one: no mutilation of the national body, no cruelties or oppressions, could dissever the Poles in spirit. They remain to-day one nation in language and in aspirations, despite a century and a half of political slavery, and through all those years the love of liberty has burned with-in them as an inextinguishable flame.

The name of Poland is derived from the word Pole, which in all Slavonic languages means a field, a plain; and it derives from the fact that the country lies in a vast productive plateau of which the River Vistula is the centre, and which has the River Oder on the west and the River Dnieper on the east. This has been the home for centuries of the Poles. In the early days of the Ninth Century, before the eastern Slavonic country had been conquered by the Normans of Roesland

and had received from them the name of Russia, the inhabitants of the country bordered by the rivers Dnieper and Oder and those living in the Vistula and Warta districts were all known under the name of Polanie, Polans. The most ancient of Russia's historical documents, the Chronicle of Nestor, dating from the beginning of the Twelfth Century, as well as the first prominent historian of Russia, Karamazin, agreed that the ancient Poles and the Polans were the same people, speaking the same language.

THE POLES A PEACE-LOVING PEOPLE

They were a kind, soft-hearted, peace-loving people. In the northwestern parts of their large country, while cultivating laboriously their ancestral rather arid soil, they developed, as is always the case where man has to fight Nature, into thrifty, energetic agriculturists; while in the south they remained somewhat indolent and poor, trusting to the extreme fertility of their land. Fond of songs and music, of dances, hospitable to excess, they were leading and easy life, to which their rich and poetic mythology lent great charm and beauty. Very soon, however, this kindly, peace-loving people, surrounded by greedy neighbors, exposed to easy invasion, in order to protect their liberty, to protect their homes, their wives, and children, were compelled to forge weapons, to learn warfare. They learned it quickly and well, and within a short time out of rustic, pastoral tribes, bound by a common danger, they became a real nation, made up of plowmen and warriors. For there could not be a real nation without a people who loved their soil, without a people who knew how to cultivate that soil in peace and how to protect it in war.

Early in the second half of the Tenth Century, under Mieszko the First, her first historical ruler, Poland was called to take her place among the Christian Kingdoms of Europe; but it was given to Mieszko's son, Boleslaus the Great, to unite all Polish lands, all Polish tribes, and to build up a political power of the very highest order.

I have told you that Poland's democratic spirit was at the root of her destruction by uneasy and covetous neighbors. It might not have happened had Poland been isolated, as you were here: she might have escaped had she been unhampered and unassailed in working out her political salvation. But just when the democratic ferment had weakened without solidifying her governmental structure, she fell prey to the unscrupulous Powers about her. Catherine II was on the throne of Russia, and when she set out to enlarge her territory at the expense of Poland, Frederick the Great, the father of Kaisercraft, aided her.

The Empress Maria Theresa of Austria pretended that the spoliation of Poland was extremely distasteful to her, but she was jealous and afraid of Frederick's growing power; and so the time was ripe for the rape of a nation.

A cattle plague in 1770 afforded excuse for invasion. Frederick threw into Poland military forces which he chose to call *cordons sanitaire*, and it was officially explained that they were necessary to prevent a spread of the epidemic. The others followed the same course, and their troops pushed forward until each occupied a prearranged area, selected as its spoil. After the epidemic had subsided, the troops were not withdrawn. They remained in Poland.

PARTITION OF POLAND

Then, on February 17, 1772, the first treaty of partition was signed at St. Petersburg between Catherine and Frederick. Later, they admitted Austria. Russia took Vitebsk, Polotsk and Mscislaw, 1,586 square miles of territory with a population of 550,000; Austria took the greater part of Galicia (but not Cracow), 1,710 square miles, with a population of 816,000; and Prussia took the maritime palatinate (minus Danzig), East Prussia (minus Thorn) and Great Poland as far as the Nitza; and the palatinates of Marienbad and Ermeland; 629 square miles, with a population of 378,000.

They seized one fourth of Poland's territory, one fifth of her population. To the remainder they graciously accorded autonomy, dependent upon their royal favor.

Before the next partition, in 1793, the personnel of the thieving triumvirate altered. Catherine remained, but in Prussia, Frederick William took up his predecessor's policies, and Francis ascended the throne of Austria.

In 1791, King Stanislaus Poniatowski, last of the Poles to rule, brought about the adoption of a liberal constitution and proclaimed religious tolerance. He extended the franchise to the town burghers, prior to that unrepresented in the Diet, and established a cabinet of ministers. Nothing could have displeased Catherine more acutely than this liberalism. She would have preferred anarchy in Poland; and Francis, a weakling, was equally disquieted.

Catherine was at war with Turkey. It seemed no moment for conquest in Poland; but she hoped to embroil the kinsmen, Francis and Frederick William, with revolutionary France, make peace with Turkey, then turn and rend Poland; and in the end that was substantially what happened. For while the armies of Prussia and Austria were being defeated by the democracy of France, Catherine sent her armies again into Poland, and gave battle to a heroic force of 46,000 men under Prince Joseph Poniatowski and Kosciuszko. For a time they stemmed the invasion. The Prussians, fearful lest Catherine would seize territory while they got none, poured into Great Poland; and on September 23, 1793, came the second partition.

Russia took the eastern provinces of Kiev, Minsk, and Bracelaw [*sic, Bracław*] and the greater part of Volhynia, an area of 90,000 square miles, with a population of three millions; Prussia got Dobrzyn, Kujavia and the most of Great Poland, with Thorn and Danzig. Poland remained only one third her original size, with a population of three and one half millions.

Kosciuszko led a revolution in 1794 against the Russians. History has told you how the whole country flamed into revolt, and how it was humiliated. The three enemy Powers rushed their armies into the little Kingdom, crushed and massacred the Poles and burned their dwellings. Catherine's hands were the reddest and so she took the lion's share of the loot. To Austria went Western Galicia and Southern Masovia; to Prussia, Podlachia and the rest of Masovia, with Warsaw; and into Russia's insatiable maw went the remainder.

A FREE POLAND AFTER THE WAR

Out of the welter of this war will come a belated justice for all these wrongs. Russia has been punished. The political system which made possible her depredations has been destroyed, and she can no longer oppose the restoration of Poland. The victorious Allies, we may be sure, will bring the other aggressors to terms. Before Germany had forced the United States into this war, President Wilson made clear his attitude. In his address to the United States Senate on January 22, 1917, he said:

I take it for granted, for instance, if I may venture upon a single example, that statesmen everywhere are agreed that there should be a united, independent, and autonomous Poland, and that henceforth inviolable security of life, of worship, have lived hitherto under the power of governments devoted to a faith and purpose hostile to their own. . . . Any peace which does not recognize and accept this principle will inevitably be upset. It will not rest upon the affections or the convictions of mankind.

After the United States had entered the war, the President reaffirmed his conviction as to Poland. In his address to Congress on January 8th, last, he gave one of his fourteen Articles of Peace as follows:

> XIII. An independent Polish State should be erected which should include the territory inhabited by indisputably Polish populations, which should be assured a free and secure access to the sea, and whose political and economic independence and territorial integrity should be guaranteed by international covenant.

Mr. Lloyd George has expressed similar convictions, and the Versailles Conference has declared that not only Great Britain, but France and Italy, are committed to them.

The interest of Germany demands a weak Poland, surrounded by provinces either directly belonging to Germany, or recognizing Teutonic supremacy. The interests of peace require a large, powerful, and economically independent Poland. This can be attained through a complete union of all provinces once belonging to the Polish crown. Only a Poland with access to the sea through Danzig will be able to maintain direct relations with England, France, and America. Danzig is to us what London is to England. And only with the mines of Silesia, her ancient province, will Poland be able to acquire economic independence of Germany, to support her surplus population and to check excessive emigration. Despite four centuries of Germanization, the Regency of Opeln, Upper Silesia, contains a peasant and workingman population genuinely Polish, indigenous to that soil without a break from prehistoric times, which was, in 1910, a million and a half strong. The people have defeated every effort at denationalization.

An economically independent, self-supporting Poland will constitute a substantial barrier to the Mittel Europa dream of dominion. No other nation stands to win so much from the defeat of the Central Empires. No other nation offers a better guarantee to the future security of Europe. Its liberation is prerequisite to the safety of the world from German greed and aggression. A peace which would leave in Germany's hand any economic whip over Poland, would be a German peace.

Poland should be restored in a manner which would satisfy the needs and wishes of the Polish nation. A new Poland should be a continuation of that which she has been, otherwise she can not find again the ideal which she has in her soul. It has in itself all the elements of vitality and progress, and it is so deeply rooted in the nature of the Polish people that it forms the psychological necessity of their existence. Polish life can not be normal if she lacks the essential elements which have given her breath. The partitions of Poland have not divided the nation. They have created a flagrant contradiction between an artificial state, established by force, and the national conscience.

If one should plan to cut out a certain part of the former Poland to make a new one, if instead of erasing the artificial confines, one should only modify their direction, it would be creating irridentisms which would fatally lead to a new crisis. If we are to have a lasting and durable peace, we must reunite in the new Poland all the Polish lands. It is evident that it would be difficult to construct a Polish state out of territories where there are no Poles. But would it be possible to build a Poland out of lands which have never formed a part of her history, if by some chance, let us suppose, due to a forced immigration, the number of Poles would reach 65 per cent. of the inhabitants?

NUMBER OF POLES INHABITING POLISH LANDS

The correct number of Poles inhabiting Polish lands is generally little known, because in compiling the statistics the interested governments always treated the ethnical problems from a viewpoint of their politics. The following calculations are based upon the only existing authority, the official statistics compiled before the war, and as such they must be accepted with the understanding that they show only the minimum of Polish elements:

I. Russian Partition.

    a. Kingdom of Poland, within the territories outlined by the Congress of Vienna (1815) of 127,684 square kilometers. Total population (including Russian troops): 13,427,180; Poles 10,232,200 (76.46 per cent.); Lithuanians: 336,900; Ruthenians: 374,280; Russians: 137,200; Jews 1,746,600; Germans, 500,000.
    b. Lithuania and White Ruthenia: 6,000,000 Poles.
    c. Ruthenia: 870,000 Poles.
    d. In Russia, the scattered Polish colonies (chiefly in the industrial districts), count approximately 600,000.

The total number of Poles in the Russian partition is 17,702,200.

II. Austrian Partition.

    a. Galicia, consisting of a part of former Little Poland and Red Ruthenia, covers an area of 78,497 square kilometers. The total number of inhabitants is: 8,200,000, composed of Poles, 4,960,000 (61 per cent.); Ruthenians, 320,000 (39 per cent.) [*sic*, 3,200,000?].
    b. Silesia of Cieszyn, with an area of 23,000 square kilometers. Total population; 434,000 with 285,000 Poles, or 65 per cent.
    c. Spisz [now Spiš in northern Slovakia], occupied by the Austrians since 1769, and to-day belonging to Hungary, has 200,000 Poles.
    d. Bukowina, has 36,000 Poles, Bosnia, 12,000 and other Austrian provinces, 24,000 Poles.

The total number of Poles in Austrian partition is 5,417,000.

III. Prussian Partition.

(Compiling the official statistics the Prussian Government employed various methods with the purpose to diminish the figures of the correct number of Poles. The recognition of the Kaszub and Mazurian dialects as belonging to separate nationalities, and other details of registry particularly unfavorable for the Poles, were the chief means of lowering the figures of Poles in the Prussian partition.

(The statistics of primary schools are a trifle more accurate than the figures of the general census, although still unfavorable to the Poles. According to the latest data (1910) the figures of Polish population in the Prussian partition are as follows:)

    a. The Grand Duchy of Posen (annexed by Prussia during the second partition of Poland in 1793) covers an area of 28,996 square kilometers, with a total population of 2,100,000 out of which there are 1,465,000 Poles, or 69.67 per cent. Out of forty-two districts thirty-three have an unquestionably predominant Polish population.

    b. West Prussia (formerly Royal Prussia) was assigned to Prussia by the Congress of Vienna in 1815. The total area is 25,553 square kilometers, with a population of 1,703,500, of which 754,500 (44.29 per cent.) are Poles. Out of twenty-nine districts fourteen have a predominance of Poles.

    c. East Prussia (Ducal Prussia). Total area: 37,000 square kilometers. Population: 543,000. The Poles number 385,000 or 70.9 per cent., with an overwhelming predominance in eight districts out of ten.

    d. Prussian Silesia. Total area: 40,355 square kilometers with a population of 2,208,000, of which 1,548,500, or 70.1 per cent. are Poles. Out of twenty-six districts, eighteen have the Polish majority of population.

    e. In Germany, outside of Polish territory, there live about 600,000 Poles. The major part of them (over 500,000) is concentrated in the industrial districts of Westphalia.

The total number of Poles in the German partition, was, in 1914, 4,751,000. Counting the increase of population from the year 1914 till 1918, we can estimate the total population of Poles in the German partition as 5,000,000.

The minimum figure, compiled by Poland's enemies, gives a total of Polish population in the Russian, Austrian, and German partitions as 25,319,200, but actually it may be accepted as certain that the total is fully thirty-five millions.

It is not to be supposed that all of these thirty-five million Poles will be included within the boundaries of the new state; for although Mr. Wilson's references to an "indisputably Polish population," and to the necessity of an outlet to the sea, have served to underscore those phases of the question, other problems present themselves. Whether we attempt to envisage the New Poland according to linguistic, cultural, economic, geographic, or historic boundaries, we find our path beset by difficulties. To work out the solution there will be, in all probability, some combination of several or all of these factors.

No Pole wishes to transgress the national individuality of the Lithuanians or Ukrainians (Ruthenians), and a scrupulous observance of their best interests may be expected from those who will exercise authority in determining their fate, and the fate of all the new nations which are to arise in Europe out of the ashes of this war. Historic Poland, prior to the partition of 1772, divided itself naturally into two sections; the Kingdom of Poland, with an area about equal to your state of Missouri, and the Grand Duchy of Lithuania; and the latter divided itself into the portions inhabited by the Luthuanians [sic] themselves and that inhabited by the Ruthenians or Ukrainians. So that the problem ahead is of great complexity. Space precludes the discussion of it in detail, but it may be possible to sketch the situation as it exists, for instance, in East Prussia, in Galicia and in those eastern provinces seized by Catherine II.

The original inhabitants of East Prussia were of Lithuanian stock, and were Germanized by the Teutonic Order. The language spoken now in the larger part of the province is German and the province itself is economically dependent on Germany. Its population is but 144 to the square mile and the obedient peasant votes at the behest of the large landowner. Those who preserve any recollection of Lithuanian origin take little interest in public affairs.

The landed proprietors are the German Junkers. This province is the stronghold of the reactionary militarist caste. The conservative extremists in the Prussian House are elected mainly by the spiritless East Prussian serfs—for in reality they are in a state of serfdom. Nowhere has the House of Hohenzollern found stauncher support. Feudal traditions and the feudal viewpoint are undisturbed to-day among the aristocracy of East Prussia, and to deprive this dangerous retrograde class of its power in German affairs, to lop this limb from the German body politic, would be political surgery of the highest order. Until that major operation is performed, we can hardly hope to witness any true democratization of the German system.

Between East Prussia and the main body of the German Empire lies West Prussia, containing Danzig, which is Poland's natural and historic seaport. I think it would not be presumptuous for me to say that West Prussia seems certain to be included in Polish territory, in which event we may expect to see Danzig become once more a flourishing city, and perhaps to achieve a population of a million. German manipulation of the currents of trade is responsible for the city's present decadence.

If, then, West Prussia were to become a part of the Polish state, and East Prussia were to remain under German dominion, it would form an isolated province, without physical contact with the parent, and might constitute a menace to the future peace of Europe. It has been suggested by some that the part of East Prussia which contains the German-speaking population, and is the seat of Königsberg, be united with Poland on a basis of home rule; by others that it be made a small independent republic, connected with Poland by a customs union and amply safeguarded as to its administrative integrity. These are but two of several solutions offered, and the advocates of both would provide that a great land reform be inaugurated, under which the large estates could be colonized by the peasantry.

Eastern Galicia has been the home of a Ruthenian national movement, known also as Ukrainian. Only 25 per cent. of the population of that part of Galicia is Polish-speaking, but the Ruthenians, in spite of their numerical strength, constitute less than 5 per cent. of the element engaged in professions and trades, aside from small farming. The natural resources of the province are great. In its western section are rich coal fields and salt mines, and in the eastern are oil fields and deposits of potassium salts. The question of the disposition of this territory is so complicated by economic and political issues that I can do no more here than indicate their nature.

The eastern provinces of Kovno, Vilna, Grodno, Minsk, Mohylov, Vitebsk, Volhynia, Polotsk, and Kiev are economically and socially the most backward of ancient Poland. They have an area of 180,911 square miles, and represent the part seized by Russia, other than the Kingdom of Poland. Their population is various. Ruthenians, White Ruthenians, Poles, and Lithuanians will be found there, and the most recent estimates of the Polish element put it at six millions; but no acceptable figures as to the other elements are at hand, because the Russian census has always been untruthful.

For a long time Russia regarded these provinces as Polish, but after 1830 she made every effort to stamp out Polish influences there, and to prevent the speaking of the Polish language, which had been used before that in the schools and in the University of Vilna, and for administrative purposes. As to the disposition to be made of this territory, some favor the organization of a separate state from the Northern Lithuanian section, and its union on a home rule basis with Poland. It is impossible to predict what the decision of those at the peace table will be. I have mentioned some of the possibilities only in the hope of acquainting you with the problems which are to be a part of the task of remaking the map of Central Europe.

I think it hardly worth while to describe the farce of Polish restoration manoeuvred by the Central Powers in the hope of making our soil a recruiting ground. It is enough to say that they failed in their schemes.

POLAND TO-DAY

What is Poland to-day? It is a vast desert, an immense ruin, a colossal cemetery. Precious works of art, valuable books, documents, and manuscripts, all the priceless proofs of our ancient, thousand-year-old culture, have been confiscated, as the operation is diplomatically called when it is performed by an overwhelming, collective force. Several large cities have been spared, preserved for the comfort of our united guests. But on the tremendous battlefront, extend-sing from the Baltic Sea to the Southern slopes of the Carpathian Mountains, all of Russian Poland, almost the whole of Austrian and even a portion of Prussian Poland have been totally ruined. Three hundred towns, two thousand churches, twenty thousand villages are no more. An area equal in size to your states of Illinois, Pennsylvania, New York, and Maine together has been laid waste.

For what could remain of a country where in many districts those huge armies of millions of men were moving forward and backward for eighteen months? Eighteen months of continuous fighting, eighteen months of incessant danger, eighteen months of uninterrupted anguish and pain, imposed upon an innocent nation! Millions of homeless peasants, of unemployed workmen, of humble Jewish shopkeepers, have been driven into open wastes. Millions of bereaved parents, of breadless, helpless widows and orphans are still wandering about in the desolate land, hiding in woods or in hollows, happy if they find an abandoned trench and in that trench, next to the body of a fallen fighter, some decaying remnants of soldier's food.

The Polish National Committee has a message for all Americans: Help us to break forever the chains which shackle and humiliate an ancient and highly civilized nation, a nation which has been for centuries one of the vital organs of progress and humanity. Each of you can help. Then the old Polish Republic, which has been murdered by three autocracies, will rise again, resurrected by the generosity of American democracy.

DOWÓDZTWO OKRĘGU GENERALNEGO POMORZE.

Grudziądz, dnia 29. kwietnia 1920.

ROZKAZ Nr. 17.

ŻOŁNIERZE!

Nadszedł czas Waszego powrotu do Ameryki, kończy się Wasza służba w szeregach walczącej Ojczyzny. Dobrowolnie przed kilku laty przebyliście ocean, by bić się o Jej wolność! Spełniliście chlubnie i uczciwie obowiązek wasz święty wobec Matki-Polski.

Na różnych frontach — w sojuszu z wolnymi ludami Zachodu — składaliście swój udział ofiar, walk i trudów, by wespół z żołnierzami starej Polski zdobyć narodowi niepodległość państwową i zabezpieczyć świat przed fizyczną przemocą pruską.

Spotyka Was też nagroda dla żołnierza polskiego najwyższa; dziś patrzycie własnemi oczyma na spełnienie się naszych najdroższych marzeń, na Polskę wolną, wielką i pełną chwały.

Dzisiaj w starych i zniszczonych mundurach opuszczacie ziemię ojczystą. Miłująca Was Polska, splądrowana przez zaborców, wyniszczona długą wojną, nie może wyposażyć swoje drogie dzieci tak, jakby tego z całego serca pragnęła i jak na to zasłużyliście.

Żołnierze, ten wytarty mundur, który zabieracie ze sobą, jest dzisiaj, dzięki męstwu żołnierza polskiego, mundurem sławy, — z tych łachmanów wołają głośno Wasze świetne czyny wojenne!

Niech pochylą się czoła Polaków amerykańskich przed powracającymi synami, którzy dla siebie nie zdobyli niczego prócz łachmanów, Polskę natomiast przystroili w purpurowy płaszcz Wolności.

Staliście się nowym węzłem łączącym silnie naszą emigrację amerykańską ze starą Ojczyzną. Wiem, że szerzyć będziecie w Ameryce miłość i przywiązanie do Polski i że zawsze, gdzie zajdzie potrzeba, staniecie silnie w obronie Matki-Polski.

Nasze serdeczne uczucia towarzyszyć Wam będą na dalszych drogach życia, a pamięć, że przyłożyliście rękę do odbudowy wolnej Rzeczypospolitej Polskiej, będzie dla Was i dla Waszych rodzin nazawsze źródłem zasłużonej dumy i niech Wam towarzyszy przez wszystkie dni Waszego życia.

Bądźcie pewni wiecznej wdzięczności Ojczyzny! I jak dotąd w szeregach, tak i na przyszłość, choć rozdzieleni oceanem, zbierać się będziemy pod Jej sztandarem i jednym porozumiewać okrzykiem:

WOLNA POLSKA NIECH ŻYJE!

Generał i Dowódca.

Odczytać przed frontem powracających do Ameryki oddziałów.

Za zgodność:
(—) **Matyasik**,
podporucznik.

COMMAND OF THE POMERANIA GENERAL DISTRICT

Grudziądz, 29 April 1920

ORDER NO. 17

SOLDIERS!

The time has come for your return to America; your service in the ranks of your fighting Fatherland has ended. Voluntarily you crossed the ocean several years ago to battle for its freedom! You have fulfilled your duty to your Mother Poland honestly and gloriously.

On various fronts — in alliance with the free peoples of the West — you have made your contribution of sacrifice, combat and labor, so that together with the soldiers of old Poland you could gain for our people national independence, and protect the world from the physical violence of Prussia.

And so the highest reward for a Polish soldier awaits you; today you see with your own eyes the fulfillment of our fondest dreams, a Poland free, great and glorious.

Today in old and worn out uniforms you leave your ancestral land. A Poland that loves you, plundered by the partitioners and devastated by long war, cannot outfit its dear children as it would wish with all its heart, and as they deserve.

Soldiers, thanks to the valor of the Polish soldier, this torn uniform that you wear is today a uniform of glory—from these tatters your magnificent military deeds cry aloud!

Let the heads of American Poles bow before their returning sons, who gained nothing for themselves but rags, yet arrayed Poland in the purple mantle of Freedom.

You have become a new link powerfully uniting our American emigrants with their old Fatherland. I know that in America you will spread love for and devotion to Poland, and that always, when the need arises, you will stand strong in defense of Poland, your Mother.

Our heartiest wishes will accompany you on your life's further paths, and the memory of how you raised your hand to rebuild a free Republic of Poland will always be for you and your families a source of earned pride, and may it accompany you all the days of your life.

Be sure of the Fatherland's eternal gratitude! And till now in the ranks, so in the future, though separated by an ocean, we will gather under Its standard and cry out as one:

LONG LIVE FREE POLAND!

[Illegible signature] General and Commander

To be read aloud before the ranks of units returning to America.

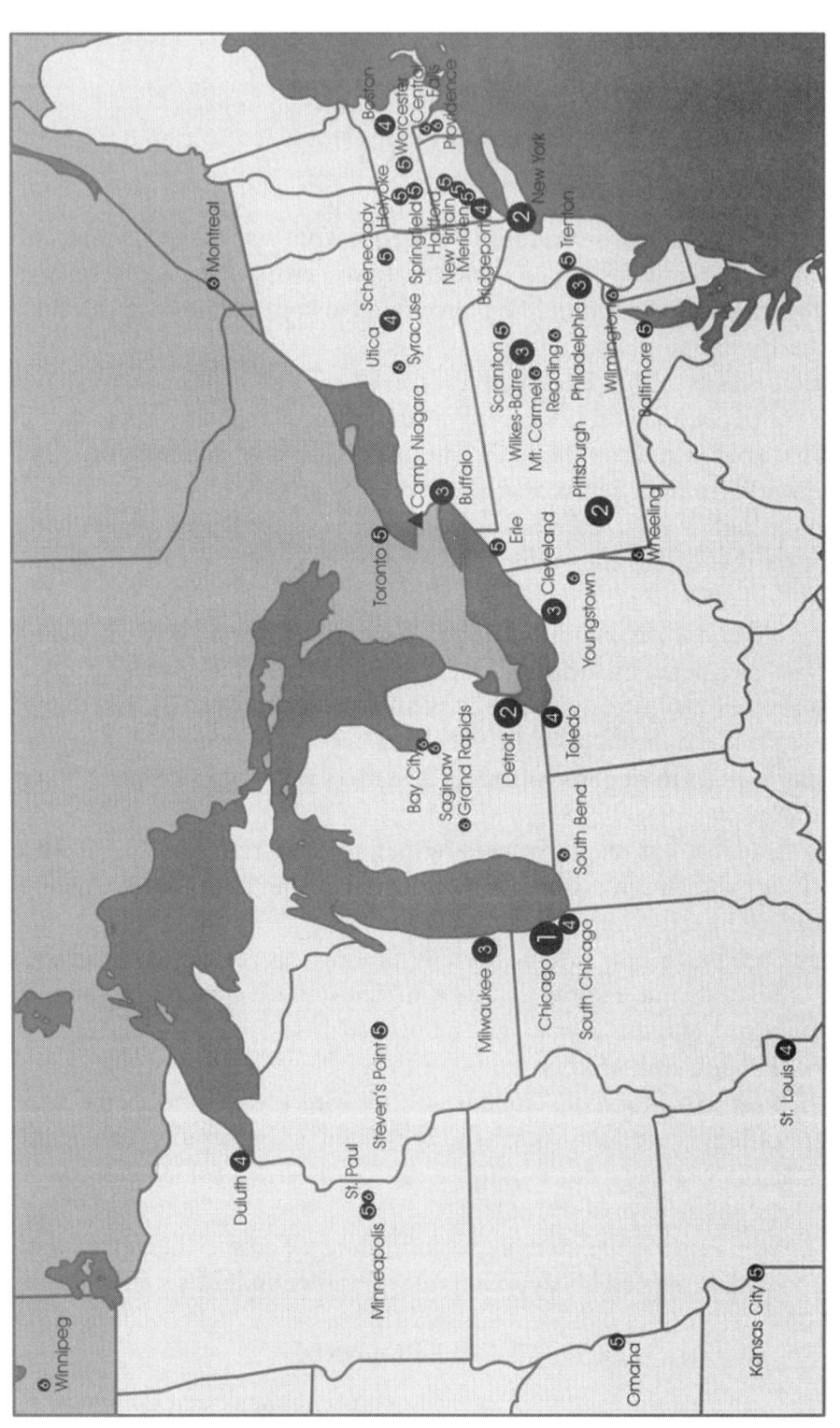

LIST OF HALLER'S ARMY/ POLISH ARMY IN FRANCE RECRUITMENT CENTERS IN NORTH AMERICA

Ctr #	City	State	Approx. # of recruits	Dates Center Was Operational
1	Milwaukee	WI	1395	October 1917 - February 1919
2	Chicago	IL	5740	October 1917 - February 1919
3	Detroit	MI	2825	October 1917 - February 1919
4	Cleveland	OH	1274	October 1917 - February 1919
5	Buffalo	NY	1818	October 1917 - February 1919
6	Pittsburgh	PA	2367	October 1917 - February 1919
7	Wilkes Barre	PA	1077	October 1917 - February 1919
8	New York	NY	3250	October 1917 - February 1919
9	Boston	MA	880	October 1917 - February 1919
10	Bridgeport	CT	854	October 1917 - January 1919
11	Schenectady	NY	214	October 1917 - February 1918
12	Winnipeg	MAN	51	October 1917 - July 1918
13	Baltimore	MD	264	October 1917 - February 1919
14	Erie	PA	453	October 1917 - January 1919
15	Grand Rapids	MI	65	November 1917 - May 1918
16	Hartford	CT	434	October 1917 - October 1918
17	Holyoke	MA	386	October 1917 - November 1918
18	Kansas City	KS	113	November 1917 - December 1918
19	Meriden	CT	178	October 1917 - August 1918
20	Minneapolis	MN	299	November 1917 - February 1919
21	Philadelphia	PA	1341	October 1917 - February 1919
22	Reading	PA	57	November 1917 - November 1918
23	Saginaw	MI	22	November 1917 - April 1918
24	Scranton	PA	135	November 1917 - June 1918
25	South Bend	IN	31	November 1917 - February 1918

26	St. Louis	MO	611	November 1917 - February 1919
27	St. Paul	MN	49	November 1917 - April 1918
28	Stevens Point	WI	290	November 1917 - June 1918
29	Syracuse	NY	73	November 1917 - February 1918
30	Toledo	OH	506	October 1917 - February 1919
31	Wilmington	DE	96	October 1917 - February 1918
32	Worcester	MA	160	October 1917 - December 1918
33	Bay City	MI	61	December 1917 - May 1918
34	Duluth	MN	635	November 1917 - November 1918
35	Youngstown	OH	57	November 1917 - July 1918
36	Mt. Carmel	PA	47	November 1917 - January 1918
37	Omaha	NE	176	November 1917 - January 1919
38	Providence	RI	94	November 1917 - September 1918
39	Toronto	ONT	255	November 1917 - January 1919
40	Wheeling	WV	78	November 1917 - October 1918
41	New Britain	CT	139	November 1917 - November 1918
42	South Chicago	IL	635	November 1917 - November 1918
43	Utica	NY	623	January 1918 - February 1919
44	Montreal	QUE	54	March 1918 - November 1918
45	Trenton	NJ	175	January 1918 - November 1918
46	Central Falls	RI	29	September 1918 - December 1918
47	Springfield	MA	427	January 1918 - February 1919
*	Camp Niagara	ONT	163	October 1917 - January 1919
**	Unidentified		311	

[The number of recruits is the best estimate possible at this time. There are some duplicates, some men are missing, and some recruits are listed in more than one recruiting center. —P. S.V.]

APPENDIX — TROOP SHIPS THAT BROUGHT *HALLERCZYCY* TO AND FROM EUROPE

Antigone

Norddeutscher Lloyd Line. Built as Neckar *by Tecklenborg, launched December 1900. Served as Boxer Rebellion troopship for Germany 1901, seized by U.S. in Baltimore April 6, 1917, renamed* Antigone. *Returned to Eastern European immigrant trade after World War I, scrapped in Baltimore September 1927.*

Chicago

Built at Penhoët, St. Nazaire. Launched in 1907 and completed for transatlantic service 1908, Le Havre to New York. Originally constructed with accommodations only for 2nd- and 3rd-Class passengers. Scrapped at St. Nazaire in 1936. This ship carried Haller Army troops from New York to France in 1918.

President Grant

Hamburg-American Line - Built by Harland and Wolff, Belfast. Launched as Servian, *completed as* President Grant, *August 8, 1907. Interned in New York August of 1914. Seized as U.S. Navy troopship April 6, 1917, served as troop and hospital ship World War II, scrapped 1952.*

Princess Matoika

Hamburg-American Line - Built as the Kiautschou, *maiden voyage December 1900. 1904 renamed* Princess Alice. *Interned in Manila August 1914, seized by U.S. Shipping Board and renamed* Princess Matoika *April 6, 1917. Renamed* President Arthur *1922, and* City of Honolulu *1927, scrapped 1933.*

46 LE HAVRE. — Compagnie Générale Transatlantique " Le Niagara ". — LL.

S.S. Niagara

Built in 1908 by Atel & Ch. de La Loire, St. Nazaire, France as the Corse *for Europe to South America, South Africa and Asia migration. The ship was purchased by the CGT French Lines in 1910 and renamed the* Niagara. *It was 9614 tons, having twin screws, two masts and one funnel. Provided service after the war as an immigration ship from Poland to South America until scrapped in 1931. The Niagara hit an iceberg April 17, 1912, only two days after the Titanic collided with the same ice field.*

406 – Haller's Polish Army in France

Above: a card showing the Rochambeau. Below: the message on the other side. See page 407 for more on this.

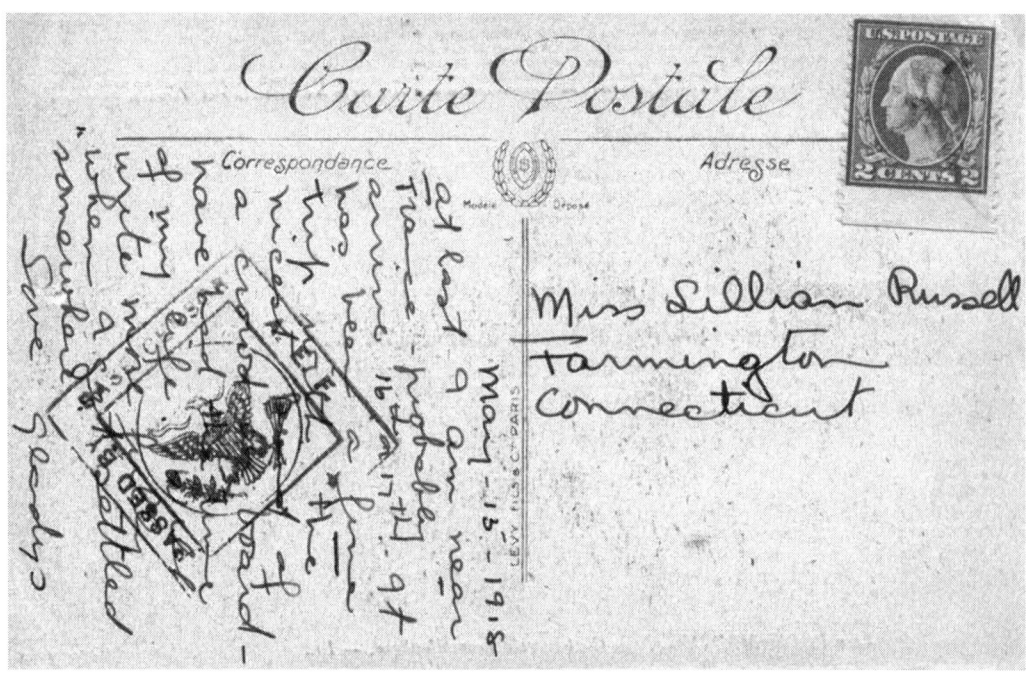

Rochambeau

Built for the CGT Line by Penhoët, St. Nazaire, 1911. Maiden voyage Le Havre to New York September 16, 1911. Originally designed with only accommodations for 2nd, 3rd, and steerage class traffic from Europe to America. 1915 Bordeaux to New York, returning to Le Havre to New York service 1918. Refitted in 1926 and scrapped in 1934.

AEF censored message on reverse of card:

Miss Lillian Russell
Farmington, Connecticut

May 15, 1918

At last I am near France - probably arrive 16th or 17th. It has been a fine trip with the nicest (?) of a crowd on board - have had the time of my life. Will write more fully when I get settled somewhere,

    Love Gladys

It appears Gladys was traveling on an eastbound U.S. troop transport in May 1918 and was destined to help out in France. It is unsure if this particular voyage carried any Hallerczycy.

THE EMERGENCE OF THE POLISH ARMY IN FRANCE

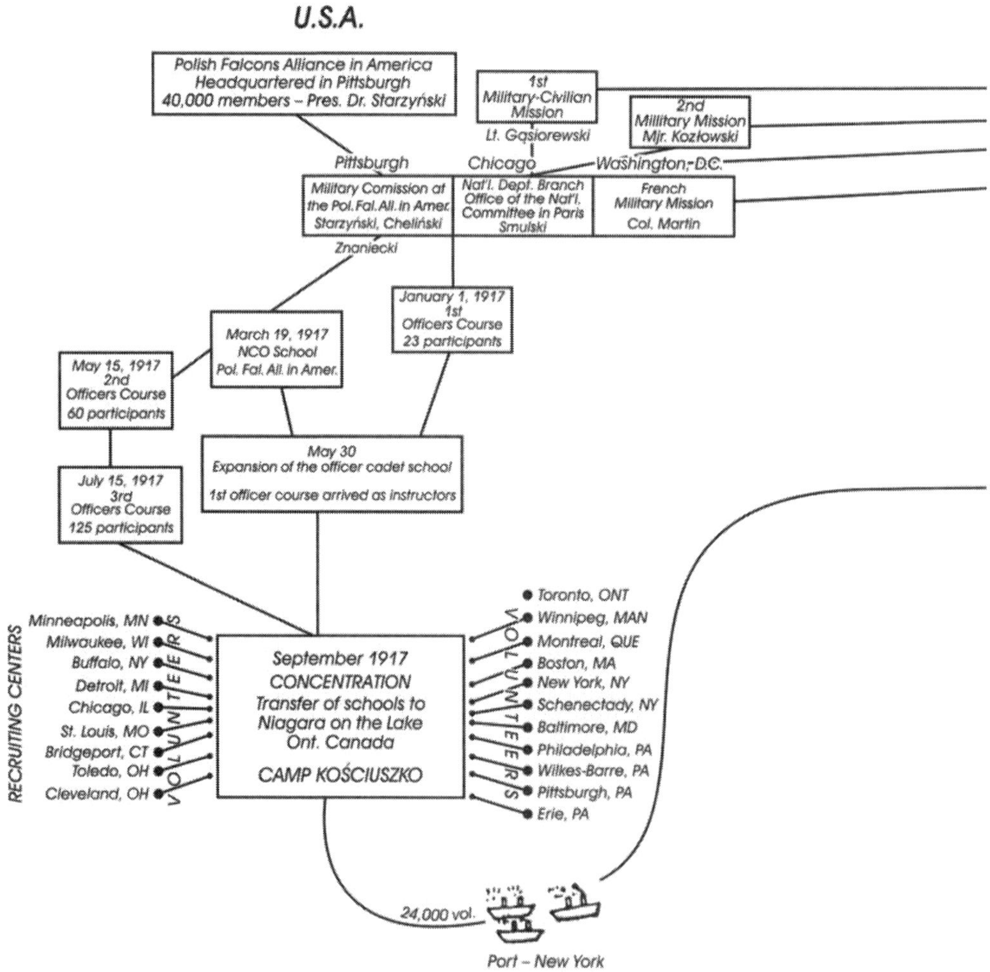

APPENDIX: EMERGENCE OF THE POLISH ARMY IN FRANCE – **409**

Translated and adapted from **WETERAN** Magazine, March 1963
(SWAP)

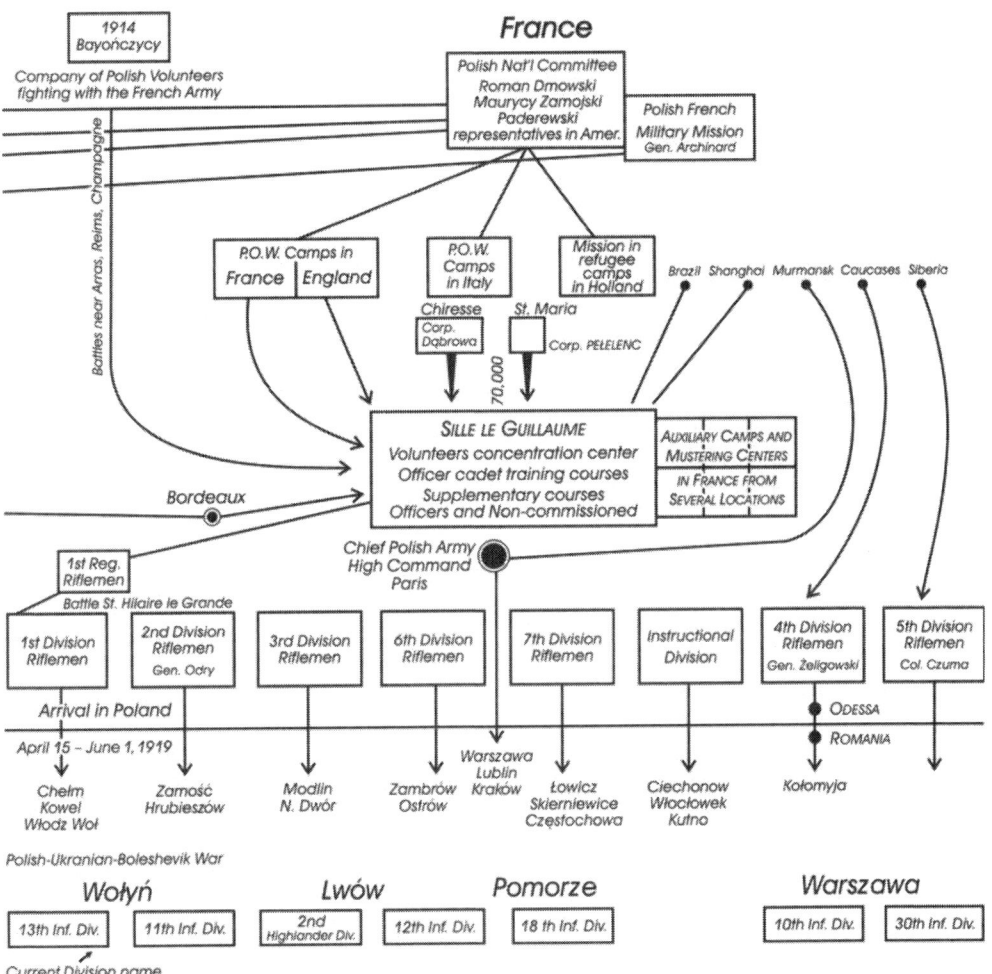

Index to Names of Persons and Places and Foreign Terms Found in the Text

This index is intended to help the reader locate information about specific persons and places, and explanations of foreign terms, mentioned in the various sections of this book. Since these sections were written by different persons at different times and under different circumstances, and do not always spell names consistently, an index of this sort will surely help draw the many different threads together to form a coherent whole.

Proper names are generally spelled as they were in the text, whether correctly or not; but when names were spelled different ways in different places, I attempted to indicate the standard spelling, if I could determine it with reasonable certainty, as well as the variants. When Polish names appeared in English-language text without diacritical marks, I added those marks only if I could verify the correct Polish spelling from another source. Unfortunately, that was not always possible. I prefer to spell Polish names with *ogonek* and *kreska* and *kropka*; but it is never a good idea to "correct" primary sources.

It seemed pointless to repeat here the long lists of surnames given in Joseph A. Borkowski's "City of Pittsburgh's Part in Formation of Polish Army: World War I 1917-1920," on pages 41-43 and on pages 52-70. Similarly, I have not repeated the lists given at the end of the regimental histories, on pages 178-185, pages 224-226; and pages 256-258. If searching for an individual's surname, please remember to look there, as well.

I also chose not to repeat the long list of place names presented in the index on page 290-297; but it would be wise to refer to that list as well as to this index, especially for help with the various forms those names can take in Polish, Russian, Ukrainian, etc. The "Aleksandrja" mentioned on page 198 is probably the same place as "Aleksandrya" on page 240, "Aleksandryja" on page 222, and "Aleksandrya" on page 291—but without further information it's impossible to be certain. Many, many places in central and eastern Europe have the same names, or very similar ones. It would be misleading to tell researchers they are the same place if it turns out they're not! Better to give each spelling separately, and let the individual researcher settle the matter to his or her own satisfaction.

The same logic applies to people's names. The Lt. E. Dickie mentioned on page 312 is almost certainly the same "Lt. Dickie" on page 329; but I listed them separately anyway. Well-meaning authors have often confused, rather than helped, when they made changes that were "obvious." I've found it best to let individual researchers decide for themselves what is obvious.

In this index, numbers in regular Roman type indicate the name is mentioned in the text somewhere on that page. Page numbers printed in bold italic typeface indicate that the name in question appears in a caption to a photograph on that page.

Abczynski, R. S. 39
Adamczak, 1st Lt. 213
Adamczak, L. Z. 29, 97-**99**, 118
Adamczak, Miss Helen (Pawlak) 38
Adamek, 2nd Lt. 167
Adampol 243
Adams, Ohio 41
Adrian Helmet 4, 10
Aeolian Building, New York 357
Alberg, M. 379
Albrecht 97
Albrycht, A. ***93***
Albrycht, W. 29, 98-**99**

Aleksandrja 198
Aleksandrya 240, 291
Aleksandryja 222
Alexander I of Russia 23
Allegheny County 71
Allegheny County Court 48, 71
Alliance College 11, ***20***, 27, 30, 100, ***117***
Alma, Miss 341
Alpine Riflemen 160
Alsace 16, 163, 165, 238, 305
Alski, Victor L. 26
Altoona, PA 40
Ambridge, PA 41, 47

Ambronay 138
Ambukowa 254
American Division 271
American Red Cross 147-148, 317, 333
Andrejewski, Madam 338, 346
Andrejewski, Mrs. Frank 346
Andruskiewicz, Lt. P. 106, 223
Andruszówka 212, 214
Annopol 200
Annówka 170, 213
Antoniny 304
Antonowicz, Z. 380
Antonówka 254, 284
Arc de Triomphe 192
Arcadia, PA 41
Archinard, General *123*, 124, 126-127, 129, *142*, 157-158, 189, 232, 235, 267
Armia Hallera 11, 15
Armia Polska we Francyi 11, 15
Armistice Day 11, 16-17, 143, 326
Armstrong, Mayor Joseph 31
Arras 155, 266
Arthur, Prince of Connaught 318
Ascher, Elizabeth C. 309, *332*, 333, 342, 344-346
ataman 227, 239
Atel and Ch. de La Loire **405**
Australia 4
Avricourt 165, 194
Awratyn 203, 206, 241
Babcia's house 9
Babi 9
Baczynska, A. 380
Bailey, Colonel 370
Bajer, Capt. 138
Bajer, Col. Michal 203, 241-244, 284
Bajończyk (plural *Bajończycy*) 154-157, 172, 185, 232-233, 266
Baltic Sea 306, 394
Baltimore 401
Baranie Perytoki 196
Baranowka 201, 204-205
Baranowski 51
Barchaczów (Barchaczew) 220, 285-286
Barnesboro, PA 40, 41
Baron, Rev. A. 40
Barry, Major 310
Bartek the Conquerer (Bartek Zwycięzca) 84
Bartman, A. 102, 161

Bartmański, Jan 35, 90, **93**, ***101***-103, ***109***, 116-***117***
Barton, Ohio 41
Bartosz 162
Baseball 349
Baśkiewicz, F. 106
Basowski, M. 106
Bastille Day 143
Batków 173
Bauer, F. 102, 161
Bayon, France 164, 166, 236, 238
Bayonne, France 134, 154-155, 232, 266
Bazalia 278
Bazalja 172, 249
Beauchamp 322
Beaver Falls, PA 41
Beckett, Mr. 334, 338, 346
Bednarko, Miss Alexandra Sophia 44
Bednarz, J. J. 102
Belarus 238, 240
Belfort 141
Bellona 211
Belvedere 365
Bełz 282
Berdyczów 201, 207, 211, 248, 274
Berecki, Col. Ryszard 136, 191-192, 199, 269
Beresteczko 167, 279
Berezina 353
Berezna 175
Bereźne 199
Berezyna 231
Berlin 87, 94, 385
Bernacki, Mr. 336
Bernard 197
Bernard, General 163, 194, 198, 240, 270-271
Berthonval 155
Bezerski, Mr. 346
Biała Cerkiew 273-275
Białas, F. 106
Białykamień 217
Biczowa 169
Bielów 198
Biernacki, Capt. of Horse, S.G. 211
Biłka Szlachecka 217-218, 281-282
Bilmin, Capt. 211-212, 222-223
Birstein, S. 39
Biskupiczki Male 254
Bismarck, Otto von 23

Blacha, S. 106
Blaine, OH 41
Błękitna Armia 15
Błudów 196
Blue Army 9, 11, 15, 270
Blue Division, The 261-289
Bobrowski, 1st Lt. 208, 210
Bobrowski, Major Stanislaw 187
Boche 137, 371, 374
Boer War 326
Bogucki, J. 29, 98
Bogusław 304-305
Boguszewski, F. 29, **93**
Boh River 243
Bohdanówka 248
Bois de Boulogne street 144
Bois de Raquette Forest, Battle of 160-161
Boleslaus (Bolesław) the Great 385, 386
Bolshevik 11, 17, 35, 47, 51, 90, 166, 209-210, 240-241, 246, 248, 255, 271-273, 275-278, 281-282, 289, 303, 306, 349, 351, 353-354, 367-369, 372, 377
Book of Golden Deeds 343
Boratyn 254
Bordeaux (France) 122, **123**, 157, 266, **407**
Borderland Riflemen 11, 149
Borek, S. 102
Borkowski, Joseph A. 18, 21, 71
Borkowski, Judge Edward 18, 21
Borowiak, Mrs. Dr. 344, 346
Borowicz, Wiktor 39
Borysov 353
Boston, MA 16, 157
Boswell PA 41
Bouillon, Franklin 113, 115
Bouzy 138
Boxer Rebellion **401**
Bożanka 254
"*Boże coś Polskę*" 132, 265, 322, 327
Bracław 387
Braddock, PA 38, 41
Branford, Major **111**
Bratałów 203, 241
Bratuszewski, S. B. 106
Brazil 11, 15, 189, 232, 305
Brażyńce 276
Brest, France 50, 157, 190
Bretagne 322 (*see also* Brittany)
Bridgeport, CT 16

Brienne-La-Château 50, 348, 358
Brieuc 360
Brittany 356, 358 (*see also* Bretagne)
Brochocka, H. 380
Bródek 220, 285, 286
Brodów 200
Brody 176, 216-217, 250, 279
Brody, County of 300
Broniki 176, 198
Brooklyn, NY 338
Brown, Mrs. Charles 341
Brown, N.H.C. 312
Brudek (Bródek?) 286
Brzesc 303
Brzeziński, B. 106
Brzoza, Pvt. Józef 209
Brzozów (in Galicia) 260
Bubacz, Jozef F. 26
Bubacz, Lt. Frank **25**
Bubnów 205
Bucholtz, Leopold 26
Buckler of Christendom 384
Budapest 302
Budionny, Semion Mikhailovich (this surname appears in various sources as *Budenny, Budienny, Budyonny, etc.*) 130, 169-171, 173-174, 211-212, 214, 217-222, 245-255, 271-275, 279-289
Budinkova, Marie 9
Budziak, L. 106
Budziskami 51
Buffalo, NY 16, 43, 49, 89-90, 115, 318, 326, 329, 333-335, 337-338, 341-345, 356
Bug River 175, 217, 221, 254, 288, 307, 370
Buhryń 200
Bukowina 390
Bukowinski 303
Burgoyne, Major Henry 345
Busk 279
Butlak, S.A. 106
Butler's Barracks 16, 326
Butowce 172, 277
Byra, Michalina 18
Byzowicz, Sgt. Jacob **25**
C.A.D.C. *see* Canadian Army Dental Corps
Caen 358
Calvados 347
Cambridge Springs, PA 11, **20**, 27, 30, 90, 100-101, 113, 117, 330

Camp Borden, ONT 4, 10, 11, 16, 103, 107, 109, *112*-113, 115-116, 310, 328, 330
Camp Chermont 183
Camp de Mailly 130 (*see also* Camp Mailly)
Camp Dix, NJ 47, 52
Camp Kościuszko 11, 49, 263, 333
Camp Mailly 235
Camp Meade, MD 47
Camp Niagara 15, 263
Camp St. Quentin 50, 235
Camp St. Tanche, Champiegnie Front 50
Camp Upton, NY 45
Campbell 326
Canadian Army Dental Corps (C.A.D.C.) 78
Canadian Officer's Training Corp (C.O.T.C.) 4, 18, 97, 98, **99**, 100-101, 104, 106-107, 109, 111-113, 118
Capdepont, General *142*
Canonsburg, PA 41
Carls Rite Hotel Toronto 96
Carnegie, PA 41
Carnegie Library, Pittsburgh, Lawrenceville, Oakland Branches 49
Carnochan, Janet **324**, 325, 341, 345
Carpathians 367, 371, 375, 394
Carter, Mr. (of the YMCA) 347, 356, 359, 362, 364
Caserbe 360
Casille-le-Guillaume 358
Catherine II 386-388, 392
Cebrów 250
Central Council of Polish Organizations 21, 49, 71
Centre d'Instruction Divisionaire (C.I.D.) 138, 164, 191, 199
centre-Chaiton 160
CGT French Lines **405**, **407**
Chalonne sur Marne 268
Chalons 348, 358
Châlons-sur-Marne 183
Chambers, Captain 375
Champagne (region of France) 11, 16, 50, 130, 134, 138-139, 141, 155, 162-165, 177, 235, 262, 268-270, 305, 348
Champs Élysées 192
Charleroi, PA 41
Châteauneuf sur Loire 191
Châteaux-Thierry 158
Chaumont 361

Chełm 51, 166, 194, 270
Chelmszczyzna (the Chełm region) 303
Ches Lee 361
Cheutonouf 50
Chicago, IL 4, 9, 16, 19, 24, 35, 37, 101, 116, 118-121, 150, 157, 186, 228, 244, 338, 342, 356
Chief of the Purchasing Mission in Paris 148
Children's Shelter of St. Catharines 339
Chmielewka 278
Chmielewski, Capt. 234
Chmielnik 244-245, 249
Cholmondeley 322
Chomora 200
Chomory sector 227
chorąży (Chief Warrant Officer) 155, 226
Chorłupy 197
Chronicle of Nestor 386
Chrycόw 276
Chwałkowski, Lt. Lucjan 30, 98-**99**, **134**, 159-160
Chwastów 212
Chwastyk, J. 102
Ciapa, J. 106
C. I. D. see *Centre d'Instruction Divisionaire*
Ciecierski, 1st Lt. Wacław 106, 243
Cieślicki, A. 106
Cieszczyk 322
Cieszyn (*German name* Teschen) 302, 367, 390
Cincinnatus, Order of 307
Ciszałowicz, Pvt. 193
citrons (French slang for "grenades") 137
City of Marseilles see *SS City of Marseilles*
Claridge, PA 41
Clarksburg, WV 41
Clemenceau, Premier 84, 124-125, 305
Cleveland, OH 16, 261, 346
Coblenz 364
Commander of the Chief Riflemen's Association 154
Commandor of the Italian Crown 307
Conemaugh, PA 41
Congress of Vienna 390-391
Connellsville, PA 40, 46
Constance 343
Cornebise, Alfred E. 350
Cossacks 170, 213, 231, 247-248, 253-254, 271, 273-274, 281, 286-289

Cossacks, Don 221
Council of State 302
Councils of Colonels 303
Coyne, A.J. 341
Crabtree, PA 44
Cracow *see* Kraków
Crescent, OH 41
Crevachamp 50
Croix Charpenters sub-sector 193
Croix de Guerre 134, 155, 161-162, 185, 226, 348, 362
Cross "De la Victoire" 258
Cross of Commander of "Polonia Restituta" 309
Cross of Valor *(Krzyż walecznych)* 184, 226, 258, 307
Cud nad Wisłą (Miracle on the Vistula) 307
Cudnów 201, 203
Curie, Marie Skłodowska 71
Curzytek, A. 38, 41
Cwiklinski, Stanislaw 39
Cybulski, Lt. 138
Cygnarowicz-Lewandowska, Mrs. Heromina 49
Cywinska, Z. 380
Czaban, W.A. 106
Czaczkowski, B. 106
Czajczynce 249
Czajkowski, W. 106
Czapla, Pvt. Baltazar 253
Czaritza (ship) 190
Czarny Ostróg 277
Czarny Ostrów 249
Czartonja 204
Czartorja 204
Czartowczyk 219
Czartowo 283
Czartowska Skala 218, 282
Czaruków 239
Czechowski, Sergt. 346
Czecz, H. 380
Czecz, Z. 380
Czeremoszne 302
Czerniawka 214
Czernica 242
Czerniszyn 221
Cześniki 174, 285, 286-287
Częstochowa 216, 302, 374
Czestochowa, Our Lady of 329

Czunów 221
Czyżewka 223
Czyzykow 173
Dąbrowa 253
Dąbrowski, J. 106, 194
Dąbrowski, Major Jerzy 229
Dabrowski's mazurka 266
Danzig (in Polish *Gdańsk*) 259, 305-306, 341, 353, 364, 372, 387, 388, 389, 392 (*see also* Gdańsk)
Daughters of Liberty, PWA 44
Davis, D.A. 347, 349, 356, 358-359, 362, 373-374
de Hallenburg Haller 298-300
de la Plaine sub-sector 193
De Latoun, Capt. 218
Debald, J. **39**
Debald, Jan 39
Dęblin 174, 306
Defenders of Lwów 17
Degrand, Baron **142**
Dekowski, Rev. Jan J. 46, **46**
Demidówka 167
Denikin, Anton Ivanovich 169, 195, 199, 201, 211, 241, 245, 272-273
Derażne 240
Deraźnia 277
d'Esperey, General Franchet 130, 158
Detloff, H. 380
Detroit, MI 16, 89, 94, 95, 101, 157, 346, 356
Devonshire, Duke of 318
Diatkowce 271
Dickie, Lt. E. 312, 329
Die-Nord, St. 236
Dienville 192, 235-236
Dilenjus, Capt. of Horse 204-205
Distinguished Service Medal 307
Division Training Center (C.I.D.) 191, 199
Dluski, Prof. 146
Dmowski, Minister of War 235
Dmowski, Roman 15, 87, 95-97, 125-127, 130, 138, 141-**142**, 157, 192, 301, 305
Dnieper River 385-386
Dobrowolska, M.R. 379
Dobrzyn 388
Dolhalevka 170
Dołżek 212-213
Dom Polski, Buffalo 337-338
Domachowska, Mrs. J. W. 44

Domachowska, Mrs. Jadwiga 44
Domachowski, Jan 39
Domaniewska, A. 380
Domaniewska, W. 380
Dombrowski 322
Dombrowski, A. 106
Dombrowski, K. 102
Domfront 360
Dominican Republic 84
Donora, PA 41
Doumergue, Senator 158
Dowbor-Muśnicki, General Józef 87, 304
Drączkowski, S. 106
Drenniki 203
Druga Wólka 218
drużyny 176
Dub 221, 283
Dubno 176, 197, 214, 279
Dubois, PA 41
Ducal Prussia 391
Dudek, W. 106
Duquesne University 44, 71
Duzynski, Rev. Czeslaw 46
Dworzec Kowelski (Kowel station) 270
Dworzecki, F. 106
Dytkowska, Helen 9
dywersanty (partisans) 255
Dżaparydz 244
Dzhaparydze 244
Dziennik Chicagoski 9, 45
Dziennik Polski 95
Dzierzgowski, P. 106
Dziewonska, W. 380
Dziob, Franciszek 30, **93**-94, 96-97, 101, 118
Dziónków 262, 274 (*see also* Dziunków)
Dziunków 130, 169-171
Dziunków, Battle of 170
Dzwonkowski, Capt. 239
Eagle Pass, TX 89
East Vandergrift, PA 41
Ecochard, General 164, 236
Edwardówka 167
Eichhorn, Marshal 304
Elizabeth, PA 42
Ellwood City, PA 42
Emilia Plater Women's Society 546, 44
Emmonshalle 364
Empress Maria Theresa of Austria 386
Emsworth, PA 24, 27

Erfurt 166
Ermeland 387
Everson, PA 40, 42
Evert, H. 379
Fabowski, 2nd Lt. 218
Fabre Sector 134, 138
Fairpoint, OH 42
Falcon Hall 46, 71
Falcons 28, 138, 233, 300
Falcons Military Committee 116
Falcons Technical Commission 28
Fanion 185
Farmers Bank Building 38
Farmington, CT 407
Farrell, PA 42
Fastów 273, 275
Faunt le Roy, Col. 277
Ferguson, R.J. 312, 329
Figura, Fr. 39
Fijalkowski, Colonel 301
Filarets 46
Filińcy 206
Filipowicze 271
Firlejówka 173
First Moroccan Division 155
First Regiment of Polish Chasseurs 347-348
Florjanówka 206, 208
Foch, Marshall 193, 236, 364
Fonder, Sgt. 161
Footdale, PA 40
Forain 165
Ford City, PA 42
Foreman High School 10
Forêt de Parroy 165
Fort George, ONT 326, 330
Fort Mississauga, ONT 326, 330
Fort Niagara, NY 49, 314, 329
Fort Pompel 138
Forty Fifth Regiment of Eastern Frontier Infantry Riflemen 228-259
Forty Fourth Regiment of Eastern Frontier Riflemen 186-227
Forty Third Regiment of Frontier Riflemen 150-185
Fowler, C.H. 312, 329
Foyers du Soldat 347-348, 356
Francis of Austria 387
Frania, Rev. F. 40
Frankenstein, E. 380

Frankfort 364
Frazet, Vice-Minister of War 113, 115
Frederick the Great 386-387
Frederick William 387
French Foreign Legion 266
French High Commission 315-316
French Honorary Legion 307
French Legion of Honor 226
French Military Cross 307
French Military Mission 122
French Minister of War 158, 232
French Mission 37
French Mission, New York 328
French-Polish Military Mission 122, 124, 130, 158, 189-190, 232-233, 267
Fronczak, Dr. Z. E. **140**, 345
Fronczak, Mrs. F. E. 346
Fronczak, Major Francis E. 103, 105, **140**, *142*
Fronsak, Col. Francis E. 36
Gabrys *see* Gawryś, T.
Gacek, Wojciech (George) 19
Gael 325
Gaje 173
Galasiewicz, F. 106
Galicia 260, 367, 375, 388, 390, 392-393
Galician Sich Riflemen 206
Galiński, W. J. 106
Galiszewski, Marcin 26, 39
Gallitzin, PA 42
Gały 176
Garrett, Rev. Canon 345
Gąsiorowski, Waclaw 108, 113-**114**, 124, 126, 156
Gawałkiewicz, W. 106
Gawronski, Stanislaw 39
Gawryś, T. (Gabrys) 29, 98-**99**
Gdańsk 87, 94, 144, 146, 341 (*see also* Danzig)
Gdeszyn 175
Geddes, Dr. 329
"General Dowbór" (armoured train) 203
George, Mr. Lloyd 388
German Junkers 392
Gevre 147
Gibson, Ambassador 349, 365
Ginter, Lt. 211
Girl's Service Battalion 335, 339
Gizycki, Major 141

Glapurski, Father 346
Glassport, PA 42
Glen Campbell, PA 42
Glendale, PA 42
Gliniany 217, 280-281
Glogowski, Rev. P. 40
Gnidawa 249
Gniezno 329
Gnutkiewicz, Fr. **93**
Godfather of the Polish Army 328, 330, 335
Godowski, T. 29, 98-**99**
Godziszewski, R. 106
Gołaszewski, W. 106
Golikov 279
Gołogory 250, 280
Gorczyca, W. 106
Gorecki, F. 2nd Lt. 106, 173
Górecki, Major 147
Gorny, M. 380
Gorwski, Mr. 357
Goryńka 277-278
Gosiewski, J. 106
Gouraud/Gourand/Goureaux, General 130, 141, *142,* 158, 160, 163, 192, 235, 305
Gouraud's French Army 348, 358
Goureaux *see* Gouraud
Grabarka (river) 279
Grabiński, Col. 194, 196, 197
Grabiński, Major 190
Grand Duchy of Lithuania 392
Grand Duchy of Posen 391
Grand Duchy of Warsaw 23
Graski, St. **140**
Graves 17
Graydon, W. L. 312
Grecki, J. 106
Greensburg, PA 40
Grey Samaritans 48
Gródek 175
Grodno 393
Grodzki, Major 173
Gruchacz, L. 106
Grudziądz 19, 397
Grudzinska, H. 380
Grupa 51
Grzebień, Capt. Bronisław 240, 243, 251
Grzesicki, General 302
Grzeszczuk 322
Guardian Angels R.C. Church 40

Gut, J.L. 106
Gutkowski, 1st Lt. 217
Gutowski 113
Gutowski, 1st Lt. Roman 209
Gwatkin, Maj. Gen. W. G. 100, 319, 328, 335
Habeas Corpus Act 384
Habrowski, Rev. M. 40
Haciski, Major 138, 162
Haduch, Ludwik 39
Haiman, M. 346
Haiman, Mrs. 338, 346
Halifax, Nova Scotia 16, 45, 190, 233, 311
Haller, Caesar (Cezary) 299
Haller Eagle 4
Haller, General Józef **259, 298**
Haller, General Stanisław 219, 220, 279, 282, 288
Hallerczyk (plural *Hallerczycy*, Polish term for a member of Haller's Army) 4, 12, 17, 19, 84, 238, **259**, 401, 407
Hamburg-American Line 12, **403, 404**
Hamilton, Ontario 340
Hamilton, W. G. 312, 329
Harajewicz, I. 380
Harenski, Jan 26
Harland and Wolf **403**
Harris, Capt. J. 311, 329
Hartford, CT 355
Haussonville 192, 194
Haute Marne 358
(Le) Havre 305 (see Le Havre)
Healy, E. P. 341
Helinski, T. M. 35, 116
Helvetia, PA 42
Henry, Mr. (L. J.) 338, 346
Hering, Mrs. 360
Hermanów 217, 251
Herron Hill 33, 38, 43-45, 48
Hessler, General 193
Hibbard 374
High Commandor, The 307
Hincman/Hintzman, Rev. 99, **99**
Hindenberg 304
Hoboken, NJ 47, 356
Hodkiewicz, Mrs. 346
Hoffman, William "Fred" 19
Hohenzollern, House of 392
Holendry 206-210, 262
Holy Family Institute 27
Holy Family Parish 71
Holy Trinity Church, Chicago **121**
Honiatycze 174
Hoover, Herbert Mr. 337
Horodek 221
Horodnica 199, 200
Horodyski, J. 48, 95-97, 100-101, 108, 113, 118
Horodyszcze 199
Horseville 50
Horyń river 167, 168, 198, 200, 240, 271, 276-277, 289
Horynka 172, 183, 215-216
Horyszow Ruski 285, 287
Hosonville 50
Hoszcza 168
Hoszczatyn 222
Hotel Bayon 124
Hotel Iroquois, Buffalo 335
Hotel Rider, Cambridge Springs PA **20**
Hotel William Penn 32
House, Col. 49
Houtzdale, PA 40, 42
Hranice 300
Hreczana 244
Hreczany 243
Hrubieszów 174, 175, 221, 254, 285, 288
Huczwa (river) 174, 175, 221, 254, 283-284, 288
Hughes, Sir Sam/Minister 92, 94
Hulanick 305
Hulsk 200
Humań 169, 213, 245, 304
Humboldt Park, Chicago 124
Hunter, Miss Betty 345
Hunter, Mrs. W. E. 344-345
Hupert, Kamil 49
Ikwa (river) 277
Immaculate Heart of Mary, R.C. Church 33, 44-46, 71
Insurrection of 1863, 23, 190, 191
Insurrectionists (1863), 190
Inter-Party Circle 305
Islen, PA 40
Italy 15, 84, 194
Iwaczów 250
Iwanicze 196
Iwanowicz 51
Iwaszkiewicz, General 279

"Iwaszkiewicz, General" (armored train) 250
Iwaszkówka 222
Jabłonne 199
Jackson, MI 358
Jagniątkowski, Capt. 122, 136
Jagniatkowski, Major 146
"Jak szybko mijają chwile" (song) 322
Jamaica 326
Janeczko, P. 102
Janiewicz 168
Janiewicze 196
Jarosinska, Z. 379
Jaroslawicze 51
Jasienska, K. 380
Jasiński (Jasieński), Col. 130, *131*, 132, **133**, 134, 136-138, 141, 143-144, 158, 164, 267-268, 280, 305
Jasinski, Lt. 197
Jatutów 253
Jaworski, Major 197
Jaworski (Chaplain) 356
Jaworski, Rev. Joseph L. **44**, 45, 122
Jędrczak, J. 106
Jelmski, Mr. 346
Jerome, PA 42
"Jeszcze Polska nie Zginęła" (now the Polish national anthem) 122, 322
Jews 127, 169, 273, 277, 283, 289, 327, 368-370, 375, 394
Johannet, Controller 316
Johnson, Lt. B. K. 312
Johnson, Carl H. 358
Johnstown, PA 42
Jonchery 183
Jorkiewies, Miss 364
Jurczyce 298-299
Jurówka 200
Kabanówka (river) 280-281
Kaczynski, Jan **25**
Kadlewicz, Jan 39
Kaiser 84, 326
Kaisercraft 386
Kajko, Lucjusz 39
Kąkolewo 51, 270
Kakolewska, H. 380
Kaleuski, Secretary 345
Kalewskis, Mr. Edmund 345
Kaliningrad 94
Kalinówka 210, 244-245, 249
Kalinowski 247
Kalisz 166
Kamień 203
Kamienna Gora 222
Kaminski, Piotr 39
Kamionka Strumiłowa 279, 282
Kancelewski, Wojciech 39
Kaniów 192, 269, 303-305
Karabasz, Antoni 39, 48
Karamazin 386
Karań 202
Karczewski, S. 106
Karczynski, Jan **25**
Kargol, W. 106
Karnicki, General 196, 239, 272-273
Karpaty 306
Kasaczun, Regina M. 299
Kaska, J. 380
Kaszub 390
Katerburg 216
Katerynówka 222-223
Kautz Family YMCA Archives, Minneapolis 18
Kawszewicz, J. 106
Kazimierska, W. 380
Kazunerski, Mr. and Mrs. Andreas 346
Kedzierski, Wlodzimierz 38
Kelly (American pilot) 17
Kendziorek, F. 102
Kenrick, Major F. B. (Kendrick) *111*, 312, 329-330
Kerensky 156
Kerk, Major *see* Kirk, Major W. F.
Kerr, Dr. 31
Kerr, Lt. H. M. 312
Kielce 302
Kiev (Polish name *Kijów*) 11, 17, 171, 197, 205, 211, 239, 245, 271-273, 275, 283, 289, 305-306, 352, 387, 393
Kijów *see* Kiev
Kiliński 162
Kingdom of Poland 385
Kirghiz 271
Kirk, Major W. F. (Kerk) *111*, 312, 329-330
Klatt, A. 29, 98-**99**
Klątwa (Klątwy) 221
Kleczkowski, Lt. 144
Klewań 197-198, 271, 289
Klich, F. 102, 170

Klimczewski, H. 106
Klitna 172, 278
Klub Polski 300
Knight of the Legion of Honor 190
Kogut, G. J. 106
Kolasa, S. J. 106
Kolchak 273
Kołobrzeg 146
Kołodzianka 200
Kolodziejczyk 322
Kołomyja 302
Komarów 174, 220, 284
Komitet Obrony Narodowej (National Defense Committee) 26
Königsberg (Kaliningrad) 392
Koniuchy 221
Korab-Laskowski, 1st Lt. Jan 226
Korczyk (river) 276, 289
Kordecki, Father 216
Kordecki, W. 106
Korosteń 176
Korostkil 202 *(see page 293)*
Korzec 168, 176, 222
Korżówka 276
Korzun-Osmołowski, Col. *131*, 136, 141, 164
Korzybski, Alfred 39
Kościuszko, Tadeusz (Thaddeus) 36, 303, 326, 360, 384, 388
Kościuszko Squadron 17, 214
Kościuszko, Army of 16, 32-35, 46, 97, 336
Kosiński, F. 106
Kosmacki, S. 39
Kostopol 199, 222
Kostopole 51
Kostrubała, Joseph G., DDS MD 4
Kostrubała, Lt. Jan Kazimierz 4, 6, 9, 80, 106, **228**, 244, **259**
Koszelewka 278
Koszelówka 172
Koszyce 300
Kotiużyńce 249
Kotlice 221
Kotovsky, Commander 172, 215, 276-278
Kovno (Kaunas, Lithuania) 393
Kowalczyk, A. 106, 201
Kowalewski, A. 106
Kowalewski, Sgt. Leon **25**
Kowalski, 1st Lt. 170

Kowalski, M. 106
Kowel 166, 196, 239,
Kowel Station (*Dworzec Kowelski*, in Warsaw) 270
Koziarowski, 2nd Lt. 204
Kozary 205
Koziatyn 169, 174, 206, 207, 210, 213, 244-245, 275
Kozicki, St. *140*
Kozieracki, 2nd Lt. 200
Kozierowski, 1st Lt. 168, 169
Kozierowski, Capt. 176
Koźlakowski, A. 106
Kozlowski, J. F. 106
Kraczow (now called Kraczew) 219
Krajewski, Leonard 29
Krajowski (Krajewski), General 172, 214-215, 249
Kraków (Cracow) 172, 218, 299-302, 352, 354, 367, 369, 375, 378, 387
Krakow, Prince Bishop of 352
Krall, Stanislaw 26
Krasiłów 172, 249, 278
Krasne 173, 196, 217, 279-281
Krasnopol 206
Krasnystaw 174
Kresse, A. 29, 98-**99**
Krob, Lieut. 346
Król, B. 29, 98-**99**
Kropiwna 176, 242
Krynicki Majdan 253
Krystynopol 219, 282
Kryze, J. 29, 98
Krzemieniec 171-173, 183, 215, 277-279
Krzewica 219
Krzysztawkiewicz, Z. 102
Krzywkowski-Wolański, Lt. 130
Krzywkowski-Woliński, Capt. 160, 162
Krzyż 146
Krzyż walecznych, see Cross of Valor
Krzyzan, Rev. Cesary 336, 345-346
Krzyżanżwka 206
Krzyzanowski 322
Księga Prawdy Dziejowej (Book of Historical Truth) 85, 86
Kubiak, F. X. 39
Kuettner, Colonel 302
Kujavia (*Kujawy,* a region of northwestern Poland) 388

Kuka 222
Kukuczka, J. 106
Kulików 282
Kulturkampf 23
Kumanowce 244
Kupczyńce 276
Kuraszkiewicz, S. 102
Kurcyusz, Major S. G. 211
Kurdek, Leonard 19
Kurowce 250
Kurowice 218, 250-252, 280-282
Kusjorski, P. 102
Kuszlin 172, 183
Kutyszcze 241
Kuzma, Timothy 18
Kuźmin 278
Kuźmiński, F. S. 106
Kwasieborski, Adam 39
Kwaśniewski, Lt. Tadeusz 106, **186**, 203, 213, 215
La Manche 347
La Sollay de Malescot, Baronnesse 300
Labat, Lieut. 319
Łabędzki, S.K. 102
Labujewski. Rev. Stanislaus R. **47**
Łabunie 253, 284, 285
Łabuńka (river) 283, 285, 287
Łabuńki 252-253, 285
Łabuńska Wola 253
Lachowce (Łachowce) 252
Łączkowski, S. 102
Lafayette Hotel 337
Lafferty, OH 42
Lake Ontario 263
Langer, Rev. J. 40
Lansing, Robert, Secretary of State 36, 115
Łasków 175
Lasków 222
Łaszczów 283
Laszki Królewskie 282
Latrobe, PA 40, 42
Laval (France) 124, 129-130, 158, 234, 266-267, 347, 356, 359-360
Ławcewicz, G. 106
Lawicz-Liszka, Major 196, 207
Lawrenceville Historical Society 71
Lawrenceville, PA 38, 44
Le Doux, J. 132, 144
Le Havre 157, 190, 233, **402**, **407**

Le Mans 266
le Mont sur Aube 138
Le Pan, Col. Arthur D. 97, 100, 103, 105, **111**, **112**, 115, 122, **308**, 309, 311, 319, 329-330, 342
League of Nations 367
Lech 329
Leechburg, PA 42
Legion of Honor 160
Leipzig 166, 364
Lenard, Sgt. Jan 239
Leopold, Emperor 300
Leprey 360-361
Lepuys 358
Lewandowski, M. 102
Lewis, Capt. J. L. 312, 329
Lewis, Lt. **111**
L'Huitre 236
Licuori, M. 380
Lignica, Battle of 383
Lilly, PA 40, 42
Lincoln, Abraham 360
Linde, General 214
Link, Z. 380
Lipno 150, 241
Lipów 262
Lipowiec 214, 221, 245-248, 274
Lipski, Rev. Wladyslaw 40
Liss, J. 102
Listewska, H. S. 26
Listowski, General 206
Lisznia 215
Litowisko 216
Little Poland, *see* Małopolska
Litwa 175, 222
Łódź 134, 173, 353, 364
Łódź Staging Battalion 250
Loire (river) 347
Łokacze 254
Lokanski, Henryk 31
London 298, 389
Łopatyn 208, 209
Lorraine (region of France) 16, 141, 143, 163-165, 235, 262, 269, 322, 348
Louis Philippe 384
Loyola University of Chicago 10
Lubar 51, 168, 201-203, 205-206, 226-227
Lublin 174, 219, 282-283
Lubomirski, Prince 338

Lubomirz 300
Łuck 51, 173, 175, 195-198, 222, 239-240, 254-255, 271, 288-289
Łuczywo, B. 106
Ług River 254
Ługa River 288
Luneville 144, 165
Lutosławski, Prof. Wincenty 127
Lwów 17, 87, 130, 166, 173-174, 195, 197, 201, 217-219, 229, 238, 248, 250, 252, 256, 271, 279-282, 300-301, 306, 367
Łyczak, A. B. 106
Łyczaków 173
Lyczakowski Cemetery 17
Lyndora, PA 42
MacCallum (American pilot) 17
Macewicze 276
Machewicz, Col. 200
Machnikowski, F. 26
Machnówka 207-208
Mackiewicz, 1st Lt. 234
Macphee, Mayor 335, 345
Madill, Maj. H. H. *111*, 312, 314, 329-330
Magdeburg 192
Magnuski, D. G. 39
Maguda, Jan 43
Mailly (France) 358
Mainz (Germany) 166
Majdan 217
Majdan Krynicki 253
Majewski, General 148
Maksymowka 304
Malcolmson, Mrs. 337
Malescot, de 300
Malinowski, A.T. 106
Malinowski, Capt. Tadeusz 138
Małkowski, Andrzej 30, *91*, 92, *93*, 94-96, 98
Mallow-Sterling Hotel 299
Małopolska ("Little Poland," region of Poland) 194-195, 239, 306
Mały Bratałów 206
Mamers (France) 11, 190, 233, 347, 360
Manche (France) 358
Manduk, Consul 345
Manduk, Mrs. 345
Mangin, General 192-193
Maniew 277
Manila *404*
Marciniak, Jan 39

Marienbad 387
Marjanówka 276
Markowice 209
Markus, Lt. 136
Marmaros-Sziget 303
Marne (river in France) 16, 235
Marriott, W.G. 312
Marszewski, M. 106
Martin, Col. James 120, 122, 315
Maslowski, Jan 26, 39
Masovia (Polish *Mazowsze*, a region of Poland) 388
Masters, Captain Charles K. 345
Masters, Margaret 334
Masters, Mr. Arthur 339, 341
Matecki, J. K. 102, 127, 138
Matejkowski, A. 106
Matula, Father 216
Matuszkiewicz, J. 106
Maurizio, M. 380
Maxims 205
Mayenne (France) 50, 129-130, 158, 190, 234, 347, 356, 358, 360-361, 363
Mazurian (of Mazury, a region of Poland) 238, 390
McAdams 362
McBride, Judge Lois M. 48
McKees Rocks, PA 42, 90
McKeesport, PA 42
McPhedran, Mrs. 341
Mecherzyńce 278
Medaille Militaire 185
Medal of Victory 226
Memorial Medal 226
Mercer, James W. 335, 346
Mercere, B. 379
Metz (now in France) 50, 143, 193, 236-237
Meuse (river) 223
Mexican Campaign 89, 147
Mexican War 27
Mexico 28, 89-90
Mexico Border Incident 27
Miączyn 221
Miąszyn 287
Michaelis, General 304
Michalin 206
Michniewicz, Z. 102
Mickiewicz, Adam 83, 333
Mickiewicz Society Hall 24

Mielcarek, Jan 26
Mierzejewski, W. 106
Mieszko the First (King of Poland) 386
Mieszkowska, Z. 380
Mikołajczyk-Małachowski, 1st Lt. 202
Mikolajow 219, 282
Mikuliński, 1st Lt. 206
Mikuliński, Capt. 208
Miller, Dr. 365
Miller, L. R. 106
Miller, Lt. Roman 106, 237
Milukov 126
Milwaukee, WI 16, 101, 260
Ministry of Foreign Affairs 148
Ministry of Military Affairs 168, 177, 289
Minoga, J. 106
Minsk (Belarus) 240, 352-353, 387, 393
Minszczyzna 304
Miracle of the Vistula 307
Miropol 51, 168, 171, 201-206, 208, 226, 227, 241, 277
Mirski, 1st Lt. 234
Misiewicz, P. 106
Misiorówka 243, 249
Mission Militaire Française 122
Missouri 392
Missuna, N. 380
mitrailleuse 193, 194, 210, 235
Mittel Europa 389
Młochowski, K. 106
Mlynarska, I. 380
Mlynarska, W. 379
Młynów 198, 289
Młynowce 215
Modlin 349-350, 353, 364
Monessen, PA 42
Modre 362
Modrzejewska, Madame 71
Mogila 219, 251, 282
Mohylov (Belarus) 393
Mokiejewski, Col. 122, **123**, 124, 126-127, **128**, 130, 266
Mołoczki 206
Montreal Standard 326
Montreal, Quebec 337, 345
Moravia 9
Moriville 193, 194
Morocco 361
Morozówka 212

Mościcki, Second Lt. Michał 146
Moscow 273, 305
Moselle (river in France) 192
Moszynska, A. 380
Motrunki 206
Mott, Dr. 355, 365, 373-374, 379
Motz, Dr. 126
Moyen Moutier (France) 165
Mozhaisk 231
Mroczko, Pfc. Michał 160
Mruczek, Blazej 26
Mscislaw (Berlarus) 387
Mt. Carmel, PA 44
Mt. Pleasant, PA 42
Mulak, J. 106
Mulholland, Thos. 341
Murmansk 83, 87, 144, 192, 269
Muscovites 202-203, 248
nachal'nik [Russian начальник*]* 282, 284
Nagierany 215
Nakwasza 216
Nałęcz-Dobrowolski, Dr. M. 87
Nancy (France) 164-165, 235, 348, 358
Napadówka 213, 245-248, 256
Napieralski, Mrs. 118
Naples 194
Napoleon Bonaparte 10, 23, 125, 196, 353
Napoleon's Vistula Legion 124
Nash, C.R. 312, 329
Nasielsk 307
Nastał Helena **260**
Nastał, Stanisław I. 18, 102, 138, **260**-261, 280
National Committee 87, 124-125, 127, 130, 146, 192, 232, 269 (*see also* Polish National Committee)
National Defence Headquarters 309
National Defense Committee 26, 94-95, 118
National Military Commission 41
National Polish Army 328
National Polish Committee 335
National Polish Department 318
National Polish Relief Committee 339
Natrona, PA 42
Naulin, General 162
Neffs, PA 42
New Britain, CT 356
New Castle, PA 40, 42
New Kensington, PA 42

New Salem, PA 42
New York, NY 12, 16, 24, 38, 45, 50, 52, 95-96, 157, 244, 259, 265, 311, 315, 334-335, 342, 347, 374, 402-403, 407
Newark Chapter I.O.D.E. 344
Newman, Madam 338
Newman, Miss Jean 338
Niagara Advance 317, 321
Niagara Bowling Club 339
Niagara Camp 310, 330
Niagara Falls, New York 317, 326, 329
Niagara Historical Society 18, 309, 321-322, 325, 333
Niagara Plains 325
Niagara-on-the-Lake, Ontario 4, 11, 16, 18, 46, 103, 115-116, 120, 157, 263, 309-310, 314, 319, 322, 330, 333, 337, 343-344, 356-357
Nice 362
"Niech Żyje Nam" 32
Niemiacze 216
Niemiec, P. J. 106
Niemielanka 176
Niski, B. 106
Nitza 387
Noce 364
Normandie 322
Normandy 358
Normans of Roesland 385
Norrdeutscher Lloyd 401
Noryskiewicz, Mrs. 346
Nôtre-Dame de Lorette 155
Nowa Sieniawka 244
Nowak, Mr. M. M. 334
Nowak, Z. F. 106
Nowakowski, S. 106
Nowochwastow 169, 211-212
Nowosiółki 196
Nowożytów / Nowo-Żywotów 274
Nuszce 250
Obarów 197-198, 255
O'Brien, Rev. A. J. 345
Oczeretnia 213-214, 246
Oczytków 245-246, 248
Oder River 385-386
Odessa 83, 144
Ognisko 373
Ognisko Domowe (Home Hearth Society) PNA 44

Oil City, PA 40
"Ojczyznę, Wolność racz nam wrócić Panie" 265
Oknin 216
Okolowicz, Mr. Josef 339
Oktawin 175
Oleksy, E. J. 102
Olewsk 51, 199
Olhopol 304
Olstynski, K. 26
Olyka 222, 289
Oratów 248
Order of Polonia Restituta 344
Organisty, W. 102
Orionotloire 358
Orlowski, Count 356
Osceola Mills, PA 42
Osielski, J. 29, 97-**99**, 118
Ossów 307
Ostaszewski, Father 336, 340
Ostróg 172, 214-215, 240, 249, 277
Ostropol 90, 130, 169, 171, 243, 276
Ostrów 51, 270
Ostrowska, M. 380
Ostrowski, Col. 148
Ostrowski, Dr. Romuald **91**
Ottawa 92, 96-97, 100, 309, 328, 335
Ottoman 384
Ozierna 171, 211-212
Pachucki, Col. Leon 136, 199, 235, 239, 269
Paderewski, Ignacy J. 15, 20, **21**, 29, **32**-33, 35-36, 46, 49, 71, 96-97, 101, 116, 118, 121, 124, 157, 306, 318, 325, 327, 330, 337, 357, 365, 370, 383
Paderewski, Madame Helena 29, 118, 325, 333-334
Painlevé, Minister Paul 108, 156, 232
Pajewski, M. 106
Pałaszewski, S. 106
Palcza 197
Palewski, Dr. Jan 199
Palikrowy 216
Paluch, M. K. 106
Pancho Villa 27
Panczyk, Jan 39
Papacy 373-374
Parade of Nations 192
Paraná, Brazil 189
Paris 16, 24, 36, 50, 87, 95, 103, 105, 108, 124-

126, 138, 141, 144, 146, 148, 154, 160, 177, 192, 199, 232, 306-306, 348, 357, 365, 370, 374
Parr, C. H. *111*, 312, 329
Partyka, S. 106
Parzyk, Stanislaus 71
Paśniewski, J. R. 106
Pasternak, F. 102
Paszków 240
Pawlak, Capt. W. A. *25*
Pawlak, W. A. 106
Pawlak-Adamczak, Mrs. Helen 49
Pawlikowski, Rev. E. 40
Pawłowicz, E. 102
Pawłówka 169
Pawlowski, Rev. B. 40
Pawłowski, W. 106
Pawołocza 211
Peace Conference 28
Pean, Col. 162
Peart 329
Pedosy 213
Pela, J. 102
Pembroke, Capt. H.E. 312, 329
Penhoët *402*, *407*
Perespa 239, 283
Perry, W. A. 27
Perzan, J. 106
Petain, Marshal 355
Petit de Mange, General 365
Petlura 51, 195, 200-201, 227, 306
Philadelphia, PA 157
Piasecki, W. 102
Piątkowski, Capt. 170-171
Pichon, French Minister 126
Piec, Idzi 38
Piekarska, Mrs. M. 44
Piekarska, Mrs. M.S. 44
Piekarski, Capt. 134, 138, 161-162
Piekarski, Col. Wacław *131*, *135*, 136, *136*
Piekarski, Frank A. 32, *48*
Piekarski, Maj. 168, 171
Pieniaki 216
Pieprzny, G. 102
Pieslak, Capt. 202
Piewce 215
Pików 249
Pikowiec 208, 210
Piła 146

Pilawa 243
Pilc, Rev. F. 40
Pilc, Rev. P 40
Pilchowski, S. *39*
Pilchowski, Stanislaw 39
Piłsudski, Józef 11, *82*-83, 86-87, 120, 126, 146, 154, 166, 174, 189, 192, 194-195, 202, 219, 238, 272, 301-302, 306, 348, 365, 368, 372
Piłsudski's Legions 17
Pinsk (Belarus) 306
Piotrków, Legion of 302
Piotrowski, Grzegorz 84
Piotrowski, Z. 102
Pitakowski, Mrs. Mary 49
Pitass, Father 336
Pittsburgh 326, 329, 356
Pittsburgh, University of 71
Plastuns 203, 205
Pliskow 170, 183, 213
Płoski, Private 209
Płoskirów (*also called* Proskurów, *see page 295*) 172, 204, 249
Plowaret 343
Plutnicki, Adam 26, *31*, 39
Pniak, Rev. A. 40
Poburzany 279
Podhajce 172
Podhorce 217, 282
Podkamień 173, 216-217
Podlachia (region of Poland) 388
Podolia (region of Ukraine) 239
Podoski, 2nd Lt. 167
Pogonowski, Iwo Cyprian 84
Pohrebyszcze 169, 212, 245-246, 274
Poincaré, Pres. Raymond 34-35, 108, 141, 156, 184, 189, 192, 232, 235, 328, 348, 358
Polak (weekly publication)191
"Polaks" 326
Polanie, Polans 386
Polish Aid Corps 303
Polish Army Association of America 49
Polish Army Veteran's Association (PAVA) 9, 18, 244, 261
Polish Catholic Union 346
Polish Central Committee 35, 36
Polish Central Relief Committee 37
Polish Citizens' Committee 335, 345-346

Polish Consulate of Buffalo 345
Polish Council of Canada 336
Polish Daily Telegram 344
Polish Defense Committee 48
Polish Falcons Alliance 27, 89-91, 94-95, 97, 100-101, 103, 107, 109, 115-116, 330
Polish Falcons Alliance Technical Committee 90
Polish Falcons Executive Board 35
Polish Falcons of America 9, 18, 24, 26-35, 37, 43-44, 47, 49, 93, 113, 124, 189
Polish Government Relief Bureau 342
Polish Military Commision 35, 37, 39-40, 314, 316
Polish National Alliance (PNA) 9, 11, 48, 90, 116
Polish National Alliance College *see* Alliance College
Polish National Army 36
Polish National Committee 36-37, 87, 103, 105, 124, 157, 305-306, 383
Polish National Library, Warsaw 18
Polish Naval Reserve 84
Polish Officers' Veteran Association 9
Polish Relief Committee 34, 48
Polish Roman Catholic Union (PRCU) 9, 116
Polish Roman Catholic Union Archives 49
Polish Scouts 307
Polish Senate 384
Polish Veterans Union, Buffalo Chapter 346
Polish White Cross 333-335, 338, 346
Polish Women's Alliance 116, 118, 338
Polish Women's Relief Auxiliary 344, 346
Polish Women's Relief organization 335
Polish Women's Relief Society 341
Polish-Russian War 149
Polish-Soviet War 11, 15
Polonia-Jutrzenka Publ. Co. 262
Polonia Restituta, Order of 344
Połonne 172, 200, 202-205, 277
Polonskiy, Commissar 170
Polotsk (Belarus) 387, 393
Polowa Kurja Biskupa 45
polskość 155
Pomerania 19, 306, 397
Pomiechowek 51
Ponchentrain Hotel, Detroit MI 94
Ponebel 198

Poniatowski, King Stanislaus 387
Poniatowski, Lt. Prince Stanisław August **114**-115, 122, 387
Poniatowski, Sub-sector 199-200
Ponikwa 216
Popov 171
Popowce 216-217
Poromów 254
Portgage, PA 40, 42
Poryck 167
Posen 371, 375 (*see also* Poznań)
Posluszny, F. 26
Pospuła, J. 106
Post Gazette 71
Post, Christian Frederick 71
"Postrach" (armored train) 201, 203
Potigny (France) 343
Potoski, Mr. Antoni 363
Powierza, H. 380
Poznań (*German name* Posen) 28, 134, 270
Poznan Army 270
Poźniak, 1st Lt. 201
Pozych, J. 32
Price, Colonel Sir William 92
Primakov, Vitaliy Markovich 172, 249
Proskurów 277 (*see* Płoskirów)
Prugar-Ketling, Capt. 196, 202
Prussian Silesia 391
Pryba, W. 102
Pryłuki 249
Prymakov 172
Prywalówka 206
Prywitów 203
Przemyśl 303
Przepisy dla powstancow 1863 roku 190
Przewalew (Przewale) 221
Przewodow 219
Przybylowicz 322
Przybyłowski, S. 106
Pszczółkowski, K. 106
Puchalski, General 302
Puck 306
Pugh 329
Pulaski, Casimir (Kazimierz Pułaski) 71
Pułaski, S. 106
Putotsky 371
Quantin 360
Quebec 329
Radków 252

Radomyśl 239
Radziwanowicz, A. 106
Radziwiłł, Maj. 122, 144
Radzymin 307
Rafajłowo 301-302
Rajce 203-204
Rajchel, Mrs. J. *48*
Rajchel, Sgt. Jan *25*
Rajki 276
Rajs, Rev. J. 40
Rajzacher, Mr. 120
Ralphton, PA 43
Ramberville 237
Raon l'Etape 192
Rarańcza 303
Ratajczyk, Jan 26
Ravines sub-sector 236
Rawa Ruska 174, 219, 252, 282
Recruiting Centers USA 398-400
Red Cross 307, 318, 333-334, 339, 364, 370
Red Ruthenia 390
Regency of Opeln 389
Regent Council of Warsaw 303-304
Reims/ Rheims 138-139, 155, 158-159, 177, 348, 358
Rembervillers 165
Republic, PA 40, 43
Reszutci, Lieut. 346
Rhine (river) 143, 269
Ribot, Minister A. 108, 156, 232
Richards, J. 312
Rider Hotel, Cambridge Springs PA *20*
Rio Grande 89
Robinson, Capt. J. L. 316
Rodzyński, Capt. Mieczysław 172, 185, 277
Rodzynski, Lt. 122, 124
Rogoziński, S. 102
Rokicki, J. 29, 98-*99*
Rolka, I. 106
Roman Catholic Church 15
Romanów 51, 201-205, 242
Romanów, Battle at 51
Romer, General 147-148, 203, 207, 215, 276-277
Rommel, Col. 282, 287
Rómmel, General 176, 185, 220
Ropalewska, J. 380
Roś (river) 169, 248
Rose, Mr. 365
Rosiak, Capt. Józef 243, 250, 255
Rośka (river) 248
Roskosz, Jan 39, 102
Ross, E.H. 312, 373, 375
Rossiter, PA 43
Rossosze 245
Rostków 173
Rowiński, Z. J. 102, 127
Równe (*also called* Rowno) 51, 167-168, 172, 175-176, 197-200, 204, 214-215, 222-223, 240, 255, 256, 271, 289
Royal Prussia 391
Rozenman, 1st Lt. Izydor 251
Rozkopane 169
Rozwadowski, Prof. J. 125, *140*
Ruciński, J.H. 106
Rudnia 205
Rudzisko 205
Rumiński, J.A. 106
Rupiński, J. 102
Rusiak, Capt. 255
Rusiecki, Capt. Wiktor 239, 241-242, 244, 246, 250-251
Rusinowo 173, 196
Russell, Miss Lillian 407
Russian Expeditionary Corps 157, 190, 233
Russian Revolution 17
Russo-Polish War 11
Ruszczyzna 220
Ruszów-Wierzba 285
Rutkowski, S. R. 106
Ryan, Mrs. William 341
Rybicki, Col. Kazimierz 256
Rycozutci, Lieut. 345
Rydlewski, Father Z. 33, 45, 46, 322, 326, 329, 334, 336, 338-339
Rylski 89
Ryszkowski, F. 39
Ryzowicz, Sgt, Jacob *25*
Rzekiecki, Henryk *114*
Rżewski, 2nd Lt. 161
Rzewuski, Stanislaw 38
Rzewuski, W. W. 102
Sadowski, Anthony 71
Saffais 143
Sagamore, PA 43
Sainte-Tanche 158, 162-163, 268, 359
Sala, Alexandra 300
"Sambra i Moza" (regimental march) 223

Sambre (river) 223
Samhorodek 169, 171, 207, 209, 211-212
Samo-Sierry 231
Samulski, T. 31, 90, 115
San Domingo 231
Santa Maria Capua Vetere 194
Santo Domingo 84
Sarny 197
Sarthe 129, 347
Sassów 217
Sawicki, 1st Lt. Bohdan 222
Sawicki, General 202, 212
Saxony 385
Scarbro, PA 43
Schafnagel, T. von 380
School of Cadets 90
Schunike, Mrs. 346
Schutz, Walter S. 347, 355-376
Sealigeon 360
Secretary of War Garrison 27, 28
Seiler, J. (Sejler) 29, 98-**99**, 197
Sembrich, Marcella 71
Sept-Saults 159
Seret River 173, 216, 250, 279
Serge, B. 29, 98
Seyda, Marjan 125
Sharpsburg, PA 43
Shneider barracks 267
Siadecki, Rev. T. 40
Siatecki, Rev. T. 46
Siberia 23, 83, 87, 144, 366
Sichow, Fort 282
Siedlce 199
Siedlecka, J. 380
Sielawa, S. 106
Sielce 222, 254
Sielec 288
Sieliszki 199
Siemierz 284
Sienkiewicz, Henryk 84, 326
Sierociński, Józef 29, 30, 35, 97, 98, **99**, 100, ***117***
Sierocki, Wladyslaw 38
Sikorska, Miss Angelina Leona 44
Sikorski, General 283, 303
Sikorski, Major 302
Silesia 17, 239, 306, 368, 385, 390
Silesia, Upper 239, 389
Sillé-le-Guillaume 129, 136, 147, 157-158, 190-191, 233-234, 343, 347
Siwicka, Mrs. Hedwig 49
Six Nation Indians 325
Skarzyński, Wincenty N. 30, 35, 80-81, 83-84, 86, **88**, **91**, **93**-96, 98-**99**, ***101***, 103-105, 107, ***109***, 110, ***111***, ***112***, ***117***, ***119***, 129, 144-***145***, 147-149
Skarzynska, Mrs. M. M. 44
Skarzynski, Mrs. Wanda M. 44
Skierski, 2nd Lt. Gen. 241
Skitka 245-246
Skorupka, Rev. Father John 307
Skwira 274
Sławuta 200, 240
Śledziak, Pfc. 203
Słucz Group 275-277
Słucz River 167-169, 171, 198, 200-202, 204, 241, 243, 271, 275-278, 289
Smakosz, V. T. 106
Smieciński, F. 106
Smith, A. G. 312, 329
Smuck, Capt. J. W. 312
Śniatycze 285
Śniechowski, 1st Lt. 222
Śnieżna 171, 211-212
Sobczak, L. (Sobszyk) 30, 94, 98-99
Sobieski, 1st Lt. 208
Sobieski, I. 106
Sobieski, John (Jan III) 384
Society of Adam Mickiewicz 27, 31
Sokal 219, 252, 282-283
Sokolowska, H. 380
Sokolowski, Ignacy 39
Solon, Lt. S. 106, 200, 207
Somepuis/Sommepuis 132, 158
Soroka 304
Sosien, Lt. S. 106, 213, 215
Sosnowski, C.A. 106
Sosnowski, J. J. 85, 86
sotniki 167
Souain 183
Souchez 155
South Africa 329
South Bend, IN 101
South Chicago, IL 16
South Fork, PA 40, 43
Southern Masovia 388 (*see also* Masovia)
Spanish Flu 326
Spiczyńce 212-213

Spisz/Spiš 390
Sprague, WV 43
Spychala, Sgt. Tadeusz **25**
Spychala, Mrs. Antoinette 44
SS *Antigone* 12, 47, **401**
SS *Chicago* **402**
SS *City of Honolulu* **404**
SS *City of Marseilles* 305
SS *Corse* **405**
SS *Czar* 190
SS *Czaritza* 190
SS *Kiautschou* **404**
SS *Kursk* 190
SS *Mercury* 47
SS *Neckar* 12, **401**
SS *Niagara* 45, 122, 265, **405**
SS *Pocohontas* 47
SS *President Arthur* **404**
SS *President Grant* 12, 47, **259**, **403**
SS *Princess Alice* **404**
SS *Princess Matoika* 47, **404**
SS *Rochambeau* **406-407**
SS *Servian* **403**
SS *Titanic* **405**
St. Bartholomew's Night 384
St. Catherine's Settlement, Toronto 46
St. Catherines, ONT 336-337, 340, 345
St. Dizier 50, 194
St. Genevieve Grammar School 9
St. Hilaire-le-Grand (France) 17, 134, 139, 143, 160, 163
St. John, ONT 265
St. John's, QUE 122, 157, 311, 314, 329
St. Joseph's Union 40
St. Mark's 326
St. Mark's Hall 344
St. Mary's 345
St. Nazaire (France) **402**, **405**, **407**
St. Petersburg 83, 387
St. Stanislaus Kostka Parish 71
St. Stanislaus Polish Church, Toronto 345
St. Vincent de Paul Cemetery (Niagara-on-the-Lake) 322, 335, 336
St. Vincent's Cemetery 326
St. Vincent de Paul Church 345, 346
Stach, L. S. 106
Stanisławczyk 167, 196
Staniszewski, A. 106
Stankiewicz, General 304
Stara Huta 176
Stara Sieniawa 243-244, 249
Stara Wieś 260
Starokonstanynów/Stary Konstantynów 130, 168, 172, 214, 242-243, 249, 277
Starzyński, Dr. Teofil A. 24, 26-28, **31**-35, 48, 90, **93**, 95-97, 99-101, 103, 108-**109**, 113, 115-**117**, 120, 124, 126, 189
Starzynski, Ignacy 26, 39
Statue of Liberty 265
Stawiszcze 169
"Steel Division" 274-289
Stępkowski, J. 106
Stestland, H. Gen. Adjutant 28
Stethem, H. 312
Steubenville, OH 43
Stevens, Miss (of Hoboken, wife of Count Orlowski) 356
Stinson, Miss 360
Stobychwa 302
Stochód 302
Stochód river 239
Stowarzyszenie Weteranów Armii Polskiej w Ameryce (SWAP) 9, 18, **99**, 244, 408-409
Strasbourg/Strasburg/Strassburg 50, 165, 237
Straszewski, Dr. Michal, Consul-General 344-345
Strypa 250
Strzembosz, J. 380
Stubla (river) 168, 197-198
Stygar, Lt. Wojciech 106, 254
Stypula, Michael 49, **50**
Styr River 167, 175, 195-196, 222, 239, 254-255, 271, 279, 289, 302
Suchomski, Pvt. Jan 237
Sujkowski, Prof. 146
Sulewski, Władysław 29, **93**, 101-102, **109**, 118
Sułkowski, Capt. Witold 242-243
Sully-sur-Loire 235
SWAP *see* Stowarzyszenie Weteranów Armii Polskiej w Ameryce
Sweeny, Rev. Father 346
Świącki, Cadet 211
Świniuchy 196
Swinnoje 243
Synoradzka, Miss Helen J. 44

Synoradzka, Mrs. Sophia 44
Sypniewski, C.W. *26*, 35, 48
Sypniewski, K. 124-126
Syski, Dr. 338
Syzyfowe prace (Labors of Sisyphus) 86
Szaniawski, Włodzimierz **114**
Szczepanski, P. A. 106
Szczepiatyn 219
Szczypiorna 302
Szelagowski, Jan 39
Szelwów 254
Szembarski, S. 102
Szepetówka 168, 200, 240, 242, 276-277
Szeptycki, Col. Stanislaus 302
Szewc, 1st Lt. 280
Szlachciński, S. 30, 98-**99**
Szujski, Władysław 155
Szwagiel, Lt. W. 106, 217
Szwedzinska, H. 380
Szwejkowski, J. 106
Szylling, Lt. Col. Antoni 172, 212, 214-217, 220, 222, 226, 246, 281, 284
Szylling, Maj. Antoni 197, 198, 202-206, 208, 210
Szymański, 1st Lt. Antoni 173
Szymański, F. 30, 98
Szymański, General 276-277
Szymański, J. 102
Szymbarski, 1st Lt. 274
Szymorowski, Edward 38, **41**
tachanki (Polish spelling *taczanki*) 173, 185, 216, 222, 247, 249, 251, 273
Tajkury 200
Tallyn, Mr. and Mrs. 346
Tanska, J. 380
Tarasink, Rev. Dr. 340
Tarczynski, Prof. Rudolph 24
Targowica 167
Targowski, Sgt. Jan 201
Tarnopol 250
Tartar 384
Taylor, A. S. 350-351, 354
Tecklenborg **401**
Telatyn 219
Tenerowicz, J. 106
Tennyson 322
Tereszpol 249
Terlecki, Lisa A. 4, 19
Teschen *see* Cieszyn

Thessaloniki (Greece) 136, 190, 235, 269
Thomson, Dr. 329
Thorn *see* Toruń
Till, Major 234
Tkach, Harry 71
Tomaszewska, H. 380
Tomaszów 284
Topule 196
Torczyn 175, 222
Toronto 10, 97-99, 103, 105, 107, 112, 310, 319, 330, 340
Toronto, University of 16, 29, 91, 97-98, 101, 106, 111, 319, 327, 329
Toruń (*German name* Thorn) 306, 387, 388
"Tovarishch Shauman" (armored train) 244
Trannes 235
Trawiński, Witold Hilary 80, 102, 127, **150**
Treaty of Riga (1921) 11
Treaty of Versailles 17, 83, 352
Treter, Olga 300
Treter, Wiktor 300
Trojanowski, Lt. Col. 199
Trotsky 282, 289
Truszkiewicz, F. 106
Trzetrzynski, Rev. J. 40
Tucza 207, 209
Tuczyn 222
Tukhachevsky 219, 250, 253
Tupadły Czarne 150
Turkowski, W. 102
Twardowski, S. J. 106
Tyrol 299
Tyszowce 221, 283, 288
Tytyjów 169
U. E. Loyalists 325
Udzin 175
Uhnów 219
Ułanów 169
Ulhówek 252
Uljanówka 247
Uniontown, PA 40, 43
Uprising of 1831 (against Russian rule) 267
Urban, L. 102
Urban, Mr. and Mrs. 346
Urban, Sgt Ludwik **25**
Urbaniak, J. H. 102, 197
Vachoux, Major 129
Valasek, Andrea 19
Valasek, Christine 9

Valasek, Dr. Charles E. 6
Vaschoux, Col. 126, 130, 138
Velle (river) 138
Verdun 141, 190, 192, 266, 269
Versailles Conference 305, 388
Versailles Treaty *see* Treaty of Versailles
Verzenay 138
Verzy 138
Veterans Association 346
Vidallon, General 143
Vienna 302
Vienna, Military Academy 300
Vilna (*now* Vilnius, Lithuania, *Polish name* Wilno) 348, 367, 372, 393 (*see also* Wilno)
Vilna, University of 393
Vimy Ridge 155, 329
Virgil Women's Institute 339
Virtuti Militari 45, 156, 183, 191, 210, 252, 255, 257, 307
Vishnevetsky, Military Commissar 171
Vistula (*river, in Polish* Wisła) 365, 385-386
Vitebsk 387, 393
Volhynia (*region in Ukraine, in Polish* Wołyń) 166, 194-195, 197-199, 200, 205, 219, 238-241, 253-255, 302, 387, 393
Volhynian Polesie 240
Vosges (mountain range in northern France) 50, 139, 143, 192-193, 236, 239, 348, 356, 361-363
Wagner, Major 329
Wakijów 254
Walaszczyk, W. 102
Waldo, Arthur 49
Walsh's Hall, Chicago 118
Wankowicz, K. 380
War Council of Paris 367
Waręż 283
Warsaw 49, 81, 87, 134, 148, 153, 166, 173-174, 186-187, 197, 217, 219, 229, 270, 277, 282-283, 302, 306-307, 336, 341, 348-349, 353-354, 364-366, 368, 370, 373, 377-378, 388
Warta 386
Washington, D.C. 16, 108, 113, 120, 315
Washington, PA 43
Wasilewski, Mieczyslaw 49
Wasyliszyn, Rev. John 40
Wasyłków 305

Waterbury, CT 368
Weber High School, Chicago 10
Weirtown, WV 43
Wenda, B. 106
Wenglicki, J. W. 106
Werbkowice 175, 221, 254, 285, 288
Wesołówka 215
Westphalia 391
White Guard 305
Więcek, 1st Lt. A. (Wiącek) 30, 98-**99**, 193, 198, 203-204, 213, 221
Więckowski, Rev. 134
Wielki Czerniatyn 169
Wielki Mytnik 244
Wielkopolski Infantry Regiment 204
Wielowiejski, J. **140**
Wienckus, Z. F. 106
Wieniawa-Długoszewski, Capt. 146
Wieprz (river) 252
Wildcat Division of Tennessee 143
Wilk, A. F. 39
Wilkes-Barre, PA 16, 299
William Penn Hotel 71
Wilno 195, 197, 238 (*see also* Vilna)
Wilson, President Woodrow 16, **28**, 32-34, 36-37, 177, 383, 388
Windber, PA 43
Windsor, ONT 90
Winnica 210, 244-245
Winniczki 173
Winniki 173, 218-219, 252, 282
Winohrady 304
Wisłocki, 1st Lt. Czesław 241-242
Wiśniowiec 216, 249-250
Wiśniowiecki, Jarema 211
Wisznowiec 172
Witkowski, Mr. 335
Witos, Premier 352
Wlodzimierz (*also called* Włodzimierz Wołyński, *see page 297*) 51, 166, 167, 175, 183, 195, 239, 270-271, 288
Wojciechowski, S. 102
Wojcieszczuk, Rev. 191
Wójcik, F. 102
Wojszcza 169
Wójtowce 244
Wojtylak, B. 106
Wolcyrz, Dr. Adam 27
Wolica Śniatycka 174, 220-221, 285-286

Wólka 173
Wołkowyja 167, 175
Wołodarka 169
Wolowska, Mrs. Honorata B. **44**, 48
Wołuczyn 253, 284
Wołyń *see* Volhynia
Women's Institute 339, 341
Worobijówka 242
Wright, E. B., Capt. 312, 316, 329
Wrobel, P. 39
Wróblewka 51, 203
Wróblewski, J. 30, 98-**99**, 118
Wróblówka 204-205
Wronowski, S. 102, 127, 161
Wudarczyk, James 71
Wujna 209
Wyczółkowski, Capt. 172, 217
Wyczółkowski, Major Stefan 153
Wyszgorodek 277
Wyszogródek 172
Wyżniany 251
Y.M.C.A. 191, 317-318, 326, 329-330, 334-335, 338, 346-380
Yorkville, OH 43
Young Eagles (of Lwów) 17
Young, Major C. R. **111**, 309, 311, **320**, 321, 326-327, 329-330, 345
Youngstown, OH 43
Ypres 329
Yudenich 273
Zabołotowce 196
Zaboryce 205
Zaborzycami [sic], Battle at 51
Zabrowski, F. **93**
Zadworze 282
Zajączkowski, W. 106
Zakopane 306, 375
Zaleska, J. 380
Załoźce 173, 216
Zamojski 372
Zamojski estate 124
Zamość 11, 130, 174, 219-221, 252-253, 256, 262, 282-285, 372
Zamoyski, Count Maurycy **140**, 157
Zamoyski, Władysław 95, 124-126
Zapalowicz, K. 380
Zaporoże Corps 241
Zarewicz, T. 38
Żarków 216
Zarzecki, W. L. 106
Zasław 172, 240, 277
Zastawie 219
Zaucha, J. **93**
Zaucha, Mrs. A. 44
Zawadsky, Mr. and Mrs. C. 346
Zawadzki, Lieut. 208, 346
Zawalew (Zawalow) 221
Zawilski, 2nd Lt. 218
Zborów 279
Zbrucz (river) 239, 277
Zdołbunów 176, 200
Zdrojkowski, Rev. J. 40
Żebrowski, S. 106
Zegarski, F. R. 106
Żeligowski, Col. 144, 305
Żeromski, S. 86
Zielecki, K. 30, 98-**99**, 118
Zieleniewski, Capt. Rafał 200, 206, 208, 209, 213
Zielinów 222
Zieliński, Chief Warrant Officer 209
Zielinski, Dr. B. M. 38
Zielona 302
Zimne 288
Zimno 175, 196
Złoczów 173, 279-280
Zmijewski, Rev. S. 40
Zmudzinska, Mrs. R. 44
Znamięcki, A. 35, 38, 116
Zozulińce 249
Zozulincy 278
Zubkowice (Zubowice) 221
Żuków 198
Zulawski, Czesław 38
Żulice 174
Zwiahel 51, **135**, 168, 176, 200, 222-223, 242, 271, 289
Związek b. Oficerów Armii Polskiej w Ameryce 9
Zwierzyniec nad Wieprzem 228
Zwinogródek 169
Zwolinski, I. 39
Żychliński, Kazimierz 116
Żydanowicz, P. F. 102
Zyglerowicz, S. 26
Żymierski, Col. Michael 305
Żytomierz 201, 207, 248, 274
Żywotow 248, 262

- NOTES -